1795

Introducing Pascal

Introducing Pascal

Seymour V. Pollack

Department of Computer Science
Washington University
St. Louis, Missouri

Holt, Rinehart and Winston

New York   Chicago   San Francisco   Philadelphia
Montreal   Toronto   London   Sydney   Tokyo
Mexico City   Rio de Janeiro   Madrid

Library of Congress Cataloging in Publication Data

Pollack, Seymour V.
     Introducing Pascal.

     Includes index.
     1. PASCAL (Computer program language)   I. Title.
QA76.73.P2P64   1983   001.64'24   83-10756

ISBN 0-03-060563-6

Address correspondence to:
383 Madison Avenue
New York, New York 10017
Published simultaneously in Canada

3   4   5   039   9   8   7   6   5   4   3   2   1

CBS COLLEGE PUBLISHING
Holt, Rinehart & Winston
The Dryden Press
Saunders College Publishing

Contents

Preface

Although Pascal made its debut in the midst of hundreds of existing programming languages, it is revolutionary in that it is the first major programming language based on a perception of programming as a systematic process. While earlier languages include features that offer varying opportunities for structured programming, the presence or absence of such features is more a matter of circumstance than design. Most of these languages were conceived and implemented prior to the emergence and crystallization of structured programming concepts. Subsequent extensions to these languages have been constrained by the necessity to remain compatible with their original syntactic rules.

Pascal, on the other hand, has no such ancestral restrictions. It reflects an explicit concern with structured programming. In fact, a major design objective is to encourage the use of constructions and practices that are associated with the production of clear, reliable programs. This is done to a large extent by incorporating language features that encourage structured programming and erecting barriers that make it awkward or difficult to avoid structured programming practices.

Given this orientation, it is useful to view Pascal as the beginning of a new generation of programming languages. This book reflects that view in that it accepts structured programming as a rational approach to program development and it presents Pascal as a reasonable vehicle for supporting this approach. There is no need at this stage of the discipline to defend structured programming and argue against the ad hoc approach that preceded it.

Pascal's organizational simplicity, when combined with the educational advantages inherent in Pascal's design, results in a powerful vehicle for developing good programming habits and acquiring the necessary programming skills relatively painlessly. Thus the student is learning to write programs in a clear and orderly way while building familiarity with algorithmic processes.

This book is designed for students who have not had previous experience with Pascal (or any other programming language for that matter). Its extensive use for example makes it equally suitable for a class or for self-study. If the student has worked with another programming language (on any system), it may be appropriate to bypass the first chapter.

There is no intent to present Pascal in its entirety. Although Dr. Nikalus Wirth, its developer, envisioned a standardized language that would be supported intact on a wide variety of computing systems, this is not quite the way events developed. Instead, various organizations, each seeking to exploit the language in some particular way, have used Wirth's standard version as a nucleus which they have embellished with an arbitrary assortment of additional features. (Some of these are seen as absolute necessities that cure basic deficiencies or oversights; others are viewed as frippery that adds unwanted complications to a language designed to be simple. Ultimately, each individual must judge the situation with respect to his or her interests.) Fortunately, these various excursions, despite their diversity, have been built around the original (standard) version so that its features form a subset of most (if not all) of Pascal's dialects.

Thus, rather than trying to accommodate the morass that such uncontrolled growth inevitably produces, this book uses standard Pascal as a vehicle for presenting well-illustrated discussions of sound programming principles and practices. (Some specialized features have been omitted and an occasional extension, explicitly earmarked as such, has been included to amplify a particular point. However, the book's flavor and direction center around standard Pascal and the principles that it embodies. The foundation thus provided makes it relatively simple for the programmer to use any additional features once he or she becomes acquainted with their operational properties.

Another feature of the text is worth noting here. Pascal is neither an "Interactive" language nor a "batch-oriented" language. Since it is intended to be a general-purpose language with particular advantages for teaching sound programming principles and techniques, it (rightly) avoids such issues. Instead, the selection of an operating mode is treated conceptually as an external process that depends on the requirements and characteristics of the particular application. As far as Pascal is concerned there are facilities for implementing a program either way. Consequently, this book pays attention to both types of implementations so that the student is not nudged toward a prejudice in either direction. Each mode has its uses, and the student is motivated to learn techniques for both so that he or she can select the proper one on a rational basis.

I would like to thank Brete Harrison and Paul Becker of CBS College Publishing and Rachel Hockett of Cobb and Dunlop for their valuable suggestions and help. Finally, my continued gratitude and love go to Sydell, Mark, and Sherie Pollack. These are truly wonderful people.

Seymour V. Pollack

Chapter One

Introduction

In this book we shall be concerned with the features of the Pascal programming language and the techniques for using them to develop effective problem solutions on a computer. Unlike the names of most other languages, Pascal is not an abbreviation for anything. The language is named in honor of Blaise Pascal (Figure 1.1), a brilliant French mathematician of the seventeenth century. He is generally credited with building the first successful mechanical adding machine. Although there is no direct historical connection, Pascal's device (Figure 1.2) is considered the starting point in a long line of arithmetic machines preceding today's electronic digital computer.

The Pascal programming language, developed by Dr. Niklaus Wirth, was introduced in 1971. Although there already were several hundred programming languages in existence at the time, it would be misleading to think of Pascal as just another one to add to the list. Pascal's importance lies in the fact that it explicitly seeks to support a view of programming as a systematic, orderly activity. While the earlier major programming languages do not promote chaos (some people will give you an argument about that), they represent ideas and attitudes about programming that date back to the early 1950s. Accordingly, these languages place primary emphasis on making it convenient to specify certain kinds of computations considered to be useful. With few exceptions, these languages pay only incidental attention to the organization of these computations and to the data on which they are performed.

Over the years, the programming process has been the subject of extensive study. As a result, we now appreciate the importance of treating a program as a manufactured product. While it is not a physical item (we do not think of a program as something that can be carried around in a bucket), it shares many attributes with a physical product: It consists of several parts (called *modules*), each of which is designed for a particular purpose. Moreover, these modules must work with each other in certain predefined ways in order for the overall assembly to function properly and effectively as a unit. This similarity to a manufactured physical item compels us to

Figure 1.1

Blaise Pascal (Courtesy of Science Museum, London)

recognize the fact that the programming process lends itself to the same orderly, systematic approach underlying the design and development of any other product. Structured design and structured programming, both of which are still evolving, stem from this recognition.

Having said all of that, we can now establish Pascal's significance: It is the first major programming language in which program design and organization are central concerns. Therefore, its primary features are arranged so that they encourage good structure by making it easy to specify. Pascal goes even further by imposing requirements that make it awkward or difficult to avoid good structure. The result is a powerful tool whose mastery can be of great help in using the computer to solve problems effectively.

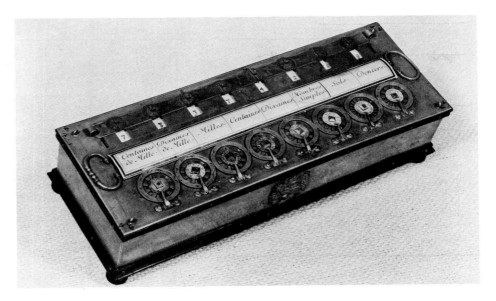

Figure 1.2

Mechanical Calculator (Courtesy of Smithsonian Institution)

1.1 SOLVING PROBLEMS SYSTEMATICALLY

The computer does not know all the answers. Strictly speaking, it does not "know" anything. Its circuits are designed to move information around in certain ways so that particular elementary operations can be performed on that information. However, it is up to us to combine these operations so that the overall effect is to produce useful results. Thus, when we use a computer to solve a problem, we are the ones who determine how the problem is to be solved, and the computer carries out the solution by following our directions. This relationship between the computer and the human programmer is an important one: It means that the programmer knows how a certain problem is going to be solved before he or she calls on the computer to help out. The method of solution, called an *algorithm,* is worked out beforehand and is expressed as a series of steps, each of which brings us closer to the final result. We bring the computer into the picture by restating the algorithm as a *program.* This is the same series of steps, described in the precise vocabulary of a programming language.

Before we can write a program, it is necessary to develop an algorithm and describe it so clearly that its conversion to a correct program is relatively uncomplicated. This is when the problem solving takes place, not when the program is written. Although there is no exact, foolproof recipe for solving problems, there are orderly steps that help increase the likelihood of a successful solution. We shall outline these steps briefly in the next few sections.

1.1.1 Identifying the Problem

It is difficult to imagine the amount of time, money, and effort spent on developing extensive, ingenious solutions to the wrong problems. Common sense would indicate that this can be avoided by making sure the problem is clearly defined before one plunges ahead and starts solving. Yet, these situations continue to arise. Recently, the people running a hospital in a certain city observed that their patients were staying one or two days longer than those admitted to other hospitals for the same types of operations or treatments. The problem was spotted immediately (or so they thought): Obviously, the physicians kept the patients too long after surgery. The hospital launched an extensive and vigorous campaign aimed at encouraging the doctors to get their patients up and moving as soon as good practice allowed. The physicians insisted they were doing that anyway, but promised to pay particular attention to this issue. Nothing changed. Finally, the real problem was discovered: A patient could not be discharged until the bill was ready, and it was taking the accounting department a day or two longer to prepare the bill than it did at other hospitals.

Because of situations like this, many organizations have made it a rule to develop and agree upon a precise, written statement of the problem to be solved before any work is started on a solution.

1.1.2 Finding a Suitable Solution

It is easy to say, "Now that we know exactly what the problem is, the next step is to find an effective way to solve it." Sure. Nothing to it. Of course, there is no step-by-step procedure that leads us from problem to solution. In fact, we cannot be sure that there is a solution just because we know what the problem is. Because of these uncertainties, this step is usually the most difficult one in the entire process. It is the one where much of the creative effort and ingenuity is concentrated. Entire libraries can be filled with writings seeking to learn the nature of this process. Several are given as references at the end of this chapter.

For our purposes, the solution to a problem takes the form of an *algorithm*. We can define an algorithm as a sequence of steps or rules that meets certain requirements:

1. An algorithm must be *finite*. That is, it must come to a stop sooner or later. For instance, suppose we were faced with the problem of producing a particular shade of blue paint. Our proposed solution is as follows:

Get a can of base paint and a can of blue coloring.
Open both cans.
Add blue coloring to the base paint until the color is right.

While this procedure seems harmless enough, it might not be finite. For example, there could be a case where the base color is too blue to begin with. According to the instructions, this is not the right color. But the procedure says to keep adding till the color is right. So, in goes more and more blue, indefinitely. This is not as ridiculous as it sounds. Remember that computers cannot exercise judgment. It is up to us to provide a specific mechanism that will guarantee a stopping point regardless of the conditions under which the algorithm operates. For this little procedure, we might specify the following revision:

Get a can each of base color, white, and blue color.
Open the three paint cans.
IF the base color is too blue,
THEN
   Add white paint, a little at a time, until the color is right.
ELSE
   Add blue paint, a little at a time, until the color is right.

We may be able to think of other situations for which this procedure will not be finite, but we shall not belabor the issue. The basic point is that there must be a way to bring our procedure to a successful conclusion.

2. An algorithm should be *precise*. This means that each of the steps must be described in such a way that it can be performed by whoever (or *whatever*) will be carrying out the process. In our little example, which lacks precision, we would have to specify the amount of blue or white paint to add (how much is "a little?"), and we would have to describe how to determine when the right color is produced. For a skilled colorist, this might be as simple as saying, "When the mixture matches this color sample, you have the right color." For someone who is less sensitive to color, the directions might be quite different: "When the mixture gives a reading between 407.5 and 423.3 on the Schmugelsky Coloramic Pigmentovacutron, you have the right color." When the algorithm is to be transformed into a computer program, the requirement for precision means that each step must be expressed in such a way that it can be carried out on a computer.

3. An algorithm should be *general*. This means that the procedure should not be so limited that it solves only one specific problem for one specific case. Instead, it should be capable of producing satisfactory solutions for a variety of cases. For example, our little color mixing procedure does what we need it to do as long as we want that particular shade of blue. We could generalize it by expanding its capabilities to include other shades of blue, or even other shades of other colors.

There are many instances where we can come up with several different solutions for a problem. For instance, suppose we are driving along and suddenly the ride becomes much bumpier without any noticeable change in the road. Moreover, steering becomes more difficult. After stopping the car and inspecting it, we find that one of the tires is flat. Before discussing possible solutions, we must agree on what the problem is. In this instance there is little difficulty on that score: Our journey has been interrupted, and we wish to resume it as soon as we can. When we state the problem that way, we can think of numerous potential solutions. Here are just a few:

1. Abandon the car and continue on foot.
2. Buy another car and continue in that one.
3. Reinflate the tire and continue the trip.
4. Get in touch with a service station and have one of their mechanics replace the tire.
5. Flag down a passing motorist and persuade that party to transport us to our destination.
6. Flag down a passing motorist and persuade that party to replace the tire.
7. Call home and get a loved one to come out and replace the tire.
8. Replace the tire ourselves and continue on our way.

Sometimes we can narrow down the choices by rejecting some as being clearly unsuitable. In our example, solutions 2 and 3 are in that category. We probably would not need much convincing to reject solutions 5 and 6 as well. After that, the choice of the most "appropriate" solution may become more complicated because what is "appropriate" will depend on the circumstances. For example, solution 1 may be best after all if we are close to our destination and we must get there promptly. Thus, in many situations, selection of an effective solution method can be the most challenging part of an information-processing project.

1.1.3 Decomposition of a Problem

Once we identify a problem, it is often impossible to solve the entire problem all at once. More likely than not, the problem is too complicated for us to be able to keep track of all the possible twists and angles at the same time. When this happens, it is useful to break up the problem into a collection of interrelated subproblems. Each of these is small enough so that we can handle it comfortably, as a complete entity. This process of *decomposition* makes it easier to develop a solution for each little problem. As a result we can produce a complete, precise definition of what each piece is supposed to do and how it fits with the connecting pieces. The stage is set, then, for each of these components to be developed separately.

To illustrate, let us return to our disabled automobile. Suppose we decided that the best solution under the circumstances was to replace the flat tire with the spare tire. When we look at the solution more closely, we can identify several steps, each of which embodies a little problem of its own:

1. Remove the spare wheel/tire and the necessary tools from the trunk.
2. Remove the wheel on which the flat tire is mounted.
3. Install the wheel on which the spare tire is mounted.
4. Place the wheel removed in step 2 in the trunk, along with the tools.

The activities required to carry out a given step become increasingly clear as we focus even more closely. For example, let us consider step 2 in more detail. The actual removal of the wheel cannot occur without some preparation.

2. Remove the wheel on which the flat tire is mounted:
    2.1 Remove the hubcap and retaining nuts from the wounded wheel.
    2.2 Find an appropriate place for positioning the jack.
    2.3 Set up the jack.
    2.4 Raise the wheel by means of the jack until the wheel no longer touches the ground.
    2.5 Remove the wheel.

If necessary, decomposition continues by dissecting each of these subproblems in turn, until each activity has been reduced to a series of simple steps that are completely understood.

The same process applies to a problem solution involving a computer. Eventually, the result will be a program, but we know nothing about that program's details at this point. Rather, the decomposition process tells us how that program divides into pieces and what each of these pieces needs to do.

1.1.4 Identification of Component Details

At this stage of the game, we do not yet know exactly how each piece identified during the decomposition will do its job. In fact, we may not know whether each of these little problems has a solution or not. The whole point of the decomposition process is to make it easier to deal with these issues one at a time. Once the pieces are known, we can focus in on each one to determine its characteristics in detail. As a result, each piece will be completely defined: We shall know what it does, what it needs to do its job, and precisely how that job is done.

The idea behind this step can be illustrated with a simple example:

Suppose our problem is to produce a device for playing phonograph records. As a result of the decomposition step, we identify the need for a number of components, one of which is a turntable on which the record is to spin. (Studies during the solution-finding stage have convinced us that it will be better to have a spinning record and a passive tone arm than to use a design in which the record stands still and the needle races around the grooves.) We know upon entering this stage that the turntable must be able to hold records of a certain size, and that it must be driven at a certain speed. Now, during this stage, we can deal with such questions as the turntable's thickness, the material out of which it is to be manufactured, the distribution of its weight throughout its surface area, and other such concerns. By the time this stage is completed, we shall have developed enough information about the turntable to enable it to be built. The same will be true for the other parts. In the case of a computerized problem solution, then, this stage produces complete specifications for each part of what eventually will be a computer program. These parts are called *program modules* or, simply, *modules,* and we shall use the term in that context. Note that we haven't written any programs yet. That comes in the next step.

1.1.5 Coding

It is at this point that we are ready to express our solution as a sequence of program statements so that a computer can be used to carry it out. If we did a reasonable job during the previous stages, this part of the process will be like a translation from one "language" to another. Although in this book we shall be translating to Pascal, it is important to point out that the description of each module should contain enough detail so that it can be restated in any one of a variety of programming languages. As a matter of fact, when the modules' details are being worked out, the particular programming language to be used does not enter the picture and should not influence that work.

The process of writing such program modules is called *coding.* It is important to understand that we are not developing a solution method at this stage. That has been done already in previous stages. We know what we want to do, and we know how we want to do it. We also know what we want to tell the computer. When we write the code, we convert the description of our intentions from a form that the computer cannot use to a form with which it can work.

Pascal itself is organized to make the coding process particularly convenient, especially when it is driven by an orderly set of specifications. We shall take full advantage of this convenience by emphasizing the preparation of clear, unambiguous descriptions for program modules. The pertinent discussion begins in Section 1.3.

1.1.6 Module Testing

After we have expressed a module in terms of programming language statements, there is no guarantee that the program will be correct. Even the most careful decomposition and analysis cannot always prevent us from overlooking something or just making a mistake. Consequently, each module, once coded, must be perfected by systematically testing it for errors, tracking them down, and correcting them. During this stage we have an opportunity to exploit one of the most conspicuous advantages of decomposition. Since the overall problem solution has been recast as an interrelated collection of smaller problem solutions, we can develop and perfect each piece separately. When the overall computer application is a large one, this has a particular advantage in that the work can be divided among several people. This is a common practice used effectively throughout industry. It emphasizes again the conceptual similarity between the development of a program and any other complex product.

1.1.7 Integration

During the final stage of the systematic development process, the pieces are put together to see whether they work as a whole. Since each module has already been checked by itself, the integration process deals primarily with the connections among them. This enables the developers to spot areas where adjustments are needed to make everything fit properly.

It is unrealistic to expect a perfect fit when all the pieces are connected for the first time. Even the most careful decomposition and planning can be subject to oversight. However, this orderly approach reduces such tendencies drastically, so that many organizations have implemented mechanisms for using and enforcing some type of systematic process for developing computer programs. Numerous specific methods have been formulated, and some of the related literature is listed at the end of this chapter.

1.2 COMPUTERS AND PROGRAMS

Before a program can produce useful results, it must be installed in a computer so that the machine's operations can be guided by the program's instructions. This section reviews that process briefly and relates the Pascal program to it.

1.2.1 A Glance at Computer Architecture

The term *computer architecture* is used to characterized the functional organization of a computing system. Attention focuses on the major equipment components, what they do, and how they are interconnected. Examination of a particular architecture may take place at various levels: A low-level analysis looks at a computer's functional characteristics in terms of its individual electronic circuits. This provides insights as to how information is moved from one place to another inside a computer and exactly how the computations are done. At a higher level, the individual circuit is "invisible" and the emphasis is on larger components. We are interested in the types of major operations that the computer performs and the way information is moved to support these operations.

All computers operate by executing instructions, each of which does something specific, such as adding two numbers, comparing two numbers, or moving an item of information from one place to another. In most machines, instructions are executed one at a time, but an increasing number of computers (*called multiprocessors*) are being designed to perform several operations simultaneously. Correspondingly, there are programming languages that enable people to implement procedures for such machines.

The major functional components of a computer system are shown in the basic architectural diagram of Figure 1.3. Note that the individual boxes may correspond to actual physical components in some types of computers but not in others. There are numerous models in which all the functional parts are packaged into a single physical unit. Regardless of the physical configuration, the fact remains that these distinct functional components exist.

The Central Processor   The heart of a computer is its *central processor.* Much of the system's computing is done by the processor, and those activities performed outside the processor are (ultimately) directed by it. The instructions that a processor executes are stored in the *main storage*

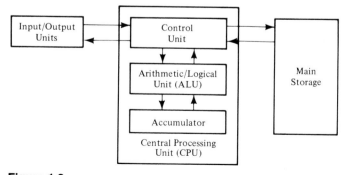

Figure 1.3

Basic Functional Components of a Digital Computer

component (sometimes called *main memory*). Data on which these instructions are to operate are stored there as well.

Main storage is divided into individual units or cells, each of which is physically capable of holding a fixed amount of information. Various types of computers are designed with different maximum main storage capacities. Regardless of a main storage component's size or construction, each of its cells has a unique *address* that defines the cell's physical location. This provides a basis for storing information, finding it, and moving it around. Such movements, then, can be considered in terms of addresses. For example, a typical activity might be described as follows: "Make a copy of the information currently stored in address 784 and store that copy in address 1077, erasing what was there before." Pascal provides bookkeeping services that make it unnecessary for the programmer to deal with these details.

When the processor executes an instruction, the actual computations are done by a group of circuits called the *arithmetic logical unit* (ALU). This component is equipped with special memory units called *registers*. One type of register is the *accumulator*. When a data item is to be used for a computation, it is brought from main storage to an accumulator, where the computation takes place. The result, then, may be transported from the accumulator to a designated location in main storage or it may be left in the accumulator for further computations.

The *control unit* runs the entire show. In order for a program to execute, the control unit must obtain the program's instructions from main storage, one at a time. Each instruction is examined to determine the type of activity being specified. Based on this information, the control unit activates only those parts of the ALU required for that activity, thereby triggering the required operation. When it is completed, the control unit repeats the process for the next instruction. Thus, the processor's main storage and ALU can be viewed as subsidiary components that provide instructions, data, or computational services in accordance with the control unit's demands.

Peripheral Components   Every computer system is equipped with one or more devices (*peripheral components*) for transporting information to or from the central processor. There are endless varieties of such devices covering a wide range of data forms, capacities, and operating speeds. Some (like keyboards) are capable only of sending information to a processor (*input devices*); others (like printers) are designed strictly for receiving information from a processor (*output devices*); still others (like magnetic disk or tape units) can be used for information transfer in either direction (*input/output devices*). As is true with the processor's major parts, peripheral components may be packaged as physically separate pieces, or they may be built-in parts of a one-piece system. A popular packaging approach for many small computers is to configure the system as four physical pieces: A printer, an input keyboard, an output video display, and a fourth box containing the processor and magnetic disk unit(s). Alternatively, systems exist in which all these components are being installed in a single briefcase.

Many peripheral units have considerable computing capabilities of their own. In a real sense, they include separate processors, so that they can direct some of their own operations. However, these activities still are subsidiary since they are started by signals from the central processor's control unit.

1.2.2 Machine Language

As noted earlier, the processor's control unit examines a program's instructions to determine what is to be done next. The kinds of instructions that can be specified for a particular machine are defined as part of that processor's design. Accordingly, if a program is to execute properly on a given computer system, its instructions must be drawn from the set of instruction types (i.e., the *machine language*) "recognized" by that processor.

Machine languages for most processors are elementary structures in which instructions are expressed as strings of 1s and 0s (i.e., *binary strings*). A simple instruction generally consists of two parts: a numerical *operation code* that specifies the activity to be performed and an *operand* that defines an address in main storage whose contents are to participate in the activity. Consequently, the control unit is designed to interpret the instruction string as two binary numbers. For example, suppose that in a certain processor's machine language, an operation code of 30, expressed as the binary string 011110, means "copy data into the accumulator." Then, if we wanted the contents of memory location 81 (expressed as the binary string 0001010001) copied into the accumulator, the instruction would look like this:

$$0111100001010001$$

At some point during its execution, the program would reach this instruction. The control unit, having determined that a data item is to be copied into the accumulator, would arrange the ALU's electronic pathways such that the only thing the ALU could do would be to copy the contents of location 81 into the accumulator.

The number of different instruction types in a machine language varies from one processor model to the next, ranging in general between extremes of approximately 20 and 300. For most systems, each machine language instruction specifies a basic operation such as simple addition or multiplication. There are special cases where the machine language includes single instructions for relatively extensive computations such as taking a square root.

Since each machine language instruction corresponds to a relatively modest amount of computation, it is likely that any algorithm of interest to its users will require a lengthy sequence of such instructions for its expression. The idea of having to write such programs is not an appealing one. Fortunately, languages like Pascal eliminate the need for this tedious work. In the next section, we examine the basic mechanism that makes this convenience possible.

1.2.3 Pascal and Machine Language

In spite of the spectacular advances in computing equipment, machine languages have not changed much. Instructions still must be presented to the control unit as a series of binary strings. Relief for the programmer, then, did not develop from this direction. Instead, it has evolved in the form of increasingly convenient programming languages that enable the programmer to communicate with the computing system on his or her terms rather than those imposed by the machinery.

Programming languages like Pascal are called high-level languages because they make it possible for programmers to describe complicated processing activities as if they were single operations. In effect, the programmer can pretend (or can be fooled into believing) that the computer is designed to handle the high-level language directly. Operating on the programmer's behalf is a *compiler*, a translating program designed to insulate the programmer from the minute details of the machine language. A compiler consists of two basic sections. The first of these embodies a complete set of the high-level language's structural rules. This enables the compiler to examine the original program (called the *source program*) and determine its computational requirements. The results of this analysis are delivered to the second section, whose job it is to convert these computational requirements to an appropriate sequence of instructions (an *object program*) in the machine language of the computer on which the program is to be executed. In general, each high-level language statement produces several simpler machine language instructions. This relationship is shown in the diagram of Figure 1.4. As part of the process, the compiler equips the object program with all of the support necessary to prevent the programmer from having to know the numerical operation codes or the actual machine locations assigned to his or her program.

The convenience of being able to describe a series of computations in terms meaningful to the programmer is just one of the benefits provided by a high-level programming language. Another important payoff lies in the language's support of *portability*. When a program is written originally in

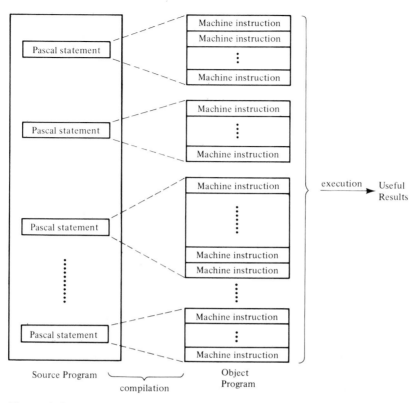

Figure 1.4

Basic Relationship Between a Source Program and an Object Program

machine language, its usefulness is tied to a particular type of computer. If its users change to another machine, or its authors wish to make it available for other machines, it is likely that the program would have to be rewritten, with a separate version being required for each type of computer. When a high-level language is used for the source program, this diversity becomes much less of a problem. If the high-level language's structural rules are standardized, a single version of the source program can be submitted to several different compilers, each of which is designed to produce a functionally equivalent object program for a different type of computer. In a sense, then, the reprogramming is done automatically. This process is shown diagrammatically in Figure 1.5.

The idea of portability is an attractive one, but it has been put into practice only with partial success. Even where standard versions of high-level languages have been defined, various language designers have added special features that enhance their versions of a particular language on one

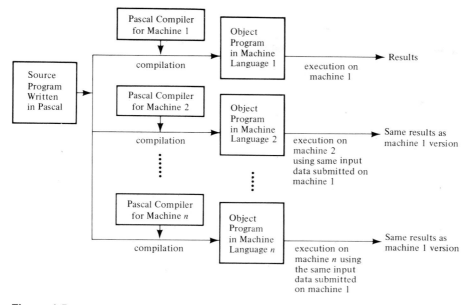

Figure 1.5

Portability of High-Level Language Programs

hand but reduce or destroy the programs' portability on the other. Because of Pascal's emphasis on simplicity and good structure, the expectation is that portability will be easier to preserve for this language.

1.3 SYSTEMATIC DESCRIPTION OF ALGORITHMS

We have seen that the transformation of a Pascal program to one expressed in machine language is an automatic process. That is, it is handled by a program (the Pascal compiler) without human intervention. Such conveniences are not readily available for the preparation of the Pascal program. For the time being, at least, it is up to the human programmer to produce a proper sequence of correct Pascal statements from some prior specifications. This is not so terrible. We can help ourselves considerably by making sure that the specifications guiding a program's construction provide the clearest possible description of what the program is to do.

A number of methods are used for expressing these specifications systematically. Many programming departments have selected one of these methods and made it part of their standard operating procedures. That is, coding of a particular program (or program module) cannot begin until a systematic description of the algorithm is prepared, examined, and approved.

A popular descriptive vehicle is one that uses *pseudocode*. The idea is to present an algorithm's specifications in a form that imitates the final program. Computations and other processing activities are expressed as narrative sentences rather than precise program statements. The exact words and phrases for these descriptions are not strictly defined. Instead, emphasis is placed on the structural framework within which these descriptions appear. The basic idea, though simple, is an important one because it is the cornerstone of structured programming:

> There are certain processing activities that serve as fundamental building blocks for all programs. Accordingly, it is possible to express any series of computations solely as a combination of these building blocks. When a program is constructed using only these components, it is considered to be a well-structured program. The reason is that such programs tend to be clearer, easier to analyze, and easier to perfect than those in which these structural concepts are not followed.

Pseudocode imposes a standardized way of expressing each of these building blocks. This makes it convenient to prepare a "well-structured" description of an algorithm. (Convenient is not the same as easy; for many applications, it still may require considerable thought and ingenuity to figure out how to express a certain computational task in terms of these structured components.) One of Pascal's great strengths is that some of its statements correspond directly to these building blocks. Consequently, conversion from pseudocode to Pascal is straightforward.

There are many versions of pseuodocode. However, the differences among them are relatively superficial, dealing primarily with the exact form for the structured components. The version selected for this book is widely used; in any event, adjustment from one form to another takes but a few minutes, with no painful side effects. We shall build our acquiantance with pseudocode by examining each of the basic structured components and seeing how it is expressed.

1.3.1 The Sequence

The simplest activity is one in which we perform a succession of tasks, one after the other. In concept, it does not matter how many tasks there are or how complicated they may be. The point is that a sequence has a beginning and an end. When we perform a sequence, we start at its beginning and come out at the end. If we choose to avoid a sequence, we avoid it entirely. Our tire-changing process in Section 1.1.3 was such a sequence.

The pseudocode representation of a sequence consists simply of a list of activities:

Do this.
Then do this.
Then do this.
. . . . . .
Finally, do this.

For example, suppose a person returned a rented car and the rental company wanted to compute the bill. Charges are based on a fixed rate per day, a fixed rate per mile, a flat fee for insurance, a charge for the gasoline needed to fill the tank when the car is returned, and a discount applied to the total. Data submitted for processing include the car's identification number, the renter's name, number of rental days, number of miles driven, gasoline charge, and discount rate. The pseudocode sequence for the process might look as shown below. [We use the word "read" to indicate the process of obtaining data (i.e., bringing information into the processor) for use in our computations and "write" to indicate the display or delivery of data from the processor to the outside world.]

Read car i.d., name, no. of days, miles, gas charge, discount.
Compute daily charge.
Compute mileage charge.
Add daily charge, mileage charge, gas charge, and insurance fee to obtain total charge.
Compute net charge by applying discount rate to total charge.
Print car i.d., name, individual charges, total charge, discount, and net charge.

1.3.2 Simple Selection: The IF-THEN-ELSE Component

Not all activities follow each other inevitably. Algorithms often require us to make a choice between two activities depending on the outcome of some test. This basic process is described by the IF-THEN-ELSE component:

IF
the condition described here is true
THEN
Perform this activity.
ELSE
Perform this other activity instead.
ENDIF

(ENDIF is a signal to indicate the conclusion of the IF-THE-ELSE structural component.) Either or both activities can be single tasks or arbitrarily long sequences. To illustrate, we shall modify our little car rental example so that not every renter gets a discount. Accordingly, we now include a test to determine whether a discount applies:

Read car i.d., name, no. of days, miles, gas charge, discount.
Compute daily charge.
Compute mileage charge.
Add daily charge, mileage charge, gas charge, and insurance fee to
   obtain total charge.
IF
   the renter received a discount
THEN
   Compute net charge by applying discount rate to total charge.
ELSE
   Compute the net rate = total rate.
ENDIF
Print car i.d., name, individual charges, total charge, discount (if any),
   and net charge.

It is often necessary to set up a situation in which a particular test lets us make a choice between doing something and doing nothing. The pseudo-code for this construction looks like this:

IF
   the condition described here is true
THEN
   Perform this activity.
ELSE
ENDIF

In cases like this, it also is acceptable to omit the ELSE. For instance, suppose we made insurance optional in the example used before. As a result, part of the sequence would be changed as follows:

. . . . . .
Compute mileage charge.
Compute total charge by adding daily charge, mileage charge, and gas
   charge.
IF
   driver signed for insurance coverage

```
THEN
    add insurance fee to total charge.
ENDIF
IF
    the renter received a discount
THEN
    . . . . . . . . .
    . . . . . . . .
```

As seen in these examples, the IF-THEN-ELSE can be included as part of a sequence. In concept, it is simply a single step in that sequence. We are saying in essence, "Now, in this next step, perform the indicated test, see how it comes out, and do the appropriate thing."

1.3.3 Cyclic Activities: The WHILE-DO Component

A third fundamental component of a well-structured program is a *loop* in which an activity (a single step or an entire sequence) may be performed over and over under control of a logical mechanism that is there to make sure the process does not run away with itself by repeating endlessly. There are several ways in which such control can be exercised, and each can be described in pseudocode. The one we shall discuss here is the WHILE-DO construction. This is the most general type of cyclic control in that any kind of loop can be described as a WHILE-DO construction. Accordingly, the other types of loop constructions are included in the pseudocode for convenience rather than necessity. These will be discussed later.

The general form for the WHILE-DO construction is as follows:

```
WHILE the condition described here is true, DO:
    Perform this activity.
ENDWHILE
```

As is true with the other types of structured components, this represents a single conceptual activity that begins with the indicated test being performed for the first time. If the condition described by the test turns out to be false, the entire loop is skipped and the next activity (the one following the ENDWHILE) is started. On the other hand, if the test's outcome is true, the entire activity inside the loop is performed once. ENDWHILE conveys the idea of a control mechanism that forces the process back to the beginning of the component, where the test is performed again. The point is that the activities inside the loop would be designed to include something that might change the outcome of the test when it is performed again. Otherwise, the outcome always would be the same, and the loop would be repeated forever. As long as the test's outcome is true, the loop's activity is performed one more time, and the process goes back to test the condition once again. As soon as the outcome becomes false, the loop is bypassed and activity continues after the ENDWHILE.

Use of the WHILE-DO component can be illustrated by expanding the car rental example so that the sequence for computing a bill can be applied to a succession of customer's data. We shall make the process general by assuming that we do not know how many returned cars there are. Instead, we shall place the previously developed sequence inside a WHILE-DO component that allows the loop to operate as long as there are data values to process:

```
WHILE there still are renters requiring bills, DO:
    Read car i.d., name, no. of days, miles, gas charge, and discount for
        the next renter.
    Compute daily charge.
    Compute mileage charge.
    Compute total charge by adding daily charge, mileage charge, and
        gas charge.
    IF
        driver signed for insurance coverage
    THEN
        add insurance fee to total charge.
    ENDIF
    IF
        the renter received a discount
    THEN
        Compute net charge by applying discount rate to total charge.
    ELSE
        Compute the net rate = total charge.
    ENDIF
        Print car i.d., name, individual charges, total charge, discount (if
            any), and net charge.
ENDWHILE
Print a terminating message indicating the end of the run.
```

This pseudocode description tells us that the sequence inside the loop will be performed once for each set of renter's data, however many sets that may be. Then, when all the bills have been computed and printed, the ENDWHILE brings the process back to the test. This time, the test fails (i.e., there are no more renters to process), and the entire loop is bypassed. As a result, the process enters the next activity, and the terminating message is printed *once.*

Problems

1. State whether you think each of the following processes qualifies as an algorithm. If it does not, indicate why it does not:
   (a) Baking chocolate chip cookies by following a written recipe
   (b) Driving home from work
   (c) Selling encyclopedia sets door to door
   (d) Curing the hiccups by holding your breath and counting to 36
   (e) Brushing your teeth
   (f) Computing the value $9 \times 6 \times 4$

2. Develop an algorithm for changing an automobile tire in accordance with choice number 6 given in Section 1.1.2. Write a pseudocode description of your algorithm.

3. Many people make a good living by telling others how they can make money in the stock market. See if you can find four or five of these "sure-fire" methods. Write a pseudocode description for each one. Is it possible to write a pseudocode description for something that is not an algorithm?

4. This problem is for those of you who are interested in jogging. Every jogger has his or her own extra-special this-is-it method for warming up. Write a pseudocode description for your favorite warm-up routine.

5. Take a look at the little car rental example in Section 1.3.3. One of the assumptions in that process is that every renter will have a gasoline charge as part of the total cost. However, it could happen that some renters may fill the tank just before returning the car. Modify the pseudocode description so that the algorithm handles this possibility.

6. The pseudocode in Section 1.3.3 describes an algorithm that prepares bills for any number of returned cars. If we wanted to find out how many bills are prepared during a run, we would have to include a way of keeping count. An easy method for doing this is to set up a counter and include a step in the processing loop that adds 1 to that counter every time a bill is produced. Modify the pseudocode from Section 1.3.3 or from Problem 5 so that the algorithm prints the number of returned cars processed along with the terminating message.

7. Starting either with the description in Section 1.3.3 or the one produced for Problem 5 or Problem 6, modify the algorithm (and the pseudocode) so that the algorithm computes the total charges billed for the run. This amount is to be printed once, just prior to the terminating message.

8. Modify the pseudocode in Problem 7 so that it describes a process that computes the average amount billed during that run (along with everything else computed in previous versions). This average amount is to be the last thing printed just before the terminating message.

9. Devise an algorithm (and describe it in pseudocode) that computes and prints the sum of the first 30 positive odd integers.

10. Modify the pseudocode description in Problem 9 so that it describes the following algorithm: Instead of computing the sum of the first 30 odd integers, it reads a positive integer named THISMANY and computes the sum of the first THISMANY integers.

11. The process in Problem 10 is based on the assumption that the value THISMANY being read in is a positive integer. Suppose we cannot make that assumption, that is, THISMANY is an integer all right, but it may not be positive. Revise the pseudocode description from Problem 10 so that the algorithm produces the sum of the first THISMANY integers if THISMANY is positive, as before. Alternatively, if THISMANY is not positive, the algorithm prints the offending value along with a message saying, "THIS VALUE IS NOT VALID FOR MY COMPUTATIONS."

12. Expand the pseudocode description from Problem 10 or 11 so that it produces a sum (or the error message) for each of a succession of input values.

13. Revise the pseudocode from Problem 12 so that, after the last input value has been read and processed, the algorithm prints the number of values read, the number of sums produced, and the number of error messages printed.

14. Devise an algorithm and write a pseudocode description for the following process: We would like to read a succession of (however many) English words. For each word, we would like to print the word, the number of letters in that word, the number of consonants, and the number of vowels. After all the words have been processed, we would like to print the number of words read, the longest word, and the shortest word. If more than one word tied for the greatest length, the *first* word having that length is the one printed. If more than one word tied for the shortest length, the *last* word having that length is the one printed.

15. (*Special Challenge*) The American Association for the Promotion of the Use of Blue Paint in Residential Environments (good old

AAPUBPRE) has taken a survey: Senior Room Observers, Room Observers, Associate Room Observers, and Apprentice Room Observers have been hired to observe rooms and report on what they find. For each room observed, the Room Observing Person records his or her Official Observer i.d. number, a preassigned room number, the kind of room it is (living room, kitchen, bedroom, bathroom, dining room, hall, library/den/study, office, laboratory/workshop, laundry/utility, family room/game room/playroom, or other), and the wall color (carmine, light green, royal blue, Hawaiian Sunset, antique white, September Mist, Azure Capri, etc.). Devise an algorithm (and its pseudocode description) that reads and processes these findings. After all the room observations have been processed, the algorithm reports the number of rooms observed, the number painted in some shade of blue, and the number using a color that (alas) is not a shade of blue. Then, the algorithm is to report the i.d. number of the observer who observed the most rooms, along with the number of rooms observed by that observer. Assume there will be no ties. Lastly, the algorithm is to report the total number of living rooms and kitchens (one number) whose colors are shades of blue.

Suggested Reading

Problem Solving

Ackoff, R., "The Art of Problem Solving," John Wiley, New York, 1978.
Banerji, R. B., "Theory of Problem Solving: An Approach to Artificial Intelligence," American Elsevier, New York, 1969.
Polya, G., "How to Solve It," Doubleday Anchor Books, Garden City, N.Y., 1957.

Systematic Program Development

ACM Computing Surveys, 6, No. 4 (December 1974), Association for Computing Machinery, New York, 1974.
Gillett, W. D., and Pollack, S. V., "Introduction to Engineered Software," Holt, Rinehart and Winston, New York, 1982, especially Chapters 1, 2, and 4.
Ramamoorthy, C. V., and Yeh, R. T., "Software Methodology," Catalogue No. EHO 142–0, Institute of Electronic and Electrical Engineers, New York, 1978.
Roman, et al., "Total System Design Methodology Assessment," Report RADC-TR-82-331, Rome Air Development Center, Griffiss Air Force Base, New York, 1982.

Computer System Architecture

Nievergelt, J., and Farrar, J. L., "What Machines Can and Cannot Do," in ACM Computing Surveys, 4, No. 2 (June 1972), pp. 81ff.

Tanenbaum, A., "Structured Computer Organization," Prentice-Hall, Englewood Cliffs, N.J., 1976, especially Chapters 1–3.

Programming Languages

Glass, R. L., "An Elementary Discussion of Compiler/Interpreter Writing," in ACM Computing Surveys, 1, No. 1, March 1969, pp. 55ff.

Chapter Two

The Pascal Program

One of Pascal's primary advantages is that it compels its users to write highly organized programs. This chapter introduces the language's basic structural features and shows how they encourage an orderly arrangement of data definitions and processing activities.

2.1 DESCRIPTION OF PASCAL

Like every other language, Pascal has a grammar, i.e., a set of rules describing the parts of the language and how they can be used to build larger components. Pascal's grammar is particularly precise because this was one of the design objectives. Natural languages grow and develop in an uncontrolled manner, so that any attempt to define a grammar for such a language necessarily must superimpose the grammar on existing usage. Since Pascal was designed from the ground up, the grammar could be defined with complete consistency and a language devised in accordance with that grammar. This makes it possible to describe Pascal's syntax concisely and unambiguously, as we shall begin to see in the next few sections.

2.1.1 Description of Pascal's Syntax

A convenient way to describe Pascal's structure precisely is to have a special language for this purpose. Such descriptive languages (called *metalanguages*) are not always obtained so easily. One of the problems is that the terms and utterances in the metalanguage can be confused with those in the language being described (i.e., the *target language.*) This is a convincing argument against the use of a natural language (e.g., English) as a metalanguage. Instead, a number of small, formal metalanguages have been devised, each with its special symbols.

The descriptive vehicle we shall use in this book is the *syntax diagram* (also called a *railroad diagram* becase of the description's general appearance). Each diagram defines a particular Pascal component by showing the legal way(s) in which that component may be constructed. A simple example from English will illustrate the idea behind a railroad diagram and the symbols used for it.

Figure 2.1(a) shows a syntax diagram for something called a *word*. We see that the diagram starts at its upper-left-hand corner with the name of the component being described. The line leading from the component's name, and the items found on that line, define the legal ways in which a word may be constructed. Thus, we see [Figure 2.1(a)] that a word can be constructed from something called a *letter*. By enclosing the name *letter* in a rectangular frame, the diagram indicates that *letter* is another component, defined by a separate syntax diagram. The definition for a letter appears in the diagram of Figure 2.1(b), which shows that a letter can be either a *vowel* or a *consonant*. The fact that this is a choice (either but not both) is indicated by a branch in the line. Since *vowel* and *consonant* are in rectangular frames themselves, there must be further definitions. Sooner or later, every component has to be defined in terms of elementary items: things that are what they are, rather than being built up from other things. Such items are called *terminal symbols*. In a syntax diagram, a terminal symbol is enclosed in a circular frame. For example, the diagram in Figure 2.1(c) defines a vowel as something that may consist of one of the five terminal symbols A, E, I, O, or U. (Notice the five alternative line branches.) Similarly [Figure 2.1(d)], a consonant is seen to consist of any one of the terminal symbols B, C, D, F, G, H, J, etc.

Referring again to Figure 2.1(a), note that the line coming out of the *vowel* designation splits into two branches. One of them brings us nonstop to the end of the diagram while the other loops back around. The first branch indicates that a word may consist of a single letter followed by nothing. On the other hand, if we take the return branch, we have a single letter followed by another letter. Having picked up a second letter, we are faced with that choice once more: If we take the nonstop route, we have constructed a word out of two letters; if we loop around again, we attach yet a third letter. Consequently, Figure 2.1(a) is a graphical way of saying that a word may consist of a letter followed by zero or more letters. "Well," you ask, "Why go through all this when you could say the same thing so clearly in English?" Now wait a minute. For simple definitions, this may be true. However, as soon as the structure becomes more intricate, the complexity of a precise and complete English description grows rapidly, and the advantages of a formal metalanguage become increasingly dramatic.

One other type of item will appear in Pascal's syntax diagrams: When a symbol is enclosed in an oval frame, it means that the symbol is a *reserved word*, i.e., part of Pascal's permanent vocabulary. As such, it serves a specific purpose in Pascal statements and may not be used in any other context. A complete set of syntax diagrams for Pascal is given in Appendix A, and many of these will be discussed individually as we work our way through the language.

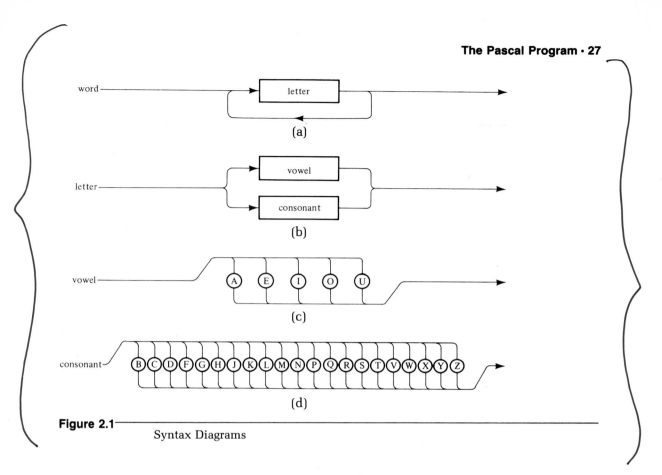

(a)

(b)

(c)

(d)

Figure 2.1

Syntax Diagrams

The use of a syntax diagram does not guarantee that the definition being portrayed is a correct one. For instance, constructions like *can't* or *well-worn* would be considered to be illegal words according to the definitions in Figure 2.1. Similarly, something like GGZUXD would be a legal word. If it is really our intent to define a word as consisting only of the 26 English letters, in any combination, fine; if not, it would be necessary to amend the definitions.

2.1.2 Description of Pascal's Semantics

The syntax of a language (no matter how it is expressed) does not describe the language completely; it defines only the structural aspects. There are additional factors relating to the meaning of the various components that establish how these components can and cannot be used. For example, let us say we are willing to accept the definition of a word given by the diagrams in Figure 2.1. That still leaves us with no information about how letters are used to form a word. As far as the structure is concerned, we start with any letter and keep adding letters till we stop. However, we know that certain combinations of letters simply are not used to form English words. For instance, one would not expect to see the letter x following an f or a k (or quite a few others, once you start thinking about it). This kind of information, and many other items like it, comprise a language's *semantics*. Unhappily, semantic information is likely to be considerably more voluminous and complex than that defining the syntax, even for small, carefully designed artificial languages like Pascal. The problem of providing complete, precise semantic descriptions continues to resist a satisfactory formal solution. Consequently, we shall have to content ourselves with semantic descriptions in narrative form. To help build familiarity with Pascal, the syntax diagrams will be coupled with appropriate semantic information so that proper structure and proper usage will be unified wherever possible.

2.1.3 Representation of Pascal Programs

Throughout the text, many of the concepts and language structures will be illustrated with Pascal statements, parts of programs, and complete programs. These will be produced as computer printouts in which reserved words will be in capital letters and programmer-defined names will be in lowercase. This will improve clarity and make it easier to learn the vocabulary. The same practice will be followed in the body of the text for consistency.

2.2 OVERALL PROGRAM STRUCTURE

At the highest level of scrutiny, every Pascal program is organized in the same basic way. As Figure 2.2 indicates, the program consists of an *identification section*, a *block*, and a concluding period. The period is not part of the block.

2.2.1 The Identification Section

The identification section is a bookkeeping item that establishes the name of the program. As a result, any Pascal program can be identified as an entity that can be made a part of some larger environment (such as a program library) or manipulated in some other useful way. There is not much to an identification section (Figure 2.3): The reserved word PROG-

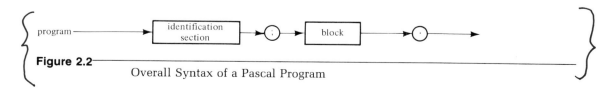

Figure 2.2

Overall Syntax of a Pascal Program

RAM is followed by the program name, and the name, in turn, is followed by a list of input/output services required by that program. (Since the interpretation of syntax diagrams still may be a little unfamiliar at this stage, we shall examine these early ones more closely than will be our practice later on.)

The program name is any identifier that the programmer wishes to attach to the program as a whole. Thus, Figure 2.3(b) defines the program name as being an identifier, and Figure 2.3(d) shows simply that an identifier may consist of a letter followed by any number of letters or digits in any combination. However, there are all kinds of places in Pascal where identifiers may appear. An identifier is constructed as shown in Figure 2.3(d) regardless of where it appears, but the meaning associated with each type of usage is a matter of semantics. Thus, when an identifier is used to name a program, we also must know that this name cannot be used anywhere else in the program.

The service list [Figure 2.3(c)] consists of one or more identifiers separated by commas and enclosed in parentheses. More specifically, these identifiers name the data sources from which the program can receive

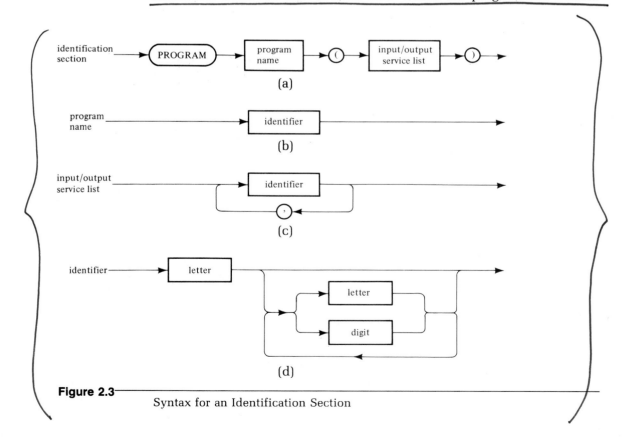

(a)

(b)

(c)

(d)

Figure 2.3
Syntax for an Identification Section

input and the destinations to which the program can deliver output. Pascal provides the two identifiers INPUT and OUTPUT for standard input and output services, respectively. The associations between these identifiers and particular services are not defined permanently. They can be changed by adjustments to the operating software within which Pascal functions. Accordingly, it is best to check with your computer department to find out how the standard input and output devices are defined at your installation. For example, the software at many installations is arranged so that a person working at an interactive terminal automatically may use that terminal as standard INPUT and OUTPUT.

For much of the work in this book, we shall use INPUT and OUTPUT as our service list. Thus, the following identification section

```
PROGRAM stockanalysis (INPUT, OUTPUT)
```

indicates the beginning of a program named stockanalysis that will require the use of the services INPUT and OUTPUT.

2.2.2 The Block

The remainder of any Pascal program is organized as a structure called a *block*. Because of its versatility, a block may be constructed in so many ways that it would be impossible to illustrate them all. Instead, it will serve us better to learn the block's syntax so that we develop an understanding of what is legal without having to examine each possible combination of ingredients. There are two principal components: a *declaration section* followed by a *processing section*. As Figure 2.4 makes clear, both sections must appear, and they must be in the order shown.

The declaration section presents a complete description of the data used in the block. Each item must be described in terms of the values it can have. When several items are to be treated as a collection, their organization must be described as well. Thus, every block unavoidably includes a complete record of its data usage. The ways in which data descriptions are constructed will be examined in detail later on. Right now, it is important to know that every block starts this way.

The processing section specifies the block's computational activities. As a start, we shall examine a block's basic construction by acquainting ourselves with Pascal's major structural ingredients. This will enable us to

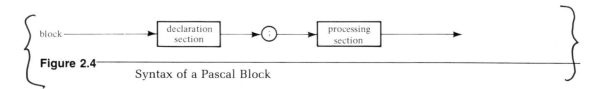

Figure 2.4 Syntax of a Pascal Block

become familiar with a block's organizational pattern without immediate concern about each detail.

2.3 FUNDAMENTAL LANGUAGE COMPONENTS

We shall examine three types of ingredients that serve as Pascal's major organizational elements within a block.

2.3.1 The Declaration

A *declaration* is used to describe some aspect of data usage in a block. The information given in it enables Pascal to set up storage allocations, bookkeeping, and other supporting activites that facilitate the performance of the computations specified in the block's processing section.

One type of declaration is the *variable declaration*. This is the mechanism whereby Pascal reserves storage and associates it with a programmer-defined name. Thereafter (throughout that block), the program can refer to that storage location by using that name. This is called a variable declaration because the value stored in the location reserved under that name is likely to change during the program's execution. As part of the declaration, the programmer also specifies the kind of data to be assigned to that variable (i.e., the *data type*). This becomes part of Pascal's description of the association. The information then is available for Pascal's use in making sure that a value to be assigned to a particular variable is of the same type as that declared for the variable.

The general syntax for a variable declaration is shown in Figure 2.5. As an example, let us compare the following declaration:

```
VAR
     numunits   :   INTEGER
```

This follows the most basic syntax: The reserved word VAR is followed by our variable name (numunits). As required by the rules (Figure 2.5), the name is followed by a colon, after which we specify the data type. INTEGER is one of the standard types recognized by Pascal. It indicates that the only kind of value that can be stored in numunits is a number with no fractional part. (The reserved word VAR was placed on a separate line and to the left of the rest of the declaration to make the declaration easier to read.)

We shall expand the variable declaration by following the inner loop of Figure 2.5's syntax diagram. This enables us to declare several variables of a given type. Thus,

```
VAR
     numunits, branches   :   INTEGER
```

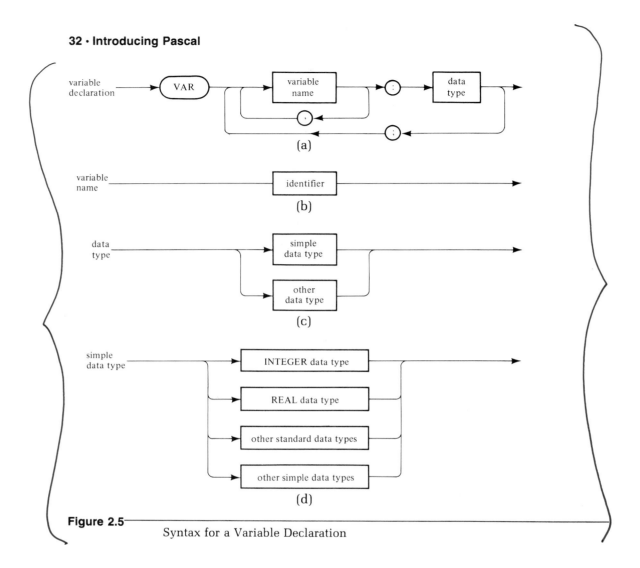

Figure 2.5 Syntax for a Variable Declaration

reserves storage for two variables named numunits and branches, respectively, with each being designed to accommodate an INTEGER value. Further expansion can take place by following Figure 2.5's outer loop and declaring variables with different data types:

```
VAR
    numunits, branches  :  INTEGER  ;
    cost                :  REAL
```

Now, our declaration reserves storage for three variables: The new addition is named cost and it will accommodate a REAL value (i.e., a number that includes a fractional portion). As Figure 2.5 indicates, a semicolon is used to separate declarations of one data type from those of another.

The variable declaration is just one kind of declaration that may appear in a block's declaration section. Now that we are acquainted with this one, the characteristics and usage of the others will easily be learned when we get to them.

2.3.2 The Statement

The *statement* is Pascal's basic unit of expression in somewhat the same way that the sentence is in a natural language. The contents of the processing section in a program's block consists of some number of statements which, when taken together, describe that block's processing activities.

A Pascal statement can be as long as it needs to be in order to express the desired activity. As Figure 2.6 shows, the statement either is *simple* or *compound*.

Simple Statements   A simple statement represents a single step in a computational process. As Figure 1.4 indicated, the work expressed by a single "step" in Pascal eventually may require several machine language instructions. Thus, we cannot establish any specific relationship between a simple statement and the "amount of computation" it specifies. Moreover, Pascal's syntax allows great flexibility in the length of a simple statement and the number of operations it can specify.

Organizationally, there are less than a dozen types of simple statements in Pascal. The one we shall introduce here is the *assignment statement*, Pascal's vehicle for expressing an explicit computation. For example, suppose the names cost and numunits refer to variables that were declared with numerical data types. Then, the following specification:

```
numunits   := 327
```

is an assignment statement in which the variable numunits is assigned a value of 327. The operation being performed is *assignment*, and := is the symbol for the *assignment operator*. Some people find it convenient to

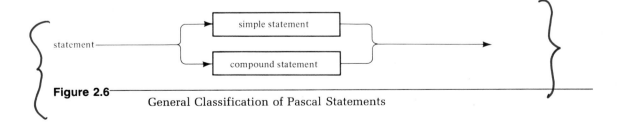

Figure 2.6   General Classification of Pascal Statements

interpret this statement as follows: "*The value in* numunits *is replaced by 327.*"

Having thus given a value to numunits, we can write

```
cost := 32.84 * numunits
```

As a result, numunits' value (327) will be multiplied by 32.84 and the value thus computed (10738.68) will be assigned to cost. [The asterisk (*) is used in Pascal to denote multiplication.] This still is a simple statement even though it requires more processing than the previous one shown. When we examine the assignment statement's syntax in detail, it will be clear that the specified computations can be extended almost arbitrarily without changing the basic structure.

Compound Statements   Although Pascal allows great flexibility in the extent of a simple statement, its syntax imposes certain limitations. For example, the assignment statement can specify an enormous string of computations, but when all the smoke clears, the result must be a single destination. There are many occasions where we would like to consider several such assignments as parts of a single conceptual activity. (This, of course, is the essence of the sequence described in Section 1.3.1) We prepare such activities simply enough, by writing the statements sequentially. Thus, the two assignment statements from the previous section form the following sequence:

```
numunits := 327 ;
cost     := 32.84 * numunits
```

The semicolon is used to separate the two simple statements and is not part of either statement. If we had shown a third statement in the sequence, another semicolon would have been used, this one placed between the second assignment statement and the additional statement. (Since the Pascal compiler has all of the syntactic rules built in, it has no difficulty in distinguishing the use of the semicolon as a statement separator from that in which it separates declarations of different data types.)

For us, then, the recognition of activities formed by sequences of simple statements is an easy matter. However, there are numerous situations where Pascal has to be able to recognize such sequences formally. One common circumstance, for example, is a simple selection (Section 1.3.2) where the activities associated with either or both of a test's outcomes require several simple statements for their respective descriptions. The way this is handled in Pascal is to write such a sequence as *a compound statement*. This is nothing more than an arbitrarily long sequence of statements separated by semicolons, starting with the reserved word BEGIN and concluding with the reserved word END (Figure 2.7). Note that BEGIN and END are not parts of the compound statement; they are brackets that define the statement's boundaries.

The syntax diagram specifies a *statement*, rather than a *simple statement*, as the component of a compound statement. At first glance, this seems innocent enough, but a look back at Figure 2.6 reminds us that a statement may be simple or compound. Thus, we have a situation in which a compound statement legally can contain a compound statement. In fact, the syntactic rule of Figure 2.7 appears to allow a compound statement consisting of nothing but compound statements. How can this be?

The feature that makes it come out all right is an escape hatch that prevents the definition from being circular: Since a simple statement is an acceptable statement (it is one of the available choices in Figure 2.6), then a sequence of simple statements meets the requirements for a compound statement (Figure 2.7). The fact that we are able to build a compound statement using only simple statements gives us something that can be used as an ingredient in another compound statement.

When a set of apparently circular definitions is provided with this kind of loophole, it is known as a *recursive definition*. We shall run into this situation repeatedly as we continue to discuss Pascal's syntax. Whenever any doubt arises, convince yourself that the definitions are not circular by finding a specific route through the diagram that meets the definition's syntactic requirements without using itself.

The compound statement forms the basic framework for a block's processing station. In structural terms, the part of a Pascal program that describes the actual algorithm is really a single statement. This is illustrated in Figure 2.8, where some details have been added to the organizational picture of Figure 2.2. Note the use of semicolons between the identification section and the block, and between the sections within the block.

2.3.3 Subprograms

When a sequence of statements is perceived by the programmer as a single activity that has uses in several places throughout a program, it is beneficial to implement that sequence as a *subprogram*. This is a separate program that can be installed inside another program in such a way that only one

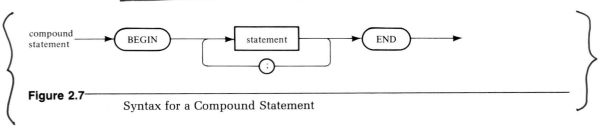

Figure 2.7 Syntax for a Compound Statement

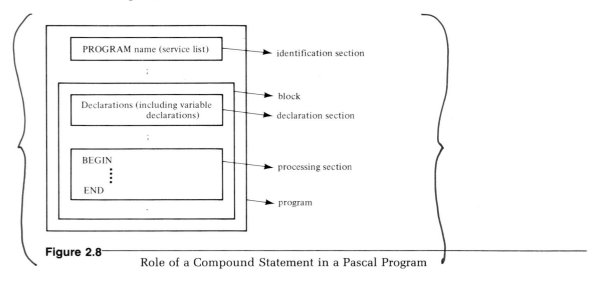

Figure 2.8 Role of a Compound Statement in a Pascal Program

copy is needed in that program regardless of the number of times the activity is needed or the number of different places from which its services are requested. Since a subprogram is much like an independent program, it offers additional conveniences: It can be developed and perfected separately. Often, this enables the programming work to be divided among several people without having the entire undertaking end up in chaos. Then, once the subprogram is known to be working, it is a simple matter to incorporate it into a larger program. Moreover, if the processing embodied in a subprogram is generally useful, it is just as easy to make it a part of many different programs as it is to install it in the program for which it may have been intended initially. In fact, Pascal has a standard library of subprograms available (automatically, through the compiler) for inclusion in any program. In addition, there are convenient facilities for writing and installing programmer-defined subprograms in the library.

Types of Subprograms   There are two types of subprograms in Pascal. The *function* provides a facility that enables its users to treat a sequence of activities as if it were a single operation. For example, Pascal has a standard function that computes the square root of the number it is given. Although it takes several Pascal statements to express the computations necessary to produce a square root, the user is unaware of this; he or she simply provides a value (an *argument*) and "asks for" its square root as if the process were as elementary as addition or subtraction. (The way this takes place is outlined in the next section.)

The *procedure* is a more comprehensive type of subprogram in that the processing described in a procedure is treated as if it were a single statement rather than merely a single operation. For example, Pascal's standard subprogram library includes a procedure whose job it is to read the next item(s) of input data. Although the underlying process is rather intricate, the programmer uses the subprogram by writing a single statement each time he or she wants a line of data brought into the processor from the outside.

Subprogram Definitions   When a programmer uses one or more subprograms from Pascal's standard library, there is no need to specify what these subprograms do. The *subprogram definitions* are part of Pascal itself. Consequently, when a programmer requests the use of a standard subprogram. Pascal recognizes the subprogram's name and automatically makes a copy of it (from the library) for inclusion in the new program. However, if the subprogram is one defined and written by the programmer, its definition must be included explicitly as part of the program.

The structure of a subprogram definition bears a close resemblance to that of a program: It consists of a subprogram identification section and a block (Figure 2.9). The subprogram identification section serves the same general purpose as does the program's identification section, and you already know what a block is. These two components provide a complete description of the subprogram's algorithm and its internal data requirements.

Earlier, it was pointed out that only one copy of the subprogram needs to be included in a program, no matter how many times it is requested from different places in the program that uses it. Now that we know how a subprogram is organized, there still is a question with regard to where the single copy is installed in the program. In keeping with Pascal's emphasis on good, straightforward program structure, there is one legitimate place for subprograms: They are part of the program block's declaration section. More specifically, they are the last items in the declaration section, after the

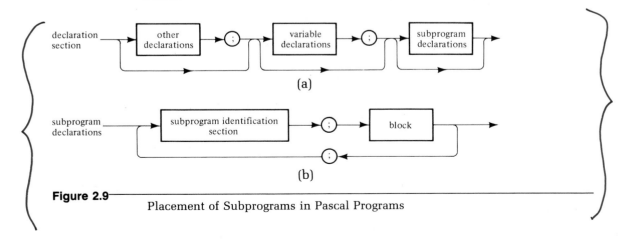

Figure 2.9   Placement of Subprograms in Pascal Programs

VAR declarations. This is indicated in Figure 2.9 as an additional detail in the program's overall organizational picture.

Here is another example where recursion shows up in our syntactic definitions: Any subprogram (regardless of whether it is a function or procedure) consists of a subprogram identification section and a block. The subprogram is installed in a program so that it becomes part of the program's block. As a result, we can have an acceptable situation where a block may consist of a number of components, and at least one of those components is itself a block.

A Pascal program may have any number of subprograms in it. All of them are placed at the end of the declaration section (after the VAR declarations) and just prior to the processing section. If there are several subprograms, their order is not important. Furthermore, functions and procedures may be intermixed. The next section explains why this is possible.

Invocation of Subprograms   Although a subprogram resembles a program, it is distinctly different in the way that it executes. The only way a subprogram can execute is by being activated by the program in which it is installed. This is why it is called a subprogram. When a program activates a subprogram, the process is known as a *call* or an *invocation,* and the program doing the activating is known as the *calling* or *invoking* program. Consequently, the physical placement of the subprogram's statements has nothing to do with its execution; the only time a subprogram can operate is when a program calls it.

In a sense, invocation turns control of the computer over to the subprogram. When the subprogram finishes executing, it returns control to the invoking program at a point immediately following the place from which the subprogram was called, and processing continues from there. The mechanisms for keeping track of these control transfers are built into the program when it is compiled and, therefore, are automatic as far as the Pascal programmer is concerned. As a result, the installation and use of a subprogram is independent of the number of places from which it is called.

Since a function's processing is intended to be perceived as a single operation, it is invoked as part of a computational statement. For example, SQRT is the reserved word for the Pascal square root function. Assuming that side1, side2, and vsum have been declared as REAL variables and side1 and side2 have numerical values currently stored in their respective locations, the statement

```
vsum := SQRT (side1 + side2)
```

computes the sum of the two values in side1 and side2. Then, the function SQRT is invoked and the sum is delivered to it as an argument on which to operate. In response to the invocation, SQRT executes and, when it is done, it delivers a numerical value equal to the square root of side1+side2. That value is assigned to vsum and the computations specified in this statement are completed. As far as the programmer is concerned, the computations (appear to) consist of three operations: addition, square root, and assignment.

A procedure is invoked by a separate statement. For example, Pascal has a standard procedure named READLN whose job it is to read the next line of input from a predefined standard input device. (A "line" may represent a line from a video terminal or other keyboard device, or it may correspond to data from a punched card.) Using the same variables from the previous paragraph, the sequence of statements

```
READLN (side1, side2)  ;
vsum := SQRT (side1 + side2)
```

describes two activities. The first, specified as an invocation of the Pascal procedure READLN, calls that subprogram and causes it to execute. As a result, READLN reads two data items from the next input line and stores them in variables side1 and side2, respectively. Then, having completed its job, READLN returns control to the program at a point just after the invocation (i.e., the next statement). Now, the computations (including an invocation of the SQRT function) are performed as described before.

2.3.4 A Sample Program

To reinforce the organizational principles discussed in the previous sections, we shall write a little program to meet the following requirements: The program is to read a line of input data containing two integer values to be stored in num1 and num2, respectively. These values are to be used to compute a third value, bigsum, by adding the smaller of the two input values to three times the larger of the two. Finally, the program is to print a line showing num1 and num2, a second line showing bigsum, and a final line of output with the message END OF RUN. There is no advance knowledge as to which input value is larger, but we are guaranteed that they are different.

There is no great difficulty in devising an algorithm for this problem. In essence, the solution method is described by the requirements. Accordingly, we can move directly to a pseudocode representation of the solution (Figure 2.10). Since the data requirements already are clear at this stage, they are described in the pseudocode, along with the processing. The expressions min(num1, num2) and max(num1, num2) are used to denote the larger and smaller of the two values, respectively. Note that there is no indication as to how these will be determined. That particular problem is simple enough so that its details need not be worked out in the pseudocode.

Declare integer variables num1, num2, and bigsum.
Read num1 and num2.
Compute bigsum = min(num1, num2,) + 3*max(num1, num2).
Print num1 and num2.
Print bigsum.
Print "END OF RUN."

Figure 2.10 Pseudocode for the Algorithm in Section 2.3.4

Inclusion or omission of such details in the pseudocode is a matter of judgment; there are no precise rules. As a reasonable guideline, bear in mind that the step from pseudocode to program statements should be as straightforward as possible.

The complete program is given in Figure 2.11. Before we look at the details, a quick comparison with Figure 2.10 will point up the strong relationship between the pseudocode and the Pascal code. We shall make this correspondence work for us as we go on.

Several new things appear in the program. All of them are fairly self-evident, and so the commentary will be brief. The material preceding the program's identification section is not part of the program. Any text enclosed by (* ..... *) or [....] is a *comment*. As such, it is printed along with the code, but it is not processed by the compiler. The practice of using comments to provide a narrative description is recommended as an aid to legibility, and we shall follow it throughout the text.

The program finds the larger of the two input values simply by comparing them and providing two alternative computations. One of these will be used depending on the outcome of the comparison. This is implemented by using Pascal's IF statement. Although this type of statement can get to be impressively complicated, this basic form is so close to the pseudocode representation of the IF-THEN-ELSE structural component (Section 1.3.2) that its action is self-evident. (The only thing missing is the ENDIF; Pascal has no ENDIF. Instead, the BEGIN and END brackets around the compound statement help establish the boundaries of the IF-THEN-ELSE component.) We shall explore this powerful statement later on. Meanwhile, Figure 2.12 shows the syntax diagram for the IF statement and the relationship between this statement and its pseudocode representation. Compare the diagrams in Figure 2.12 against the statement in Figure 2.11 to make sure the structure is clear.

A fitting partner to Pascal's READLN procedure is WRITELN. It comes as no surprise that WRITELN produces a line of output on a predefined (standard) output device (usually a printer or video display tube). The information to be produced is specified in parentheses. In strict terms, the desired output is the argument delivered to the procedure WRITELN. Since

```
(************************************************)
(*                 PROGRAM EX201                *)
(************************************************)
(* THIS PROGRAM READS TWO INTEGERS NUM1 AND NUM2 *)
(* AND COMPUTES BIGSUM, THE SUM OF THE SMALLER   *)
(* OF THE TWO PLUS 3 TIMES THE LARGER OF THE TWO *)
(* INPUT VALUES. THE RESULTS ARE PRINTED, ALONG  *)
(* WITH A TERMINATING MESSAGE.                   *)
(************************************************)

PROGRAM ex201 (INPUT, OUTPUT) ;

VAR
  num1, num2, bigsum  :  INTEGER;

BEGIN
   READLN (num1, num2)  ;
   IF
      num 1 < num2
   THEN
      bigsum := num1 + 3 * num2
   ELSE
      bigsum := num2 + 3 * num1 ;
   WRITELN (num1, num2)   ;
   WRITELN (bigsum)    ;
   WRITELN ('END OF RUN.')
END.
```

Figure 2.11
Pascal Code for the Problem in Section 2.3.4

there are three invocations of WRITELN in the program, there are three lines of output. The last of these prints (displays) the *literal* message given in parentheses. Pascal distinguishes literal text from variable names by looking for the apostrophes that begin and end all literal specifications. If we had put apostrophes around num1, for instance, the program would have printed the characters num1 instead of the value stored in the location associated with the name num1. To reinforce this difference, Figure 2.13(a) shows a line of input for this program, and Figure 2.13(b) shows the resulting output.

2.3.5 Interactive Programs

Many Pascal compilers are implemented on computing systems where the expected mode of operation is *interactive*. That is, a program running on such a system engages in a dialogue with the user during which it requests

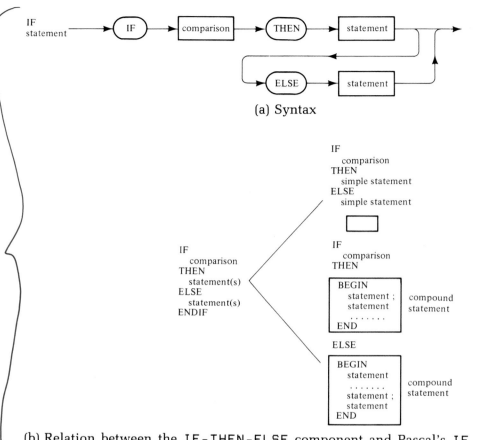

(a) Syntax

(b) Relation between the IF-THEN-ELSE component and Pascal's IF
statement

Figure 2.12

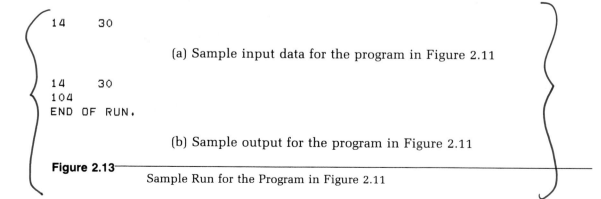

```
14      30
```

(a) Sample input data for the program in Figure 2.11

```
14      30
104
END OF RUN.
```

(b) Sample output for the program in Figure 2.11

Figure 2.13

Sample Run for the Program in Figure 2.11

information and uses it to guide subsequent processing activities. The interactive operating environment is set up so that, when a program makes such a request, it stops and waits for the user to supply the necessary input. Thus, the programmer has an opportunity to design programs whose conduct can be controlled while they are running. In contrast, a program written for *batch operation* is designed so that all of its input data have to be made available to it before it starts running. Then, once started, everything is automatic; the program runs its course with no intervention from the user. The example in Figure 2.11 is intended for batch operation.

If this same program were to be run in an interactive environment, it probably could be made to operate, but it would not be a particularly effective program. Here is what would happen in many systems: To reflect the predominance of interactive computing, the Pascal implementation would be arranged so that the standard input source would be the user's keyboard and the standard output destination would be the user's video display. Consequently, the program would stop just before the READLN statement. If the user, sitting at the terminal, knows exactly how the program is designed, he or she would type in values for num1 and num2, the two items needed by the program before it can continue processing. Once these values are submitted, the READLN statement can be executed and the subsequent activities can be performed.

Instead of assuming that the user knows exactly what to do whenever an interactive program stops and waits, it is much better to equip such a program with output messages that tell the user what is needed and what his or her choices are. Such a message is called a *prompt* or *promptline*. For small, simple programs such prompts may not seem important. However, in more realistic cases, a program may contain dozens of such preplanned stopping points, each with its own set of requirements that the user must fulfill properly. If the user does not receive clear detailed guidance on the spot (i.e., issued by the program itself), he or she simply will not use the program, saying some R-rated things in the process. In some cases, it may even be desirable to display a message after the input has been read to indicate that the data have been received, thereby assuring the user that his or her part of the dialogue was successful.

The interactive version of the previous example (Figure 2.14) illustrates these concepts. Prior to the READLN statement there is an output statement that delivers the prompt to the user's terminal. Immediately after the READLN statement there is an additional output statement that displays the values just read. Such a display (whether in printed form or on the screen) is called an *echo*. A sample run for this interactive version is shown in Figure 2.15. To make sure that the idea of the user-program dialogue is clearly established, the figure includes markings (not part of the program) to indicate who is "saying" what.

```
(******************************************************************)
(*                     PROGRAM EX202                            *)
(* THIS PROGRAM PERFORMS THE SAME PROCESSING AS THE ONE SHOWN *)
(* IN FIGURE 2.11. THE ONLY DIFFERENCE IS THAT THIS VERSION IS*)
(* WRITTEN FOR INTERACTIVE USE. ACCORDINGLY, IT IS EQUIPPED   *)
(* MESSAGES ASKING FOR INPUT AND ACKNOWLEDGING ITS RECEIPT.   *)
(* THE FIRST WRITELN STATEMENT AFTER THE IF STATEMENT IS DE-  *)
(* LETED SINCE IT WOULD NOW BE REDUNDANT.                     *)
(******************************************************************)

PROGRAM ex201 (INPUT, OUTPUT)  ;

VAR
    num1, num2, bigsum  :   INTEGER  ;

BEGIN
    WRITELN ('PLEASE TYPE INTEGER VALUES FOR num1 AND num2')  ;
    READLN (num1, num2)  ;
    WRITELN ('num1 IS ',num1,' num 2 IS ',num2,' THANK YOU.')  ;
    IF
        num1 < num2
    THEN
        bigsum := num1 + 3 * num2
    ELSE
        bigsum := num2 + 3 * num1  ;
    WRITELN (bigsum)  ;
    WRITELN ('END OF RUN.')
END.
```

Figure 2.14

Interactive Version of the Program in Figure 2.11

```
EX202:      PLEASE TYPE INTEGER VALUES FOR num1 AND num2

 USER:      14   30 <RETURN>

            (<RETURN> indicates that the user ended
            the input by hitting the RETURN key.)


EX202:      num1 IS 14 num2 IS 30 THANK YOU.

            104

            END OF RUN.
```

Figure 2.15

Sample Run for the Interactive Program in Figure 2.14. (Double spacing and dialogue labels are for illustrative purposes.)

(*Note:* Although the Pascal statements for interactive programs are identical to those used for batch programs in many implementations, your implementation may require minor programming adjustments for interactive processing. Check with your instructor to make sure that the appropriate ground rules are well established and understood.)

1. Look at Figure 2.11 and explain why there is no semicolon just before the reserved word END.
2. An unsigned integer consists of at least one digit, and a digit may be any of the characters 0 through 9. Prepare a set of syntax diagrams for these definitions.
3. A signed integer can be a positive integer or a negative integer. Using the material from Problem 2 as a basis, prepare syntax diagrams for a complete definition of a signed integer. (Remember that +36 and 36 mean the same thing.)
4. We shall use the term *number* to refer to a general numerical value. For example, 0, −36, 184.507, −0.00743, +44., .208, and +300.003 all are numbers. Prepare a set of syntax diagrams to convey this definition. Use as much of the material as possible from the previous problems.
5. Modern science has made it possible for us to dial a long distance telephone number directly. Prepare a syntax diagram for such a number.
6. The Peerless Floogle Company identifies each type of manufactured parts with a part number consisting of one or two letters followed by a three-digit integer followed by a vowel. The first of the three digits is used as a category classification and ranges from 1 to 5. Prepare a syntax diagram for such a part number. (If you do not know what a Peerless floogle is, you are cautioned against buying one.)
7. In the land of Fneh, accountants are held in high esteem. Thus, when a person becomes a certified accountant there, he or she is given a new name as part of the ceremony. All accountants' names are hyphenated. On the left side of the hyphen are three consonants (any three can be used) followed by two vowels, both of which have to be the same. On the right side of the hyphen are two digits, both of which have to be the same. Depict this syntax diagrammatically.
8. Referring to Problem 7, suppose the authorities in Fneh decided to modify the rules for constructing highly esteemed accountants' names so that the first and third letters in the group of three con-

sonants had to be the same. (The second letter is whatever it is.) How would you handle that in the definition?

9. Prepare a syntax diagram for an automobile tire size. (This will require a little research.)

10. Write the Pascal code for each of the following declarations:
    (a) Three INTEGER variables named COUNT1, COUNT2, and COUNT3
    (b) Two REAL variables named velocity and time
    (c) Combine (a) and (b) in a single declaration

11. Assuming that v1, v2, and v3 are declared as INTEGER variables, specify the value stored in v3 as a result of each of the following sequences. Treat each sequence independently.
    (a) v3 := 404 ;
        v3 := 17
    (b) v1 := −897 ;
        v2 := 61 ;
        v3 := v1 − 4
    (c) v1 := −200 ;
        v2 := 16 ;
        v3 := v1 + 2*v2
    (d) v3 := 688 ;
        v2 := 31 ;
        v3 := v3 − v2 − 43 (remember that := means "is replaced by")

12. Supply the necessary semicolons for each of the following sequences:

(a)
```
BEGIN
    statement
    statement
    statement
    statement
    statement
END
```

(b)
```
BEGIN
    statement
    statement
    BEGIN
        statement
        statement
    END
END
```

(c)
```
statement
statement
BEGIN
    BEGIN
        statement
        BEGIN
            statement
            statement
        END
    END
END
```

(d)
```
statement
BEGIN
    BEGIN
        statement
        BEGIN
            statement
            statement
        END
        statement
    END
    statement
END
```

```
(e)  PROGRAM prob12e (INPUT,OUTPUT
     VAR
         bk,m5,str : INTEGER
         arcs,sides : REAL
     subprogram definition
     BEGIN
         statement
         statement
         statement
     END
```

13. The Pascal compiler uses a variety of signals (such as colons, semicolons, and parentheses), along with reserved words, to aid in its analysis of source programs. Consequently, the physical placement of the statements is of no concern to Pascal as long as they are in proper sequence. It is of concern to us, however, since legibility and clarity are important programming objectives. This is why we have been using an indented format (as exemplified in Figure 2.11), and we shall continue to do so. In light of this introduction, reformat the following program so that its appearance follows this practice:

```
PROGRAM writedown(INPUT,OUTPUT);VAR orig,pct,valuenow:REAL;numyrs
:INTEGER;BEGIN READLN(orig,pct,numyrs);WRITELN(orig,pct,numyrs);
valuenow:=orig*(1.00-0.01*pct*numyrs);WRITELN(valuenow)END.
```

14. Show the output that would be produced by the program in Figure 2.11 for each of the following lines of input:

(a)	348	27	(b)	−41	6
(c)	30	−56	(d)	−303	−32

15. Modify the program in Figure 2.11 so that the first line of output is printed immediately after the input values are read.

16. Prepare a pseudocode description and a Pascal program to meet the following requirements: We would like to read three integer values num1, num2, and adjuster. These values are to be printed immediately after they have been read. Then, the program is to compute bigval as follows: Add adjuster to the larger of the two values num1 and num2 and multiply that sum by 4. The value thus obtained is to be added to the smaller of the two values num1 and num2. Print a second line of output showing bigval. Then, print a final line of output saying RUN COMPLETED.

17. Prepare a Pascal program from the following pseudocode description:

Declare integer variables num1, num2, num3, smallest,
    largest, and range.
Read values for num1, num2, and num3.
Print a line with num1, num2, and num3.
Assign num1 to smallest.
IF
    num2 is less than smallest
THEN
    Assign num2 to smallest.
ENDIF
IF
    num3 is less than smallest
THEN
    Assign num3 to smallest.
ENDIF
Assign num1 to largest.
IF
    num2 is greater than largest
THEN
    Assign num2 to largest
ENDIF
IF
    num3 is greater than largest
THEN
    Assign num3 to largest
ENDIF
Print the values of smallest and largest on a line.
Compute range = largest - smallest.
Print a line showing range.
Print a final line saying RR   N COMPLETED.

(Expectedly, > is Pascal's symbol for "greater than.") sing no more than two simple sentences, describe the process presented above. Show what the output would be for the following line of input:

-27 40 12

Chapter Three

Preparation of Programs

Pascal's emphasis on program clarity is seen both inside and outside the language itself. By now, enough of the syntax has been examined to establish the idea that there are intentionally close ties between the structural components of a well-constructed program and their expression as Pascal statements. This chapter will provide an opportunity to explore that relationship further. In doing so, additional statement types will be introduced, thereby expanding the programming possibilities.

Proper use of Pascal's features takes us only part of the way toward the production of a "good" program. It is not enough for the program to compute correct results efficiently. One of the most predictable aspects of computer applications is that they are likely to change. This is a natural process. As an application's usage grows, its users recognize more and more capabilities (unanticipated earlier) that they would like to see as part of the application. Consequently, a program, seen as being good and wonderful at first, often becomes a bothersome obstacle in the way of progress in a surprisingly short time. The message is clear enough: An important quality of a good program is that it is easy to change.

This places the program's listing in a central position. After serving as a reference document during the program's development, the listing continues to act as a focal point for changes. Whenever a program is modified, the change is denoted by altering the most recent version of the listing to produce a new one reflecting the change. In this chapter we shall establish coding conventions that emphasize clarity and enhance the listing's usefulness.

3.1 STRUCTURAL COMPONENTS AND PASCAL CODE

In this section, a structured program's basic components will be examined again. This time, we shall concentrate on building the relationships between these components and their expression in Pascal. Once the Pascal representations have been defined, we shall look at convenient ways of writing (typing) them so that their intended meaning is easy to see.

3.1.1 Sequences and Compound Statements

The direct correspondence between a structural sequence and a compound statement (Section 2.3.2) needs no further elaboration. In general, it is a good idea to use a separate line (or punched card) for each simple statement. When a sequence of statements is gathered inside the BEGIN . . . END brackets, the resulting compound statement is easy to represent clearly when we write it down. As Figure 3.2(a) indicates, legibility is enhanced when the body of the statement is indented two or three spaces in from the BEGIN and END. The indentation, plus the fact that BEGIN and END are on separate lines by themselves, make the sequences's structure conspicuous.

There can be reasonable exceptions to the practice of placing each simple statement on a new line. A typical case is one where there are related elementary statements, each of which performs the same kind of activity (e.g., a group of variables being set to zero). In this situation, placement of several statements on the same line [as illustrated in Figure 3.1(b)] does not detract seriously from the statements' clarity.

3.1.2 The IF-THEN-ELSE Component and the IF Statement

Figure 2.12 established the fact that there is a close correspondence between Pascal's IF statement and the pseudocode representation of the IF-THEN-ELSE component. This resemblance is emphasized by writing the IF statement with the same kind of indentation used in the pseudocode. To illustrate, we shall show part of Figure 2.10's pseudocode in more detail. Specifically, the computation of b i s um will be broken down more minutely to include a description of how the minimum and maximum values are determined [Figure 3.2(a)]. The corresponding Pascal code in Figure 3.2(b) shows how clearly the indented form conveys the statement's intent.

Another, more compact way sometimes is used to write the IF statement. Figure 3.2(c) shows the same mechanism as the one in Figure 3.2(b) with the reserved word IF, the comparison, and the reserved word THEN all on the same line. As far as the Pascal compiler is concerned, the statements in Figures 3.3(a) and 3.2(b) are syntactically and semantically identical. Usually, Figure 3.2(c)'s format is restricted to those IF statements in which the comparison is small and simple enough so that everything fits on the same line without crowding. The structure of such a comparison is exemplified by the test following the word IF in Figure 3.2:

```
BEGIN                   BEGIN
    statement  ;            statement   ;
    statement  ;            a := 0 ; b := 0 ; c := 0;
    ......                  statement   ;
    ......                  ......
    statement               ......
END                         statement
                        END


    (a)                     (b)
```

Figure 3.1
Representation of a Compound Statement

Two values are compared against each other. The rule under which the comparison takes place is specified by a *relational operator*. For instance, the < operator in Figure 3.2 represents a rule that says, "If the first of the two values currently being compared is less than the second one, the outcome is true; otherwise it is false." The operator < is one of Pascal's six basic relational operators. These are shown in Table 3.1. (Other types of comparisons are possible and will be explained later; meanwhile, we shall have plenty to do with just these six.)

```
IF                              IF
   num1 is less than num2           num1 < num2
THEN                            THEN
    Compute bigsum = num2+3(num1)       bigsum := num2 + 3 * num1
ELSE                            ELSE
    Compute bigsum = num1+3(num2)       bigsum := num1 + 3 * num2
ENDIF
      (a) Pseudocode representation       (b) Pascal specification
```

```
IF num1 < num2 THEN
  bigsum := num2 + 3 * num1
ELSE
  bigsum := num1 + 3 * num2
```

(c) Alternative layout for Pascal representation

Figure 3.2
The IF-THEN-ELSE Component as a Pascal IF Statement

Table 3.1 Relational Operators

Operator	Meaning
<	Less than
<=	Less than or equal to
=	Equal to
<>	Not equal to
>=	Greater than or equal to
>	Greater than

Since the activity associated with a comparison's outcome is expressed as a Pascal statement, there is complete freedom with regard to how simple or extensive that activity can be: When an activity cannot be expressed as a simple statement, the programmer merely specifies it as a sequence (i.e., a compound statement), and the syntax rule for the IF statement still is obeyed. This was seen in Figure 2.12. To explore this decision structure further, Figure 3.3 shows a representation of an IF statement in which some variable named velocity is compared to another value named criticalv. If the two values are equal (i.e., if the outcome of the comparison is true), the program will execute the entire sequence specified within the compound statement. If not, that statement will be ignored and the program will execute the alternative simple statement instead. Indentation of the compound statement emphasizes the fact that, in concept, it is a single activity related to one of the two possible outcomes of the true-or-false test.

```
IF
    velocity = criticalv
THEN
    BEGIN
        statement ;
        statement ;
        ........
        ........
        statement
    END
ELSE
        statement
```

Figure 3.3 Pascal IF Statement with a Compound Statement as a Consequent Activity

3.1.3 Example 3.1

We shall illustrate the use of these features by developing a program to meet the following requirements: Real values val1 and val2 are to be compared with a third value cutoff. Those values smaller than cutoff (this may be true for neither of them, one of them, or both of them) are to be used in computing the following results:

1. sum1, the sum of the eligible values
2. prod1, the product of the eligible values
3. sumsqr1, the sum of the squared eligible values

Those values not smaller than cutoff (this may be true for neither of them, one of them, or both of them) are to be used in computing the following values:

1. sum2, the sum of the eligible values, each multiplied by a real adjustment value named adjust
2. prod2, the product of the eligible values
3. sumsqr2, the sum of the squared eligible values

sum1 and sum2 are to be printed on a separate line, followed by a second line for prod1 and prod2, and a third line for sumsqr1 and sumsqr2. The input value for cutoff is on a separate line (input card), followed by val1, val2, and adjust in that order, all on the next input line. If no values appear in a particular sum, product, and sum of squares, their respective values are to be printed as zero. val1 and val2 always will be positive, their values never falling below 10.5. adjust's value also will be positive, never less than 0.25.

The heart of the solution method lies in a comparison to determine whether a value is less than cutoff or not. Once this comparison is set up, it can be specified for val1 and val2 in turn, along with the appropriate actions. Specification of the comparison is handled easily enough, in terms of an IF-THEN-ELSE component, as shown in the pseudocode of Figure 3.4. Since sum1, sum2, sumsqr1, and sumsqr2 all are quantities to which values may be added, we shall give them starting values of zero so that the additions will make sense. prod1 and prod2 need initial values for the same reason, but in those cases a value of 1 is used. In accordance with the problem's requirements, then, we must remember to change prod1 or prod2 to 0 if its final value is 1. (What conclusion would you draw from the observation that prod1 or prod2 had a value of 1 after val1 and val2 were processed?)

Since the actions required for each comparison's outcome cannot be described by single statements, they must be formulated as compound statements. The resulting program is shown in Figure 3.5. One additional

Declare real variables val1, val2, cutoff, adjust, sum1, sum2, prod1, prod2, sumsqr1, and sumsqr2.
Set sum1, sum2, sumsqr1, and sumsqr2 to 0.
Set prod1 and prod2 to 1.
Read cutoff, val1, val2, and adjust.
Print the input values.
IF
    val1 is less than cutoff
THEN
    Add val1 to sum1.
    Multiply prod1 by val1.
    Add the squared value of val1 to sumsqr1.
ELSE
    Multiply val1 by adjust and add the result to val2.
    Multiply prod2 by val1.
    Add the squared value of val1 to sumsqr2.
ENDIF
IF
    val2 is less than cutoff
THEN
    Add val2 to sum1.
    Multiply prod1 by val2.
    Square val2 and add the result to sumsqr1.
ELSE
    Multiply val2 by adjust and add the result to sum1.
    Multiply prod2 by val2.
    Square val2 and add the result to sumsqr2.
ENDIF
IF
    prod1 or prod2 has a value of 1
THEN
    Assign it a value of 0.
ELSE
ENDIF
Print sum1, sum2, prod1, prod2, sumsqr1, sumsqr2.
Stop.

Figure 3.4
Pseudocode for Example 3.1

item needs attention: In computing sumsqr1 and sumsqr2, another one of Pascal's built-in functions has been introduced: SQR simply takes the value it is given and squares it.

3.1.4 The WHILE Component and Pascal's WHILE Statement

Pascal's WHILE statement (Figure 3.6) presents a direct representation of the processing for the WHILE-DO component: The test with which the statement starts determines whether the rest of the statement will be executed or skipped over. If it is executed, its conclusion is followed auto-

```
(******************************************************************)
(*                        EXAMPLE 3.1                           *)
(******************************************************************)
(*   THIS PROGRAM COMPUTES SUMS, PRODUCTS, AND SUMS OF SQUARES  *)
(*   FOR INPUT VALUES VAL1 AND VAL2 THAT MEET CRITERIA WITH     *)
(*   RESPECT TO A THIRD VALUE (CUTOFF). VALUE(S) BELOW CUTOFF   *)
(*   ARE USED TO COMPUTE SUM1, PROD1, AND SUMSQR1, AND THE      *)
(*   OTHER(S) IS (ARE) USED TO COMPUTE SUM2, PROD2, AND SUMSQR2.*)
(******************************************************************)
PROGRAM EX301 (INPUT, OUTPUT) ;
VAR
   VAL1, VAL2, CUTOFF, SUM1, SUM2, PROD1, PROD2,
   SUMSQR1, SUMSQR2, ADJUST :   REAL ;

BEGIN
   PROD1 := 1 ; PROD2 := 1 ;
   SUM1 := 0 ; SUM2 := 0 ; SUMSQR1 := 0 ; SUMSQR2 := 0 ;

   READLN (CUTOFF) ;
   READLN (VAL1, VAL2, ADJUST) ;
   WRITELN ('CUTOFF:  ', CUTOFF) ;
   WRITELN ('VAL1:  ', VAL1, ' VAL2:  ', VAL2) ;

   IF
     VAL1 < CUTOFF
   THEN
      BEGIN
         SUM1 := SUM1 + VAL1 ;
         PROD1 := PROD1 * VAL1 ;
         SUMSQR1 := SUMSQR1 + SQR(VA11)
      END
```

Figure 3.5

Program for Example 3.1

```
ELSE
  BEGIN
     SUM2 := SUM2 + ADJUST * VAL1 ;
     PROD2 := PROD2 * VAL1 ;
     SUMSQR2 := SUMSQR2 + SQR(VAL1)
  END ;

IF
  VAL2 < CUTOFF
THEN
  BEGIN
     SUM1 := SUM1 + VAL2 ;
     PROD1 : PROD1 * VAL2 ;
     SUMSQR1 := SUMSQR1 + SQR(VAL2)
  END
ELSE
  BEGIN
     SUM2 := SUM2 + ADJUST * VAL2 ;
     PROD2 := PROD2 * VAL2 ;
     SUMSQR2 := SUMSQR2 + SQR(VAL2)
  END

IF
  PROD1 = 1
THEN
  PROD1 := 0 ;
IF
  PROD2 = 1
THEN
  PROD2 := 0 ;
WRITELN ('SUM1:   ',SUM1,'  SUM2:   ',SUM2) ;
WRITELN ('PROD1:  ',PROD1,'  PROD2:  ',PROD2) ;
WRITELN ('SUMSQR1:  ',SUMSQR1,'  SUMSQR2:  ',SUMSQR2) ;
WRITELN ('END OF RUN.')
END.
```

Figure 3.5

Program for Example 3.1 (Continued)

matically by a return to the test and the possibility of repeating the activity. Thus, the WHILE statement gives us a framework for a loop controlled automatically by a test at its beginning. Typically, the test is a comparison like those used in the IF statement. An outcome of "true" enables the program to do the processing described by the simple or compound statement attached to the WHILE.

For instance, suppose we wanted the sum of the first 24 odd integers. (You'd be surprised; there has been a growing demand for this lately.)

sum24 will be the variable in which the sum is accumulated and count will serve two purposes. First of all, it will keep track of the number of times we go around the loop. At the same time, we can use it to determine the next number to add to sum24. [If count has some value n, the nth odd number is $2*(n-1)$. Thus, each time we go through the loop, we shall add 1 to count and $2*(\text{count}-1)$ to sum24.] To get things started, we initialize count to 1 and sum24 to 0. The resulting program fragment (Figure 3.7) conveys the intent clearly. Its structure is emphasized by indenting the compound statement relative to the WHILE part. (The same would have been done even if the activity in the loop were just a simple statement.) Note that the return to the test is automatic; there is nothing in the loop (or in the syntactic rule of Figure 3.6) that says explicitly, "Go back to the WHILE part and perform the test again." The WRITELN procedure is executed once, only when the test fails (i.e., count exceeds 24).

3.1.5 Example 3.2

The loop in Figure 3.6's program segment was set up to repeat a certain number of times (i.e., 24). (Later, we shall introduce more convenient ways to do that.) This is just one way to control the operation of a loop. There are many circumstances in which the number of cycles is unimportant or irrelevant. One such situation is seen here: We shall expand Example 3.1 by requiring that the program handle a succession of input sets. (As before, an input set consists of a value for each of the variables cutoff, val1, val2, and adjust.) The program is to leave two blank lines between each set of printed results, and the message END OF RUN is to follow the last set. There is no advance information regarding the number of input sets in a run.

The pseudocode (Figure 3.8) is not terribly different from the previous version (Figure 3.5). Basically, all that needed to be done was to enclose the processing section (except for the terminating message) inside a WHILE-DO component. (Addition of two blank lines is a minor detail.) The first input set is read outside the loop to get things started.

Now that we have decided what to do, we need to determine how to do it. The pseudocode says (rather blithely) that the loop is to continue going around as long as there is a set of input values to process, no matter how many input sets we have processed already. How can we tell then the input has run out? There are all kinds of ways. For instance, the requirements in

Figure 3.6

Syntax for the WHILE Statement

```
     · · · · · · · · · ·
     · · · · · · · · · ·
sum24 := 0              ;
count := 1              ;
WHILE count <= 24 DO
    BEGIN
        sum24 := sum24 + 2*(count-1) ;
        count := count +1
    END
WRITELN ('SUM24:    ',sum24)

     · · · · · · · · · ·
     · · · · · · · · · ·
```

Figure 3.7

Construction of a Loop with the WHILE Statement

Example 3.1 stated that val1 and val2 never were less than 10.0. We can use that restriction to provide a special signal: an input set, placed after the last one we wish to process, in which val1 is some value conspicuously less than 10.0 (say, −1.0). Then, the program can include a test based on that signal. "Data" used in this way are known as *dummy data*. This is illustrated by the fragment shown below:

```
READLN (cutoff) ;
READLN (val1, val2, adjust) ;
     · · · · · · ·
     · · · · · · ·
WHILE val1  >= 10.0  DO
    BEGIN
     · · · · · ·
     · · · · · ·
    END
     · · · · · ·
     · · · · · ·
```

Although this approach is straightforward, it requires the user to remember to include the special dummy input set at the end of each run. Another way is provided by the standard function EOF. Pascal sets up an EOF value for each source of input. This value is either TRUE or FALSE. (Data with such characteristics are called *boolean* data.) Right now, we are using only one input source (the standard one, named INPUT), so that we need to concern ourselves solely with EOF(INPUT). (For many Pascal implementations, EOF(INPUT) and just plain EOF are equivalent.) At the start of program execution, EOF(INPUT) is initialized to FALSE, and it

Declare real variables val1, val2, adjust, sum1, sum2, prod1, prod2, sumsqr1, sumsqr2.
Set sum1, sum2, sumsqr1, and sumsqr2 to 0.
Set prod1 and prod2 to 1.
Read the first set of input data.
WHILE there are input values to process DO:
    Print the input values just read.
    IF
        val1 is less than cutoff
    THEN
        Add val1 to sum1.
        Multiply prod1 by val1.
        Square val1 and add the result to sumsqr1.
    ELSE
        Multiply val1 by adjust and add the result to sum2.
        Multiply prod2 by val1.
        Square val1 and add the result to sumsqr2.
    ENDIF
    IF
        val2 is less than cutoff
    THEN
        Add val2 to sum1.
        Multiply prod1 by val2.
        Square val2 and add the result to sumsqr1.
    ELSE
        Multiply val2 by adjust and add the result to sumsqr2.
        Multiply prod2 by val2.
        Square val2 and add the result to sumsqr2.
    ENDIF
    IF
        prod1 or prod2 has a value of 1
    THEN
        Assign it a value of 0.
    ELSE
    ENDIF
    Print sum1 and sum2.
    Print prod1 and prod2.
    Print sumsqr1 and sumsqr2.
    Print two blank lines.
    Read the next input set.
ENDWHILE
Print a terminating message.
Stop.

Figure 3.8
Pseudocode for Example 3.2

stays that way as long as any attempt to read data from INPUT is successful. When such an attempt fails (there is no more input to read), EOF (INPUT) automatically changes to TRUE. This mechanism, then, gives us the basis for a simple test: As long as EOF (INPUT) is FALSE, we know that the most recent attempt to read was successful, and we can continue processing. This can be expressed as follows:

```
WHILE NOT EOF(INPUT) DO
    BEGIN
      processing statements
    END
```

(The reserved word NOT is a *boolean operation* that changes a value of TRUE to FALSE, and vice versa. In effect, we are saying, "While EOF (INPUT) has a value of FALSE, we want to perform the processing described by the attached statement.") The resulting program is shown in Figure 3.9, and input and output for a sample run is given in Figure 3.10. The WRITELN statements without specified output produce blank lines. A closer look at Figure 3.10 provides further insight into the end-of-file mechanism: The test for end of file is performed at the beginning of the WHILE-DO loop. If EOF is false, the entire loop is repeated once more; if not, the entire loop is bypassed. Numerical values are shown here in *floating-point form*. In this notation, each value is accompanied by an exponent (the E+nn or E–nn) that indicates the power of 10 by which the number is to be multiplied to obtain the proper magnitude. For instance, the first value of cutoff (which we know to be 20 from the input) is printed as 2.000000E+01. This means that the value being represented is 2.000000 times 10 to the first power. The system uses this notation automatically unless we instruct it explicitly to do otherwise. We shall see how to do that a little later on. (Some systems may use slightly different notation. For instance, 20 may appear as 2.00000E1 or 0.20000E2, but the idea is the same.) Since a boolean data item is defined as one with a possible value either of TRUE or FALSE, the test in the WHILE statement does not show any comparison. In essence, it says, "If the value of EOF (INPUT) is true (i.e., if the most recent attempt to read input data was successful), go ahead and work your way through the loop again. If not, skip the loop and continue beyond it."

3.2 PROGRAM STRUCTURE AND APPEARANCE

As seen in the previous examples, the use of indentation is helpful in highlighting individual program statements and their contribution to the structures in which they appear. This section offers additional ideas that tend to improve the clarity of the program as a whole. There is considerable

```
(**********************************************************)
(*                    EXAMPLE 3.2                         *)
(**********************************************************)
(*   THIS PROGRAM DOES THE SAME PROCESSING AS IN          *)
(*   EXAMPLE 3.1. HOWEVER, THE PROCESSING IS REPEATED     *)
(*   FOR AN ARBITRARY NUMBER OF SUCCESSIVE INPUT SETS.    *)
(*   THE END-OF-FILE INDICATOR IS USED TO STOP THE RUN.   *)
(**********************************************************)
PROGRAM ex302 (INPUT, OUTPUT) ;
VAR
    val1, val2, cutoff, adjust, sum1, sum2,
    prod1, prod2, sumsqr1, sumsqr2 :   REAL ;

BEGIN
    sum1 := 0; sum2 := 0 ; sumsqr1 := 0 ; sumsqr2 := 0 ;
    prod1 := 1 ; prod2 := 1 ;
    READLN (cutoff) ; READLN (val1, val2, adjust) ;

WHILE NOT EOF(INPUT) DO
    BEGIN
        WRITELN ('CUTOFF:  ',cutoff) ;
        WRITELN ('VAL1:  ',val1,'  VAL2:   ',val2,
                 ' ADJUST:  ',adjust) ;

        IF
          val1 < cutoff
        THEN
          BEGIN
            sum1 := sum1 + val1 ;
            prod1 := prod1 * val1 ;
            sumsqr1 := sumsqr1 + SQR(val1)
          END
        ELSE
          BEGIN
            sum2 := sum2 + val1 * adjust ;
            prod2 := prod2 * val1 ;
            sumsqr2 := sumsqr2 + SQR(val1)
          END ;
        IF
          val2 < cutoff
        THEN
          BEGIN
            sum1 := sum1 + val2 ;
            prod1 := prod1 * val2  ;
            sumsqr1 := sumsqr1 + SQR(val2)
          END
```

Figure 3.9

Program for Example 3.2

```
      ELSE
         BEGIN
            sum2 := sum2 + val2 * adjust ;
            prod2 := prod2 * val2 ;
            sumsqr2 := sumsqr2 + SQR(val2)
         END ;
      IF
         prod1 = 1 ;
      THEN
         prod1 := 0 ;
      IF
         prod2 = 1
      THEN
         prod2 = 0 ;
      WRITELN ('SUM1:   ',sum1,'  SUM2:   ',sum2) ;
      WRITELN ('PROD1:   ',prod1,'  PROD2:   ',prod2) ;
      WRITELN ('SUMSQR1:   ',sumsqr1,'  SUMSQR2:   ',sumsqr2) ;
      WRITELN ('        ') ;
      WRITELN ('        ') ;
      READLN (cutoff) ;
      READLN (val1, val2, adjust)
   END ;

WRITELN ('END OF RUN.')
END.
```

Figure 3.9

Program for Example 3.2 (Continued)

payoff in taking the small amount of extra effort to prepare a highly legible program listing.

3.2.1 Program Layout

An important factor in a program's clarity is its relation to the pseudocode from which it is developed. (Don't tell me that you know of places where the pseudocode is written *after* the program for the sole reason of keeping the boss happy. Such places are dwindling in number, and the remaining ones are destined to wallow in swamps of their own making.) Since the pseudocode emphasizes the structural components used to express an algorithm, similar emphasis in the code helps strengthen the correspondence between the two. For this reason is it a good idea to separate each component from its neighbors by one or more blank lines. If the component is a subprogram, it is even better to arrange the listing so that each function or procedure appears on a separate page. Similarly, if a program listing

```
20
12          30          0.5

24
40          25          0.4

18
32          15          0.1
```

(a) Sample input

```
CUTOFF:   2.000000E+01
VAL1: 1.200000E+01  VAL2: 3.000000E+01  ADJUST: 5.000000E–01
SUM1:   1.200000E+01   SUM2:   1.500000E+01
PROD1:  1.200000E+01   PROD2:  3.000000E+01
SUMSQR1:  1.440000E+02   SUMSQR2:  9.000000E+02


CUTOFF:   2.400000E+01
VAL1:   4.000000E+01   VAL2:  2.500000E+01   ADJUST:  4.000000E–01
SUM1:   0.000000E+00   SUM2:   2.600000E+01
PROD1:  0.000000E+00   PROD2:  1.000000E+03
SUMSQR1:  0.000000E+00   SUMSQR2:  2.225000E+03


CUTOFF:   1.800000E+01
VAL1:   3.200000E+01   VAL2:  1.500000E+01   ADJUST:  1.000000E–01
SUM1:   1.500000E+01   SUM2:   3.200000E+00
PROD1:  1.500000E+01   PROD2:  3.200000E+01
SUMSQR1:  2.250000E+02   SUMSQR2:  1.024000E+03


END OF RUN.
```

(b) Sample output

Figure 3.10

A Sample Run for Example 3.2

shows that a structural component crosses a page boundary, an appropriate specification can be inserted at the beginning of that component so that it will start on a new page in the next version of the listing. If left to its own devices, a compiler generally will print (or display) a fixed number of lines on each page of the program listing. Thus, when that many lines have been printed, a new page is started automatically regardless of anything else.

Facilities to force the start of a new page or to leave a blank line in a program listing have nothing to do with the Pascal language. Rather, they are conveniences included as part of the compiler, but they are not treated as part of the program. Consequently, these services are specified in different ways for different versions of Pascal. For instance,

```
%PAGE
```

is the way a new page is signaled in IBM's VS Pascal. When the VS Pascal compiler comes across this specification, it prints the next Pascal statement at the top of a new page regardless of the amount of room still remaining on the previous page of the listing. Your instructor will show you how such controls are specified for your particular implementation.

3.2.2 Program Documentation

An important aspect of systematic program design is to keep careful records of each stage of the process. Thus, the pseudocode documents the algorithm, and the program listing documents the implementation of that algorithm. In a sense, the listing is the ultimate record of the programming project. The use of comments, in addition to the layout techniques discussed in the previous section, can make the listing even more helpful.

As you already have guessed from the example programs, a comment is anything the programmer wants it to be. The Pascal compiler recognizes a special signal that indicates the beginning of a comment. Everything after that signal simply appears on the program listing as is; the compiler makes no attempt to analyze it as part of the program. This continues until a special signal appears again, thereby indicating the end of the comment. In our examples, (* and *) are the beginning and concluding signals, respectively. These are recognized by many versions of Pascal. Alternatively, { and } often are used for this purpose. (Some compilers recognize either set, some only one.)

Comments, when carefully constructed, can be helpful additions to the listing. A good practice is to include a comment at the beginning of a program that explains what the program does. The amount of detail, of course, will depend on the individual situation. In general, this comment would explain the algorithm (if it needs explaining) and define the important variables used in the program. Sometimes it is helpful to include some information about the program's structure. For example, if a program includes one or more user-defined subprograms (i.e., those other than Pascal's built-in functions and procedures), it is useful to indicate briefly what their names are and what they do.

This introductory comment usually is the most extensive one in the program. In many instances, it may be the only one. When additional comments are included inside a program, they generally are minimal (one or two lines), their main purpose often being to explain the processing specified by a particular structural component. If the processing is easy to discern from the statements, the comment is unnecessary, unless it helps to explain why the processing is done in that way and/or why it is done at that point. If the processing is intricate or complicated, the comment should be an explanation of the process and not a paraphrase of the individual statements. What not to do is illustrated best by the classic paraphrase shown below. Although the original occurrence is enshrined in the Computer Monument in Bilgewater, New Mexico, new ones keep showing up daily:

```
(*Add 3 to chrvalue and store the result in TTLVALUE*)
TTLVALUE := CHRVALUE + 3
```

It is not necessary for you to contribute to this list of useless comments. The industry has more than enough already.

Pascal allows a comment to appear on the same line as a program statement. However, it usually is better to keep the comments on separate lines. They are more conspicuous that way.

Problems

1. Write the appropriate Pascal statement(s) for each of the following descriptions. Assume that $v1$, $v2$, $v3$, $v4$, $v5$, $v6$, etc. are real variables and $j1$, $j2$, $j3$, $j4$, $j5$, $j6$, etc. are integer variables. Assume further that all the variables have known values in them.

   (a) IF

       $v1$ is greater than $v2 + v3$

   THEN

       Compute $v4$ as $6v1$.

   ELSE

       Compute $v4$ as $8(v2+v3)$.

   ENDIF

   (b) Compute $v4$ as the sum of the largest and smallest of the values $v1$, $v2$, and $v3$.

   (c) IF

       $j1$ is no greater than 90

   THEN

       do nothing.

   ELSE

       Assign twice $j2$'s value to $j3$.

       Compute $j4$ as 18 more than $j3$.

       Print $j1$, $j2$, $j3$, and $j4$ on four separate lines.

   ENDIF

(d) IF
  j1 is at least as large as j2
  THEN
  Compute j3 as j1 times the smaller of j2 and j4.
  ELSE
  Compute j3 as j1 times the larger of j2 and j4.
  ENDIF
  Print j1 and j2 on one line, followed by j4 and j3 on another.

(e) Compute v3 as the ratio of the smaller of v1 and v2 to the larger of v1 and v2. (Division of real numbers is specified as / in Pascal.) Compute v4 as v3's reciprocal. Then, print v3 and v4 on the same line.

(f) $v5 = \sqrt{v1^2 + v3^2} - \sqrt{v4}$

(g) $v5 = (\sqrt{v1} + \sqrt{v3})^2$

(h) $j1 = \sum_{i=1}^{i=6} i$

(i) $j2 = 8!$

(j) $j3 = j4!$

(k) Compute j3 as the sum of the first 7 multiples of 6.

(l) Compute v5 as the average of v1, v2, v3, and v4. Print v5.

(m) Compute j5 as the sum of all integers larger than 100 and smaller than 10000 that are multiples of 12. (*Note:* Here is a case where a little thought could produce a better algorithm than one that might come to mind right away.)

(n) $j4 = j1^7$

(o) $j1 = j4^{j2}$

2. Write a complete Pascal program from the following pseudocode description:

Declare real variables hrsworked, payrate, strtpay, ovtmpay, grosspay, netpay, dues, fedtax, sttax, soclsec, ttldec.

Declare integer variable idnum.

Read idum, hrsworked, payrate.

Compute strtpay (strtpay=payrate*hrsworked for first 40 hours).

Compute ovtmpay (ovtmpay=1.5*payrate for hrsworked over 40).

Compute grosspay = strtpay+ovtmpay.

ttldec =sum of fedtax (23% of grosspay), sttax (5.5% of grosspay), soclsec (6.9% of grosspay), and dues (3% of grosspay).

Compute netpay = grosspay − ttldec.
Print idnum, hrsworked, payrate.
Print strtpay, outmpay, and grosspay.
Print each deduction.
Print netpay.
Stop.

Note: hrsworked may be less than 40. Run your program with the following values: idnum=674, hrsworked=48, payrate=8.85.

3. Revise the program of Problem 2 so that it processes any number of input sets. Add the following input sets to your test run:

   idnum=240, hrsworked=24, payrate=10.00
   idnum=912, hrsworked=56.5, payrate=7.72

4. Take another look at Figure 3.6. Now explain why it is legal to have a WHILE statement inside another WHILE statement.

5. Modify Example 3.2 so that it is an interactive program.

6. Clavicle Industries, Ltd. bought a DOLDRUM-7 computer system for $266,550 which they would like to write off in six years. Using the straight-line method, this would mean that in each of the six years, the system would decrease in value by a fixed amount such that its value would be zero at the end of the sixth year. Write a pseudocode description and a Pascal program that prints the initial value of the system followed by a line for each year of the write-off period showing the value of the system at the end of that year. (If you look ahead to the next problem, you will see that it is advisable to treat the initial value and the write-off period as input values.)

7. Revise the program in Problem 6 so that it produces the same kind of information for any number of initial values and write-off periods. In addition to the values from Problem 5, test your program with the following data:

   Initial value: $76000   Write-off period: 12 years
   Initial value: $644225   Write-off period: 3 years
   Initial value: $44000   Write-off period: 7 years

8. Dirk Del Mannikin and his crack team of archaeologists are investigating his theory that an advanced civilization flourished on earth tens of thousands of years ago. Not only was this civilization supposed to have had computers, but there were whispered hints that there may even have been a version of Pascal. Oh my. Now, word has come from far-off SmoozleKarpp that some peculiar writing was found by a peasant while she was digging for kvoobs (a fungoid delicacy that grows nowhere else). In the process of showing it to various people, the kvoob

lady accidentally let it be seen by the mayor's son, known affectionately to all SmoozleKarppers as Hey Stupid. Hey had attended the entire third morning of a two-week Intensive Computer Workshop. Therefore, he was able to recognize the writing as an ancient computer program. (That is why his excited father contacted Del Mannikin.) The helpful son also pointed out that time had rubbed away many of the semicolons in the program. (During that morning he had learned about semicolons.) Accordingly, he copied the program and began putting in semicolons with his usual enthusiasm. In the general hubbub, nobody noticed a local goat sneak over and grab the writing. By the time the alarm was raised, the precious morsel had been eaten, down to the last fragment. Hoo boy. Consequently, when Del Mannikin showed up the next day, all that was there for him was Hey's copy. Here is what it said:

```
PROGRAM quecosa(INPUT,OUTPUT);VAR;v1,v2,upv1,upv2,dnv1,dnv2;:INTEGER;
BEGIN;READLN(v1,v2);upv1:=v1;dnv1:=v1;upv2:=v2;dnv2:=v2;WHILE NOT EOF
(INPUT)DO;BEGIN;IF v1>upv1 THEN upv1:=v1;IF v2>upv2 THEN upv2:=v2;
IF v1<dnv1 THEN dnv1:=v1;IF v2<dnv2 THEN dnv2:=v2;READLN(v1,v2);END;
WRITELN('UPV1:  ',upv1,'  UPV2;  ',upv2);WRITELN('DNV1:  ',dnv1,
'  DNV2:  ',dnv2);END.
```

(You might blame Hey for going wild with semicolons, but he had nothing to do with the rest of it; he copied it just the way it was recorded.)

(a) Rewrite the program in a form that makes it easier to read and analyze.

(b) Remove the extra semicolons.

(c) Write a brief description (2 to 3 sentences) of the processing done by this ancient program.

(d) Insert appropriate comments in your revised (reformatted) programming. "Appropriate comments" are those meant to help document the program, not those expressing your opinion of the program or the problem.

Chapter Four

Data

A program's effectiveness is tied to the way its data are organized and managed. Pascal emphasizes this by providing a powerful set of features for describing the types of data and the properties that a programmer wants them to have in a program. Moreover, these features are enforced by rules that make it impossible for the programmer to omit data definitions. Thus, every Pascal program includes a complete record of its data requirements. This chapter introduces the mechanisms for data description and examines their use.

4.1 DATA TYPES AND THEIR REPRESENTATION

No one can hope to list all the data types that might be useful. There are certain fundamental forms, however, that are applicable to a wide range of problems, and computers are designed to recognize and deal with them. For instance, all digital computers can handle integers, and many can process numbers with fractional portions. These are part of Pascal's standard data facilities. In addition, Pascal offers an extensive bookkeeping mechanism that enables the programmer to define his or her own data types for a particular program.

4.1.1 Numerical Data

Pascal recognizes two kinds of numerical data: INTEGER and REAL. Since we have used them before, there is no need here for great detail.

Integers   Although most computers are built to work with binary integers (i.e., integers expressed to a base of 2), Pascal provides the necessary insulation that allows the programmer to use positive and negative integers in the familiar decimal form. Thus, the numbers 3, −101, 0, 3857, and −29 are all legitimate integer values and are referred to as *integer constants*. Numbers such as 38.6, −4.0, or 179. are *not* acceptable as integer constants because they have fractional portions. (The decimal point, even without anything after it, is enough to imply a fractional portion.) A value such as

3,407 is unacceptable (it will be rejected by Pascal even though it is an integer) because of the embedded comma.

The largest acceptable positive or negative integer usually depends on the type of computer being used rather than Pascal itself. For the typical minicomputer, the range generally is −32768 to +32767. Larger systems (such as the IBM 370/303X/43XX series) allow a wider range (in excess of plus or minus 2 billion). Your instructor will tell you the range for your particular system.

Real Numbers Numbers with fractional portions are called *real numbers* in Pascal's terminology. Here again, the programmer can use familiar decimal notation. Thus, values such as 18.8, 0.0061, 0.0, −5493., and −.072 are all acceptable REAL values *(real constants)*.

Pascal also accepts REAL constants written in *floating-point notation*. This form provides a convenient way to write large or small values whose expression in conventional form would require many zeroes at the beginning or end of the values. For example, a number like 0.000000826 is awkward to read and susceptible to error. The situation can be improved by rewriting the value as 8.26×10^{-7}. This *scientific notation* provides the basis for floating-point notation, which is just a more concise way of writing the same thing. For instance, the REAL constant 0.000000826 can be specified in Pascal as 8.26E−7 or 0.826E−6. The 0.826E−6 tells us (and Pascal) that if we multiply 0.826 by 10 to the −6th power, the result (0.000000826) is the value being expressed.

There is no "official" form for floating-point notation. For example, 3.7E5, 0.37E+6, 0.37E+06, 370E3, 370.0E+03, and 370000E0 all represent the same value (370000.0), and all are acceptable to Pascal. Despite this flexibility, it is best to select a particular form as a standard and use it consistently. A popular standard (and the one we shall use) is to adjust the exponent (the number following the E) so that the value to the left of the E is expressed as a single nonzero integer digit and a fraction. Applying this practice to the example values used above, 0.000000826 would be written 8.26E−7, and 370000.0 would be expressed as 3.7E5.

As is the case with integers, there are limitations on the expressible real values depending on the particular computer being used. There are two aspects to this: The *magnitude range* refers to the sizes of the largest and smallest expressible REAL numbers. An IBM 370 type of computer, for example, is equipped to deal with real numbers as large as roughly plus or minus 10^{75} and as small as approximately 10^{-75}. A real value of zero (0.0 or 0.0E0), of course, also is expressible. However, any attempt (on this type of machine) to specify a real value larger than zero but smaller than about 10^{-75} will not be accepted simply because the machine cannot recognize it. The second type of restriction relates to the *precision* of a real value, i.e., the maximum number of significant digits that can be used. Computers like the IBM 370, for instance, can handle about 16 digits of precision. This means that values like 2.736004 or 6.348907211538064E3 are acceptable in such a system, but values like 147.086217994523178 or 4.1079255386501228753E−1 are not. Note that a number like 0.00000000000000002038 is fine because there are only four significant digits. We can see this more clearly be rewriting the value as 2.038E−18. On the other hand, 4.00000000000000002038 is unacceptable. (Why is that?)

As outlined previously (Chapter 2), real variables are defined within the VAR declaration:

```
VAR
    variablename   :   REAL
```

4.1.2 Character Data

Besides storing numerical values and performing arithmetic on them, computers can store and manipulate nonnumeric values as well. This capability is provided by representing such data as individual *characters*. Computers are designed to recognize a standardized collection of characters called a *character set*. This set consists of letters, numerical digits, and special symbols like punctuation marks and basic mathematical signs such as + and −. Two such character sets are in widespread use: the EBCDIC (Extended Binary Coded Decimal Interchange Code) and ASCII (American Standard Code for Information Interchange). These are tabulated in Appendix B.

Individual characters can be combined in any desired way to form *character strings* of any length. The meaning of a particular character or string of characters is determined by the programmer, not by the machine. As far as the machine (or Pascal) is concerned, a string consisting of the six characters W3J.$E is just as legitimate as one consisting of the five characters BLOOM or the six characters 570329. When a character string consists solely of numerical digits (as does 570329 in the previous sentence), it still is a character string, not a number. It is up to us to determine what kinds of character strings we want to produce, what they mean, and how to use them.

When we want to specify a particular character or character string in Pascal, we write it as a *character constant* or *string constant*. This is done by placing an apostrophe at the beginning and end of the string. Thus, the character value B would be specified in Pascal as the character constant 'B'. Similarly, the character string 570329 would be written as the character constant '570329'. This enables Pascal to distinguish it from the integer constant 570329. Some versions of Pascal accept either quotation marks or apostrophes as brackets (known in the trade as *delimiters*) for character constants. (Your instructor will tell you whether that is true for your implementation.) This means that either '570329' or "570329" would be acceptable. We shall use the apostrophe as the delimiter throughout the text.

To specify a character constant in which an apostrophe is one of the characters (or the only one, for that matter), we show two apostrophes for each one to be included. Pascal "knows" this rule, so that only one apostrophe is stored. Thus, the character string constant 'CAN''T' specifies the five characters C, A, N, apostrophe, T. A character constant consisting of a single apostrophe, then, is specified as ''''.

A character variable, whose capacity is fixed at a single character, is declared as follows:

```
VAR
     variablename  :   CHAR
```

4.1.3 Boolean Data

A computer's decision-making capabilities generally are supported by simple mechanisms that operate like simple light switches: They are either "on" or "off." The usefulness of such a mechanism stems from our ability to test its state at a given instant and select a particular action based on the outcome. These decision aids, called *logical switches, binary switches,* or *boolean switches,* are represented in Pascal by *boolean data.* There can be only two boolean constants and, in Pascal, these are TRUE and FALSE. We shall see that numerous decision processes, including the IF-THEN-ELSE activity, use a boolean value as the crucial logical factor.

Declaration of boolean variables follows the same form used for other types:

```
VAR
     variablename  :   BOOLEAN
```

Recall [Figure 2.5(d)] that we established the standard data types as being part of a larger category (simple data types). Now we can restate that definition more completely by including the four standard data types within the larger context of simple data types. These definitions appear in Figure 4.1.

4.1.4 Names for Constants

The ease with which we can use constants is emphasized by the fact that we have included them in various computations without any fuss. Hidden behind an innocent statement such as

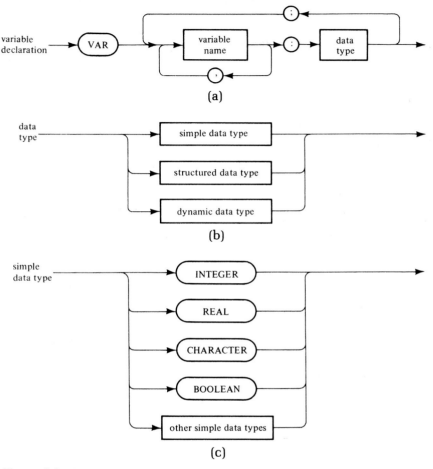

(a)

(b)

(c)

Figure 4.1

Declaration of Pascal Variables

```
result := 3.2 * aval - 6.17 * bval
```

is a collection of activities whereby Pascal recognizes the need for two REAL constants (3.2 and 6.17), produces them, and finds places to store them so that they are available when the program is run. All of this takes place without any explicit declarations by the programmer. The appearance of the constants in the statement is enough to trigger this activity. There are occasions, however, when the programmer wants to call attention to a constant by declaring it. Pascal has a specific feature for this purpose. Its use enables the programmer to give names to constants, after which those names may be used in other parts of the program as references to those values. In many instances, named constants can help greatly in clarifying the meaning of a particular computation. For instance, instead of specifying the value 3.14159 for pi in the statement

```
circum := 3.14159 * diam
```

we can declare pi as a named constant (named ₱i) in which case we can write

```
circum := ₱i * diam
```

and Pascal will "know" enough to use 3.14159.

Declaration of Named Constants   Pascal's syntax for naming constants is embodied in the syntax shown in Figure 4.2. Applying this to the example of ₱i, the declaration

```
CONST
    ₱i = 3.14159
```

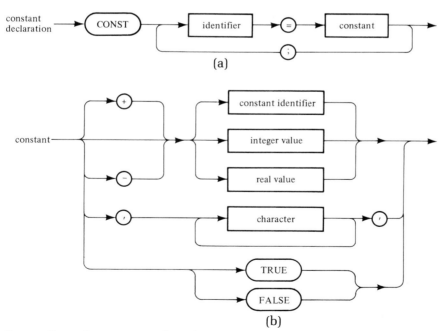

(a)

(b)

Semantics: A constant identifier is a name already associated with a constant earlier in the CONST declaration.

Figure 4.2

establishes ₽i as being synonymous with 3.14159. Similarly, the declaration

```
CONST
    blank = ' '
```

associates the name b l an k with a single blank character.

As Figure 4.1 indicates, the several named constants may be defined together. Thus,

```
CONST
    ₽i = 3.14159  ;
    blank = ' '
```

names the two constants mentioned before. The CONST declaration always goes ahead of the variable declaration. This is seen in Figure 4.3, where the declaration section's syntax is developed in more detail than the basic form given originally in Figure 2.9(a). (The additional components in the declaration section will be introduced later.) As Figure 4.3 shows, all these ingredients have certain positions in the declaration section. Regardless of the presence or absence of other declarations, CONST always precedes VAR.

Standardized Named Constants   In addition to the CONST facility described before, Pascal includes two permanently named constants. Besides the boolean constants TRUE and FALSE, Pascal provides the following standard names:

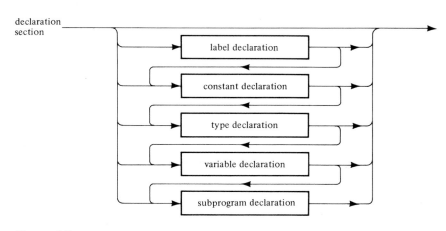

declaration section

- label declaration
- constant declaration
- type declaration
- variable declaration
- subprogram declaration

Figure 4.3
Construction of a Declaration Section

MAXINT: The largest possible integer value that can be recognized by the particular computer being used. When a Pascal compiler is implemented on an IBM 370 type of machine, for example, MAXINT is fixed at a value of 2147483647.

NIL: A designation indicating a location of "nowhere." This will be useful when we deal with dynamic data types.

4.2 PROGRAMMER-DEFINED DATA

The data types described thus far relate directly to a computer's physical facilities for recognizing and processing such data. Any other type of data, regardless of how *we* express them or what they may mean to *us*, ultimately must be transformed into numbers, characters, or boolean values before a computer can do anything with them.

Pascal includes bookkeeping structures that handle these transformations automatically. For instance, let us suppose that a particular program becomes easier to prepare if it can make use of a data type called citrus. When a data item is a citrus, it may have one of the values grapefruit, lemon, lime, orange, or tangerine. Any other value (like tangelo, or cucumber, or 7) is illegal because we say it is. We can include the definition of a citrus as part of the program's declarations. As a result, Pascal sets up mechanisms for recognizing the allowable values and spotting the illegal ones. The new data type then is available for use throughout the program. It is as if the machine had been designed to recognize a citrus just as it recognizes an INTEGER or a BOOLEAN value.

4.2.1 Definition of Nonstandard Data Types

Any and all programmer-defined data types are described in a TYPE declaration whose syntax is shown in Figure 4.4(a). To establish the basic form, we shall define the citrus data type mentioned before:

```
TYPE
    citrus = (grapefruit, lemon, lime, orange, tangerine)
```

The information given to the right of the = sign specifies (in this instance) all the possible values for the citrus data type. When we specify a list of acceptable values for a citrus, we tell Pascal that a citrus is an *enumerative* data type. This is one of several kinds of simple data types. Recall (Figure 4.1) that this class includes the four standard types, along with a category we initially called "other simple types." The enumerative data type is one of them [Figure 4.4(b)]. Classes other than simple types will be introduced a little later in the chapter.

The TYPE declaration (if there is one) is placed immediately prior to the VAR part of the declaration section. If a CONST declaration also happens to be included, it goes before the TYPE declaration. These three declarations (CONST, TYPE, and VAR, in that order) form the basic declaration section in simple programs (Figure 4.3). A LABEL declaration (introduced later but not used extensively) may appear before the CONST declaration. Subprogram declarations are included after the VAR declaration. These have been introduced in Chapter 2 and they, too, will be brought in as the plot develops.

4.2.2 Enumerative Data Types

We often deal with information that falls (or is pushed) into discrete categories. Thus, an undergraduate college student is (officially) either a

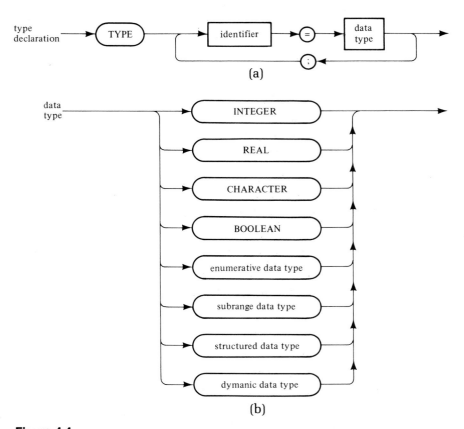

Figure 4.4 ──

Construction of a TYPE Declaration

freshman, sophomore, junior, or senior. Similarly, a current American coin is either a penny, nickel, dime, quarter, half-dollar, or dollar. Data that can be categorized this way may be organized as an enumerative data type (Figure 4.5). Using `studentyr` and `coin` as the respective data type names for the two examples just mentioned, the declaration for these types would look like this:

```
TYPE
    studentyr = (freshman, sophomore, junior, senior) ;
    coin = (penny, nickel, dime, quarter, halfdollar, dollar)
```

Declaration of Enumerative Data Definition of a nonstandard data type merely establishes its existence. It gives us the opportunity to treat the new type as if it were one of Pascal's predefined types. Accordingly, we can declare one or more variables of that type. For example, assuming the `TYPE` declaration for `studentyr` and `coin` given before, we can write something like this:

```
VAR
    studentstatus   :   studentyr  ;
    money, change   :   coin  ;
    count           :   INTEGER
```

As a result, we have a variable named `studentstatus` whose type is `studentyr`, meaning that it can have one of the four legal values defined for that type. In addition, we have two variables (`money` and `change`) both of type `coin`. Each of these may assume one of the six values defined for the type `coin`. Declaration of `count` as an ordinary integer variable was included for good measure just to show that variables of all data types are intermixed in one declaration. Real values cannot serve as a basis for an enumerative data type.

Assignment of Values for Enumerative Data Types An enumerative variable can be given a value by means of an ordinary assignment state-

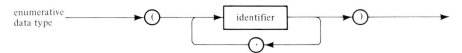

Semantics: The list of identifiers specifies the acceptable values for the data type.

Figure 4.5
Enumerative Type Declaration

ment. For example, assuming the TYPE and VAR declarations specified earlier, we can write a sequence such as

```
money       := dime   ;
studentstatus := sophomore   ;
change      := money
```

in which case the variables money and change each will have a value of dime, and studentstatus will have a value of sophomore.

Comparative Values of Enumerative Data   Even though the values associated with the data type coin in the previous example are words, they are not character strings. That is why the value on the right side of the assignment operator (:=) in each of the previous three statements was written without the apostrophes required for character string constants. For example, the statement

```
money := dime
```

was not written as

```
money := 'DIME'
```

because the value dime is conceptually different from the character string 'DIME'.

It is convenient (and not farfetched) to think of an enumerative data type as being supported by a table (invisible to the programmer) in which each value is represented by a code. For the type coin defined earlier, this table can be imagined as shown in Table 4.1. Similarly, freshman, sophomore, junior, and senior would be associated, respectively, with codes of 0, 1, 2, and 3. The codes are not arbitrary. They correspond to the order in which the values are listed in the TYPE declaration. Since

Table 4.1   Internal Coding for the Data Type coin

Value	Internal Coding
Penny	0
Nickel	1
Dime	2
Quarter	3
Half-dollar	4
Dollar	5

penny was listed first, its internal code is 0, nickel's internal code is 1 because it was listed second, and so on. These codes are not numbers. No arithmetic can be done with them, nor are they directly accessible to the programmer. They indicate the *ordinal positions* of the values, thereby ranking them relative to each other. Thus, because dime appears earlier in the list than quarter, Pascal treats the value dime as being "less than" quarter. As a result, it is possible to compare such values in an IF-THEN-ELSE construction. For instance, assume that coin has been defined in a TYPE declaration as before, some variable named money has been declared as being of type coin, and money has been assigned some value. Now, we can say something like this:

```
IF
    money <= quarter
THEN
    action1
ELSE
    action2
```

The test in the IF statement is as simple as it looks. If the value in money is no greater than quarter (i.e., if it is penny, nickel, dime, or quarter), the outcome is TRUE and action1 is taken. In other words, the programmer exercises control over the relative values for new data types by selecting the order in which he or she lists those values in the TYPE declaration.

We shall explore additional mechanisms for enumerative data later on. The purpose at this point was merely to introduce them as part of the language's data declaration facilities.

4.2.3 Subrange Data Types

A subrange data type is one whose values are taken from a wider range of possibilities, with the restrictions being imposed by the meaning of the data. For instance, suppose we wanted to report an automobile's weight to the nearest pound. It certainly is possible to represent such a value with an ordinary integer, in which case we could declare a variable named mycarwt as follows:

```
VAR
    mycarwt  :  INTEGER
```

That means we can store any integer value in mycarwt as an "acceptable" automobile weight. If the value does not make sense (a car weight of −32 pounds, for example, does not make sense), it is up to the programmer to make sure that the program is safe from such situations.

Pascal provides the opportunity for a more automatic safeguard that allows the programmer to define a new data type in which the range of permissible values is specified. To illustrate, let us suppose that we are willing to agree that 1200 pounds is the lightest possible automobile weight, and 12000 pounds is the heaviest weight. We can use these limits to define a new data type:

```
TYPE
    autowt = 1200..12000
```

This says that autowt is being defined as a subrange data type whose values may be integers ranging anywhere from 1200 to 12000. Pascal recognizes the two extreme values as integers, and the two periods indicate the acceptability of everything (every integer value, in this case) inbetween. The general syntax is shown in Figure 4.6.

Now, we can define mycarwt as

```
VAR
        mycarwt  :   autowt
```

thereby setting up a variable for which the program will accept any integer in the range specified in the TYPE declaration. Any attempt to violate that range (for that variable) anywhere in the program will be rejected automatically. Subrange data types also can be defined using character values. For instance,

```
TYPE
    letter = 'A'..'Z'
```

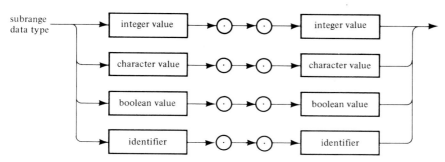

Semantics: The item to the left of .. must be "less than" the one to the right ('A' < 'B', FALSE < TRUE). Identifier refers to a value declared for an enumerative data type.

Figure 4.6
Subrange Type Declaration

defines a data type whose values are single characters taken from the 26 uppercase letters of the alphabet. Now we can write

```
VAR
    initial  :  letter
```

in which case a variable named initial can only have 1 of 26 possible values. It is illegal to define a subrange for REAL values. (Why is that a sensible restriction?)

Subranges of standard data types can be specified for individual variables without the need for separately defined data types. For example, the declarations

```
VAR
    initial  :  'A'..'Z' ;
    mycarwt  :  1200..12000
```

produce the same results as shown before. Since the acceptable values for both variables are subranges of standard types, Pascal recognizes them and no corresponding TYPE declarations are required. Thus, instead of being a variable of the autowt type, mycarwt now has been declared as an INTEGER variable with a limited range of legitimate values. Similarly, initial now is a CHARACTER subrange variable.

4.2.4 Subranges for Nonstandard Data Types

It also is possible to define a subrange for an enumerative data type because of the relation between the relative values and their positions in the declared list. To illustrate, consider the following sequence:

```
TYPE
    day = (mon, tue, wed, thu, fri, sat, sun) ;
    grade = (a, b, c, d, f) ;
VAR
    weekday  :  mon..fri ;
    passgrade :  a..d
```

As a result of these declarations, the variable named weekday may have one the five values mon, tue, wed, thu, or fri. Similarly, the variable passgrade may have one of the four values a, b, c, or d. Of course, the VAR declarations would be meaningless if the full ranges had not been defined in appropriate TYPE declarations.

Our purpose, for now, has been to introduce the concept of enumerative and subrange data types as reasonable extensions of the standard data facilities. Once we have acquired additional fluency with other language features, we shall put these types to work.

4.3 ORGANIZATION OF DATA

The simple declaration of a variable or a named constant does more than signal our requirement for a place to store something. It also defines the type of data to be stored, and it can even impose restrictions on the range of acceptable values.

There is another aspect of data definition not yet considered. Thus far, each item has been declared as a separate unit with no inherent relation to other data items. When we specify a computation, we connect some of these items with each other to help fulfill the purpose of the particular algorithm. Outside of that computation, these connections no longer exist and the data, once again, are individual, independent items. Such values are called *simple values* or *single values,* and the variables we have been declaring and using all along are *simple variables* or *single-valued variables.*

There are many useful problem solutions that require their data to be organized into various kinds of collections. These collections, called *data structures,* are characterized by certain relationships among their individual members. Each type of data structure has its own set of relationships, and these define the kinds of data that can belong to a particular structure. In addition, there are rules associated with each data structure that prescribe the kinds of operations available for it. Thus, each data item in a collection must be viewed as a member of that group, subject to the restrictions that may be imposed by the operating rules.

We can devise a limitless variety of data structures, each with its own organizational properties and operating rules. The need for such inventions depends on the kind of problems we are trying to solve. Certain data structures have been found to be useful in such a wide variety of applications that they have become standardized: Accepted terminologies have grown up around their characteristics, and their use is taught as a distinct subject. In recognition of their general usefulness, several of these data structures are supported in Pascal by *structured data types* (Figure 4.7). "Supported," in this context, means that the language is equipped with bookkeeping mechanisms that make it convenient for the programmer to set up and work with these structures. When such support is not available (as would be the case when a programmer needs a new kind of data structure), it is up to the programmer to bridge the gap between the way he or she wants to view the data and the way the data actually are organized in the machine. Methods and techniques for doing this are beyond the scope of this text. However, familiarity with some of the standard data structures will make it easier to deal with these issues in later work. Accordingly, this section takes a first look at some of the major data organizations and their representation in Pascal.

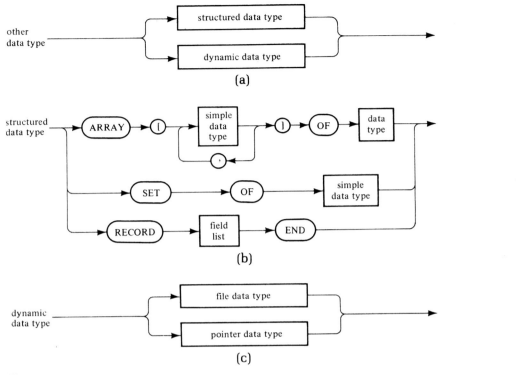

Figure 4.7 Structured Data Types

4.3.1 Arrays

An array is a collection of items with the following organizational characteristics:

1. All of the members (*elements*) have to be of the same data type.
2. The number of elements in an array is fixed for a given usage. That is, once the size of an array is defined, it stays that way. There are no computational operations whose results expand or contract the array. (We can pretend that an array changes its size by defining a big array and then using only part of it.)
3. All the elements have to be located next to each other, in a certain order. Whether this is actually the case inside the computer is of secondary importance. The point is that this is the way an array is viewed by a person using it, and all array operations are based on that view. Consequently, Pascal (or any other programming language, for

that matter) must make any arrangements that may be needed to validate that view.

4. Any and all elements of an array are accessible at any time.
5. An array has a specific first element whose location serves as a reference. That is, any element in an array is identified in terms of its location relative to the first element.

To illustrate these fundamental properties, we shall declare a simple array and work with some of its elements:

```
VAR
    lengths  :  ARRAY [1..8] OF INTEGER  ;
        . . . . . . . . . .
        . . . . . . . . . .
    lengths[1] := 26  ;
    lengths[3] := 14  ;
    lengths[2] := lengths[3] - lengths[1]
        . . . . . . . . . .
```

The declaration instructs Pascal to reserve enough storage for eight integer values under the collective name lengths. Hence, whenever the name lengths is mentioned, it refers to all eight elements, not to any one in particular. All the values will be of the same type (INTEGER in this case). There are no values yet; as is true with any other declaration, we have only bookkeeping. The information inside the square brackets defines the way to identify each of lengths' elements. (Such an identifier is called an *index*.) In this case, the index is an integer ranging from 1 through 8. This is how Pascal "knows" that lengths is to have eight elements. Furthermore, the index specification informs Pascal that the first element (the reference element) is to be named lengths[1], the next (second) element is to have the name lengths[2], and so on, up through lengths[8]. Thus, the declaration produces the data organization shown in Figure 4.8, thereby satisfying the structural requirements for an array.

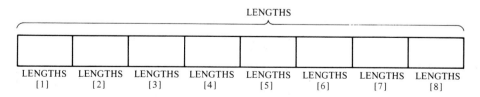

Figure 4.8

Array Organization

Now we can turn our attention to the assignment statements in the sequence given above. Since each array element has its own identifier, we can isolate it from the other elements and treat it just like an ordinary scalar variable. When the array index is applied to a particular element, the resulting index value is called a *subscript*. Thus, the first element has the subscript [1], and so on. Once this notation is clear, we can see that there is nothing special about the three assignment statements in the little example. As a result of these statements, three of lengths' eight elements now have values. This result is shown in Figure 4.9.

Automatic Loops for Arrays   An activity often applied to arrays is the systematic processing of its elements in succession. Pascal's FOR statement makes this easy to do. To illustrate, suppose we have the following declaration:

```
VAR
    lengths   :   ARRAY [1..8] OF INTEGER  ;
    i         :   INTEGER ;
      . . . . . . . . . .
      . . . . . . . . . .
  FOR i:=1 TO 8 DO
     READLN (lengths[i])
      . . . . . . . . . .
```

As a result, eight input values will be read and stored, respectively, in lengths[1] through lengths[8]. Control mechanisms associated with the FOR statement regulate the loop so that its single READLN statement is executed exactly eight times. The variable i (the *index variable*) is set to an initial value of 1 (in response to the FOR statement's directions) and is increased by 1 automatically for each repetition. A *limiting value* (8 in this case) stops the cycling. Since the FOR statement's index variable also is used to designate the subscript in the READLN statement, the element specified by the READLN changes with each repetition.

The activity in such a loop can be extended as desired by using a compound statement to specify it. Suppose that we wanted to compute the sum of lengths' elements. Using sumlengths for this purpose, we can write the following fragment:

26	-12	14	?	?	?	?	?

Figure 4.9 Manipulation of Individual Array Elements

```
VAR
    lengths      :
    i, sumlengths  ,
        . . . . . . . . . .
        . . . . . . . . . .
sumlengths := 
FOR i:=1 TO ⌐
    BEGIN
        REA⌐
        su⌐
    END
        . . . . . . . . .
```

Now, each time an elem.
part of that cycle through u.
statement, it still allows exact.

Other Data Types as Array Indices

subscript values for Pascal arrays. Charact.
subrange data types, can be used to identify i.
course, the data type to be used as the index has u
declaration. For instance, consider the following de.

```
TYPE
    letter = 'A'..'Z'  ;
VAR
    whichletter  :  letter ;
    codes        :  ARRAY [letter] OF INTEGER
        . . . . . . . . . .
```

First, we defined a data type named letter whose values can be taken
from the 26 characters 'A' through 'Z'. Once declared, this subrange type
can be used as an index for an array, and that is just what is done in the
declaration for codes: We set up an array of integers that is indexed by the
letters data type. This means that codes has 26 elements, the first of
which is codes['A'], the second is codes['B'], and so on. Thus, the
statement

```
codes['L'] := 37
```

assigns a value of 37 to the twelfth element in array codes.

An enumerative or subrange index identifies individual elements just
like an integer index does. Consequently, its use to regulate a loop requires
no special considerations. To illustrate, we shall assign a value of 180 to
each of codes' first 16 elements and a value of –61 to each of the last 10.

the declarations given above, the following two statements do

```
hichletter := 'A' TO 'P' DO
odes[whichletter] := 180    ;
 whichletter := 'Q' TO 'Z' DO
 codes[whichletter] := -61
```

4.3.2 Other Structured Data Types

Pascal recognizes other structured data types whose usefulness will become more apparent when we gain additional experience with the language. Consequently, we shall just mention them briefly to acquaint you with their fundamental properties.

Sets A set (in Pascal) is a collection of data items with the following characteristics:

1. Members (elements) of a set all must belong to the same data type. The type from which a set's members are drawn is called the *base type*.
2. The REAL type cannot be used as a base type.
3. The number of elements in a set is not fixed. Sets may grow or shrink to fit the particular occasion at any instant. A set may be *empty* (i.e., it may have no values at all).
4. Each eligible value may appear in a set only once.
5. Sets are manipulated in their entirety. Consequently, there is no explicit relationship between individual elements and respective locations. A reference to a set is a reference to all the elements (if there are any) in that set at that time.

The definition of a set (Figure 4.10) must show the values that are eligible for membership in that set. For example, the declaration

```
VAR
    winners  :  SET PF 10974, 20063, 41798, 62875
```

defines a set named winners with a base type of INTEGER. Thus, elements of winners must be INTEGER values, but not just any integers. Membership is restricted to the four values shown in the definition. winners could consist of any one of these values, any two of them, any three, all four, or none at all (the empty set). Similarly,

```
VAR
    lastsix  :  SET OF 'U'..'Z'
```

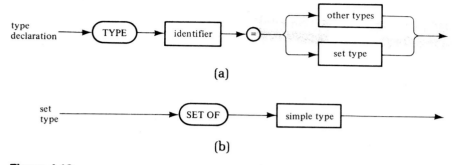

(a)

(b)

Figure 4.10

Declaration of a Set

declares lastsix to be a set variable whose values could be any or all of the characters U, V, W, X, Y, Z, or empty.

Programmer-defined data types also may be used as elements in sets. Consider the following caloric example:

```
TYPE
    topping = (hotfudge, marshmallow, pineapple,
                 butterscotch, nuts) ;
VAR
    goo  :  SET OF topping
```

This says that the variable goo is a set whose members may consist of any, all, or none of the five values listed for the enumerative type topping.

Set variables can be given values via simple assignments. Assuming the previous declarations of lastsix, the statement

```
lastsix := {'Z','W','X'}
```

assigns the three characters 'Z', 'W', and 'X' to lastsix, replacing whatever may have been there before. The statement

```
lastsix := {}
```

assigns the empty set to lastsix.

Records   When it is convenient to organize a collection of data in which the individual items may be of different types, we do so by constructing a *record*. Each type of record to be used in a program is defined by a TYPE declaration whose syntax is shown in Figure 4.11.

For example, somebody's birthdate could be constructed as a record.

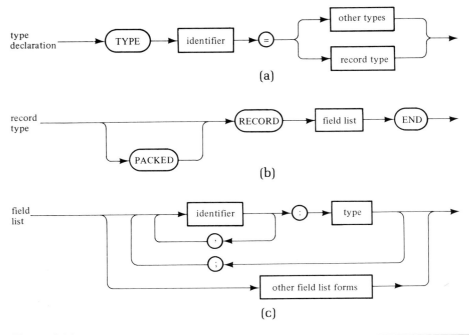

(a)

(b)

(c)

Figure 4.11 Declaration of a Record

Let us say that the date consists of a month (a two-digit integer), a day (a two-digit integer), and a year (a four-digit integer). The declaration

```
date = RECORD
    month : INTEGER ;
    day   : INTEGER ;
    year  : INTEGER ;
L=NO
```

defines a data type named `date` as consisting of the components shown. Each component in a record is called a *field*. Then, the declaration

```
VAR
    birthdate, hiredate : date
```

defines two record variables, each consisting of the three components listed in the TYPE declaration.

Each component of a record may be treated as if it were a single-valued variable of the particular data type. The WITH statement is used to avoid ambiguities that could arise because of the use of the same component name in different records. (For instance, both `birthdate` and `hiredate` have components named `day`.) If we write the statement

```
WITH hiredate DO
   BEGIN
        month := 7 ;
        day : = 7 ;
        year := 1983 ;
   END
```

there is no doubt that we are dealing with `hiredate` and not `birthdate`. Another way to provide an unambiguous reference is to *qualify* a component's name by using the record's name as a prefix. Thus, the individual assignments

```
hiredate day : = 7 ;
birthdate day : = 23
```

speak for themselves.

4.3.3 Dynamic Data Types

Pascal handles two other data types, named *files* and *pointers*, whose properties differ from those of types discussed so far. These are called *dynamic data types* to indicate that their *structures* (as well as their size) may change during the course of a program's execution. We already have an intuitive idea of what files are. Pointers are used to refer to variables for which storage is not allocated until the program runs and a particular instruction requests the creation of a variable. Uses of dynamic data types (and techniques for dealing with them) will be discussed later.

 *Problems*

1. The values shown below may or may not be legal Pascal integer constants. Point out the illegal ones and indicate what is wrong with them.
   (a) 26.5   (b) −0   (c) 128
   (d) 3,627   (e) −48.0   (f) 414−

2. The values shown below may or may not be legal Pascal real constants. Point out the illegal ones and indicate what is wrong with them.

(a)	312.4	(b)	−7,08.8	(c)	226.48426
(d)	−5	(e)	680,449.320,447	(f)	−.8
(g)	.008	(h)	0.0089	(i)	1000.03−
(j)	2E3	(k)	.2E3	(l)	−.2E3
(m)	−417.42E−4	(n)	27E−27	(o)	8.0E.6
(p)	E3	(q)	−3.16E−3.16	(r)	2.E+0
(s)	2.0E+00	(t)	17.17E−17	(u)	6E−.06

3. Specify the number of significant digits in each of the following values:

(a)	36	(b)	−20	(c)	8000.0
(d)	5.7	(e)	57	(f)	0.000005700
(g)	81.264	(h)	810.0264	(i)	−0.00005712
(j)	3.2E6	(k)	871.8E−3	(l)	2.1E+04

4. Express each of the following as a real constant in floating point using the text's standard form defined in Section 4.1.1:

(a)	−808	(b)	41.4	(c)	21.8673
(d)	−.007414	(e)	365407.88	(f)	−86E−2
(g)	21573283.6	(h)	3.1E−7	(i)	668 × 10
(j)	0.000746E8	(k)	0.0004872E−02	(l)	−41.04 × 10

5. Which of the following are illegal Pascal character constants? Why?

(a)	BRAN	(b)	'7..E'	(c)	'A7..W'
(d)	'E25W6J	(e)	'ALES''	(f)	ST'B4'
(g)	'....'	(h)	'T''A'''	(i)	'$@'E'+07'

6. Set up each of the following declarations:
   (a) Declare a real constant named gravity with a value of 32.164.
   (b) Declare an integer constant named upperlimit with a value of 208.
   (c) Declare three character constants named spaces, dashes, and dots with respective values of six blanks, four hyphens, and seven periods.
   (d) Declare two boolean constants named yessir and youbet, each with a value of TRUE.
   (e) Declare a real constant named duckbill with a value of 318000000, an integer constant named goornisht with a value of zero, and a character constant named empty with a value of the five characters 'EMPTY'.

7. Write declarations for each of the following:
   (a) A data type named tones consisting of the 12 notes in our musical system. (bflat is such a note.)

(b) A data type named homestyle consisting of the standard kinds of single-family dwellings. (ranch and capecod are examples.)

(c) A data type named mmmmm consisting of the flavors at your favorite ice cream parlor.

(d) A data type named melon consisting of the various kinds of melons commonly available.

(e) A data type named allplus consisting of all nonzero positive integers.

(f) A data type named starter consisting of the first eight letters of the alphabet.

(g) A data type named ranks consisting of the ranks (in order) in the United States Army, and a variable named brass (of type ranks) whose values are limited to second lieutenant and higher.

8. Write a declaration for each of the following:

(a) A 12-element array named act of real numbers indexed by integers from 1 through 12. Name the fifth element in the array.

(b) A 5-element array named wd of characters indexed by integers from 1 through 5. Name the second element in the array.

(c) A 26-element array named listwd of integers indexed by the characters 'A' through 'Z'. Assign a value of –8 to the ninth element.

(d) Declare an array of REAL values named freq indexed by the data type tones defined in Problem 7(a). How many elements are there in freq?

(e) Declare an array of characters named codes indexed by the starter data type defined for Problem 7(f). Write two assignment statements, the first of which places the character constant 'K' in the fourth element of codes, and the second of which copies the value from the fourth element into the sixth one.

(f) Declare an array of REAL numbers named bonus indexed by the data type ranks defined for Problem 7(g). Now write the statements necessary to assign a value of 540.75 to each element of the array. Declare any additional variables you may need.

(g) Using the array declaration prepared for the previous problem [8(f)], write the statements necessary to assign a value of 898.50 to those elements of bonus corresponding to second lieutenant and higher. Declare any additional variables you may need.

9. Write the necessary declaration(s) defining each of the following data types:

(a) evens, a set consisting of the first 12 positive even integers.

(b) psquares, a set consisting of the first 10 perfect squares.

(c) baseball, a set consisting of the nine fielding positions (e.g., b1 is first base, lf if left field, etc.). The base type is named positionb.

(d) football, a set consisting of the 11 traditional football positions (e.g., le is left end, rh is right halfback, etc.). The base type is named positionf.

10. Write a sequence of statements to produce each of the following:

(a) Define a data type named cardvalue with values consisting of the 13 types of playing cards (e.g., 2, 3, 4, . . . , ten, jack, queen, king, ace). Then, using cardvalue as a base type, construct three variables: allcards, a set consisting of all 13 cards; facecards, a set consisting of the high cards (10 and up), and lowcards, a set consisting of cards 2 through 9.

(b) Using positionb and baseball from Problem 9(c), define outf as a set consisting of the outfield positions, inf as a set consisting of the infield positions, and btry as a set consisting of the battery positions.

11. I Scungili di Bensonhurst is a community basketball league consisting of six teams. The coaches, players, and fans are interested in statistics showing the performance at each position during each game. Accordingly, every time a game is played, the league prepares two cards (lines), one for each team. Each card (line) contains a collection of input data consisting of the game number (each game of the season is given a unique integer identification), the team number (the teams are numbered 1 through 6), and the number of points scored for each of the five positions. The points are listed in the following order: left guard, left forward, center, right forward, right guard. For example, the following input line

$$54 \quad 3 \quad 15 \quad 12 \quad 23 \quad 11 \quad 18$$

shows that during game number 54, team 3's left guard(s) scored 15 points, 12 points were scored by the people playing left forward, the center position scored 23 points, the right forward position accounted for 11 points, and the right guard position added 18. Your program is to compute and print a line for each position showing the total number of points scored, and the average number scored (per game) for that position. Then, after those five lines of output, the program is to leave a blank line and print the overall statistics (the total number of points scored for all positions, along with the overall average points per game for an individual position). Use a team number of zero to terminate the run.

12. Define each of the following everyday collections of data as a record type:
    (a) Your driver's license
    (b) Your library card
    (c) The part of the Table of Contents describing Chapter 2 of this book
    (d) Your VISA, MASTERCHARGE, DINER'S CLUB, or AMERICAN EXPRESS credit card
    (e) The information on a postage stamp
    (f) Your monthly telephone bill

Chapter Five

Arithmetic in Pascal

Pascal does an excellent job of insulating the programmer from the machine's relatively limited scope of arithmetic capabilities. Extensive computations can be specified as expressions that resemble conventional algebraic formulas. As a result, we have been able to treat the construction and use of these arithmetic capabilities naturally. This chapter builds on our previous experience to present a more detailed picture of these features.

5.1 THE ASSIGNMENT STATEMENT

The power and flexibility of Pascal's assignment statement are hidden behind a deceptively innocent syntax. Before delving into the statement's marvelous properties, we shall make sure that the fundamental rules are clear.

5.1.1 Basic Syntax

As Figure 5.1 indicates, the assignment statement establishes a relationship between an expression which produces a value and a variable which receives that value. The operation, *assignment*, denoted by :=, transfers the value to its destination, replacing what was there before. Thus, in the statement

```
timer := 0
```

the value currently in the variable named `timer` is replaced by zero, the value of the expression on the right-hand side of the assignment operator. The zero, representing the simplest kind of expression (but an expression nevertheless), is just one instance of a pattern that enables us to build an endless variety of expressions (including rather complicated ones) while working with the same structural rules.

97

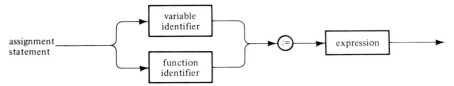

Semantics: The data type of the destination (variable or function identifier) must be compatible with that of the value of the expression.

Figure 5.1

Assignment Statement Syntax

Replacement (or assignment) is a key concept here. Recall that we can make sense out of a statement like

```
timer := timer + 1
```

by emphasizing the separation between replacement and computation. The expression describes a particular arithmetic task: Take the value in the variable named t i m e r and add one to it, thereby producing a new value. Period. There is nothing in the *expression* to tell Pascal what happens next. That information is supplied by the replacement operator and the destination named to the left of the := operator. Thus, we can imagine that there is an instant, just before the replacement occurs, when t i m e r still has its original value and the new value is suspended somewhere (in a temporary storage place) poised and ready, eager to be sent speeding homeward. This idea will make it easier to understand and use the concepts that follow.

5.1.2 Semantics of the Assignment Statement

The specifications at the bottom of Figure 5.1 tells us several things about the assignment statement that cannot be conveyed by the syntax:

1. When Pascal completes the computations specified by an expression, it produces a value of a particular data type. Selection of the result's data type is no accident; rather, it is determined by a set of internal rules applied to the ingredients of a particular expression. If that expression is constructed in violation of these rules, the computations cannot be performed.
2. The destination variable, too, has a specific data type, assigned as part of its declaration. Consequently, it has nothing to do with the data type of the value of an expression until the two are brought together in an assignment statement. The way an expression is evaluated and the nature of its result are not influenced by the destination variable.

3. When an expression is evaluated, there is no reason to expect that the data type of the resulting value will be the same as that of the destination variable. Consequently, the assignment operation requires more than a transfer of the expression's value to the destination. There must be an associated mechanism that examines the respective data types of the result and destination. If they are the same, the transfer proceeds without further processing. If the data types differ, the appropriate data conversion takes place *if it can*, so that the data type of the value finally transferred matches that of the destination variable. Even if the expression itself is constructed in accordance with Pascal's rules, and the computations take place as specified, final assignment still may not occur because the result's data type cannot be converted to that of the destination. For example, the expression may produce a real numerical value, and the destination variable may have been declared as a programmer-defined enumerative type. Pascal's compatability rules for arithmetic assignmets are summarized in Table 5.1.

4. Compatability of the two items on either side of the := operator also includes concern about whether the involved variables are scalar or not. For instance, the assignment will not work if the destination variable is a scalar variable and a variable in the expression refers to an array.

The next few sections will explore the rules governing the use of Pascal's arithmetic facilities and the construction of assignment statements specifying arithmetic computations.

5.2 BASIC ARITHMETIC OPERATIONS

Pascal deals with two sets of arithmetic operations: those performed on integers (producing integer results) and those performed on real numbers (producing real results). After examining these separately, we shall be ready to look at them in combination.

5.2.1 Addition, Subtraction, and Multiplication

Addition, subtraction, and multiplication, denoted by +, −, and *, respectively, for both types of arithmetic are straightforward. Unlike conventional algebra, however, multiplication always must be shown explicitly. Thus, if v1, con, and pr are INTEGER variables, Pascal will reject

```
pr := conv1
```

or

```
pr := con v1
```

Table 5.1 Arithmetic Assignment Rules for UCSD Pascal

		Data Type of Destination Variable		
		REAL	**INTEGER**	**INTEGER SUBRANGE**
D a t a T y p e o f R e s u l t	R E A L	no conversion necessary	illegal; compiler will reject	illegal; compiler will reject
	I N T E G E R	conversion will take place	no conversion necessary otherwise,	acceptable if the expression is a constant; otherwise, uncertain
	I S N U T B E R G A E N R G E	illegal; compiler will reject	illegal; compiler will reject	no conversion necessary

or

```
Pr := con (v1)
```

The multiplication operator must be shown:

```
Pr := con * v1
```

The same is true for multiplication of real numbers.

5.2.2 Division

Because of its nature, division receives special handling in Pascal.

Division of Real Values   The symbol / denotes real division. That means that both divisor and dividend have to be real values, and Pascal will produce a real result. Thus, if bflag and total are declared as REAL, the assignment

```
bflag := total/4
```

will not be accepted, whereas

```
bflag := total/4.0
```

will be all right.

Division of Integer Values   The symbol DIV specifies division of one integer by another, thereby producing an integer quotient. There is no remainder because there are no provisions for keeping one. Thus, the expression

```
18 DIV 20
```

causes a computation in which the integer 18 is divided by the integer 20, producing a quotient of zero. The remainder (0.9) is trekked off to a desolate tundra in the Yukon where it is unceremoniously dumped on a growing pile of remainders to be frozen and forgotten. A separate symbol is used for integer division to emphasize the different type of arithmetic. Real values cannot be used with the DIV operator.

In many applications the remainder is not needed, and integer division is used specifically to produce an integer quotient. (The process of removing the fractional part is called *truncation*.) However, Pascal provides an integer operation that makes the remainder available. No, it does not bring it back from the frozen wastes; the remainder is produced by a separate process using the MOD operation. For example, the expression

```
18 MOD 20
```

divides the integer 18 by the integer 20, producing a *remainder* expressed as an integer (18 in this case). With this operation, the quotient is discarded (scientists still have not figured out where *it* goes). Similarly the expression

```
18 MOD 3
```

produces a remainder of zero, the amount left over when 18 is divided by 3. If we want to divide an integer value by another one and obtain both the quotient and remainder, it requires two operations. For example, if ttl, quot, and remain are all declared with type INTEGER, the sequence

```
quot := ttl DIV 9 ;
remain := ttl MOD 9
```

places the quotient in quot and the remainder in remain. Assuming a value of 34 for ttl, quot will receive a value of 3 and remain will be assigned a value of 7.

5.2.3 Other Arithmetic Operations

The basic operations discussed in the previous sections are supplemented by a collection of standard *built-in functions*. Each of these permanently installed subprograms provides a mathmatical process made to appear (to the programmer) as a single arithmetic operation. Examples of such functions, i.e., SQR and SQRT, were seen earlier, and others will be discussed in the next chapter.

5.3 CONSTRUCTION OF ARITHMETIC EXPRESSIONS

The arithmetic expressions we have used thus far have been rather simple, so that we have been able to write them intuitively. When it comes to more ambitious computations, it will be necessary to become familiar with Pascal's rules of construction.

Starting with a general syntactic definition [Figure 5.2(a)], we classify an expression as being either a simple expression or a comparison expression. A simple expression, in turn, is categorized as being either an arithmetic expression or a simple boolean expression [Figure 5.2(b)]. We shall be concerned in this chapter with arithmetic expressions. Accordingly, we define the arithmetic expression as shown in Figure 5.2(c).

Recall the simple assignment statement in Section 5.1.1:

```
timer := 0
```

Comparison of the expression (0) with Figure 5.2(c) identifies the zero as a single arithmetic term. The second assignment statement in that section, namely,

```
timer := timer + 1
```

has an expression (timer + 1) that follows the alternative loop in Figure 5.2(c): There are two arithmetic terms (timer and 1) connected by the + operator.

5.3.1 Arithmetic Terms

Figure 5.3 shows the construction of an arithmetic term. We see that, in its most elementary form, an arithmetic term can consist of a single arithmetic

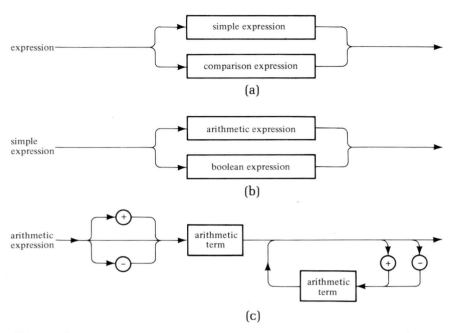

Figure 5.2 General Characterization of Pascal Expressions

factor. This is exactly the case with each of the terms in the two expressions just examined. The zero in the first assignment statement, for instance, is an arithmetic expression consisting of a single arithmetic term, and that term consists of a single arithmetic factor. In other words, the zero, in this particular appearance, is a factor, a term, and a complete expression. On the other hand, t i m e r and 1 in the second statement each are terms consisting of a single factor, but neither one is a complete expression. The two of them, brought together by the +, form a complete arithmetic expression. Now we can take a look at an expression such as

18 DIV 20

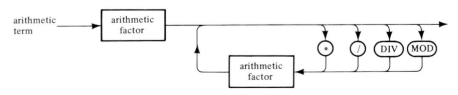

Figure 5.3 Construction of an Arithmetic Term

in light of what Figure 5.3 shows. We see that the 18 and the 20 are *not* individual arithmetic terms. Instead, each is an arithmetic factor and the two of them, when connected by the D I V operator, form a single arithmetic term.

5.3.2 Arithmetic Factors

For convenience, arithmetic factors are classified in Figure 5.4(a) as simple arithmetic factors and extended arithmetic factors. We shall limit our present discussion to the simple arithmetic factors. The extended possibilities will be introduced at appropriate points later on. The first two possibilities in Figure 5.4(b) are already familiar. Now, when we see a statement such as

```
adj := x - y + 6 * wrth
```

we can recognize that the expression consists of three terms: x, y, and 6 * wrth. x and y are factors, and the 6 * wrth consists of the two factors 6 and wrth.

The third possibility will be explored in more detail in Chapter 6, but

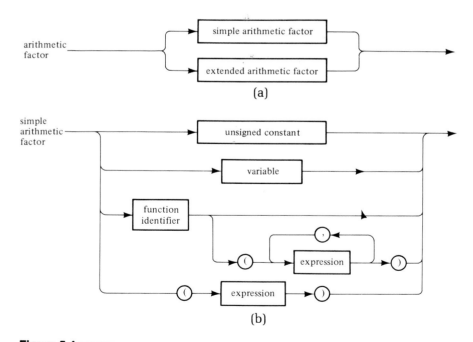

(a)

(b)

Figure 5.4

Syntax for a Factor

some initial discussion is appropriate here. An example of this kind of factor is

```
SQRT(225)
```

We know from Chapter 2 that the activity triggered by this reference causes the built-in function SQRT to work on the value 225 and to deliver its square root to the expression in which it is used. The value thus delivered is just another factor in that expression. (Of course, it may be the only factor in the expression, but it is a factor in any case.) The component inside the parentheses is designated as an expression, thereby allowing such usage as

```
SQRT (x + 3 * y)
```

or even

```
SQRT (x + 3 * SQRT(y))
```

This usage is clear enough. However, the designation of an expression as a possible component of a factor raises a peculiar issue: If we work our way back through the series of syntactic definitions in Figures 5.4, 5.3, and 5.2, we remind ourselves that this whole discussion started with the decomposition of an arithmetic expression into terms and, ultimately, into factors. This leaves us with the seemingly awkward situation in which an expression is defined (ultimately) as being part of itself. This is another instance of a recursive definition. By the time we find that a factor can be built by attaching a parenthesized expression to a function name, we already know enough ways of building complete expressions so that the definition makes sense.

The fourth possibility in Figure 5.4 simply indicates that an expression can be enclosed in parentheses to form a factor for potential use in a more complicated expression. When we discuss Pascal's arithmetic rules in the next section, we shall see that the characterization of a parenthesized expression as a factor fits nicely with those rules.

5.4 PASCAL'S RULES FOR DOING ARITHMETIC

There is virtually no practical limit to the length or complexity of arithmetic expressions in Pascal. Yet, the Pascal compiler must be prepared to handle any and all such expressions properly. The only way this can be assured is to define a set of carefully constructed rules that govern Pascal's behavior and to design the compiler so that these rules are followed to the last detail. This section examines the rules and applies them to a variety of situations.

5.4.1 Use of Real and Integer Values in Arithmetic Expressions

Arithmetic expressions can be built from a mixture of REAL and INTEGER values. When a computation is to be performed with two different types of numbers, Pascal will convert the INTEGER value to REAL. For example, if pwr is declared as REAL, the expression

```
2 * pwr
```

will cause Pascal to convert the 2 into an equivalent REAL factor (2.0) for use in the multiplication. The result of the multiplication will be a REAL value that is available for further arithmetic or assignment, depending on the contents of the rest of the statement. In general, Pascal is designed to take a safe approach. Consequently, arithmetic operations with mixed values cause conversion from INTEGER to REAL rather than the other way around. Thus, the expression

```
2 * pwr - 8
```

forces Pascal to convert the 2 to a REAL value. The multiplication then produces a REAL result. Before the subtraction takes place, the 8 is converted to REAL. Thus, the final value of the expression is REAL even though two of the three original values were INTEGER.

As Section 5.2.2 pointed out, there are two exceptions to the use of mixed arithmetic values: The DIV and MOD operations require INTEGER values. However, an INTEGER term still can be part of a legitimate arithmetic expression containing REAL terms. For instance, the expression

```
3.6 * pwr + 28 DIV 17 - 5.5
```

consists of three terms: the REAL term obtained by multiplying the two REAL factors 3.6 and pwr; the INTEGER term obtained when 28 is divided by 17; and the REAL term consisting of the single factor 5.5. In order to complete the computations, Pascal will convert the INTEGER quotient (1) to REAL (1.0), so that the final result will be REAL.

5.4.2 Precedence of Arithmetic Operations

In order to process arithmetic expressions consistently, Pascal follows a set of rules that define the relative priorities of the various arithmetic operations. These rules, called *precedence rules*, force Pascal to perform certain operations before others. The scheme is as follows:

1. Computations are performed from left to right. It is possible for Pascal to get to the end of an expression without having completed the

computations. When this happens, the left-to-right tour is repeated as many times as necessary.

2. Multiplication and division (*, /, DIV, and MOD) are processed before addition (+) and subtraction (−).
3. Addition and subtraction are performed last.

Thus, in the expression

```
pwr - res/ind * ext + plc
```

the evaluation proceeds as follows (assume all variables are REAL):

1. res is divided by ind, producing a REAL result. For convenience, let us call that intermediate result result1.
2. result1 is multiplied by ext, producing another partial result. Let us call that result result2.
3. Pascal, reaching the end of the expression and finding no more multiplication or division to perform, goes back and starts again. The work left to be done is

   ```
   pwr - result2 + plc
   ```

   Accordingly, the next operation is prw − result2, producing a REAL value which we shall call result3. (Temporary storage for this value is handled automatically, as it is for all intermediate results.)
4. Finally, result3 and plc are added together to produce the final value.

These rules make it awkward to write certain kinds of expressions. For instance, the simple algebraic expression

$$\frac{pwr - res}{ext + plc}$$

would cause some inconvenience if additional tools were not available. This shortcoming is remedied through the use of parentheses, as the next section shows.

5.4.3 Parentheses in Arithmetic Expressions

Pascal is designed so that the programmer can use parentheses "naturally." That is, parentheses can help divide an expression into easily recognizable components that establish the overall meaning simply and clearly. As Figure 5.4 indicates, an expression enclosed in parentheses becomes a factor in a larger expression. This means that by putting parentheses around a group of terms or factors, we can force Pascal to pay attention to the parenthesized material and perform the computations described there ahead of others. Stated another way, *expressions in parentheses receive highest priority, ahead of multiplication and division.* To illustrate, suppose a, b, c, and d all were declared as REAL. The expression

```
a - b / c + d
```

is processed according to Pascal's arithmetic rules:

1. Pascal does a left-to-right tour looking for parentheses. Finding none, it goes back and starts again.
2. The division b/c is performed. Let us call the temporary result r.
3. Finding no more multiplications or divisions, Pascal starts a new tour.
4. Pascal does a − r1, and a new result (call it r2) is produced.
5. Finally, r2 and d are added to develop the final expression value.

Now, let us see the effect of parentheses. If we modify the expression so that it says

```
( a - b ) / ( c + d )
```

the evaluation will proceed differently, even though the same rules are followed:

1. Pascal, finding a parenthesized expression, will produce a value for *that* expression, following the same rules it always does. In this case, the expression consists only of two terms. Thus, the subtraction a − b will be performed, producing a temporary result we shall call d1.
2. Continuing on its tour, Pascal finds another parenthesized expression. Accordingly, it applies its rules to that expression until its computations are completed. Here again, there are only two terms, so that a single tour takes care of it. The addition c + d is performed, leaving a temporary result we shall call d2.
3. Working with the modified expression
   ```
   d1 / d2
   ```
   Pascal starts a new tour. The remaining division is performed, producing the final result.

Note that the parentheses enabled Pascal to perform addition and subtraction before it did the multiplication.

Pascal will accept parentheses even when they are not needed. For instance, the expressions

```
a - b / c + d and a - ( b / c ) + d
```

produce exactly the same results. Consequently, if there is even the slightest doubt about how Pascal will handle a particular expression, it is a good idea to remove that doubt by using parentheses.

Parenthesized expressions may be placed inside other parenthesized expressions. (This is implied by Figure 5.4, but you have to stare at it a little while to see why: Since an entire expression can be placed inside parentheses, one of the factors in *that* expression can itself be a parenthesized expression.) This type of construction is called *nesting,* and it may be used to any desired extent. Thus, an expression such as

```
4.11 * (a + b * (c - 6)) / (SQRT (8.7 * (a + c)) - b)
```

is acceptable. (If you look back in Section 5.3.2, you will note that nested parentheses were used in an expression in which SQRT was used twice. No emphasis was necessary since such usage is "natural" and easy to follow.)

5.4.4 Example 5.1

We shall illustrate some simple arithmetic by writing a program that reads a sequence of four-digit positive integer values. Each value is to be printed on a separate line. If at least one of the digits in a particular value is a 7, the message SPECIAL VALUE is to be printed alongside the value. After all the values have been processed, the program is to a leave a blank line and print the number of values read and the number of special values. 7028, 1720,

```
Define value, tvalue, numvalues, numspecials, digit.
Initialize numvalues, numspecials.
Read the first input value.
While there still are input data to process, Do:
      Add 1 to numvalues.
      If
         any of value's digits is 7
      Then
         Add 1 to numspecials.
         Print value and message: SPECIAL VALUE.
      Else
         Print value.
      Endif
      Read the next value.
Endwhile
Print numvalues and numspecials.
Stop.
```

Figure 5.5
Pseudocode Description for Example 5.1.

and 2177 are examples of special values. The EOF function (see Example 3.2) will be used to terminate the run.

The program's structure is straightforward (Figure 5.5). We need call attention only to the use of the DIV and MOD operations to isolate a value's individual digits: If tvalue is such a value, then

```
(******************************************************************)
(**                        EXAMPLE 5.1                        **)
(******************************************************************)
(** VALUE IS A 4-DIGIT POSITIVE INPUT VALUE;                  **)
(** TVALUE IS A TEMPORARY WORK AREA FOR VALUE;                **)
(** NUMVALUES AND NUMSPECIALS ARE COUNTERS FOR INPUT VALUES;  **)
(** DIGIT IS AN INDIVIDUAL DIGIT EXTRACTED FROM VALUE.        **)
(** SIGNAL IS TRUE IF VALUE IS A SPECIAL VALUE, FALSE IF 55   **)
(** NOT. NOTE THAT SIGNAL IS SET TO FALSE FOR EACH VALUE.     **)

(******************************************************************)
Program ex501 (INPUT, OUTPUT)  ;
CONST
  zero = 0 ;    seven  = 7 ;     ten = 10 ;
VAR
  value, tvalue, numvalues, sumspecials, digit   :    INTEGER   ;
  signal  :  BOOLEAN  ;
BEGIN
  numvalues := zero ; numspecials := zero ;
  WRITELN ('ENTER THE FIRST VALUE.') ;
  READLN (value)  ;
  WHILE  NOT EOF(INPUT)  DO
    BEGIN
      tvalue := value  ;
      numvalues := numvalues + 1  ;
      signal := FALSE ;
      WHILE tvalue <> zero DO
        BEGIN
          digit := tvalue  MOD ten  ;
          tvalue := tvalue DIV ten  ;
          IF
            digit = seven
          THEN
            BEGIN
              numspecials := numspecials + 1  ;
              signal := TRUE  ;
              tvalue := zero
            END
          ELSE
        END  ;
```

Figure 5.6

Program for Example 5.1

```
      IF
          signal = TRUE
      THEN
          WRITELN (value,' SPECIAL VALUE')
      ELSE
          WRITELN ('VALUE: ',value)   ;
          WRITELN ('ENTER THE NEXT VALUE.")   ;
          READLN (value)
    END   ;
WRITELN ('          ')   ;
WRITELN ('NO. OF ITEMS PROCESSED:   ',numvalues)   ;
WRITELN ('NO. OF SPECIAL VALUES:   ',numspecials)
END .
```

Figure 5.6

Program for Example 5.1 (Continued)

```
      tvalue MOD 10
```

gives us its rightmost digit. By assigning that to some other variable, we can make it available for subsequent processing. On the other hand,

```
      tvalue := tvalue   DIV   10
```

removes the rightmost digit and places what is left back in tvalue. Thus, by applying these two operations, we have the basis for a mechanism for extracting and examining an integer's individual digits. The Pascal statements for this program are given in Figure 5.6.

Problems

1. Assume the following declarations:

```
CONST
  maxdev = 20 ;
  refr = 8.5 ;
TYPE
  indic = 1..maxdev ;
VAR
  cl1, cl2, cl3    :    ARRAY [indic] OF REAL ;
  txr, swb, yval   :    REAL ;
  num, nval, amt   :    INTEGER ;
  u, v, g          :    indic
.................
```

Assuming further that each of the variables has a value, indicate which of the following statements are illegal and show why:

(a) `txr := txr + swb`

(b) `refr := refr - 0.2`

(c) `num := num + indic + maxdev * v`

(d) `u := v - g DIV u`

(e) `v := maxdev * g DIV v`

(f) `swb := maxdev * g DIV v`

(g) `yval := refr * maxdev DIV txr`

(h) `v+g := yval - txr`

(i) `txr := maxdev * txr`

(j) `u,g := maxdev`

(k) `yval := num/amt + refr`

(l) `v := refr`

(m) `g := cl2/cl1[v]`

(n) `cl2[maxdev] := yval - refr`

(o) `u := num + cl1`

(p) `num := num + amt (nval + maxdev)`

(q) `amt := cl1[v] + cl2[u]`

(r) `txr := swb * (num + nval)/yval`

(s) `swb := (cl1[txr] + refr)/yval`

(t) `cl1[v] := maxdev * (yval+/swb)`

(u) `cl2[yval] := refr * (cl1[u] - refr * (cl3[u] + swb))/(g*txr)`

(v) `swb := (maxdev + 4)*(refr-(nval DIV num)*(cl2[u] + v*cl3[v])))`

2. Using the declarations given in Problem 1, write a Pascal expression for each of the following algebraic expressions:

(a) $\dfrac{amt}{nval} - r$

(b) $\dfrac{num}{amt + 4}$

(c) $txr(yval) - refr$

(d) $uvg(txr + amt)$

(e) $nval\left(\dfrac{u}{v} \dfrac{numtant}{txr}\right)$

(f) $\dfrac{refr}{10.2}\left(\dfrac{u + txr - v}{g(num + 2)} + maxdev\right)$

(g) $\dfrac{trx + refr}{v}\left(\dfrac{num\left(amt - g\left(v + \dfrac{u - 6}{nval + 3}\right)\right)}{(swb - refr)\left(\dfrac{g + v}{yval(u + 5)}\right)}\right)$

3. List the factors and terms for each of the expressions developed for Problem 2. (*Note:* Some of the terms may also be factors.)
4. Indicate the data type for the result in each of the expressions in Problem 2.
5. Using the declarations from Problem 1, assume the following values:

    0.1, 0.5, and 0.8 for txr, swb, and yval, respectively
    2, 6, and 17 for num, nval, and amt, respectively
    3, 5, and 12 for u, v, and s, respectively

    Indicate the value produced for each of the following:

    (a) txr * swb
    (b) txr * (swb + u)
    (c) u * (maxdev + v DIV s)
    (d) swb + yval / (refr * txr)
    (e) (u + v) DIV (maxdev - s) * txr
    (f) s - (maxdev * txr / (num + nval * s DIV v)
    (g) (amt DIV (num + nval - maxdev) + txr * amt) / yval * nval
    (h) num * ((txr - u) - (refr * (nval + s DIV u)) * (swb + num))

6. Expand the program in Example 5.1 so that it computes and prints the sum of the digits for each input value in addition to the information already being produced. (For instance, if the input value is 4365, the sum of its digits is 18.)
7. Revise the program in Example 5.1 or in Problem 6 so that it prints the message SPECIAL VALUE next to the value if it has exactly one 7 in it, and it prints the message extRa SPECIAL VALUE next to the value if it has two or more 7s in it. Thus, 4070 is a special value, but 7074 and 7877 are extra special values. Indeed they are.
8. Write an interactive version for either of the programs specified in Problems 6 and 7.
9. Input for this problem consists of an unknown number of three-digit positive integer values. Write a program that counts the number of values in which the middle digit is numerically equivalent to the sum of the outer two. For example, the numbers 264 and 880 are such values while 212 and 074 are not. Print each input value on a separate line. If a particular value meets the criterion described above, print the message SPECIAL VALUE on the same line. After the last value has been processed (use a value of zero to terminate the run), print the number of special values.
10. Write an interactive version of the program described in Problem 9.
11. Expand the program in Problem 9 or 10 so that, in addition to printing

the number of special values, the program prints the largest special value encountered during the run, the smallest special value, and the average special value.

12. Suppose startval is the original dollar value of a product (to the nearest cent) and salvageval is the salvage value. When the straight-line depreciation method is applied over nyrs years, the yearly decrease in value is

$$\frac{startval - salvageval}{nyrs}$$

Write a program that reads a sequence of input groups, each group consisting of startval, nyrs, and salvageval. For each group, the program is to print a line showing the input data. This is followed by a line for each year showing the year number and the (depreciated) value of the product at the end of that year. Use a startval of zero to terminate the run.

13. Another way to compute depreciation is based on the assumption that a product, starting with a value of startval, loses a constant percentage of its *current* value each year until it reaches salvageval. For instance, if startval is 5000.00 and the fractional loss per year is 0.1 (i.e., 10%), then the loss over the first year is 10% of 5000.00, or 500.00. Thus the value at the end of the first year is 4500.00. The loss over the second year is 10% of 4500.00, or 450.00, so that the product has a value of 4050.00 going into the third year, and so on. Write a program that reads and processes a series of input groups where each input group consists of startval, lossrate (expressed as a fraction), nyrs, and salvageval. For each input group, the program is to print a line repeating the input data. After that, it is to print a line for each of the nyrs years showing the year number and the (depreciated) value of the product at the end of that year. You may assume that nyrs always will be small enough so that the depreciated value will not fall below lossrate*startval. Terminate your run as in Problem 12.

14. Modify the program in Problem 12 so that it does not make any assumptions about nyrs. Specifically, this version must regulate the computations so that, if necessary, it cuts them off when the current (depreciated) value falls below lossrate * startval. For instance, if startval is 100.00 and lossrate is .2, the computations should be stopped as soon as the current value falls below .2 * 100.00, or 20.00.

15. Modify the program from either Problem 12 or Problem 13 so that it will produce one of two types of output for each input group: Depending on the contents of that input group, the program will print a

year-by-year report as before, or it will print only one line (after the input values are repeated) showing the depreciated value after n y r s have gone by. Include comments in your program specifying the input requirements for each option.

16. A popularly held (though unproven) claim is that every positive even number can be expressed as a sum of two prime numbers. (For instance, 28 = 23 + 5, or 62 = 59 + 3). Write a program that reads in successive integer values (one per line or card). For each integer read, the program is to produce a line of output consisting of the input value followed by two prime numbers whose sum equals that of the input value. If a particular value is not a positive even number, the program is to print a line showing the value followed by the message THIS VALUE IS INAPPROPRIATE. After the last value has been processed, the program is to leave a blank line and then print the total number of input values, the number of values processed, and the number of values rejected as being inappropriate.

17. Write an interactive version of the program described in Problem 16.

18. If we plot the two points on rectangular coordinates (Figure 5.7), we can describe their positions in terms of their coordinates (x 1 , y 1) and (x 2 , y 2). Then if we draw a straight line through those points, that line can be described in terms of its slope a 1 and intercept a 0 as defined by the equations in Figure 5.7. Write a program that reads a succession of input values. Each group consists of four coordinate values: (x 1 , y 1) and (x 2 , y 2) in that order, with all four values appearing on a single line or card. For each group read, the program is to print two lines of output. The first repeats the input values, and the second gives the slope and intercept of the resulting straight line. You may assume that the points in each input pair will have different

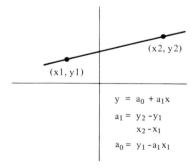

$$y = a_0 + a_1 x$$
$$a_1 = \frac{y_2 - y_1}{x_2 - x_1}$$
$$a_0 = y_1 - a_1 x_1$$

Figure 5.7

Straight-Line Equation from Two Points

Y-coordinates. Run your program with the following input:

$$
\begin{array}{cccc}
1.00 & 1.00 & 2.00 & 2.00 \\
1.00 & 2.00 & 2.00 & 4.00 \\
-8.5 & 2.5 & 1.5 & -3.5 \\
3.8 & 6.75 & 8.5 & 3.25
\end{array}
$$

19. Revise the program in Problem 18 so that it no longer makes the assumption specified there. Include the following test data in your run:

$$
\begin{array}{cccc}
1.00 & 3.00 & 1.00 & 7.85 \\
-5.00 & 2.00 & 5.00 & 2.00
\end{array}
$$

20. Expand the program from Problem 18 or 19 as follows: Each input group now consists of six values describing three points. The order is $(x1,y1)$, $(x2,y2)$, and $(x3,y3)$. For each group processed, print two lines. The first line shows the input values. The second line shows the slope and intercept for the straight line through $(x1,y1)$ and $(x2,y2)$ as before. In addition, the program is to print one of two messages on that second line: If the third point lies on the line drawn through the first two, the message is to say POINT 3 LIES ON THE LINE. If not, the message is to say POINT 3 DOES NOT LIE ON THE LINE.

21. *(Special Challenge)* Revise the program for Problem 20 so that each input group consists of a line or card giving $(x1,y1)$ and $(x2,y2)$, followed by an unknown number of cards or lines, each one containing a third point $(x3,y3)$. For each group, the first line of output shows $(x1,y1)$ and $(x2,y2)$. Then, for each additonal point processed, the program is to print a line showing that point's coordinates and one of the two messages specified in Problem 17, depending on whether that point fell on the line described by $(x1,y1)$ and $(x2,y2)$. Thus, there will be a sequence of third points to test against a a particular line. After that sequence has been processed (it will be up to you to determine how to detect the end of such a sequence), the program is to read in the next set of $(x1,y1)$ and $(x2,y2)$ values and go through the process again with a new collection of third points.

Chapter Six

Extended Arithmetic with Built-In Functions

Pascal's basic arithmetic operations are supplemented by a collection of built-in functions, each of which allows the programmer to treat a relatively complicated arithmetic process as if it were a single operation. This facility makes it easier to express extensive computations in terms that are close to conventional mathemathical notation, so that the resulting programs convey their intent directly and clearly. Since no collection of built-in functions can be complete, these are designed to serve as reasonable building blocks for more complex computations in addition to providing commonly used facilities on their own. This chapter examines Pascal's arithmetic functions and some of the computational opportunities that they present.

6.1 "EQUAL" VALUES ARE NOT ALWAYS EQUAL

Before discussing the various computational aids provided by Pascal's arithmetic functions, we shall introduce an important hazard of computer arithmetic so that it can be recognized and avoided.

There are times when a simple computation will produce a result that is not exactly right. An answer that is supposed to come out 8.7 may be 8.6999998 instead. "Big deal," you say. In human terms, the difference may be nothing to get excited about, and we can decide that 8.6999998 is "the same as" 8.7. However, when this small discrepancy occurs as part of an automatic computation, there is no one there to make such a judgment. As far as the computer is concerned, 8.6999998 definitely is *not* the same as 8.7. Consequently, if `result` is a computed REAL value, a simple test such as

```
IF result = 8.7 THEN ........
```

will fail more often than we think it will because of small differences that *we* would be willing to overlook. Similarly, two variables (one of them read and the other computed, let us say) may be "equal" for our purposes, but they will fail a test for equality because of a difference in the last place.

We cannot do anything about the machine's arithmetic. However, we can adjust the way we specify arithmetic to force actions that will avoid these effects. The next section describes built-in functions that help support computational adjustments.

6.2 COMPUTATIONAL FUNCTIONS

6.2.1 The ABS Function

This function simply delivers the absolute value of its single REAL or INTEGER argument. Thus, ABS(-87.4) is 87.4 and ABS(518) is 518. One way to overcome the effects of the uninvited small differences discussed in the previous section is to define a range within which such differences can be ignored. For example, suppose we have a program in which a REAL value htloss is computed. A certain action is to be taken when htloss is equal to some value critval. We are willing to accept a value as high as critval+.0002 or as low as critval-0002 as being "equal to" critval. The ABS function gives us a convenient way of specifying this range as part of a test:

```
IF ABS(htloss-critval) <= 0.0002 THEN
   action1
ELSE
   action2
```

Of course, the acceptable range may vary for each situation.

6.2.2 The ROUND Function

The ROUND function brings a real value to the nearest integer. Thus, ROUND(83.7) produces 84, and ROUND(83.4) produces 83. By combining this function with some simple computations, we can provide a powerful facility for controlling computational results.

For example, suppose we were performing the following computation (assume all the variables are REAL):

```
newbal := oldbal + oldbal * rate * time
```

newbal represents an amount of money to be printed to the nearest cent. One effective way to do this is to round newbal to two places after it has been computed. However, since the ROUND function produces only an integer, it cannot be used directly. Instead, we multiply by 100, apply the ROUND function, and then divide by 100 to obtain the proper value. to illustrate, suppose the value newbal is 4207.8096247. If we apply ROUND directly, i.e.,

```
newbal := ROUND(newbal)
```

The function produces a value of 4208. Since the rounded value is to be assigned to newbal (which is REAL), the program converts the 4208 to 4208.0000000 and stores *that* value in newbal. this is not what we want. Instead, we can write

```
newbal := ROUND(newbal * 100.0)/100.0
```

First, newbal is multiplied by 100 to produce an intermediate value of 420780.9624700. Next, that value is rounded, resulting in 420781, the nearest integer, and this value, when divided by 100.0, produces 4207.8100000.

The same general technique can be used to round to some other desired number of places. For example, if we wanted to round newbal to the nearest dime, we would multiply and divide by 10.

6.2.3 The TRUNC Function

Another mechanism for computational control is the TRUNC function. As its name implies, it truncates to the nearest integer. Thus,

```
TRUNC(4207.8096247)
```

produces 4207 [recall that ROUND(4207.8096247) produces 4208, whereas TRUNC(396.4721408) and ROUND (396.4721408) both produce 396]. TRUNC (-4207.8096247) produces −4207. (This function also can be used with a long integer argument to convert the value to regular integer form as long as the argument's value is between -MAXINT and MAXINT.)

6.2.4 The ODD Function

This function provides a convenient way of determining whether an integer value is odd. ODD *(value)* produces a value of TRUE if *value* is odd; a value of FALSE is produced when *value* is even. Thus, the expression ODD (717) produces a value of TRUE.

6.3 ALGEBRAIC FUNCTIONS

Four of Pascal's functions provide convenient mechanisms for specifying common algebraic operations.

6.3.1 The EXP and LN Functions

Each of these functions uses a REAL or INTEGER value (submitted as a constant, variable, or expression) to produce a REAL value. The value given to the EXP function is used as an exponent to produce the value of e (the base of natural logarithms) raised to that exponent. Thus, EXP(2) = e^2 = 7.3890560, and EXP(-1.92) = $e^{-1.92}$ = 0.1466069.

LN *(value)* produces the natural logarithm of *value*. The programmer must make sure that the argument given to LN is greater than zero. If it is not, the program will stop and an error message will be displayed.

Pascal-20, implemented on Digital Equipment Corporation's DECSYS-TEM-20, provides an additional logarithmic function in its extended library: LOG computes the common (base 10) logarithm of the single argument submitted to it. The same is true for UCSD Pascal.

6.3.2 The SQRT and SQR Functions

SQRT is familiar and needs no further discussion except for one thing: It is up to the programmer to make sure that the argument given to SQRT is (or works out to be) a positive value or zero. A negative value causes an error message to be printed, and processing terminates. As was seen earlier, SQR computes the square of the REAL or INTEGER value given to it.

6.3.3 Exponentiation

We can use Pascal's algebraic functions to raise a numerical value to a specified power. For instance, suppose we wanted to raise 3.54 to the 1.76th power and store the result in REAL variable mpr. A convenient way to do this is by combining the EXP and LN functions:

```
mpr := EXP(1.76 * LN(3.54))
```

Similarly, if we want to raise the term b×t-1 to the (n+4)th power and assign the result to xpn, we would say

```
xpn := EXP((n+4) * LN(b×t-1))
```

In certain special situations, it is more desirable to compute exponents another way. One frequently occuring circumstance involves the computation of the polynomial P, where

$$P = A_0 + A, X + A_2 X^2 + A_3 X^3 + \cdots + A_n X^n$$

This formula can be rewritten as follows:

$$P = A_0 + X(A_1 + X (A_2 + X (A_3 + \cdots)) \ldots)$$

If we were to complete the process of factorization for a fourth-order polynomial (N = 4), we would get

$$P = A1 + X(A2 + X(A3 + X(A4 + X(A5))))$$

This formulation, called *Horner's method*, provides us with a computational approach for polynomials that is less complicated than the more general method using EXP and LN. To use it, we create a data structure in which the coefficients A1, A2, etc. are represented as an array. If $numcoeff$ is the number of coefficients in the array (let us say that $numcoeff$ is 7), Horner's method can be specified as shown in Figure 6.1.

```
CONST
  numcoeff = 7 ;
VAR
  i           :  INTEGER ;
  poly, X     :  REAL ;
  a           :  ARRAY [1..numcoeff]  OF REAL ;
            ....................
            ....................
(***  IN CHAPTER 4 WE INTRODUCED THE FOR STATEMENT AS ***)
(***  A WAY TO REPEAT A LOOP A CONTROLLED NUMBER OF   ***)
(***  TIMES. THE STATEMENT ENABLES US TO INITIALIZE   ***)
(***  AN INDEX VARIABLE, AFTER WHICH PASCAL AUTOMA-   ***)
(***  TICALLY ADDS 1 TO IT EACH TIME THROUGH THE LOOP.***)
(***  WE CAN INITIALIZE AN INDEX VARIABLE AND FORCE   ***)
(***  PASCAL TO SUBTRACT 1 FROM IT EACH TIME BY USING ***)
(***  THE PASCAL WORD DOWNTO. THUS, THE FOLLOWING LOOP***)
(***  STARTS WITH I SET TO NUMCOEFF, THEN, AFTER EACH ***)
(***  TRIP THROUGH THE LOOP, I IS REDUCED BY 1.
  poly := 0 ;
  FOR i := numcoeff DOWNTO 2 DO
    poly := x * (poly + a[i]) ;
  poly := poly + a[1]
            ....................
            ....................
```

Figure 6.1 ——

Horner's Method for a Polynomial with Seven Coefficients

6.3.4 Trigonometric Functions

Standard Pascal includes three built-in functions for fundamental trigonometric computations: SIN *(value)* computes the sine of *value*, and COS *(value)* produces the cosine of *value*. The argument for either function may be REAL or INTEGER, and both functions expect their respective arguments to be in radians. Thus, if we wanted the sine of 31 degrees, we could request it by specifying

```
CONST
  pi = 3.14159
    . . . . . . . . . .
  sinofx := SIN(31 * pi/180.0)
```

Similarly, if xdeg is an angle in degrees and we want its tangent, we might convert to radians and store the result in a separate variable xrad and then compute the tangent:

```
  . . . . . . . . . . . . . .
xrad := sdeg * pi/180.0 ;
tanofx := SIN(xrad)/COS(xrad)
  . . . . . . . . . . . . .
```

Other basic trigonometric functions are readily computed from SIN and COS.

Pascal-20 provides alternate functions for sine and cosine in which the angle can be expressed in degrees. The names for these extended functions are SIND and COSD, respectively.

A single function, ARCTAN, provides access to the inverse trigonometric computations. ARCTAN uses the REAL or INTEGER argument submitted to it to compute a REAL value representing an angle in radians. Computation of the inverse tangent in degrees, then, could proceed as shown below, assuming the earlier declaration for pi:

```
xrad := ARCTAN (x)  ;
xdeg := xrad * 180.0/pi
```

Since xdeg is a REAL value, the angle thus represented is expressed in degrees and fractions of a degree. Consequently, transformation of the fractional part to minutes (if that is desired) involves a separate step but a simple one:

```
xminutes := ROUND((xdeg - TRUNC(xdeg)) * 60.0)
```

Other inverse trigonometric functions are computed easily enough starting with ARCTAN. For instance, if sinval contains a REAL value and we want its inverse sine in a variable named myangle, we can obtain it by specifying

```
myangle := ARCTAN(sinval/SQRT(1.0-SQR(sinval)))
```

Similarly, if cosval is a REAL variable whose inverse cosine is to be assigned to yourangle, the computation is

```
yourangle := ARCTAN(SQRT(1.0-SQR(cosval))/cosval)
```

Pascal-20 makes the inverse sine and cosine available directly by including the additional functions ARCSIN and ARCCOS, respectively. Some Pascal implementations recognize the name ATAN as an alternative for ARCTAN.

6.3.5 Hyperbolic Functions

Standard Pascal provides no built-in facilities for the direct computation of hyperbolic functions. However, their computation from available functions is straightforward enough. For instance, if x is a REAL variable whose hyperbolic sine we want in hypsin, the appropriate computation would be

```
hypsin := 0.5  *  (EXP(x)-EXP(-x))
```

The hyperbolic cosine, assigned to a variable named hypcos, would be handled like this:

```
hypcos := 0.5  *  (EXP(x)+EXP(-x))
```

The hyperbolic tangent is simply the hyperbolic sine divided by the hyperbolic cosine. Pascal-20 makes the three basic hyperbolic functions available directly by providing SINH, COSH, and TANH in its extended library.

Inverse hyperbolic functions are no more difficult. If x is a REAL variable whose inverse hyperbolic sine, cosine, and tangent are to be assigned to invsinhx, invcoshx and invtanhx, respectively, the following statements will fulfill these requirements:

```
invsinhx := LN (x+SQRT(SQR(x)+1.0)) ;
invcoshx := LN (x+SQRT(SQR(x)-1.0)) ;
invtanhx := 0.5 * LN ((1.0+x)/(1.0-x))
```

6.3.6 Other Computational Functions

The standard built-in functions described thus far (except for those noted) are available in every implementation designed to meet the standard for

Pascal. However, for many of these implementations, the standard represents a minimum requirement rather than a limiting one. Consequently, various versions seek to offer additional functions with the idea of providing more convenience for the programmer using a particular version. This section looks at several computational functions in that category.

The FLOAT Function   IBM's VS Pascal implementation, designed for use on its 370/303X/43XX computer types, includes a function for explicit conversion from INTEGER to REAL. For example, if we wanted the ratio of INTEGER variables t t l and num as a real value with the fractional portion intact, we could obtain it directly by specifying

```
FLOAT(ttl)/FLOAT(num)
```

The MIN and MAX Functions   The MIN function, also part of the extensions in IBM VS Pascal, selects the lowest value of a list of numerical values and/or expressions given to it. (MAX selects the highest value.) The functions will deliver a value having the same type as the members of the list. Thus,

```
MIN(32.7, 18.91, 708.95)
```

results in a value of 18.91, while

```
MAX(86, -107, 2, 41)
```

returns a value of 86. Real and integer values may appear in the same argument list, in which case the function returns its result as a real value. Note that MIN and MAX produce the proper values, but they do not indicate the source. For instance, the assignment

```
topmost := MAX(xval, tcount, y-4.4)
```

puts the list's maximum value in topmost, but there is no information to indicate which member of the list supplied the maximum.

The EXPO Function   Another version of Pascal (which we shall call Stanford Pascal), implemented by Stanford University's Linear Accelerator Center for IBM 370/303X/43XX computer types, offers a built-in function named EXPO to help determine the current magnitude of real values. This function is based on the use of 16 as a numerical base for representing real (floating-point) values in the above mentioned computers: Each value is expressed (in base 16 arithmetic) as a fraction between 0.0 and 1.0 and an integer exponent indicating the power of 16 by which that fraction has to be multiplied to obtain the proper magnitude. (The hardware is designed to perform the necessary adjustments automatically.) Thus, the value 1.0 is stored as a fractional portion of 0.1 (that is, 1/16) and an exponent of 1, meaning that the machine produces the proper value by multiplying 1/16 times 16 to the first power. Similarly, a value of 256.0 is stored as a fractional portion of 0.1 and an exponent of 3. [Multiplication of 1/16 times 16 to the third power (4096) produces the desired value 256.] (For that matter, any value that is at least 256.0 but less than 4096.0 will have an exponent of 3 in its internal representation; the fractional portion, of course, will change.)

EXPO (*value*) (where *value* is a real expression) produces the exponent used in the internal representation. For instance, EXPO(1) = 1, EXPO(16) = 2, EXPO(256) = 3, EXPO(1.0/16.0) = 0, EXPO(128) = 3, and so on.

Production of Random Numbers Many computer applications require *random numbers*. These are values taken from an available selection (i.e., from a *domain* of values) where a particular choice is no more or no less likely than any of the other choices. For instance, when we throw a single die, we are choosing a value at random (if the die is honest) from a domain consisting of the values 1, 2, 3, 4, 5, and 6. The chance of getting any of these six values is the same as that of getting any of the others. Similarly, when we toss a coin, the domain consists of two values (heads or tails), and the side on which the coin lands after a given toss is a random event.

The applications using random numbers often require such values from domains offering thousands and even millions of choices. Preparation of computing systems that are capable of producing truly random numbers requires equipment whose cost and complexity rules it out for all but a few special systems. Instead, computational techniques are used to generate numbers whose behavior approximates that of random numbers. Such values are called *pseudorandom numbers,* and the algorithms that produce them are called *pseudorandom number generators.*

VS Pascal and Pascal-20 include such a generator, available by invoking the built-in function RANDOM. This function computes a real value between 0.0 and 1.0 using the value it computed the last time it was invoked in that program. Consequently, it needs a value (called a *seed*) to get started. The programmer must provide the seed by initially invoking RANDOM with some nonzero value as the argument. (A large odd value is recommended for this purpose.) If a programmer knows that his or her VS Pascal or Pascal-20 program will require pseudorandom numbers, it is a good idea to include the initial invocation as part of the other initialization activities at the beginning of the program. For instance, if randval is the REAL variable in which RANDOM is to deliver its value, then a statement like

```
randval := RANDOM(1769937)
```

will get the computation started. Then, each subsequent invocation can specifiy

```
randval := RANDOM(0)
```

thereby informing the function to use the previous value.

In this type of pseudorandom number generator, the domain from which the numbers are drawn is limited by the internal construction of the machine on which it is implemented. For the IBM systems mentioned before, this means that RANDOM can produce over 4 billion different values between 0.0 and 1.0. The DECSYSTEM-20 allows roughly 16 times that many possibilities. (The specific dependency on machine type will be examined when we look at a pseudorandom number generator in a subsequent chapter dealing with the construction of functions and procedures.) Another characteristic of this computational technique is that, starting from a particular seed, it computes each value in its domain in some particular (seemingly random) sequence and then starts over. With over 4 billion values in the domain, this is not a big problem. However, it does mean that RANDOM always will compute the same value from a given seed. Consequently, depending on the application, it may be advisable to design your program so that the seed value can change every time the program is used.

The range of values delivered by RANDOM (0.0 to 1.0) is designed to be as general as possible. Consequently, it is likely that the value, as received, may not be in the range required by the program. Tranformation is straightforward. For instance, suppose we wanted to simulate the throwing of a single die. To do so we need to convert the value delivered by RANDOM (between 0.0 and 1.0) to an integer in the range 1–6. If randval is RANDOM's product and throw is the INTEGER variable in which the converted value is to be stored, we can perform the transformation as follows:

```
throw := TRUNC(6.0 * randval) + 1
```

6.4 ARITHMETIC WITH PROGRAMMER-DEFINED VARIABLES

The built-in functions described thus far can be used with subrange data based on the INTEGER data type. This capability is just a natural extension of ordinary numeric processing and needs no elaboration. When it comes to enumerative types, however, the arithmetic capabilities are limited, and the relationship between these capabilities and Pascal's ordinary arithme-

tic facilities is rather specialized. Consequently, this topic will be considered in a separate chapter.

Problems

1. Write Pascal expressions for each of the following:

   a. $\sqrt{X^2 + Y^2}$

   b. $\dfrac{X^2 + A}{Y^2 - B}$

   c. $\sqrt{X^2 + |Z|Y^2}$

   d. $\dfrac{X^2 + \left(\dfrac{A}{B}\right)^{-1}}{\ln\left(X^2 + \dfrac{A}{B}\right)}$

   e. $\sqrt{\sin X \cos X}$

   f. $\ln\left(e^{2x} + \dfrac{1}{2e^x}\right)$

   g. $\sqrt{\dfrac{xy^2}{1 + \cot(x + 2)}}$

   h. $\ln^2\left(\left(\dfrac{x + y}{x - y}\right)^2 + \dfrac{X \tan Y}{Y \tan^2 X}\right)$

   i. $\dfrac{X(Y^3 + \ln |Y|)}{1 + Y}$

   j. $\dfrac{\ln X \sinh (Y + X^2)}{e\sqrt{2x^2 + \tan 2Y}}$

2. Among the algebraic equations given below, there may be some that
   require more than one Pascal statement to represent an equivalent set
   of computations. For each expression, write the necessary statement
   or statements to produce the required result. If you need to specify
   additional variables (for temporary storage, perhaps), you may
   assume that t1, t2, t3, etc. have been declared as REAL. Assume
   further that each variable name (except for the temporary one) is one
   letter long.

   a. $z = \sqrt{x^2 + 2y^4}$

   b. $w = (\sqrt{x^2 + 2y^4})^3$

   c. $y = \left(\dfrac{x + \ln |w|}{x + \ln w^2}\right)^{z/2}$

   d. $z = \dfrac{3.5(y + \sqrt{y^3})}{e^{x+\sqrt{y}}}$

   e. $p = \dfrac{ax^{b+2}e^{x+2}}{c^2(x + a)^3}$

   f. $r = \left(\dfrac{dvh}{m}\right)^{.8} \left(\dfrac{mc}{k}\right)^{.4}$

3. If variable x is declared as REAL and y is declared as INTEGER, fill in the expression in the statement

    Y := expression involving x

    so that x and y follow the relationship implied by these sample values:

x	y
0.0	0
0.5	0
1.0	0
2.8	0
3.0	1
3.6	1
4.75	1
5.88	1
6.0	2
6.7	2
8.95	2
9.00	3

4. Write a Pascal program that reads a succession of input values arranged so that each line consists of four different integer values r, s, t, and u. Display each input line (on a separate line) right after it is read. After all the lines have been read and displayed (use EOF to determine this), display a line showing smallsum, the sum of the smallest value from each input line, and a final line showing bigsum, the sum of the largest value from each input line.

5. Rewrite the program specified in Problem 4 so that it can process several (an arbitrary number) collections of input lines. After each collection, the program is to display smallsum and bigsum for that collection and then leave two blank lines before starting the output for the next collection. It is up to you to determine how to separate the collection.

6. Write a program that reads a positive integer into a variable named limit (limit<50). Starting with INTEGER variable i set at 1 and proceeding up to and including limit, the program is to display i, i^2, LN(i), and $\sqrt{N(i)}$ on a line for each value of i. Include appropriate column labels at the top of the output page.

7. Write a program that reads a positive integer into a variable named limit(limit<20) and displays a table showing the logarithms to the base 2 of all integers starting with 1 up to and including limit. Each line of the table is to show an integer value and its logarithm to

the base 2. The values of the logarithms should be rounded to five places.

8. Modify the program described in Problem 7 so that the output table starts with the highest value (limit) and its base 2 logarithm and displays the entries in decreasing order. The final line of output, then, will be the value 1 and its logarithm.

9. Generalize the program in Problem 7 or 8 as follows: Input consists of two positive integers, both greater than 1. The first value, to be stored in a variable named base, indicates the base to which the required set of logarithms is to be computed. The second input value, limit, serves the same purpose as Problem 7 or 8.

10. Write the appropriate Pascal statement(s) for each of the following computations. In each case, store the final result in a variable named rslt.

    a. Round the value 8.7 to the nearest integer.
    b. Round the value 172.99 to the nearest tenth.
    c. Adjust the value 346.81 to the largest integer that does not exceed the original value.
    d. Round the value 8612.84 to the nearest thousand.
    e. Round the value in REAL variable visc to the nearest hundredth.
    f. Bring the square root of the value in variable smax to the nearest integer.
    g. Round the largest of the variables st, br, and wh to four decimal places.
    h. Round the sum of the largest and smallest of the values in REAL variables f1, f2, f3, f4, and f5 to the nearest thousandth.

11. The East Poopik Symphony Society has launched its annual campaign and the contributions are pouring in. There are six categories for such donations: groupie ($5), member ($25), fan ($50), patron ($100), pussycat ($500), and oboy ($1000). Each contribution is recorded on a separate line consisting of the identification number (an integer) and the amount (one of those given above). Write a program that computes and prints the number of donors in each category. Use an identification number of zero to terminate the run, and print each category on a separate line. For example,

    GROUPIES: 41
    MEMBERS: 189
    FANS: 212
    ....

    After the final category, print a final line showing the total number of donors and the total amount contributed.

12. Modify the program in Problem 11 to meet the following additional requirement: The Society's Ruling Board has found it is losing many contributions because people object to the predefined amounts. To correct the situation, a new donor category has been added: The freespirit category covers those contributors who wish to give an amount other than those specified on the society's tasteful Donor Card Future Pledge Form and Raffle. Now, in addition to the output specified before, the revised program is to produce a line (after the oboy category) showing the number of donors in the freespirit category, the total amount of their donations, and the average donation size in this category. The last line still shows the total number of donors (including freespirits) and the total amount donated. The input does not change. (Remember that freespirits may donate amounts that are not whole dollars.)

13. The Natural Herbal Food Works manufactures wholesome-looking confections to be sold under local brand names. The basic mixture, to which desired flavoring and coloring is added, consists of two ingredients whose relative proportions are determined strictly by price. Ingredient A (you do *not* want to know what it is) costs 51 cents a pound and B (the good stuff) costs $1.17 a pound. Write a program that computes mixtures for a succession of requirements. Each input set consists of a batch number (a six-digit integer), total number of pounds in the mixture, and the final price per pound. The final price is the amount charged. To cover its costs and to make a reasonable profit, the Natural Herbal Food Works sets its price at double its costs for ingredients A and B in a given blend.

   Output for each input set is to show the batch number, weight of the order, price per pound, and the weights of A and B used to fill the order. If a set of specifications present an impossible situation (for example, the required price is too low), display a line with that batch number, along with the message REQUIREMENTS CANNOT BE MET. On the other hand, if a price is too high (that is, the required price is greater than what the Works regularly charges), the Natural Herbal Food Works (whose proprietors, after all, are not pigs) wants the program to display the batch number, the message REQUIRED PRICE IS EXCESSIVE, and an additional line showing the batch number (again) and the total amount of excess (required total price — actual total price).

14. Prices change. To reflect this, write the program for Problem 14 so that each set of input consists of a batch number, total pounds, and final price as before. However, the first input set is to be preceded by a single line showing the current prices (per pound) for A and B, in that order.

15. Good news. The Natural Herbal Food Works has decided to expand by opening an international sales division. What this means is that orders will be coming in from customers who will specify their requirements in kilograms and dollars per kilogram. The Works will note this by changing the form of its input data so that an odd batch number will indicate that weights are in pounds (and prices are on a per pound basis), while an even batch number will specify everything in terms of kilograms. Modify the program in Problem 14 or 15 accordingly.

16. The Pancreas County Highway Authority has to define the path of a road through an expanse of mountainous terrain. For each mountain, the authority must decide whether to tunnel through or go around it. Figure 6.2 summarizes the problem for a portion of the distance. In this figure, p1 and p2 define the points under consideration. If the direct route is used, a tunnel must be built at a cost tunnelcost. If the mountain is to be circumvented, the road must detour from point p1 at an angle alpha, then make a right angle (well, we can consider it a right angle) and continue to point p2. In any event, there is a construction cost kmcost associated with each kilometer of road-way (exclusive of tunnel costs) that may change for each section. Data for this project are prepared so that each line contains the following information for a given section:

Section number (section), a three-digit integer
Number of mountains in section (mtns), either one or zero
tunnelcost, in dollars
Kilometers from p1 to p2 (p1p2) to the nearest .1 km

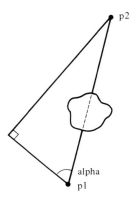

Figure 6.2
The Pancreas County Tunnel Dilemma

kmcost in dollars per kilometer, to the nearest dime
The integer portion of alpha, in degrees
The fractional portion of alpha, in minutes (to the nearest minute)

Write a program that decides whether to tunnel or detour for each section of road that is read in. The output should contain the following information: section number and total distance for each section, for direct as well as detour route; cost for each section using the alternative approaches; minimum cost for the total road project, along with the corresponding highway length; and total cost with no detours, along with that highway length.

17. A wide variety of mathematical functions can be computed as series in which the accuracy of the function value depends on the number of terms used in the computation. For example, we can get a value of e, the base of natural logarithms, from Pascal by using the EXP function with an argument of 1.0. This value, which turns out to be 0.2718281E+01, can be computed from the series

$$e = 1 + \frac{1}{1!} + \frac{1}{2!} + \frac{1}{3!} + \frac{1}{4!} + \cdots$$

We can examine the effect of each additional term by evaluating the series with one term, two terms, etc., and comparing each of the results with the reference value. Thus, for e, the comparison would look like this:

No. of Terms	Series Value	Ser. Val. – Ref. Val.
1	0.1000000E+01	−0.1718281E+01
2	0.2000000E+01	−0.7182810E+00
3	0.2500000E+01	−0.21828190E+00
4	0.2666667E+01	−0.5161400E−01
5	0.2708334E+01	−0.9947400E−02
6	0.2716667E+01	−0.1613700E−02
7	0.2718056E+01	−0.2252000E−03
8	0.2718230E+01	−0.5140000E−04
	etc.	

We can see that by the eighth term, the computed value agrees with the reference value to four decimal places. Prepare such a table for each of the following functions. Obtain the reference value by invoking the appropriate Pascal function or by constructing an appropriate computation if Pascal does not have a function for direct computation.

$$\sin x = x - \frac{x^3}{3!} + \frac{x^5}{5!} - \frac{x^7}{7!} + \frac{x^9}{9!} - \cdots \qquad \text{(use } x = 0.5)$$

$$\cos x = 1 - \frac{x^2}{2!} + \frac{x^4}{4!} - \frac{x^6}{6!} + \frac{x^8}{8!} - \cdots \qquad \text{(use } x = 0.5)$$

$$\ln x = 2 \left[\frac{x-1}{z+1} + \frac{1}{3}\left(\frac{x-1}{x+1}\right)^3 + \frac{1}{5}\left(\frac{x-1}{x+1}\right)^5 + \cdots \right] \qquad \text{(use } x = 2.0)$$

$$\tan^{-1} x = x - \frac{x^3}{3} + \frac{x^5}{5} - \frac{x^7}{7} + \ldots \qquad \text{(use } x = 0.5)$$

$$e^x = 1 + x + \frac{x^2}{2!} + \frac{x^3}{3!} - \frac{x^4}{4!} + \ldots \qquad \text{(use } x = 2.5)$$

18. The distance between two points $(x1, y1)$ and $(x2, y2)$, when plotted on rectangular coordinates, can be computed by the formula

$$\sqrt{(x2 - x1)^2 + (y2 - y1)^2}$$

Write a program that reads and processes sets of four points $(x1, y1)$, $(x2, y2)$, $(x3, y3)$, and $(x4, y4)$. For each set, the program is to compute and display the distances between all pairs of points. Each set is to produce a line for each distance showing the coordinates of the points and the distance between them. Leave a blank between input sets.

19. Modify the program in Problem 18 so that it produces three additional lines of output for each input set processed. The first additional line is to show the largest of the distances computed for that set of points, followed by a line showing the smallest distance, and a final line showing the average distance. Each of these additional lines is to be labeled clearly.

20. When an airplane sets out to fly in a certain direction, that direction may be affected by a prevailing wind. For example, an airplane traveling due west at 585 miles per hour may encounter a wind blowing due south at 45 miles per hour (Figure 6.3). This means that after, say, an hour of flying under these conditions (without correcting for them), the plane would have traveled 585 miles west and 45 miles south.

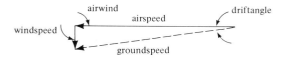

Figure 6.3

Diagram for Problem 20

In order to correct for this effect, it is necessary to determine the ground speed of the aircraft (groundspeed) and the drift angle (driftangle). Using variable names airspeed and windspeed for air speed and wind speed, respectively, and using airwind to refer to the angle between the aircraft heading and the wind direction (90 degrees in the example of Figure 6.3), we can use the law of cosines to solve for groundspeed.

$$\text{groundspeed} = \sqrt{\text{airspeed}^2 + \text{windspeed}^2 - 2\ \text{airspeed}(\text{windspeed})\cos(\text{airwind})}$$

and the law of sines to help us to solve for driftangle:

$$\frac{\text{groundspeed}}{\sin(\text{airwind})} = \frac{\text{windspeed}}{\sin(\text{driftangle})}$$

Write a program in which an input set consists of airspeed, windspeed, and airwind (the latter in degrees). For each set, the program is to reproduce (echo) the input, using one line for each value accompanied by its name. Then, the program is to display groundspeed and driftangle on one line. driftangle is to be shown in degrees. Leave a blank line between sets of output. Run your program with the following input sets.

airspeed	windspeed	airwind
325.0	0.0	0.0
280.0	10.0	0.0
300.0	20.0	180.0
300.0	55.0	90.0
400.0	50.0	120.0

21. (This problem is intended for those students whose Pascal implementation has a RANDOM built-in function.) Assume num is declared as an INTEGER variable. For each of the following requirements, write the appropriate Pascal statement(s) to store the specified kind of value in num. Declare any temporary variables you might need.
    a. A random integer with the value 1, 2, 3, 4, or 5
    b. A random integer with the value 10, 20, 30, 40, or 50
    c. A random integer with the value 5, 6, 7, or 8
    d. A random integer with the value 0, 1, 2, 3, or 7
    e. A random integer with the value −3, −2, −1, 0, 1, 2, or 3
    f. A random integer with the value 1, 2, 3, or 4 where the value 4 is twice as likely to turn up as any of the others
    g. A random integer representing a value obtained by throwing an honest pair of dice. (Note: Merely having a number from 2 through 12 does not imitate the throwing of a pair of honest dice.)

Chapter Seven

Introduction to Input-Output Operations

Our use of the READLN and WRITELN procedures with the standard INPUT and OUTPUT files exploits only part of Pascal's facilities for transmitting individual data items between the central processor and the outside world. This chapter looks more closely at these input/output processes and at the mechanisms behind them.

7.1 READLN **AND** WRITELN **OPERATIONS**

READLN and WRITELN are based on a view of a file as a series of characters followed by a special end-of-file marker. Such a file is called a *text file*. The characters in a text file are punctuated further by additional markers called *end-of-line-indicators,* or *line separators*. (We shall refer to the end-of-line indicator as <eol>.) These are invisible to the programmer, but they can be detected by Pascal. Consequently, they can be used to influence the appearance of output text and to help control certain input processes. The length of a line in a text file is not fixed. Instead, it is simply the number of characters (including blanks) between two line separators.

When we use READLN, we are telling Pascal to interpret the characters in a text file in accordance with certain rules. By the same token, a call to WRITELN dictates the way the resulting text file is prepared.

7.1.1 The READLN **Procedure**

When we use READLN in the form employed thus far, we tell Pascal to assume that each value in a text file has a certain appearance:

1. An integer value consists of a string of numerical characters (the digits 0 through 9) that may or may not be preceded by a sign. Pascal

recognizes the end of an integer value by the appearance of the first nonnumeric character. (This usually is a blank.) For example, suppose nv is an INTEGER variable and the current line of the INPUT text file looks like this:

$$-47 <eol>$$

Then, if we were to say

READLN (nv)

Pascal would find the first eligible character (the minus sign in this instance) and continue reading until it found the first blank to the right of the last digit. The resulting string of three characters (minus sign, 4, and 7) would be converted automatically to the internal form used by the processor to represent integers, and the value thus produced would be stored in nv. Pascal would skip over the subsequent blanks and stop after reading the <eol>. The same rules apply to integer subrange data values.

2. A real value consists of a string of nonblank numerical characters preceded by an optional sign and punctuated by those symbols acceptable in a real constant. The "end" of a real input value is reached when Pascal finds a character that does not belong in a real constant (e.g., a blank). Thus, if rate and cwt are REAL variables, and our input line looks like this,

$$3.274 \ -8.871E\text{-}4 \ <eol>$$

the input request

READLN (rate, cwt)

results in the storage of 3.274E0 and −8.871E-4 in rate and cwt, respectively.

3. Since a CHAR value always consists of a single character, Pascal finds such a value (when requested to do so) simply by using the next character in the file. For example, if initial is a CHAR variable (and nv, rate, and cwt are defined as they were earlier), then

READLN (nv, rate, initial, cwt)

applied to the input line

$$361 \quad 3.274 \quad W \quad -8.871E\text{-}4 \ <eol>$$

will produce values of 361, 3.274E0, and –8.871E-4 in nu, rate, and cwt, respectively, and a blank in initial. After finding and converting the 361 to integer form, Pascal finds the 5-character string 3.274, converts that to a real number and stores it in rate. The very next character (the one after the 4), which is a blank, is stored (without conversion, of course) in initial. Finally, Pascal looks for (and finds) a character string (-8.871E-4) representing a real value, converts it to real form, and stores the result in cwt. In doing so, Pascal skips over the W since it already has found a character value for initial, and, at that point, is looking for a real value. If we wanted a W in initial, our input line (assuming the same READLN request) would have to say

$$361 \quad 3.274W \quad -8.871E-4 \ <eol>$$

READLN is designed to look for <eol> and use it as a signal to conclude its activity. For example, assuming variables nu, rate, and cwt as before, suppose we prepare the following line of input:

$$24 \quad -311.56 \quad 6500.7 \quad 487 \quad 608.723 \ <eol>$$

Then, when we say

```
READLN (nu, rate, cwt)
```

the program reads the first three values, converts them, and stores them in nu, rate, and cwt, respectively. Then, it moves across the rest of the line until it finds the <eol>. As a result, the next item ready to be read is the first item on the next line. The values after the third value (i.e., the 487 and 608.727) are skipped over and lost.

It is possible to use READLN without specifying any list of variables. The form

```
READLN (INPUT) or simply READLN
```

causes the program to move across the INPUT file until it finds and reads the next <eol>.

7.1.2 Example 7.1

The Sostenuto Piano Company keeps the following line of data for each piano sold:

Name	Description	Form
serial	Serial number	Integer
piano	Type of piano (U = upright; S = spinet; C = console; B = baby grand; G = grand; L = large grand)	Character
pianowt	Piano weight to the nearest pound	Integer
price	Selling price, dollars and cents	nnnnn.nn
yrofsale	Year in which piano was sold	Integer
custloc	Customer location (two-character state code; e.g., NY = New York; FS = foreign sale)	Character array

We shall write a program that determines, for a specified time span (e.g., from 1974 through 1977) how many of each type of piano were sold. The algorithm is straightforward: An initial line of input will specify a starting year startyr and an ending year endyr. After these values are read and stored, the data for each piano will be read in succession and used (if the year of sale is in the specified range) to update the counter for the appropriate piano type. As the pseudocode in Figure 7.1 indicates, this process will be repeated as long as the end of the input file has not been reached. Once

Define serial, pianowt, yrofsale, startyr, endyr, num-
       sold for each type of piano, price, custloc, and
       piano.
Initialize numsold for each piano type.
Read startyr and endyr.
WHILE
there is input to be processed
   Read a set of input values for a piano that was sold.
   IF
      the piano was sold between years startyr and endyr
   THEN
      increment the number sold for that piano type.
ENDIF
ENDWHILE
Print headings.
Print piano type and number sold for each type.
Print terminating message.
Stop.

Figure 7.1

Pseudocode For Example 7.1

the last data line has been brought in and examined, the results will be printed and the program will conclude.

The first line of input (startyr and endyr) is handled easily enough by recording the two values on a line, e.g.,

$$1947 \qquad 1960 \text{ <eol>}$$

and saying

```
READLN (startyr, endyr)
```

Subsequent input data are processed by a loop, each cycle of which brings in another line containing values for INTEGER variable serial, CHAR variable piano, INTEGER variable pianowt, REAL variable price, INTEGER variable yrofsale, and the two-element CHAR array custloc. We must make sure that numerical values are separated by nonnumeric characters. At the same time, the character data must be positioned in such a way that we do not (mistakenly) force the program to take one of the separating blanks and use it as an input value: In our example, this means that the character value for piano must be placed immediately after the integer value for serial; a separating blank between the two would be picked up and used. Blanks may appear between piano and pianowt, and price, and between price and yrofsale. The final value for a given piano, i.e., custloc, must appear immediately after yrofsale for the same reason given in the case of piano. Thus, a typical line of input would look like this:

$$187006G \qquad 655 \qquad 8755.98 \qquad 1967TX \text{ <eol>}$$

The READLN call for each line of piano data looks like this:

```
READLN (serial, piano, pianowt, price,
yrofsale, custloc[1], custloc[2])
```

To help enhance the program's clarity, we shall define an enumerative data type named pianotype, and we shall convert the character value for piano to the corresponding name for the appropriate pianotype. The resulting program is shown in Figure 7.2 and a sample run is given in Figure 7.3. Take special note of the loop that initializes the elements of numsold to zero. The *index* that controls and monitors the number of cycles through the loop (pianosize) is not an ordinary integer. Instead, it is a programmer-defined variable which takes on values that do not appear to be integers. However, we know (from Section 4.2.2) that Pascal associ-

```
(******************************************************************)
(**                      EXAMPLE 7.1                           **)
(******************************************************************)
(** THIS PROGRAM READS A SUCCESSION OF DATA VALUES, EACH LINE  **)
(** DESCRIBING THE SALE OF A PIANO BY THE SOSTENUTO PIANO CO.  **)
(** THESE VALUES ARE PRECEDED BY A STARTING YEAR AND ENDING    **)
(** YEAR WHICH BRACKET A TIME SPAN TO BE CONSIDERED DURING THIS**)
(** RUN. FOR EACH TYPE OF PIANO, THE PROGRAM PRINTS THE NUMBER **)
(** SOLD DURING THE SPECIFIED TIME SPAN.                       **)
(** VARIABLES:                                                 **)
(**    SERIAL: A PIANO'S IDENTIFICATION NUMBER                 **)
(**    PIANO: TYPE OF PIANO (U=UPRIGHT, S=SPINET, C=CONSOLE,   **)
(**                         B=BABYGRAND, G=GRAND, L=LARGEGRAND)**)
(** PIANOSIZE: AN INTERNAL (ENUMERATIVE) VARIABLE DERIVED      **)
(**            FROM PIANO                                      **)
(** PIANOWT: A PIANO'S WEIGHT                                  **)
(** YROFSALE: THE YEAR A PARTICULAR PIANO WAS SOLD             **)
(** PRICE: A PARTICULAR PIANO'S SELLING PRICE                  **)
(** CUSTLOC: TWO-LETTER CODE INDICATING CUSTOMER'S LOCATION    **)
(** NUMSOLD: THE NUMBER OF PIANOS (OF A PARTICULAR TYPE) SOLD  **)
(**            DURING THE SPECIFIED TIME SPAN                  **)
(** STARTYR, ENDYR: STARTING AND ENDING YEARS                 **)
(******************************************************************)
PROGRAM ex701 (INPUT,OUTPUT) ;
TYPE
    pianotype = (upright, spinet, console, babygrand,
                 grand, largegrand, mislabel ;
VAR
    serial, pianowt, yrofsale, startyr, endyr  :  INTEGER ;
    numsold  :  ARRAY[pianotype] OF INTEGER ;
    price  :  REAL ;
    custloc  :  ARRAY[1..2] OF CHAR ;
    piano  :  CHAR ;
    pianosize  :  pianotype ;
BEGIN
    FOR  pianosize := upright TO mislabel  DO
       numsold[pianosize] := 0  ;
    READLN (startyr, endyr)  ;
    WHILE NOT EOF(INPUT)  DO
       BEGIN
          READLN (serial, piano, pianowt, price,
                  yrofsale, custloc[1], custloc[2] ;
          (*** CHECK WHETHER YEAR SOLD IS IN RANGE ***)
          IF  (yrofsale >= startyr) AND (yrofsale <= endyr)  THEN
             BEGIN
                (*** FIND THE PIANO TYPE ***)
```

Figure 7.2

Program for Example 7.1

```
         IF  piano = 'U'  THEN  pianosize := upright
         ELSE IF  piano = 'S"
             THEN  pianosize := spinet
             ELSE IF  piano = 'C'
                 THEN pianosize := console
                 ELSE IF  piano = 'B'
                     THEN  piano := babygrand
                     ELSE IF  piano = 'G'
                         THEN  pianosize := grand
                         ELSE IF piano = 'L'
                             THEN  pianosize := largegrand
                             ELSE  pianosize := mislabel   ;
         (*** NOW THE APPROPRIATE COUNTER IS        ***)
         (*** EXPRESSED SIMPLY AS NUMSOLD[PIANOSIZE] ***)
         numsold[pianosize] := numsold[pianosize] + 1
      END
   END  ;
(*** ALL DATA HAVE BEEN PROCESSED. TIME TO WRITE THE OUTPUT ***)
WRITELN ('SOSTENUTO PIANO REPORT')                      ;
WRITELN ('SALES FROM YEAR ',startyr, ' THROUGH ',endyr) ;
WRITELN  ;
WRITELN ('UPRIGHTS: ',numsold[upright])   ;
WRITELN ('SPINETS: ',numsold[spinet])   ;
WRITELN ('CONSOLES: ',numsold[console])   ;
WRITELN ('BABY GRANDS: ',numsold[babygrand])   ;
WRITELN ('GRANDS: ',numsold[grand])   ;
WRITELN ('LARGEGRANDS: ',numsold[largegrand])   ;
WRITELN ('mislabeled: ',numsold[mislabel])   ;
WRITELN  ;
WRITELN ('END OF RUN.')
END.
```

Figure 7.2

Program for Example 7.1 (Continued)

ates the sequence of values defined for an enumerative data type with corresponding internal numerical values. Consequently, given the TYPE definition for pianotype, the statement

```
FOR pianosize := upright TO mislabel   DO
                        etc.
```

sets up a loop that will go through exactly seven cycles.

7.1.3 The WRITELN Procedure

Each call to the WRITELN procedure produces output with a concluding <eol>. Note that WRITELN *does not start a new line*. The <eol> placed by

```
1947       1960
100U   340   1875.00   1948KY
101S   300   2100.00   1950LA
102C   410   3000.00   1956NY
103B   600   4000.00   1951NY
104B   665   5400.50   1958NJ
105G   800   8000.98   1949NY
106L  1400  12500.85   1959CA
107S   280    995.99   1960NY
```

(a) Input

```
SOSTENUTO PIANO REPORT
SALES FROM YEAR           1947THROUGH           1960

UPRIGHTS:              1
SPINETS:               2
CONSOLES:            1
BABY GRANDS:            2
SUPERGRANDS:           1
GRANDS:           1
MISLABELED:          0


END OF RUN.
```

(b) Output

Figure 7.3

Sample Run for Example 7.1

WRITELN at the end of the list of output values means that *the first value written by the next output statement* will start a new line. [Look at Figure 7.3, and see if you can explain why there is only one blank line before Example 7.1's output. Recall (Figure 7.2) that there are two blank WRITELN calls before the value of numsold[upright] is displayed.] Thus, if INTEGER variable nv has a value of −31 and rate and cwt have respective values of 3.274 and −0.0008871, the procedure call

WRITELN (nv, rate, cwt)

produces a line like this:

bbbbbbbb-3131bbbbbbb3.2740000EObbbbbb-8.8710000E-4 <eol>

(Remember, b represents a blank.) Of course, we cannot see the <eol>. If we had written

```
WRITELN (nv, cwt) ;
WRITELN (rate)
```

instead, the result would have been two shorter lines, i.e.,

bbbbbbbbb-31bbbbbbb3.2740000F0   <eol>

bbbbbbb-8.8710000E-4   <eol>

It is up to the programmer to provide separation between the displayed values. Thus, if we say

```
WRITELN (nv, ' ',rate,' ',cwt)
```

Pascal will obey, producing

$-$31bb3.2740000EObb-8.8710000E-4   <eol>

WRITELN, like READLN, can be used without an output list. The result is that the program writes an <eol>, after which it is ready to write on the next line. For instance, assuming the previous values for nv, rate, and cwt, the sequence

```
WRITELN ('NV: ',nv) ;
WRITELN  ;
WRITELN ('CWT: ',cwt,'  RATE: ',rate)
```

produces two lines of written output with a blank line between them:

NV: bbbbbbbbb-31

CWT: 3.2740000EObbRATE: -8.8710000F-4

(Now that the point has been made several times, we shall stop showing the <eol> at the end of each line except where it might be necessary for clarification.)

7.2 THE READ AND WRITE PROCEDURES

Individual input/output items in text files can be controlled by means of the READ and WRITE procedures. Each time one of these procedures is called, it reads (or writes) one data item and stops, with no consideration being given to <eol>s.

7.2.1 Properties of READ

To see how the READ procedure operates, let us assume that nu, total, maxnum, and zsum are INTEGER variables, and given the following lines of input data:

24	311	6500
7	631	7200
0	79	400

if we say

```
READ (nu)
```

the program will read the first value on the first line and store it as an integer in nu. Once that activity is complete, the program is ready to read the next value (i.e., the 311). Of course, it is up to the programmer to ask for it and to specify an appropriate destination. On the other hand, if we had said

```
READLN (nu)
```

the variable nu still would have received a value of 24. However, the program would have skipped over the 311 and 6500, and the next available input value would have been 7. If we were to say

```
READ (nu, total, maxnum, zsum)
```

the program, after reading the first three values and finding an end-of-line indicator, simply would go to the next line and get the fourth value (7). Then, the next available input value would be 631. When we use the same list of variables with READLN instead of READ, namely,

```
READLN (nu, total, maxnum, zsum)
```

and apply this to the same text file, we store the same four values, but the next available input item is 0 and not 631. (The 631 and 7200 would be skipped in READLN's relentless quest for an <eol>.) Additional comparisons between READ and READLN are shown in Table 7.1.

Although the READ procedure is not strongly affected by end-of-line indicators, the programmer can bring them into the picture by using Pascal's EOLN built-in function. EOLN produces a boolean value depending on the presence or absence of an end-of-line indicator. Whenever the program begins reading from a new input line, EOLN automatically is set to FALSE. As soon as the end of that line is reached, EOLN automatically changes to TRUE. Accordingly, the programmer can test for the end of a line in the

Table 7.1 Comparison of READ and READLN Procedures

nv, total, maxnum, zsum are declared as INTEGER variables; input for each example consists of the following four lines:

24	311	6500
7	631	7200
0	79	400
−6	32	511

Input operations(s)	nv	total	maxnum	zsum	Next value
READLN (nv, total, maxnum)	24	311	6500	?	7
READ (nv) ; READ (total) ; READ (maxnum)	24	311	6500	?	7
READ (total) ; READ (nv) ; READ (zsum)	311	24	?	6500	7
READLN (nv) ; READLN (total); READLN (maxnum)	24	7	0	?	−6
READ (nv, total); READ (maxnum, zsum)	24	311	6500	7	631
READLN (nv, total) ; READLN (maxnum, zsum)	24	311	7	631	0
READLN (nv, total) ; READ (maxnum, zsum)	24	311	7	631	7200
READ (nv, total); READLN (maxnum, zsum)	24	311	6500	7	0

standard INPUT file simply by testing EOLN(INPUT) or just EOLN. (Since such a test on a line of output makes no sense, Pascal has no trouble interpreting EOLN by itself as a specific reference to the standard INPUT file.) Thus, suppose we had to know how many data items there were on a particular input line, and there was no guarantee as to the exact quantity. We could set up a little loop using READ to bring the items in one at a time (into a variable we shall call invalue) and a counter (which we shall call numval) to keep track of the number. Our loop could look like this:

```
numval := 0 ;
WHILE NOT(EOLN) DO
BEGIN
        READ (invalue) ;
        numval := numval + 1
        . . . . . . . . .
        process invalue
        . . . . . . . . .
END ;
WRITELN ('THIS LINE HAS ',numval,'VALUES.')
        . . . . . . . . .
```

7.2.2 Input of Character Arrays

If we want to read a string of characters, we must work our way around Pascal's restriction that limits CHAR variables to single characters. (Some Pascal dialects include extensions that overcome this restriction, but we shall limit our discussion to the standard version.) The most direct way to do this is to provide CHAR arrays for such strings and then read the data into the arrays one element (i.e., one character) at a time. Suppose we wanted to store a string representing somebody's name. Based on our knowledge of the application being considered, we would determine how long a name we would have to accommodate. To illustrate, we shall use a maximum length of 20. Then, the declaration

```
VAR
    surname : ARRAY [1..20] OF CHAR
```

will give us the desired capacity. If we assume i and idnumber to be INTEGER variables, the line of input

30672HARRISONbbbbbbbbbbbbbbbbbbbb <eol>

can be read properly with the sequence

```
READ (idnumber) ;
FOR  i := 1 TO 20  DO
   READ (surname[i]) ;
READLN
```

After the integer value (30672) is brought in by the initial READ, the loop picks up a character during each of its 20 cycles, beginning with the next character (H). As a result, the letters HARRISON will be stored in surname[1] through surname[8], and the remaining elements (surname[9] through surname[20]) will be filled with the next 12 blanks from the INPUT file. The final READLN after the loop forces the program to the end of that input line, so that the next value available for input is the first value on the next line.

7.2.3 Properties of WRITE

The WRITE procedure is related to WRITELN in the same way as READ is to READLN: After WRITE has completed its activity, the program is ready to write in the next position of the current output line. If we should use the WRITE procedure with a list of data items that overflows the line, the program simply fills the line and (after adding an <eol>) continues writing on the next one. The number of items placed on a single line depends on the number of characters assigned to each item by the particular Pascal implementation. For example, IBM's VS Pascal uses the following lengths:

1. Integer values are displayed as 12-character strings with the values occupying the rightmost positions. Excess positions are filled with blank characters. (-387 would appear as bbbbbbbb-387.)
2. Real values are displayed using 20 positions. As is the case with integers, the values are right-justified, with excess positions being filled with blanks. (472.64 would appear as bbbbbbb4.7264000E+02.)
3. A single position is used to display each character value.
4. Boolean values are displayed in the rightmost positions of a 10-character field, the rest being filled with blanks (i.e., bbbbbbTRUE or bbbbbFALSE).

Character strings stored in CHAR arrays can be written into the OUTPUT file using the same technique described for input (Section 7.2.2).

Now that we have looked at both output procedures, the role of the <eol> can be seen more clearly by looking at a direct comparison between WRITE and WRITELN using the same output list. Using INTEGER variables nv and numval with respective values of 31 and 416, and REAL variable xarea with a value of 5028.96, the specification

```
WRITELN ('NV: ',nv,' XAREA: ',xarea,'NUMVAL: ',numval)
```

produces the line

```
NV: bbbbbbbbbb31   XAREA: bbbbbbb5.0289600E+03   NUMVAL: bbbbbbbbbb416
```

If we wanted to produce the same result using WRITE, we would have to say

```
WRITE ('NV: ',nv) ;
WRITE (' XAREA: ',xarea) ;
WRITE (' NUMVAL: ',numval) ;
WRITELN
```

or

WRITE ('NV: ',nv,' XAREA: ',xarea,' NUMVALL: ',numval) ; WRITELN

Without the concluding WRITELN, there would be no <eol> after the third value.

7.3 FORMAT CONTROL OF DATA VALUES

The use of READ, WRITE, READLN, and WRITELN discussed so far depends on Pascal's automatic internal mechanisms to deal with individual data items. Although this reliance on Pascal simplifies input/output processes, it forces the programmer to give up some control over data transmission. Consequently, Pascal enables the programmer to exercise full control over output data formats. In addition, many Pascal implementations provide an extension to standard Pascal that permits the programmer to control input data processing. This is done by means of a simple extension to the information specified in READ, READLN, WRITE, and WRITELN. (If your particular implementation adheres strictly to the Pascal standard, you may omit Sections 7.3.1 and 7.3.2.)

7.3.1 Control of Input Data Formats

When the programmer assumes more direct control of the form in which his or her input data are presented, he or she accounts for every column in the input file. This is done by specifying the length of each input variable along with its name. For example, if nv is an INTEGER variable, the specification

READ (nv:6)

instructs Pascal to use the next 6 characters in the INPUT file as the value to be converted and stored in nv.

READLN (nv:6)

forces the program to take the value from the next 6 characters of the line and move to the <eol>.

Although the length specification forces Pascal to use the designated number of characters, it does not change the rules for recognizing and accepting legitimate data values. For instance, if we are at the beginning of a new line whose first 12 characters are

31Tbb92084WK

(b still represents a blank) and we request a value for INTEGER variable nv by saying

```
READLN (nv:6)
```

the program will scan the first 6 characters as directed. As long as it finds numeric characters, it will treat them as part of the value to be converted and stored. In this instance, the T signals an end to the integer (since it is not a numeric character), and so the value stored in nv is 31 and the remaining four characters (T, two blanks, and a 9) are ignored. The next available position in INPUT to be scanned in response to a READ is the seventh one on the current line, (i.e., the one containing a 2).

The primary use for the input length specifier (assuming it is included in a particular extended version of Pascal) is to facilitate the handling of well-regulated collections of input text files in which each line contains a set of values for the same variables, presented in the same sequence and placed in the same positions as they are on the other input lines.

7.3.2 Example 7.2

We shall adjust the program in Example 7.1 to handle input data in which the data items are in fixed positions on the input lines:

Positions	Name
1–6	serial
7–10	blanks
11	piano
12–15	blanks
16–19	pianowt
20–24	blanks
25–32	price
33–36	yrofsale
37–40	blanks
41–42	custloc

The first two input values (startyr and endyr) will be recorded in columns (positions) 1–4 and 11–14 of the first line. This is handled easily enough by saying

```
READLN (startyr:10, endyr:4)
```

By specifying a field length of 10 for startyr, we take care of the first 10 positions of the input line. Only the first four of these supply the actual value for start yr. Since the remaining six positions are blank, they are skipped over, thereby setting the file to the eleventh character in the line, i.e., the first character of endyr. The field length of 4 forces the use of the next four characters for endyr, and the processing is complete for that line. (Would we have gotten the same result in this case without using field lengths in the READLN call?) A READLN call with length specifiers also will be used to read the data for each piano. The blanks between the values will be handled by including their positions in the field lengths of the variables immediately preceding them. Thus, the READLN call for each line of piano data looks like this:

```
READLN (serial:10, piano:5, pianowt:9, price:8:2,
        yrofsale:8, custloc[1]:1, custloc[2]:1)
```

Note that the 5-character field length for piano forces the program to take the first of these 5 characters and skip over the other 4. Since the first one is at position 11 on the input line, this gets the character that we want and ignores the ones that we do not want.

There are two field lengths attached to price in the READLN call. Since price will receive a REAL value (in dollars and cents), we need to specify the number of decimal places in the input value, as well as the value's overall length. Thus, the :8:2 says that the value will appear on the input line as a string of 8 characters, 2 of which will be decimal places. This describes everything from a magnificent large grand priced at, say, 25769.88 down to a cute little spinet costing b4723.00. The rest of the program, of course, is unaffected.

7.3.3 Control of Output Formats

The presentation of output in convenient (easily read) form is an important part of any successful computer program. Consequently, standard Pascal (and all of its extended versions) enable the programmer to describe each position of an output text file. (We shall use the standard OUTPUT file in our discussion, but the same ideas apply to any output text file.)

Format control is provided by specifying each variable in an output list together with a field length that indicates the number of positions the variable will occupy on the line. We shall look at how this works for each of the standard data types.

Control of Pages　Unless otherwise directed by the programmer, Pascal uses its own internal mechanisms to determine when to start a new output page. We need not resign ourselves to this tyranny if we do not want to. The PAGE procedure forces the start of a new page. For the standard OUTPUT file, the call is

PAGE(OUTPUT) or simply PAGE

Format Control for Integer Values When we specify an output field length for an integer value, Pascal uses a position for each digit and an additional position for the sign. For instance, if reltime is an INTEGER variable whose range is known to be between -880 and +400, we need at least four positions to display its value. Thus, the specification

WRITELN ('   RELTIME=',reltime:4)

applied to a reltime value of -423 will produce

bbbbbRELTIME=-423 <eol>

For a reltime value of 317 the display would be

bbbbbRELTIME=b317 <eol>

(The positive sign is not shown; its place is occupied by a blank.) If the specified field length is greater than that required for the value, Pascal places the value in the rightmost positions and fills the extra ones with blanks. With reltime at 27, for instance, the WRITELN specification given above would produce the display

bbbbbRELTIME=bb27 <eol>

We can separate integer output values with a specific number of blanks by using an intentionally longer field for each value. For instance, knowing that reltime never will need more than four positions for its display, a specification of reltime:9 guarantees a string of (at least) five blanks before the value.

If we do not provide adequate length for an integer value, Pascal displays as many of the rightmost digits as the length allows, and the rest are lost. The specification

WRITELN ('bbbbbRELTIME=',reltime:2)

applied to a reltime value of -726 produces the display

bbbbbRELTIME=26 <eol>

This is not good, so be a sport with your blanks.

Formatted Display of Real Values   Real values can be displayed in floating-point form (the form used thus far) or conventional form. When we want a conventional display, we must tell Pascal how many positions to allocate for the overall value and how many of those to use for decimal places. This information is specified by the form

name:overall length:decimal places

For instance, if REAL variable velocity has a current value of -327.064, the specification

WRITELN ('bbbbbVELOCITY=',velocity:8:3)

would produce

bbbbbVELOCITY=-327.064 <eol>

Note that the overall length has to include a space for the decimal point and one for the sign. (As is the case with integer values, a blank replaces the sign for positive values.) Differences between specified lengths and required lengths are handled in the same way as they are for integers. Examples are shown in Table 7.2.

When a real value is to be displayed in floating-point form with a length controlled by the programmer, the length is described by a single specification. Enough length must be provided to accommodate a two-digit exponent value, an exponent sign, the letter E, a decimal point, a single digit to the left of the decimal point, and a sign (or a blank if the sign is positive). If we add all of that together, it means that the length must be at least seven positions greater than that required to show the desired number

Table 7.2   Formatted Output of Real Values in Conventional Form

Results of WRITELN (' VELOCITY=',velocity:lgth:dec)

velocity	lgth	dec	Result
-327.064	8	3	bbbbbVELOCITY=-327.064
-327.064	11	3	bbbbbVELOCITY=bbb-327.064
-327.064	11	4	bbbbbVELOCITY=bb-327.0640
-327.064	8	4	bbbbbVELOCITY=327.0640
-327.064	7	2	bbbbbVELOCITY=-327.06
-327.064	9	1	bbbbbVELOCITY=bb-327.06
81.27	8	3	bbbbbVELOCITY=bb81.270
81.27	7	3	bbbbbVELOCITY=b81.270
81.27	7	6	bbbbbVELOCITY=.270000

of fractional digits. Using our `velocity` value of -327.064 as an example, the specification

```
WRITELN ('bbbbbVELOCITY=',velocity:12)
```

produces

bbbbbVELOCITY=-3.27064E+02 <eol>

Our specified length of 12 provides the seven positions for the standard material as described before, thereby leaving five positions for the fraction. Extra length is absorbed in the fraction. For instance, the same value, displayed by

```
WRITELN ('VELOCITY=',velocity:15)
```

produces

bbbbbVELOCITY=-3.27064000E+02) <eol>

An insufficient length specification produces results that tend to vary with different Pascal implementations. Many versions take care of the standard requirements (exponent value, exponent sign, etc.) first and use whatever (if anything) is left to show fractional digits. Other, more elaborate implementations use a predefined number of fractional digits (i.e., a default length) and add sufficient length to an inadequate specification to reach that minimum. The best thing to do is to make sure that you specify enough length (at least 10, certainly) to guarantee a reasonable floating-point display.

Formatted Display of Character Data   A character value, normally occupying a single position in an output text file, can be included as part of a larger field. To illustrate, suppose the character value 'T' in variable `dtype` is displayed by saying

```
WRITELN ('bbbbbbbDTYPE=',dtype:4)
```

The result is

bbbbbbbDTYPE=bbbT <eol>

Formatted Boolean Output   If the programmer wants to override Pascal's predefined format for boolean output (see Section 7.2), he or she may include a length specifier in the output list. Given enough length, the program places TRUE or FALSE in the rightmost positions and fills the remaining ones with blanks. When the length specifier is too small for the entire word, many Pascal implementations place an abbreviated form (T or F) in the rightmost position. To illustrate, assume that BOOLEAN variables outcome and answer have respective values of FALSE and TRUE. Then, if we display them with

```
WRITELN ('bbbbbOUTCOME IS ',outcome:6,' WHILE ANSWER IS ',answer:3)
```

the resulting line will show

bbbbbOUTCOMEbISbbFALSEbWHILEbANSWERbISbbT

7.3.4 Example 7.3

We shall expand the processing in Example 7.1 even further to include more elaborate output. In addition to showing the number of pianos sold for each type, the output is to show the total weight of pianos sold, the total price, and the average price, all for each type. Results are to be displayed in tabular form, accompanied by appropriate headings. The required format is given in Figure 7.4.

Since the processing is not appreciably more complicated than it was for the previous two versions, we shall concentrate on the design of the output format. Our first heading is 23 characters long. Using a page width of 80 positions, this means that we have 80 − 23 or 57 unused positions to be split into (more or less) equal lengths on either side of the heading. Accordingly, the heading will be preceded by 29 blanks to provide the appropriate centering, and the WRITELN call would look like this:

```
                 SOSTENUTO PIANO COMPANY
       SUMMARY OF PURCHASES FOR YEARS 1969 THROUGH 1977

PIANO TYPE     NO. SOLD    TOTAL WT.     TOTAL PRICE      AVG. PRICE
UPRIGHT            2          1356      $    9133.00     $   4566.50
SPINET             3          2776      $   44178.48     $  14726.16
CONSOLE            1           997      $    9750.99     $   9750.99
BABYGRAND          1          1105      $   12300.00     $  12300.00
SUPERGRAND              1            1550      $  20000.00     $  20000.99
GRAND      1        2112      $  23456.88     $  23456.88
MISLABEL           1           776      $   10000.00     $  10000.00

END OF RUN
```

Figure 7.4

Sample Output for Example 7.3

```
(*********************************************************************)
(**                        EXAMPLE 7.3                          **)
(*********************************************************************)
(** THIS PROGRAM IS SIMILAR TO THE ONES FOR THE PREVIOUS TWO    **)
(** EXAMPLES. IN ADDITION TO THE SALES FIGURES, IT PRINTS THE   **)
(** TOTAL WEIGHT SOLD FOR EACH TYPE, AS WELL AS THE AVERAGE     **)
(** PRICE FOR EACH TYPE.                                        **)
(** TWO ADDITIONAL VARIABLES ARE USED:                         **)
(**    TOTALPRICE: TOTAL SALES AMOUNT FOR A GIVEN PIANO TYPE    **)
(**    AVGPRICE: AVERAGE PRICE PAID FOR A PIANO OF A GIVEN TYPE **)
(*********************************************************************)
PROGRAM ex703 (INPUT,OUTPUT)  ;
TYPE
    pianotype = (upright, spinet, console, babygrand
                 grand, largegrand, mislabel)  ;
VAR
    serial, pianowt, yrofsale, startyr, endyr  :  INTEGER   ;
    numsold, totalwt  :  ARRAY[pianotype] OF INTEGER  ;
    price, realnum  :  REAL  ;
    totalprice, avgprice  :  ARRAY[pianotype] OF REAL  ;
    custloc  :  ARRAY[1..2] OF CHAR  ;
    piano  :  CHAR  ;
    pianosize  :  pianotype  ;
BEGIN
    FOR  pianosize := upright TO mislabel  DO
       BEGIN
          numsold[pianosize] := 0  ;
          totalwt[pianosize] :=0  ;
          totalprice[pianosize] := 0.0
       END
    READLN (startyr:10, endyr:4)  ;
    WHILE  NOT EOF(INPUT)  DO
       BEGIN
          READLN (serial:10, piano:5, pianowt:9, price:8:2,
                  yrofsale:8, custloc[1]:1, custloc[2]:1)  ;
          (*** CHECK WHETHER YEAR SOLD IS IN RANGE ***)
          IF  (yrofsale >= startyr) AND (yrofsale <= endyr)   THEN
             BEGIN
                (*** FIND THE PIANO TYPE ***)
                IF  piano = 'U'  THEN  pianosize := upright
                ELSE IF  piano = 'S'
                     THEN  pianosize := spinet
                     ELSE IF  piano = 'C'
                          THEN  pianosize := console
                          ELSE IF piano = 'B'
                               THEN  pianosize := babygrand
```

Figure 7.5

Program for Example 7.3

```
                                ELSE IF  piano = 'G'
                                   THEN  pianosize := grand
                                   ELSE IF  piano = 'L'
                                      THEN  pianosize := largegrand
                                      ELSE  pianosize := mislabel  ;
             (*** NOW THE APPROPRIATE INDEX IS ***)
             (*** EXPRESSED SIMPLY AS PIANOSIZE ***)
             numsold[pianosize] := numsold[pianosize] + 1    ;
             totalwt[pianosize] := totalwt[pianosize] + pianowt ;
             totalprice[pianosize] := totalprice[pianosize] + price
          END
       END  ;
(*** ALL DATA HAVE BEEN PROCESSED. TIME TO WRITE THE OUTPUT. ***)
FOR  pianosize := upright TO mislabel  DO
    BEGIN
        realnum := numsold[pianosize])  ;
        avgprice[pianosize] := totalprice[pianosize]/realnum
    END  ;
PAGE  ;
WRITELN ('                                     ',
         'SOSTENUTO PIANO COMPANY')  ;
WRITELN   ;
WRITELN ('                    SUMMARY OF PURCHASES FOR YEARS ',
         startyr:4,' THROUGH ',endyr:4) ;
WRITELN  ;
WRITELN  ;
WRITELN ('        ','PIANO TYPE',','        ','NO. SOLD  ',
         'TOTAL WT.  ',' ','TOTAL PRICE',
         '      ','AVG. PRICE') ;
WRITELN ;
WRITELN ('           ','UPRIGHT    ',numsold[upright]:10,
         totalwt[upright]:11,'    $',
         totalprice[upright]:10:2,'     $',
         avgprice[upright]:10:2   ;
WRITELN ('           ','SPINET     ',numsold[spinet]:10,
         totalwt[spinet]:11,'    $',
         totalprice[spinet]:10:2,'     $',
         avgprice[spinet]:10:2)   ;
WRITELN ('           ','CONSOLE    ',numsold[console]:10,
         totalwt[console]:11,'    $',
         totalprice[console]:10:2,'     $',
         avgprice[console]:10:2)   ;
WRITELN ('           ','BABYGRAND ;,numsold[babygrand]:10,
         totalwt[babygrand]:11,'    $',
         avgprice[babygrand]:10:2)   ;
```

Figure 7.5
Program for Example 7.3 (Continued)

```
    WRITELN ('               ','GRAND       ',numsold[grand]:10,
           totalwt[grand]:11,'     $',
           totalprice[grand]:10:2,'       $',
           avgprice[grand]:10:2  ;
    WRITELN ('               ','LARGEGRAND',numsold[largegrand]:10,
           totalwt[largegrand]:11,'     $',
           totalprice[largegrand]:10:2,'       $',
           avgprice[largegrand]:10:2) ;
    WRITELN ('               ','MISLABEL   ',numsold[mislabel]:10,
           totalwt[mislabel]:11,'     $',
           totalprice[mislabel]:10:2,'     $',
           avgprice[mislabel]:10:2)  ;
    WRITELN ;
    WRITELN ('          END OF RUN.')
END.
```

Figure 7.5

Program for Example 7.3 (Continued)

```
    WRITELN ('bbbbbbbbbbbbbbbbbbbbbbbbbbbbbbbb',
            'SOSTENUTO PIANO COMPANY')
```

The second heading includes the input values for the starting year and concluding year. A total of 48 positions are involved (from the S in SUMMARY through the rightmost digit of the concluding year), so that a left margin of 16 positions centers the text on an 80-position line. Our output call, then, says

```
    WRITELN ('bbbbbbbbbbbbbbbbbSUMMARY OF PURCHASES FOR ',
            startyr:4,' THROUGH ',endyr:4)
```

We shall start the column headings in the positions shown in Figure 7.4. When we include the appropriate number of blank characters, the output descriptions look like this:

```
    WRITELN ('bbbbbbbbbbbPIANObTYPE','bbbbbNO.bSOLDbb',
            'TOTALbWT.bb','TOTALbPRICEbbbbb',
            'AVG.bPRICE')
```

Each line of output starts with a character string constant that names the type of piano. (Remember, we cannot use an enumerative variable's values for input or output.) We shall use a common length of 10 so that the format is consistent for all seven types. The length specifiers for numsold and totalwt include the blanks that precede the respective values. A separate character constant ('bbbbb$') supplies the string of blanks and the dollar sign required in front of t o t a l p r i c e and a v g p r i c e. To illustrate, the output specification for grand piano results will say the following:

```
WRITELN ('bbbbbbbbbb','GRANDbbbbb',numsold[grand]:10,
         totalwt[grand]:10,'bbbbb$',totalprice[grand]:10:2,
         'bbbbb$',avgprice[grand]:10:2)
```

The revised program is shown in Figure 7.5.

Assume the following declarations for Problems 1 to 3:

```
VAR
    trwt, pvol, roof  : REAL ;
    xct, obs, nmax, side  :  INTEGER ;
    ltr, sym, vwl  : CHAR
```

and the following four lines of input:

```
                    31bbbb47.08bb6bb-9bbb85.1
                    -2806.9bbb77bbbRWB
                    3J -42 K A C61
                    5 508 4M7
```

1. Show what will be stored in the variables listed in each of the following sequences. Treat each problem independently.
    (a) `READ (xct, pvol, obs)`
    (b) `READLN (xct, pvol, obs)`
    (c) `READ )pvol ;`
         `READ (trwt) ;`
         `READ (xct)`
    (d) `READLN (nmax, pvol, roof, nmax)`
    (e) `READLN (obs, roof, nmax, xct) ;`
         `READLN (sym) ;`
         `READ (trwt)`
    (f) `READ (obs) ;`
         `READLN (pvol, trwt) ;`
         `READ (ltr, vwl) ;`
         `READLN (roof) ;`
         `READLN (sym, xct)`

(g) READ (obs, pval) ;
    READLN ;
    READLN (vwl, ltr) ;
    READ (trwt, xct)

2. Show the output produced by each of the following sequences. Treat each sequence independently.

(a) READ (obs, pval) ;
    WRITELN (pval, obs, pval)

(b) READLN (xct, roof, side, nmax) ;
    READLN ;
    READ (obs) ;
    READ (sym) ;
    WRITELN (obs, sym, ' ', side) ;
    WRITE ('ROOF =', roof) ;
    WRITE ('NMAX IS ', nmax, xct)

(c) READLN ;
    READ (pvol, xct) ;
    READ (vwl, sym) ;
    WRITELN (xct, pvol) ;
    WRITE (sym) ;
    WRITELN (xct, vwl, sym, xct) ;
    WRITE (LTR)

(d) READLN (side, trwt, nmax) ;
    READLN ;
    READ (obs, sym) ;
    READLN ;
    READ (side) ;
    WRITELN ('sym = ', sym:1, side:6, obs) ;
    WRITELN ;
    WRITE ('OBS = ', obs:12, trwt:15, trwt:14:3) ;
    WRITE (nmax)

(e) READ (obs, roof) ;
    WRITELN (roof:15, roof:15:5) ;
    WRITE (obs, obs:6) ;
    READ (xct, side) ;
    READLN ;
    READ (trwt) ;
    READLN (nmax) ;
    WRITE (trwt:12:3) ;
    WRITELN ;
    WRITELN (side:7, xct:8, nmax)

3. (This problem applies only to those people using a version of Pascal that supports input statements with field lengths.) Write the READ

and/or READLN call(s) needed to produce the following values in the indicated variables. Treat each problem independently. (Remember, we still are using the declarations and input given for Problem 1.)

(a)   pvol : 31.0
       roof : 47.08
       trwt : 6.0

(b)   obs : −28
       pvol : 6.9
       side : 3
       nmax : −42

(c)   xct : 3
       sym : '3'
       ltr : J
       side : 5
       nmax : 8

4. Write a program that reads in sets of 4 three-digit integers (call them wval, xval, yval, and zval) and displays them in ascending order, one set to a line. Each input set is on a separate line. If all four input values in a given set are equal to each other, print only their sum. The numbers may be positive, negative, or zero. Use end of file to stop the run.

5. Write an interactive version of the program specified for Problem 4. Make sure you include appropriate prompt messages.

6. Eastern Incendia's great political enemy is Northwestern Euphoria. (So much so, in fact, that when the High Command wants to call a meeting of Incendian intelligence agents, it is necessary to charter six buses to bring back the contingent from Euphoria.) Anyway, nothing warms the Incendian beaurocratic heart as much as news of the capture of secret Euphorian documents. Accordingly, each time such a feat is executed, an input line is created showing the agent's initials (all Incendians have four names), the number of documents captured (sometimes in the thousands), the documents' total weight to the nearest gram, and a score from 1 to 9, depending on the relative importance of the booty. When a group of such input sets has been accumulated, it is run through a program that computes and displays a Mathematical Heartwarming Score for each set. The MWS (as the High Command affectionately refers to it) is computed as

$$\text{MWS} = 0.283 \ ndoc(wt)^{\ 1.75/score}$$

where ndoc is the number of documents captured, wt is their weight, and score is the scored value. The three highest scores are singled out for commendation.

Write a program that finds the top three document collectors. (It is possible in this scheme for all three prizes to be won by the same agent.) For each winner, the program is to print a line showing the initials, the number of documents captured, and the MWS. Label your output clearly.

7. Modify the previous program based on the recognition that there may be ties in MWS values. Being quite generous, Eastern Incendia wants to award duplicate commendations. That is, it wants to give commendations for the top three scores, even though one or more of them may have been achieved by several agents. With the assurance that there will never be more than two duplicate scores at any level, arrange to display the output described before, for each of the agents having one of the top three scores.

8. Haig Bareboodjian, powerful rug merchant, is the world's leading specialist in four highly popular rug designs. His agents comb the major weaving centers (and some minor ones too) making sure that Big HB is kept up to date on who is weaving what where. This information is sent to him in code, and it eventually is typed into a terminal. For each run, the following data are acquired:

Representative's initials (3 letters)
Rug's identification number (4-digit integer)
Design code (1, 2, 3, or 4)
Country of manufacture (1 = Pilvoonia, 2 = Halvahstan,
    3 = Smenfh, 4 = Qamranq, 5 = Tfimfim)
Rug length, to the nearest inch (nnnn)
Rug width, to the nearest inch (nnnn)

Write a program that produces a one-page report summarizing the data about the rugs in production. For each design, print the number of rugs, total rug area (in square yards), and the number of countries in which that design is being produced. Include appropriate headings.

9. Haig Bareboodjian (the same Haig Bareboodjian from Problem 8) operates in a hectic world where prices fluctuate rapidly. Accordingly, he finds it useful to know the potential value of the rugs currently in production. Toward this end, modify the program in the previous problem so that prior to the input described before, it reads the current month and year, and four values giving the respective prices, in dollars per square yard, for each of the four designs. Then, for each rug, the revised program is to produce a line of output giving the rug's i.d., the representative's initials, the numerical code for the country in which the rug is being woven, the length and width (in feet, to the nearest foot), the area in square yards (to the nearest square yard), and the price. After data for all the rugs have been processed, the program

is to print a line showing the number of rugs processed, the total square yardage, and their total value. Prepare your output so that it follows the format shown in Figure 7.6.

10. The El Warpo Company sells ¾-in.-thick plywood in three grades: finished, semifinished, and pwg (please wear gloves). Finished plywood sells for $1.78 per square foot, semifinished for $1.45 per square foot, and pwg for $1.19 per square foot. These plywood sheets come in various standard rectangular sizes.

Sales summaries are to be produced on a daily basis. Each line of input describes the sale of a quantity of sheets of a given grade and size to a specified customer on that day:

Item	Format
Date of sale	mm dd yy (e.g., 03 28 82)
Customer number	Six-digit (unsigned) integer
Grade	1, 2, or 3 (1 = finished)
Number of sheets purchased	nnn
Length (in feet and inches)	nn nn (e.g., 7 6 = 7 ft, 6 in.)
Width (in feet and inches)	Same as length

All orders for a given customer are grouped together, and these data are preceded by a separate line showing today's date. Write a program that processes a day's sales and produces the following output:

· A line for each input line showing the input data (except for the date), the total area in square feet (with fractional square feet truncated), and the price for that material
· A line for each customer showing the total number of square feet purchased and the total price
· A set of lines after the last customer line (starting on a new page)

```
                       HAIG BAREBOODJIAN
                     RUG SUMMARY FOR 10/82
          DESIGN 1:  $42.50 PER SQ. YD.     DESIGN 2:  $61.70 PER SQ. YD.
          DESIGN 3:  $88.15 PER SQ. YD.     DESIGN 4:  $53.35 PER SQ. YD.

I.D.      REP       WHERE       LENGTH      WIDTH      AREA,       COST
                    WOVEN                              SQ. YD.
3276      MHP       2           14          10         16          $nnnnn.nn
1008      CYD       1           22          12         29          $nnnnn.nn
```

Figure 7.6
Output Format for Problem 7.8

showing the number of customers processed, average order size (in square feet), and the average sales amount for the orders

A suggested arrangement is shown in Figure 7.7.

11. After a number of embarrassing episodes, El Warpo found that it cannot be certain that all the input lines for a given run will show the same date. Consequently, modify the program for Problem 10 so that it finds and rejects all input lines with the wrong date. After displaying the summary for the run, the revised program is to show an additional line indicating the number of lines thus rejected.

12. (*An American Tradition*)In a recent landmark decision, the Supreme Court let stand a historic ruling by a lower court: It is a misdemeanor to publish and distribute a text, booklet, film, or videodisc on programming (in any language) in which the Indian Problem does not appear at least once. Your author, above all, is law abiding. Consequently, in the interest of Good Government, here is the Indian Problem: In 1624, there was disquiet among the normally tranquil Canarsie Indians. The problem was Manhattan Island. Long an unkempt, noisy eyesore on the otherwise orderly Indian landscape, things on the island were going from bad to worse. The bars were getting rowdier by the day, the rivers and inlets were literally filling with garbage, and there were places where innocent citizens actually were in physical danger. Numerous Council meetings were held to determine What to Do about That Stinking Rock. At the height of this perplexity, who should appear but Peter Minuit and a group of set-

```
                        EL  WARPO  PLYWOOD  CO.
                     SALES  SUMMARY  FOR  mm/dd/yy
CUST        GRADE       NO. OF     LENGTH      WIDTH       TOTAL       TOTAL
NO.                     SHEETS                             AREA        PRICE
nnnnnn       2            44       10' 6"       3' 2"     nnnnn.nn    $nnnnn.nn
nnnnnn       1            16        9' 0"       6' 0"     nnnnn.nn    $nnnnn.nn
                     ***  SUMMARY  FOR  CUSTOMER  nnnnn  ***
      TOTAL  AREA:  nnnnn.nn SQ. FT.        TOTAL PRICE:     $nnnnn.nn
```

(a) Output for an individual customer (Problem 7.9)

```
EL WARPO PLYWOOD CO.
OVERALL SUMMARY FOR mm/dd/yy
NUMBER OF CUSTOMERS PROCESSED:     nnn
AVERAGE ORDER: nnnnnn.nn SQ. FT.
AVERAGE ORDER AMOUNT: $nnnnnn.nn
```

(b) Overall summary

Figure 7.7

tlers interested (no, eager) to persuade the Canarsies to part with this real estate. The settlers offered about $24 worth of trendy costume jewelry and reasonably good theatrical accessories, and the Indians discussed the matter among themselves. A short time later, they told the settlers that it was a deal, and the land changed hands. (It is a matter of historical record that no single Canarsie giggled until the settlers were miles away.) Within hours of the exchange, the smiling Canarsies sold the merchandise to a troupe of Bohemian gypsies for $28.75. They bought $4.75 worth of nifty fishing lures (from those selfsame gypsies) and put the remaining $24 into the Succotash Fund, a conservative investment vehicle paying 6%, and There The Money Has Sat. Since then, the Canarsies have turned their attention to other matters, and nobody has paid much attention to the money in the Succotash Fund. What is needed is a program to let the people know what has been happening. Write a program that reads in the current year (thisyear) and produces a year-by-year display showing the value of the $24 plus accrued interest from the year 1624 through thisyr.

13. In this version of the program, the output is to be limited to 50 years on each page. Every time a new page is started, the program is to print the column headings.

14. As a more challenging version of the previous problem, write a program that reads two integer values startyr and endyr. In response to these values, the program is to display the value of the Canarsie's investment for each year in the specified range.

15. Here is another, more involved version of the Indian Problem: Read in five values for five different interest rates. (For instance, an input value of 6.5 represents an interest rate of 6.5 percent, i.e., 0.065.) The program is to produce an expanded version of the table in Problem 11: Each line is to show a particular year and the value of the $24 and accrued interest for each of the five interest rates.

16. The Deluxe Version of the Indian problem is similar to Problem 15 with one specific exception: Input consists of anywhere from one to five interest rates. Accordingly, the number of columns in the output table will depend on the number of input values. (A single input value will produce a two-column table like the one in Problem 12, and five input values will duplicate Problem 15.)

17. When somebody borrows money to buy something like a house, an automobile, a personal computer, or other major appliance, the conditions of the loan are arranged so that the interest is a fixed fraction of the amount owed at that time. For instance, suppose somebody borrows $10,000 and the interest rate is 1.5% per month on the unpaid balance. That means that the initial payment must include interest amounting to 0.015 * 10000, or $150. Then, suppose that, in addition

to the interest, the borrower pays off $200 of his loan. As a result, the next monthly payment will require interest amounting to 0.015 * (10000–200), or $147.

As a convenience to the lender as well as the borrower, such loans usually are arranged so that the monthly payments are set at a fixed amount. The distribution of that fixed amount between interest and loan repayment will vary with each payment, the first payment having the highest fraction tied up in interest, and the last payment contributing little or nothing to interest. Given an initial loan amount loanamt, the annual interest rate annrate, and the number of payments numpay, the monthly payment can be computed as

$$\text{mnthrate (loanamt)} \left[\frac{(1 + \text{mnthrate})^{\text{numpay}}}{(1 + \text{mnthrate})^{\text{numpay}} - 1} \right]$$

where mnthrate is annrate/12. The program is to produce an initial line of output showing the loan number, amount of the loan, and number of monthly payments. A second line is to show the amount of the (fixed) monthly payment. Then, after two blank lines, the program is to produce a table in which each line shows the payment number, balance owed prior to that payment, amount of the payment credited toward the loan, amount of payment used for interest, and the new balance owed. These five columns are to have appropriate headings, and the headings are to be repeated at the top of each new page. The program is to be designed so that it processes any number of loans.

18. Write an interactive version of the installment loan program described in the previous problem. The program should accept the appropriate input values for a loan and, in response, the output should indicate the monthly payment. As before, the program should be designed to process any number of loans. Be sure to include clear, unambiguous prompt messages.

Chapter Eight

Decision and Control Structures

The capabilities that we have used thus far represent only part of Pascal's resources for specifying decision-making processes. In this chapter, we look at some more ambitious decision mechanisms and some additional ways of constructing them conveniently.

8.1 SIMPLE SELECTION: THE IF STATEMENT

Extensive use has enabled us to characterize the IF statement's service: It lets us set up a comparison between two values such that there are two possible outcomes: TRUE or FALSE. Each outcome is associated with a corresponding action expressible as a Pascal statement. This is reflected in the syntax diagram in Figure 2.12 and repeated for convenience in Figure 8.1(a).

The opportunities presented even by this basic selection process go beyond those explored earlier. Consequently, we shall spend a little time in this section on extending these possibilities.

8.1.1 Construction of Comparisons

Figure 8.1(a) does not say much about what a comparison is or how to build one. We did not miss this information because the comparisons used so far were constructed "naturally," without the need for detailed attention to their exact syntax. Now, the structural rules become important if we are to take advantage of the IF statement's flexibility.

The structure of a comparison is developed in Figure 8.1(b). We see that the relational operater, defined earlier in Table 3.1, is used to combine two expressions to produce a test whose outcome is TRUE or FALSE. For example, if vel and maxvel are REAL variables, the construction

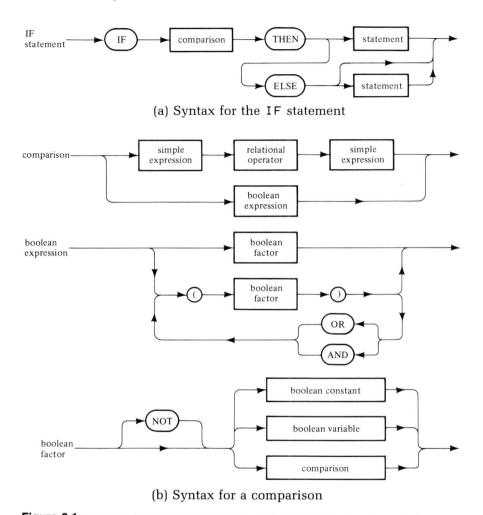

(a) Syntax for the IF statement

(b) Syntax for a comparison

Figure 8.1

(a) Syntax for the IF statement
(b) Syntax for a comparison

```
2.3 * SQRT (vel) < 0.8 * maxvel
```

describes a comparison whose outcome is TRUE if 2.3 times the square root of the current value in vel is less then 0.8 times the current value in maxvel. The semantic considerations require us to make sure that the two expressions brought together by the relational operator are reasonable partners in the comparison. For example, comparison of two integer values would be reasonable, but comparisons of a character with an integer value probably would not be.

We can expand a comparison's possibilities by noting that the outcome of a comparison, being either TRUE or FALSE, is nothing more than a boolean value. Since the IF statement's only concern is with testing such a value, it does not "know" where the value came from or how it was developed. This means that the boolean expression, which also produces a value of TRUE or FALSE, can serve as a comparison to be processed by the IF statement. Accordingly, Figure 8.1(b) shows the boolean expression as being one type of comparison. The next few sections discuss the uses of this added flexibility.

8.1.2 Comparisons Between Nonnumeric Values

It is not necessary to base decisions solely on numerical comparisons. Besides enabling the programmer to set up comparisons between characters and boolean values, Pascal also accepts comparisions between programmer-defined data values.

Comparisons Between Characters   Suppose we have the followng sequence:

```
VAR
    letter, symbol  :   CHAR
        . . . . . . . . . . .
    symbol := 'Z'
    READLN (letter)
        . . . . . . . . . . . .
```

It is clear that we can set up a decision rule like this:

```
IF letter = symbol THEN
    action1

ELSE
    action2
```

The program will perform *action1* if letter has the same character as symbol, and will perform *action2* if the two characters are different. However, such comparisions need not be limited to equality or nonequality. It is legal to write, say,

```
IF letter < symbol THEN
    action1

ELSE
    action2
```

What happens is this: Since each type of character has its own internal numerical representation, a comparison between two characters translates eventually to a comparison between two numerical quantities. Thus, the example given above will produce a value of TRUE if the internal numerical representation of the character in letter is less than the number used to represent the uppercase letter Z, i.e, the value previously stored in symbol.

Internal representations for the various types of characters are assigned as part of a processor's permanent design in accordance with a particular code. Such a code is called a *collating sequence*. There are two collating sequences in common use: the American Standard Code for Information Interchange (ASCII) and the Extended Binary Coded Decimal Interchange Code (EBCDIC). (The available characters, together with their respective numerical representations, are tabulated for the two collating sequences in Appendix B.) One code system is not "better" or "worse" than the other. (Your instructor will tell you which one is used in your computer.) In both systems the numerical sequence is in alphabetical order, so that 'A' is "less than" 'B', 'B' is "less than" 'C', and so on. In the EBCDIC system, letters have lower internal numerical representations than digits (0 through 9), and in the ASCII system the reverse is true. Further discussion is to be found in Section 13.1.3.

Comparisons Between Programmer-Defined Data Values   The scope of expressible decision rules is broadened further by the ability to compare enumerative data values. This is done by taking advantage of the sequencing implied by the delcaration of an enumerative data type. For instance, in Example 7.1 we defined a data type named pianotype and a variable of that type named pianosize:

```
TYPE
    pianotype = (upright, spinet, console, babygrand,
                 grand, largegrand, mislabel)
          + + + + + + + + + + + + + + + + + + + + + +
VAR
    pianosize  :  pianotype
```

Given these declarations, the decison rule

```
IF pianosize <= console THEN
    action1

ELSE
    action2
```

triggers *action1* if ᴘⁱᵃⁿᵒˢⁱᶻᵉ is anything equal to or greater than ᶜᵒⁿ‐ ˢᵒˡᵉ (namely, ᶜᵒⁿˢᵒˡᵉ, ᵇᵃᵇʸᵍʳᵃⁿᵈ, ᵍʳᵃⁿᵈ, ˡᵃʳᵍᵉᵍʳᵃⁿᵈ, or ᵐⁱˢ‐ ˡᵃᵇᵉˡ).

8.1.3 Extended Comparisons

Decisions often require tests in which several conditions have to be considered. Construction of such tests is handled conveniently by using boolean operations to combine comparisons.

Tests Based on Multiple Comparisons   When we want to set up a test in which several conditions have to be met, we can use Pascal's AND operation for that purpose. For example, suppose we are conducting a medical investigation calling for the selection of certain patients' records from a large collection. Each patient's information includes:

An identifying number (ᴘᵗⁿᵗⁱᵈ)
Year of birth (ᵇⁱʳᵗʰʸʳ)
Sex (ˢᵉˣ): 0 = female, 1 = male
Height (ʰᵗ) in inches
Weight (ʷᵗ) in pounds
Result of the Foop test (ᶠᵒᵒᴘ), a REAL number
Result of the Poznik color test (ᴘᵒᶻⁿⁱᵏ): 0 = no color, 1 = trace, 2 = light, 3 = medium, 4 = heavy color

Let us say that we are interested in reading the data for each patient and printing the patient identification numbers for those individuals between the ages of 30 and 40. To do this, we can define a variable ᵗʰⁱˢʸʳ and read into it the value for the current year. An additional variable named ᵃᵍᵉ will be used to store the computed age (ᵗʰⁱˢʸʳ ‐ ᵇⁱʳᵗʰʸʳ) for the patient whose record is currently being processed. The corresponding part of the declaration section might look like this:

```
• • • • • • • • • •
VAR
    ptntid, birthyr, sex, ht, wt, poznik,
    thisyr, age   :   INTEGER ;
    foop : REAL
• • • • • • • • • • •
```

After reading the data for a particular patient and computing ᵃᵍᵉ, we can determine whether that patient falls in the required age range by testing ᵃᵍᵉ against each of the limits:

```
. . . . . . . . . . . .
READLN (thisyr)
. . . . . . . . . . . .
READLIN (ptntid, birthyr, sex, ht, wt, foop, poznik)    ;
age  := thisyr - birthyr ;
IF   (age >= 30)   AND   (age <= 40) THEN
     WRITELN (ptntid)
. . . . . . . . . . . .
```

Now the value of ptntid will be printed only if both outcomes are TRUE.
    Note that if we were to write

```
IF   (age >=30 AND <= 40)   THEN
     WRITELN (ptntid)
```

the Pascal compiler would reject it because the structure is improper. The
AND operator must connect two complete comparisons.

    Suppose we wanted to be even more selective and print identifications
numbers only for male patients between the ages of 30 and 40. This requires
three comparisons, all of whose outcomes must be TRUE before the patient
is selected:

```
. . . . . . . . . . . .
  IF         (age >= 30)
     AND  (age <= 40)
     AND  (sex = 1)     THEN
     WRITELN (ptntid)
. . . . . . . . . . . .
```

Tests based on more extensive combinations of criteria can be built in the
same way. The only limit is that imposed by the programmer to keep such
structures from becoming too involved.

Tests Based on Choices   Sometimes a decision is based on one of several
tests, any of which is sufficient to trigger the associated action. Referring to
the data in the previous section, suppose we wanted to select the following
patients and print their identification numbers:

    Male patients with Foop readings above 32.7
    Female patients with Foop readings above 40.4

Two comparisons are required to identify eligible male patients. These are
combined, as before, with the AND operation. Thus,

```
. . . . . (sex = 1)   AND   (foop >   32.7. . . . .
```

selects the male patients. Similarly, female patients are selected by the combination

```
.....(sex = 0)   AND   (foop > 40.4).....
```

The choice between these two possibilities is specified by using Pascal's OR operation:

```
IF      (sex = 1)   AND   (foop > 32.7)
    OR  (sex = 0)   AND   (foop > 40.4)   THEN
      WRITELN (ptntid)
```

Negative Tests   Another type of circumstance requires a decision based on a negative outcome. For instance, suppose our medical study required the selection of all patients *except* males over 52. We can describe such a decision rule by saying.

```
IF      (sex = 1)   AND   (age <= 52)
    OR  (sex = 0)
THEN
      WRITELN (ptntid)
```

Even though we achieve the desired result, the decision rule is not de-scribed in the way we intended. It is sufficiently complicated to require us to stop a moment and figure out what it says. Pascal's NOT operation enables the programmer to specify such decision rules more naturally. To illustrate, we shall rewrite the previous test using this operation:

```
IF  NOT((sex = 1)   AND   (age > 52))   THEN
      WRITELN (ptntid)
```

The same general construction applies to more intricate decision rules. For instance, let us select all patients except men over 60 and women over 55:

```
IF   NOT  ((sex = 1)   AND   (age > 60)
               OR  (sex = 0)   AND   (age > 55))
THEN
      WRITELN (ptntid)
```

8.2 DECISION NETWORKS WITH MULTIPLE TESTS

A course of action cannot always be determined by a single test, no matter how complex that test may be. Often, it is necessary to set up a procedure that must work its way through a series of tests before a final decision can be made. To illustrate this type of situation, suppose the patients in our previous example are to receive a specific amount of a therapeutic drug based on their sex and the Foop test result:

Males with a Foop result less than 35.5 receive 500 units of the drug
Males with a Foop result of at least 35.5 receive 630 units
Females with a Foop result less than 27.6 receive 420 units
Females with a Foop result of at least 27.6 receive 520 units

The appropriate dose is to be reported in an INTEGER variable named dose. Then, instead of printing information only for certain patients, we would like to display the i.d. and dose for each patient in the population.

Until now we have worked with tests that varied in their complexity but produced a single outcome whose value immediately determined what action to take. In the situation just described, a single test is not enough. We have to go through a series of tests before we learn everything we need to know to select the correct response. In other words, we need a decision structure in which the outcome of the first test tells us which test to perform next.

Such test series are easily built by using an IF statement whose THEN or ELSE portion consists of another IF statement. (A quick check of Figure 8.1 shows that this structure is consistent with Pascal's rules.) The result is called a *nested IF construction*. To represent the test series for our example, we simple can follow the rules stated before:

```
. . . . . . . . . . . . . . . .
READLN (ptntid, birthyr, sex, ht, wt, foop poznik)  ;
IF  (sex = 1)   THEN
    IF  foop < 35.5   THEN
        dose := 500
    ELSE
        dose := 630
ELSE
    IF foop < 27.6   THEN
        dose := 420
    ELSE
        dose := 520  ;
WRITELN (ptntid, dose)
. . . . . . . . . . . . . . . .
```

Here, as is true in many other types of nested constructions, indentation is of considerable help in keeping track of which ELSE goes with which IF. Nested IF constructions can be extended as far as desired; however, the programmer is well advised to place his or her own limits on the maximum degree of nesting to use. When it appears necessary to exceed that limit, this often can be taken as a good sign that the underlying decision structure is too complicated and needs further study. Sometimes, nesting may be so extensive that the resulting indentation forces the statement off the end of the line to be gobbled up by one of the four giant tortoises that hold up the Earth. Beware.

There is no guarantee that every decision structure will be symmetrical. There will be countless situations in which the first test will produce two possible outcomes, one of which produces a final decision without further testing while the other leads to a long series of additonal tests. As long as we have a clear idea of the decison rules, their systematic representation in Pascal will give us no trouble. For instance, let us define a new decision structure for our patients and their dosages. We have an improved drug whose dosage for females can be fixed at one standard level, but the amount given to males depends on age as well as Foop result:

females
The standard dose is 465 units.
males

age	*Foop results*	*dose*
less than 34	less than 35.5	400 units
less than 34	at least 35.5	520 units
at least 34	less than 41.4	580 units
at least 34	at least 41.4	665 units

The pseudocode is shown in Figure 8.2, and the corresponding Pascal statements appear in Figure 8.3.

8.3 MULTIPLE SELECTION: THE CASE STATEMENT

Another type of realistic test situation is one in which there are more than two possible outcomes. Each outcome is associated with a particular action that is to be taken when that outcome occurs. For instance, suppose that the situation with our patients becomes more complicated because of the introduction of yet another medicine. The only way to make full use of its improved effectiveness is to tie the dosage to a more extensive set of criteria involving the Poznik test result as well as some other factors. This is shown in Table 8.1.

8.3.1 Basic Structure of the CASE Statement

In the example of Table 8.1 the decision rule pivots on a test that can have five different outcomes, and there is a specific activity associated with each outcome. The programming structure that describes this kind of situation

....
Read thisyr.

....
Read a patient's record.
Compute the patient's age (thisyr - byr).
if
 the patient is male
then
 if
  the patient's age is less than 34
 then
  if
   the patient's Foop result is less than 35.5
  then
   set dose to 440
  else
   set dose to 520
  endif
 else
  if
   the patient's Foop result is less than 41.4
  then
   set dose to 580
  else
   set dose to 665
  endif
 endif
else
 set dose to 465
endif

Figure 8.2
Pseudocode Description of a Nested Decision Structure

(one in which a decision rule is based on a test that has more than two possible outcomes) is called a *CASE component.* It occurs often enough so that Pascal has a separate CASE statement with which such rules can be specified easily. The syntax, shown in Figure 8.4, allows the programmer to represent the multiple selection directly, regardless of the number of choices required. For our example, the variable motivating the selection is poznik, and the five alternatives follow immediately. This is shown in Figure 8.5

In this example, poznik acts like a multiway switch that guides the program toward one of the five alternative actions. Each action is associ-

```
...................
 READLN (thisyr)
...................
 READLN (ptntid, byr, sex, ht, wt, foop, poznik) ;
age := thisyr - byr ;
IF  sex = 1  THEN
   IF  AGE < 34  THEN
       IF foop < 35.5 THEN
          dose := 440
       ELSE
          dose := 520
   ELSE
       IF  foop < 41.4  THEN
          dose := 665
   ELSE
       dose := 564
 WRITELN (ptntid, dose) ;
...............
```

Figure 8.3

A Multilevel Decision Rule Expressed as a Nested IF Statement

ated with a particular value, so that when poznik has a value of 2, for instance, the program will proceed directly to the statement tagged with that value. Once that action is completed, the other actions are ignored and the program continues at a point immediately after the concluding END. The programmer shold make sure that the CASE statement has an action for

Table 8.1 An Example of a Situation Motivating a CASE Construction

Poznik test outcome	Dosage
Category 0 (no color)	0.82 unit for each pound of weight
Category 1	0.74 unit for each pound of weight and 0.11 unit for each year in the person's age
Category 2	140 units for males, 166 units for females
Category 3	0.90 units for each pound of weight. Subtract 0.10 unit for each year for males or 0.12 unit for each year for females.
Category 4	For males. 0.93 unit per pound of weight less 0.05 unit per year. Subtract 18.5 units if Foop test exceeds 50.6.
	For females: 0.86 unit per pound of weight plus 0.027 unit per year. Subtract 10.6 units for females over 55 if Foop test results below 35.6.

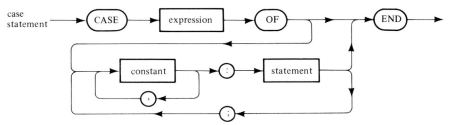

Semantics: The constant(s) must be consistent with the types of values computed from the expression.

Figure 8.4

Syntax for the CASE Statement

```
+ + + + + + + + + +
READLIN (thisyr)
+ + + + + + + + + +
READLIN (ptntid, byr, sex, wt, ht, foop, poznik ;
age := this year - byr ;
CASE   poznik   OF
   0:     dose := 0.82 * wt ;
   1:     dose := 0.74 * wt + 0.11 * age ;
   2:     IF sex = 1   THEN
             dose := 140
          ELSE
             dose := 166 ;
   3:     IF sex = 1   THEN
             dose := 90 * wt - 0.10 * age
          ELSE
             dose := 90 * wt - 0.12 * age ;
   4:     IF sex = 1 THEN
             BEGIN
               dose := 0.93 * wt - 0.05 * age ;
               IF  foop > 50.6  THEN
                   dose := dose - 18.5
             END
          ELSE
             BEGIN
               dose := 0.86 * wt + 0.027 * age ;
               IF      age > 55
                 AND  foop < 35.6   THEN
                   dose := dose - 10.6
             END
END ;
WRITELN (ptnid, dose)
+ + + + + + + + + +
```

Figure 8.5

Implementation of Decision Structure for Section 7.3.1

every possible outcome. If a particular usage produces no match and the program is allowed to proceed through the CASE, the result will be undefined.

8.3.2 Identical Actions for Different Outcomes

All the actions associated with a CASE do not have to be different from each other. For instance, suppose it were to turn out that dosages for category 3 (from Table 8.1) could be computed the same as for category 2. This can be specified by attaching both outcome values to the appropriate action. For our example, the revised statements would appear as shown in Figure 8.6.

8.3.3 Multiway Switches with Programmer-Defined Values

The selection capabilities of the CASE statement can be applied to situations where the choices are values other than integers. Decision rules can be set up to select from any group of alternatives as long as the choices are

```
* * * * * * * * *
CASE poznik  OF
   O  :  dose := 0.82 * wt ;
   1  :  dose := 0.74 * wt + 0.11 * age ;
  2, 3 : IF sex = 1  THEN
             dose := 140
          ELSE
             DOSE := 166 ;
     4 :  IF sex -= 1 THEN
          BEGIN
             dose := 0.93 * wt - 0.05* ;
             IF  foop > 50.6  THEN
                dose := dose - 18.5
          END
          ELSE
          BEGIN
             dose := 0.86 * wt + 0.027 * age  ;
             IF     AGE > 55
               AND  foop < 35.6  THEN
                dose := dose - 10.6
          END
END ;
WRITELN (ptntid, dose)
* * * * * * * * * *
```

Figure 8.6
CASE Construction with Identical Actions for Multiple Outcomes

clearly defined. For instance, if we defined a data type named season and declared a variable of that type as follows:

```
TYPE
    season = (winter, spring, summer fall)
            ................
VAR
    timeofyear : season
            ................
```

then, assuming timeofyear had a value assigned to it, we could use it as a switch to select one of four actions:

```
CASE  timeofyear  OF
    winter : action for winter      ;
    spring : action for spring      ;
    summer : action for summer      ;
    fall   : action for fall
END
```

8.4 EXPLICIT TRANSFER OF CONTROL

Although Pascal provides specific statement types for the major control structures, there may be occasions where an explicit transfer to some other part of the program is useful. A situation where this might be applied is one in which a loop is to be provided with an opportunity for a sudden exit in midcycle.

Such transfers are specified by Pascal's GOTO statement whose general form is

GOTO *label*

where *label* is a numerical tag (i.e., an unsigned integer) attached to the destination statement. For example,

GOTO 24

indicates that the next statement to be executed is the one labeled 24. That statement, then, would have the label 24 attached to it, i.e.,

24: statement

This statement may appear anywhere in the program, but it must be the only one labeled 24. Moreover, every label must be declared like the other identifiers. This is done at the beginning of the declaration section [i.e., immediately after the identification section and immediately prior to the TYPE declarations (if there are any)]. Thus, the declaration

```
LABEL
   10, 18, 26, 334, 71
```

informs Pascal that there will be five labeled statements somewhere in the program, and that their label numbers will be as shown.

Problems

1. Indicate the output produced by each of the independent sequences given below. (*Note:* Some of these sequences may contain errors that prevent any output from being produced.) Assume the following declarations and assignments:

```
CONST
 yes = TRUE    ;
 no = FALSE    ;
TYPE
 doublereed = (englehorn, oboe, bassoon, contrabassoon)   ;
 cartype = (coupe, sedan, stawag, convert, sports)   ;
VAR
 r1, r2, r3, r4  :  REAL  ;
 num1, num2, num3   :  INTEGER  ;
 ltrs  :  ARRAY  [1..4] OF CHAR  ;
 wdi, sym  :  CHAR  ;
 test1, test2  :  BOOLEAN  ;
 blaser  :  doublereed  ;
 flivver, liz  :  cartype  ;
 r1  := 4 ;
 r2  := 5 ;
 num2  := 2 ;
 num3  := 6 ;
 ltrs [1] := 'M' ;
 wdi := '*' ;
 sym := ' '  ;
 test1 := yes  ;
 blaser  := oboe
```

    (a) If no THEN
            WRITELN (r1, r2, num2, num3)

```
(b)  IF test1 = yes THEN
       ltrs[2] := wdi        ;
       ltrs[3] := sym        ;
       ltrs[4] := ltrs[3]
     ELSE
       ltrs[2] := sym        ;
       ltrs[3] := ltrs[1] ;
       ltrs[4] := ltrs[3] ;
       FOR  num1 := 1 TO 4   DO
         WRITELN (ltrs[num1]:4)
(c)  r4 := 0  ;
     IF r1 * r2 < SQR(num2 * num3 DIV 3)   THEN
       BEGIN
       r4 := r1 * ( r2 + num2)  ;
         ltrs[2] := ltrs[1]   ;
         ltrs[3] := ltrs[1] ;
         WRITELN (ltrs[3], ltrs[2], r4)
       END
     ELSE
       BEGIN
         r3 := num2 * ( r1+r2) ;
         r4 := r4 + 0.5 * r3 ;
         ltrs[2] := wdi ;
         WRITELN (r4, r3, wdi, ltrs[1], ltrs[2])
       END
(e)  IF blaser <= bassoon THEN
       flivver := convert
     ELSE
         flivver :- sedan ;
     IF flivver >= staway THEN
       BEGIN
         num3 := num3 * SQR(num2) :
         r3 := r1 * ( r1+r2) ;
         WRITELN (num3, r3)
       END
     ELSE
       WRITELN ( r2:12, num2:10, r1:12, num1:10)
(f)  IF NOT(yes AND test1) THEN
       r4 := r1 * r2/( r1+r2)
     ELSE
       ltrs[1] := wdi ;
     WRITELN ( r4:12, ltrs[1]:6)
(g)  IF (num2 <= SQR(num1)) Or (sym <= wdi) THEN
       FOR num1 := 2 TO 4 DO
         ltrs[num1] * = ltrs[1]
     ELSE
```

```
BEGIN
  For num1 := 2 TO 4 DO
    ltrs[num1] := wdi ;
    r4 := (r1+r2)/(r1 * r2)
  END ;
WRITELN (r4) :
WRITELN ;
FOR num1 := 1 TO 4 DO
WRITE (ltrs[num1]:4)
```

(h)   IF (TRUNC(r1 * r2) DIV num3 < num2num3) OR (blaser >= englhorn) THEN
```
    num1 := ROUND(r1 * r2) DIV (num2+num3)
ELSE
    IF wdi < ltrs[1] THEN
    BEGIN
      num1 := ROUND ((num2+num3)/r2) + num2 ;
      ltrs[1] := 'N'
    END
    ELSE
      num1 := TRUNC ((num2+num3)/r2) - num2
WRITELN (ltrs[1]:8, num1:8, ltrs[f1]:6)
```

2.   Write a sequence of statements to represent each of the specifications given below. Use the same declarations and initial assignments shown for the previous problem.

(a)   After reading in values for r1 and r2, set num1 to 3 if r1 is greater than r2; otherwise set num1 to 4.

(b)   Read a value for ltrs[3].

IF
   ltrs[3] has a vowel in it
THEN
   set sym to '@'
ELSE
   set sym to '*'
ENDIF

(c)   Read a value for wdi.

IF
   wdi's value is 'A' through 'R'
THEN
   double the value in num2
ELSE
   subtract 1 from the value in num2
ENDIF

(d) Read a value for sym.

```
IF
   sym is between 'a' and 'm' and 'N' and 'Z'
THEN
   set wdi's value to '&'
ELSE
   set wdi's value to '%'
ENDIF
```

(e) Read values for r2, r3, and r4. Assign to r1 a value equal to the sum of the two largest input values.

(f) Read values for num1, num2, and num3. Store the square of the largest odd number in r1, the sum of the odd values in r2, the overall sum in r3, and the square of the largest even number in r4. Whenever a value cannot be produced (e.g., there are no odd values among those read in), store a zero for that result.

3. aval, bval, cval, and dval are declared as INTEGER. For the following sequence:

```
IF bval = 2 * aval THEN
IF cval = 4 * dval THEN
IF bval = cval-4 THEN
zval := 12
ELSE
IF aval = dval+6 THEN
IF cval = aval+14 THEN
zval := 22
ELSE
zval := 11
ELSE
zval := 31
ELSE
zval := 41
```

state the value of zval when

(a) aval is 10, bval is 20, cval is 24, and dval is 6.
(b) aval is 9, bval is 20, cval is 24, and dval is 6.
(c) aval is 10, bval is 20, cval is 24, dval is 7.
(d) aval is 3, bval is 6, cval is 4, and dval is 5.
(e) aval is 2, bval is 4, cval is 8, and dval is 16.

4. A series of five-digit decimal integers are available, one per input line. Write a program that counts and prints (displays) the number of values read in and the number of values ending with a 6 and evenly divisible by 4.

5. Values for integer variables ʋ a l 1 and ʋ a l 2, respectively, are recorded on an input line. There is an arbitrary number of input lines.
   Write a program that performs the following processing:
   (a) Counts and displays the number of pairs of values in which the
       product is not more than 10 times the ratio of the first value to
       the second
   (b) Computes the sum of the products of all pairs meeting the
       criteria in (a)
   (c) Computes the product of the sum of all the pairs in which both
       values are even.
   (d) Counts the number of times the digit 2 appears in the data.
   Zero is a legitimate value, but no two members of a pair will have
   identical values. Provide appropriate labels for all output.

6. Write a program to perform the following processing: Each input line
   contains a three-digit positive integer value ᴘ o s i n t ᶃ r. If the rightmost (third) digit is equal to the sum of the other two digits, that
   number is to be shown on a separate line along with the message THIS
   IS A SPECIAL NUMBER. If not, there is to be no output for that
   number. Thus, 246 and 729 are special numbers while 264 and 381
   are not. A run may consist of any number of input values. After the
   last value is processed, the program is to show the number of values
   that met the requirement described before (s ᴘ e c i a l s) and the number of values that did not (r e ᶃ u l a r s). Here are some suggested
   input values:

$$303$$
$$627$$
$$718$$
$$339$$
$$336$$
$$347$$
$$112$$

7. Generalize the program in the previous problem so that it processes
   any number of runs. Insert three blank lines to separate consecutive
   runs, and keep track of the number of runs. Before the first line of
   output for each run, show a line that says "RUN NUMBER nn." After
   the last run, start a new page and show the number of runs, total
   number of values read, total number of special values, and total
   number of regular values.

8. Here is a more challenging version of the previous problem: We still
   are reading positive integer values. However, the number of digits is
   not fixed. If a particular number reads the same way in either direction, the program is to show the value, along with the message "THIS

IS A SYMMETRICAL NUMBER." If not, there is to be no output for that input value. Thus, 8228, 757, 4004, 47574, and 88 are symmetrical numbers while 6161, 20, 32732, and 9 are not. As in the previous problem, there may be any number of runs, each consisting of any number of input values. For each run, the program is to show the number of symmetrical values (numsym), their sum (sumsym), the total number of values (numval), *their* sum (sumval), and the ratio of sumsym to sumval, rounded to three places. After the last run, on a separate page, the program is to show the number of runs (numruns), the total number of symmetrical values (ttlsym), and the total number of values (ttlnumval).

9. Write an interactive version of the program specified in Problem 6, 7, or 8.

10. Write a program that reads three integer values lower, middle, and upper. These values are different from each other, with lower being the smallest, and upper being the largest. These values are followed by a succession of integers (which may be positive, negative, or zero), one to a line. After the last integer has been read and processed, the program is to produce the following output:

First line: The number of values read (not counting lower, middle, or upper)
Second line: The number of values less than lower
Third line: The number of values greater than lower but less than middle
Fourth line: The number of values greater than middle but less than upper
Fifth line: The number of values greater than upper
Sixth line: The number of values equal to lower, middle, or upper

11. This is a more intricate version of the previous problem: Input still consists of three integers followed by an arbitrary number of additional integer values. The difference is that the three initial input values are not guaranteed to be in any numerical order. Moreoever, they are not guaranteed to be all different. Consequently, the program must determine whether they are. If they are, the program is to proceed as in the previous problem, producing the results indicated there. If they are not all different, the program is to produce one of the following messages, depending on the situation:

ALL THREE TEST VALUES ARE EQUAL.
THE TWO HIGHER TEST VALUES ARE EQUAL.
THE TWO LOWER TEST VALUES ARE EQUAL.

12. Write an interactive version of the program described in Problem 10 or 11.

13. The Pampered Pancreas (known affectionately as The P-squared) is a limited-menu restaurant specializing in mediocre food, a fact hidden only with partial success by a bewildering collection of prefab cutesy decorations and a folk guitarist with severe vocal problems. One of the P-squared's popular specialties is a prepackaged Dinner for Eight (reservations 3 days in advance, please) whose basic cost is $62.00. For that amount, each Pampered Pancreas Patron (known as a P-cube to the Innermost Crowd) gets a salad, an entree, a beverage, and a dessert. Fantastic. This sounds simple enough, but it gets a little involved because of the conditions under which the items are selected:

(a) Everybody gets the same salad.

(b) There are three entrees (beefarama, ultrachicken, and supercod). The fixed price entitles the group to eight entrees, but at least three of them must be beefarama, at least two of them must be ultrachicken, and at least one must be supercod. Beyond that, the other choices may be of any of the three types.

(c) Everybody gets any of the three beverages on the menu. (Well, limited is limited.)

(d) P-squared offers two desserts: Sunset and Paradiso. (I don't know what they are either.) Four of the desserts must be from each type.

Of course, the diners have the right to deviate from these rules, but it will cost them:

(e) If less than three beefaramas are ordered, there is a $2.00 penalty for each one less. If less than two ultrachickens are ordered, there is a $1.75 penalty for each one less.

(f) If more than eight beverages are ordered, there is an additional charge of $1.50 each for the first five and $1.25 each beyond that.

(g) Sunsets are $1.80 each and Paradisos are $1.95 each. If diners order less than four desserts of either type, there is no credit for the unordered dessert. For instance, if a party of eight gets six sunsets and only two paradisos, they are charged $3.60 extra for the two additional sunsets.

The P-squared would like a program that computes and displays a total amount to be billed for each party of eight. Input (for each party) consists of eight lines. Each contains the party number (an integer), the number of beefaramas, the number of ultrachickens, the number of supercods, the number of beverages, the number of sunsets, and the number of paradisos. This series of input sets is preceded by a single line showing today's month, day, and year. For each party, the program is to produce five output lines: The party number, total surcharge for entrees, total surcharge for beverages, total surcharge for dessert, and the total amount billed. Leave a blank line between output sets and include appropriate labels for the various items shown. Precede the first output set with a line showing today's date, and follow the last output set with three blank lines and an additional output line showing the number of parties and the total amount billed.

14. In this version of Problem 13, use the same decision rules and produce the same output. However, the results for each party are to appear on a single line of a five-column table equipped with appropriate column headings. The date still goes at the top as before. After all the sets have been processed, the program is to leave two blank lines and then show an additonal line containing the string "TOTAL" in the first column (where the party number was shown for the individual sets) and the various total figures in the other four columns.

15. Write a program that computes a date (month/day/year) given a starting date and an elapsed time period in years, months, and days. That is, each input line consists of six integer values: starting month (startmo), starting day (startday), starting year (startyr), number of elapsed years (years), number of elapsed months (months), and a number of elapsed days (days). These are used to compute a final date (finalmo, finalday, finalyr). Each input set produces three lines of output. For instance, the input line

7 7 1982 3 4 16

will give the following output:

```
STARTING DATE: 7/ 7/1982
ELAPSED TIME: 3 YEARS, 4 MONTHS, 16 DAYS
FINAL DATE: 11/23/1985
```

Leave a blank line between output sets. The following assumptions apply here:
(a) All data will be in the twentieth century.
(b) months will never exceed 12, days will never exceed 31, and years will always be sized so as not to violate (a).
(c) All starting dates will be valid.
(d) All time lapses will be forward, that is, the final date will always be later in time than the starting date.

16. Here is a slight variation on the previous problem. Instead of specifying the elapsed time in years, months, and days, an input set in this instance consists of the first three values as before and the elapsed

time *in days.* The first and third lines of output remain as they were, and the second line changes in accordance with the modified input.

17. In this problem, produce a version of the program in either of the previous two problems where the output is arranged as a table in which the output produced for each set appears a single line. If you select Problem 13 as a basis, your table will have five columns (starting date, elapsed years, elapsed months, elapsed days, and final date). The requirements from Problem 14, on the other hand, suggest a three-column table (starting date, elapsed days, and final date). In either version, include appropriate column headings.

18. To complicate things a bit further, write a program that meets the requirements given in Problems 15, 16, or 17 with one exception: Assumption (c) no longer holds. The only thing we can say about the first three input values is that they will be integers. This means that not only will you have to check for ridiculous dates (e.g., 14/42/1978), but it will also be necessary to check dates that are legal to make sure that assumption (a) is not violated. If you find a starting date that will not meet these conditions, produce a line of output showing the date and the message "IMPROPER STARTING DATE," and go on to the next input set.

19. Now we shall complicate the elapsed time problem further by removing assumption (b) (see Problem 15). Thus, an elapsed time period of 0 years, 14 months, and 47 days, for example, is acceptable under these relaxed rules. Write the program requested in Problem 13 or 14 with assumptions (b) and (c) removed.

20. As a final complication, write the program specified for Problem 19 with the additional stipulation that assumption (a) is removed. This leaves only assumption (d), and the more adventurous may remove that one as well.

21. Write an interactive version of the program specified in Problem 15, 16, 17, 18, or 19.

22. Here is a research question: Pick your favorite (or least favorite) airline and find out how many different ways there are to determine what it costs to fly between two particular cities. Then, having defined the information you need to make the computations, write a program that reads this information and computes the appropriate cost. Some suggested journeys are listed below. A few are easier than others, but remember that all of them are subject to such considerations as class of flight, family plans, group plans, length of stay, and advance reservations. Have a good trip.
    (a) Saint Louis to Kansas City
    (b) Philadelphia to Pittsburgh
    (c) New York to Chicago

(d) New York to Miami
(e) New York to Los Angeles
(f) New York to London
(g) New York to Las Vegas
(h) New York to Washington, D.C.
(i) New York to Honolulu
(j) Washington, D.C. to Chicago
(k) Washington, D.C. to Los Angeles
(l) Chicago to Honolulu
(m) Chicago to London
(n) Los Angeles to London
(p) Tyler, Texas to Syracuse, New York

Chapter Nine

Cyclic Processes

Chapter 2 discussed the loop's fundamental importance as a structural component, and we have made frequent use of Pascal's facilities for building and controlling such loops. In this chapter we elaborate on these features and take a more detailed look at the kinds of repetitive processes that they support.

9.1 LOOPS FOR COUNTING: THE FOR STATEMENT

A commonly used type of cyclic process is one consisting of a specified number of trips through a loop. It is not necessarily true that the number of trips is the same every time the cyclic process is used, but that number, whatever it is, always is known at the start of the process. Pascal's FOR statement (Figure 9.1) makes the construction of such loops convenient because the program automatically maintains a counter that keeps track of the cycles and automatically cuts off the repetitions when the required number has been completed.

Example 9.1

A simple illustration will remind us how easily such loops are built: In this example we shall compute the sum sumval and the sum of the square roots sumroots of eight real input values, each one of which will be read, in turn, into a variable newval. In addition, we shall find the largest of these eight values (largestval). An integer named counter will be used to keep track of the number of cycles through the loop.

The heart of the resulting program (Figure 9.2) is the FOR loop in which each of the eight cycles brings in an input value, uses it to update sumval and sumroots, and to replace the current value for largest if appropriate.

9.1.1 Loops with Varying Numbers of Cycles

Since the number of cycles in a FOR loop need not be specified as a constant (it may be an expression, as Figure 9.1 indicates), we have an opportunity to vary the number of cycles each time the looping process is

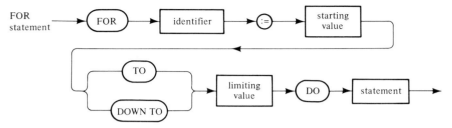

Semantics: Starting value and limiting value are expressions whose values must be such that starting value must not be greater than limiting value when TO is specified; alternatively, starting value must not be less than limiting value if DOWNTO is used.

Figure 9.1

Syntax and Semantics for the FOR Statement

used. This is illustrated by revising the requirements in Example 9.1 so that, instead of reading and processing exactly eight values each time the program is run, the modified version, which also is interactive (Figure 9.3), reads an initial input value that tells the program how many subsequent values to read and process. The index that monitors the number of cycles (counter in this example) is changed automatically as part of the control mechanism built into the FOR statement. *The programmer does not and should not change the index by anything he or she specifies in the loop.*

9.1.2 Automatic Decrementation in FOR Loops

Another form of the FOR statement enables the programmer to set up a loop in which an index is initialized and then decreased (*decremented*) by 1 before each cycle. In this form, the reserved word TO is replaced by the reserved word DOWNTO to indicate explicitly that the index will be decreased by 1 automatically. The initial and final index values, which may be specified as constants or more extensive expressions, must be consistent in that the initial value must be greater than the final value when DOWNTO is used. It is up to the programmer (and not Pascal) to make sure that the program specifies the proper direction in which the index value is to change (i.e., TO for automatic increase by 1, DOWNTO for automatic decrease by 1). If there is any inconsistency (for instance, if the FOR statement says TO and the starting value for the index is greater than its final value, the program skips the entire FOR statement.

This feature was used to compute a polynomial value (Figure 6.1). To illustrate another use of this form, we shall declare an array letters of 18 characters and read them in reverse order. That is, the first input character will be stored in letters[18], the second in letters[17], and so on:

```
VAR
    which   :   INTEGER   ;
    letters :   ARRAY [1..18] OF CHAR
                . . . . . . . . . . . . . . . . .
    FOR  which  := 18 DOWNTO 1  DO
        READ (letters[which])


(**********************************************************************)
(**                          EXAMPLE 9.1                          **)
(**********************************************************************)
(** THIS PROGRAM ILLUSTRATES THE CONSTRUCTION OF A SIMPLE COUNTING **)
(** LOOP. A LOOP IS SET UP IN WHICH EACH OF ITS EIGHT CYCLES READS **)
(** A REAL VALUE FOR newvalue, ADDS IT TO sumval, ADDS ITS SQUARE  **)
(** ROOT TO sumroots, AND COMPARES ITS VALUE TO largest, REPLACING **)
(** largest IF THE NEW VALUE EXCEEDS IT.                           **)
(**********************************************************************)
PROGRAM  ex901    (INPUT, OUTPUT)  ;
VAR
    counter  :  INTEGER  ;
    newval, sumval, sumroots, largest  :  REAL  ;
(**********************************************************************)
(** largest WILL BE INITIALIZED TO A SMALL VALUE SO THAT THE FIRST **)
(** INPUT VALUE WILL BE SURE TO REPLACE IT UPON COMPARISON.        **)
(**********************************************************************)
BEGIN
    sumval := 0.0  ;
    sumroots := 0.0  ;
    largest := -1.0E40  ;
    WRITELN ('TYPE THE NUMBER OF INPUT VALUES FOR THIS RUN AND
              HIT <RETURN>.');
    FOR  counter := 1 TO 8  DO
        BEGIN
            WRITELN ('TYPE IN THE NEXT newval AND HIT <RETURN>.');
            READLN (newval)  ;
            sumval := sumval + newval  ;
            sumroots := sumroots + SQRT(newval) ;
            IF  newval > largest  THEN
                largest := newval
        END ;
    WRITELN ('LARGEST OF EIGHT INPUT VALUES:  ',largest) ;
    WRITELN ('SUM OF EIGHT INPUT VALUES:  ',sumval) ;
    WRITELN ('SUM OF SQUARE ROOTS:  ',sumroots)  ;
    WRITELN  ;
    WRITELN ('END OF RUN.')
END.
```

Figure 9.2———————————————————————————————————————

Pascal Statements for Example 9.1

```
(**********************************************************************)
(**                          EXAMPLE 9.2                            **)
(**********************************************************************)
(** THE LOOP IN THIS PROGRAM STILL GOES THROUGH A PREDEFINED        **)
(** NUMBER numnew OF CYCLES, BUT THAT NUMBER IS AN INPUT VALUE      **)
(** THAT CAN CHANGE FROM RUN TO RUN.                                **)
(**********************************************************************)
PROGRAM ex902  (INPUT, OUTPUT)  ;
VAR
    numnew, counter  :  INTEGER  ;
    newval, sumval, numroots, largest  :  REAL  ;
BEGIN
    sumval := 0.0  ;
    sumroots := 0.0  ;
    largest := -1.0E40  ;
    READLN (numnew)  ;
    WRITELN ('NUMBER OF VALUES TO BE READ:  ',numnew)  ;
    FOR  counter := 1 TO numnew  DO
       BEGIN
          READLN (newval)  ;
          sumval := sumval + newval ;
          sumroots := sumroots + SQRT(newval)  ;
          IF  newval > largest  THEN
             largest := newval
       END  ;
    WRITELN ('LARGEST OF ',numnew, ' VALUES: ',largest)  ;
    WRITELN ('SUM OF ',numnew,' VALUES:  ',sumval)  ;
    WRITELN ('SUM OF ',numnew ,' SQUARE ROOTS:  ',sumroots)  ;
    WRITELN ;
    WRITELN ('END OF RUN.')
END.
```

Figure 9.3

Pascal Statements for Example 9.2

9.1.3 Use of the Loop Index in Computations

Although the index in a FOR loop is to be changed only by the automatic mechanism built into the FOR statement, it can participate in any computations specified within the loop. For example, suppose we wanted to compute the quantity hfact, where

$$hfact = \sum_{lower}^{upper} tracker \, LOG(tracker)$$

In this formation, lower and upper are integer values that define the limits of the computation and may vary from one instance to the next. Accordingly, we shall show them as input values:

```
VAR
    lower , upper, tracker  :    INTEGER ;
    hfact   :   REAL ;
      . . . . . . . . . . . . . .
    READLN (lower, upper) ;
    hfact := 0.0   ;
    FOR  tracker := lower TO upper  DO
       hfact := hfact + tracker * LOG(tracker)
      . . . . . . . . . . . . . . .
```

Note that, although the index (c o u n t e r in this example) plays a dominant role in the computations, its value is not affected by those computations.

9.1.4 Loops with Programmer-Defined Indexes

Examples 7.1 and 7.2 (Figures 7.2 and 7.5) included a FOR loop with an index variable of type p i a n o t y p e—an enumerative type defined in the programs themselves. As Section 7.1.2 explained, Pascal can manage such counters by using the internal sequencing associated with the list of values in a TYPE declaration. For example, suppose we make the following declarations and assignments:

```
TYPE
    luggage = (makeupcase, overnight, airplane, weekend,
               pullman, trunk, omigod)  ;
VAR
    grip, littlecarrier, bigcarrier   :   luggage
      . . . . . . . . . . . . . . . . . . . . . . .
    littlecarrier := overnight   ;
    bigcarrier := pullman
      . . . . . . . . . . . . . . . . . . . . . . . .
```

Then the loop

```
FOR grip := littlecarrier TO bigcarrier DO
                       action
```

will execute four times. So would the loop

```
FOR grip := pullman DOWNTO overnight DO
                     action
```

9.2 MORE GENERAL EVENT-CONTROLLED LOOPS

Attainment of a predetermined number of cycles is just one kind of event that can be used to control the behavior of a loop. There are more general situations where the number of cycles is not crucial in determining whether a loop should continue or not. Instead, some other circumstance serves as the basis for such a decision. For example, it often makes sense to build a loop whose activity continues to repeat as long as input values are available, a practice we have used frequently throughout the book. This section looks at additional considerations in the construction and use of such loops.

9.2.1 The WHILE Statement Revisited

Our extensive use of the WHILE-DO construction (and the corresponding WHILE statement) makes it unnecessary to dwell on its properties here. One point worth reemphasizing is that the placement of the test at the entrance to the loop's processing activities makes it possible to include situations in which the loop is not entered at all.

For example, suppose we were to add each successive real input value testvalue to a sum sumoftests as long as testvalue exceeds some minimum value minvalue. Assuming all the necessary declarations, our code might look like this:

```
READLN (minvalue)   ;
sumoftests := 0.0   ;
READLN (testvalue)   ;
WHILE  testvalue > minvalue DO
   BEGIN
       sumoftests := sumoftests + testvalue   ;
       READLN (testvalue)
   END ;
                              next statement
```

The loop pays no attention to the number of input values used. Consequently, if the first value of testvalue turns out to be too small (i.e., not greater than minvalue), the test in the WHILE statement fails even before the first cycle, and the entire loop structure is bypassed.

9.2.2 The REPEAT-UNTIL Structure

A special case of the WHILE-DO loop occurs when the programmer wishes to guarantee at least one cycle through the loop regardless of the number of additional cycles that may be completed. This type of situation occurs often enough so that it has been characterized as a distinct structural component, i.e., the REPEAT-UNTIL construction. The basic property of

```
REPEAT
     activity
UNTIL this condition is true.
```

Figure 9.4————————————————————————————————

Pseudocode Representation for the REPEAT-UNTIL Construction

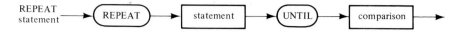

Figure 9.5

Syntax for the REPEAT Statement

this type of loop is that the test which controls continued cycling is at the end of the loop (rather than at the beginning, as is the case in the WHILE-DO construction). Moreover, the test is expressed in such a way that an outcome of TRUE breaks the loop and forces the process to move to the next activity. Alternatively, an outcome of FALSE sends the program back through the loop for another cycle. The pseudocode representation of this loop is shown in Figure 9.4.

Pascal's REPEAT statement (Figure 9.5) is a direct expression of this structure: The activity specified after the reserved word REPEAT is performed once before any determination is made to repeat the process or move on. To emphasize the difference between the WHILE-DO and RE-PEAT-UNTIL components, we shall compare two similar programs. The basic intent is to read a succession of values for real variable pval and compute the sum of their logarithms sumlogpvals. Figure 9.6 shows a

```
(********************************************************)
(** THIS PROGRAM COMPUTES smlog, THE SUM OF THE LOGS    **)
(** OF AN ARBITRARY NUMBER OF INPUT VALUES FOR pval, THE **)
(** PROCESSING LOOP IS SHOWN IN TWO VERSIONS,           **)
(********************************************************)
     PROGRAM   whileuntil (INPUT, OUTPUT)  ;
     VAR
         pval, smlog   :   REAL  ;
```

```
BEGIN                           BEGIN
   smlog := 0,0  ;                 smlog := 0,0  ;
   READLN (pval)  ;                READLN (pval)  ;
   WHILE  NOT EOF  DO              REPEAT
       BEGIN                          BEGIN
           smmlog := smlog+pval ;         smlog := smlog+pval ;
           READLN (pval)                  READLN (pval)
       END  ;                         END
   WRITELN ('SMLOG: ',smlog)       UNTIL  EOF ;
END,                               WRITELN ('SMLOG: ',smlog)
                                 END,
```

Figure 9.6

Comparison Between WHILE . . . DO and REPEAT . . . UNTIL Constructions

common set of declarations followed by alternative procedural sections. The version on the right is designed to expect at least one input value. If that actually is the case, the two versions will produce the same results. In the extreme case where there are no input values (such things can and do

```
loop specification 1
    BEGIN
        statement   ;
        statement
        ..........
        loop specification 2
            BEGIN
                statement   ;
                statement
                ..........
                loop specification 3
                    BEGIN
                        statement
                        ..........
                        statement
                    END ;
                statement
                ..........
            END ;
            statement ;
            statement
            ..........
            loop specification 4
                BEGIN
                    statement
                    ..........
                    statement
                END
    END
```

loop specification is either FOR index := start TO finish DO
                or   FOR index := start DOWNTO finish DO
                or   WHILE test outcome is true DO
                or   REPEAT
                          activity
                    UNTIL test outcome is true

Figure 9.7

Construction of Nested Loops

happen), the more general version on the left will operate as usual, but the alternate construction will terminate with an error message.

9.3 NESTED LOOPS

Many situations call for cyclic processes which themselves contain other cyclic processes. For instance, the second hand of a clock must go through a complete set of (60) movements for the minute hand to move one notch. Similarly, the minute hand must go through a complete set of (60) movements for the hour hand to move one notch. Loops contained in other loops are said to be *nested*. Pascal's facilities for building such processes are easy to use because they are direct extensions of the fundamental FOR, WHILE, or REPEAT statements. Since the cyclic activity for any of these forms can be expressed as a compound statement, that statement may consist of a sequence that includes another loop. *That* loop, in turn, may itself incorporate a complete loop, and so on. These relationships, examples of which are depicted in Figure 9.7, make it possible to extend nested loop systems to any desired level without changing the overall structure. Note that the

```
Define 6-element array HT, indexes I and K, switch NOSWAP.
Read HT.
DO for the first 5 elements of HT using index I:
    Initialize NOSWAP to TRUE.
    DO for HT[6] down to HT[I+1] using index K:
        IF
                HT[K] is greater than HT[K-1]
        THEN
                Exchange HT[K] and HT[K-1].
                Set NOSWAP to FALSE.
        ELSE
        ENDIF
    ENDDO
    IF
        NOSWAP is TRUE
    THEN
        Sort is complete; exit from the loop.
    ELSE
    ENDIF
ENDDO
Display the sorted array.
Display terminating message.
Stop.
```

Figure 9.8

Pseudocode for Example 9.3

nesting possibilities are completely general: A FOR loop may be nested in a WHILE loop or a REPEAT loop, and so on. When a FOR loop is nested in another FOR loop, the programmer must make sure he or she uses different index variables for each loop.

```
(***********************************************************************)
(                              EXAMPLE 9.3                             )
(***********************************************************************)
(   THIS PROGRAM SORTS A 6-ELEMENT INTEGER ARRAY IN DESCENDING ORDER   )
(   USING A BUBBLE SORT TECHNIQUE. THE NORMALLY INSIDIOUS GOTO IS      )
(   USED TO PROVIDE A QUICK EXIT FROM THE SORTING LOOP WHEN FURTHER    )
(   EXAMINATION OF THE ARRAY IS DETERMINED TO BE UNNECESSARY.          )
(   NOTE THE PLACEMENT OF THE LABEL DECLARATION.                       )
(***********************************************************************)
PROGRAM   ex903 (INPUT, OUTPUT)  ;
LABEL
   99  ;
CONST
   arraylimit = 6  ;
VAR
   ht  :  ARRAY[1..arraylimit] OF INTEGER  ;
   i, k, temp ht  :  INTEGER  ;
   noswap  :  BOOLEAN  ;
BEGIN
   FOR  i := 1 TO arraylimit  DO
     READ (ht[i])  ;
   FOR  i := 1 TO arraylimit-1  DO
     BEGIN
       noswap := TRUE  ;
       FOR  k := arraylimit DOWNTO i+1  DO
         IF
           ht[k] > ht[k-1]
         THEN
           BEGIN
             temp ht := ht[k] ;  ht[k] := ht[k-1] ; ht[k-1] := tempht ;
             noswap := FALSE
           END  ;
       IF  noswap  THEN GOTO 99
     END  ;
99: WRITELN ('SORTED ARRAY:')  ;
   FOR  i := 1 TO arraylimit  DO
     WRITE (ht[i]:8)  ;
   WRITELN  ;
   WRITELN ('END OF RUN.')
END.
```

Figure 9.9

Program For Example 9.3

Example 9.3

A good way to summarize these fundamental cyclic processes (as it has been since Neanderthal Man stumbled on the first loop uncharted eons ago) is to set up a program that reads in elements for a one-dimensional array and processes them so that the final array has its elements arranged in descending order (i.e., the largest value in the first element, etc.). To keep our attention focused on the processing itself, we shall use a small (6-element) integer array named ht.

The algorithm selected for this example is called a *bubble sort* because larger values are systematically "bubbled" toward one end of the array while the smaller elements percolate their way toward the other end. In addition, the algorithm includes a signal (the BOOLEAN variable noswap) that prevents unnecessary cycling if the elements are already in proper order. A pseudocode description is given in Figure 9.8.

A simple loop brings the array's elements into the processor, and a similar process displays them. (No, we cannot transmit an entire array with a single READ, READLN, WRITE, or WRITELN.) The program itself is shown in Figure 9.9. Of special interest is the appearance of a GOTO

```
Original Array:  7      2    4    9    6  3

i = 1;   k = 6:  7      2    4    9    6  3
         k = 5:  7      2    4    9    6  3
         k = 4:  7      2    9    4    6  3 (NOSWAP = FALSE)
         k = 3:  7      9    2    4    6  3
         k = 2:  9      7    2    4    6  3
                                         (NOSWAP = TRUE)
i = 2;   k = 6:  9      7    2    4    6  3
         k = 5:  9      7    2    6    4  3 (NOSWAP = FALSE)
         k = 4:  9      7    6    2    4  3
         k = 3:  9      7    6    2    4  3
                                         (NOSWAP = TRUE)
i = 3;   k = 6   9      7    6    2    4  3
         k = 5   9      7    6    4    2  3 (NOSWAP = FALSE)
         k = 4   9      7    6    4    2  3
                                         (NOSWAP = TRUE)
i = 4;   k = 6   9      7    6    4    3  2 (NOSWAP = FALSE
         k = 5   9      7    6    4    3  2
                                         (NOSWAP = TRUE)
i = 5;   k = 6   9      7    6    4    3  2
```

SORT COMPLETE.

Figure 9.10
Step-by-Step Example of the Bubble Sort (Worst Case)

statement. This is a special situation in which this dreaded statement simplifies the processing: When the value in noswap tells us that the program has worked its way through a cycle without having to rearrange any elements, we can conclude that the array is sorted and needs no further treatment. Consequently, we would like to stop the cyclic process abruptly, right at that point, even though the FOR statement "expects" more cycles. Under those circumstance, the GOTO statement gives us a clean, direct getaway.

If the exact operation of an algorithm leaves some questions, a helpful technique is to "walk through" its operations as if we were the processor. We shall do that for the sorting loop of this example by starting with the array

$$7 \quad 2 \quad 4 \quad 9 \quad 6 \quad 3$$

and seeing the effect of each individual cycle. Using the same index variables (i and k) defined in the program, the results of such a walk-through are given in Figure 9.10.

1. Write the Pascal statement(s) necessary to implement each of the following processes. Assume all necessary declarations.
   (a) Find the sum of 20 successive input values for integer numsold, and store the sum in totalsold.
   (b) Read an integer value breakval. Then, add each of the next 23 input integer values (each of which is stored in newval) either to lowsum if it is less than breakval or to highsum if it is not.
   (c) Read an integer value howmany and then compute the square root of the sum of the natural logarithms of the next howmany input values. Each of these values will be a real number to be stored in nextval.
   (d) Compute sumfirstm, the sum of the first m positive integers. The value for m is to read as input.
   (e) Compute sumfirstoddm, the sum of the first m odd integers. The value for m is to read as input.
   (f) Compute numberofprimes, the number of prime numbers in the first m prime integers. The value of m is read as input.
   (g) Expand the statements in (f) so that they also produce bigprime, the largest prime number in the first m positive integers.
   (h) Compute numberofsevens, the number of times the digit 7

appears in the positive integers ranging from input value low to 999. Assume low is always a positive integer less than 999.

2. Rewrite the program in Example 9.2 so that processing repeats automatically for an arbitrary number of sets of input values.

3. Write a program that reads sets of input consisting of two positive integers m and n. For each set, the program is to produce a table in which there is a line for each integer i between m and n. Each line shows i, its square, its cube, its square root, and its logarithm. There is no guarantee that m and n are different, nor is it assured that m is always the smaller of the two when they are different.

4. Write a program that produces the same kind of table as that specified for Problem 3. The difference is that, instead of restricting the input values to integers, each table is produced in response to three real input values: lowval, the lowest value, hival, the highest value, and increment, the amount to be added to the current value to produce the basis for the next line of the table. For example, input values of

$$1.0 \quad 50.0 \quad 0.2$$

would produce a table whose first line shows the square, cube, etc. of 1.0, the second line shows similar information for 1.2, the third line for 1.4, and so on up to and including 50.0. Assume increment is always greater than zero and that hival is always greater than lowval.

5. Write the same kind of program described for the previous problem, but do not make either of the assumptions stipulated there.

6. Revise the program in Example 9.3 so that it processes any number of input sets.

7. Revise the program in Example 9.3 so that it processes arrays of 20 elements.

8. Revise the program in Problems 6 or 7 so that it sorts the elements in ascending order (lowest value in ht[1], etc.

9. In the distant land of Poopikonia, the unit of currency is the Riegloch. There are three Zoopchiks to the Riegloch, seven Glepniks to the Zoopchik, eleven Fnivs to the Glepnik, and four Digidehs to the Fniv. Write a program that counts the number of ways to make change for a Riegloch.

10. Revise the program in Problem 9 so that it displays each combination-producing change for a Riegloch as long as that combination does not include any Fnivs.

11. Revise the program in Problem 8 so that it will process arrays of 20 elements or less. Each array is preceded by an integer value elements that specifies the number of elements in the array that follows.

Chapter Ten

Subprograms

A major attribute of a well-constructed program is its clarity—success at conveying succinctly and accurately the processing activities embodied in it. To enhance a program's clarity, we would like to focus on the procedural steps required by the *algorithm* and submerge our concern with the detailed expression of those steps in the *program*. This is exactly what we do when we use one of Pascal's standard (permanent) subprograms or write one ourselves: By expressing the action in the main program as a single statement or operation, we are able to pretend that the processing is really accomplished in one step; details of the activity, hidden away in a subprogram, can be as extensive and/or tedious as they need to be without upsetting this illusion.

Example 10.1

We can see how to submerge the operating details of an activity by rewriting Example 9.3 from the previous chapter. In that program there is a pair of nested loops that sorts an array. The size and complexity of these loops is dictated by the algorithms used and by Pascal's properties. However, our view of this activity is considerably simpler: "Sort the array's elements in descending order."

To bring the program in Example 9.3 closer to this view, we shall move the sorting process out of the main program and convert it into a separate subprogram whose description will appear in the declaration section. In its place (in the main program) will be a simple request for the rearrangement to be performed. This reorganization is shown in the overall structure of the revised program (Figure 10.1). The sorting process is recast as a *procedure*. The statement that uses *(invokes)* the procedure simply specifies the procedure's name (arraysort) and a value (ht) on which the procedure is to operate. The procedure, in response, produces results that are *returned* to the invoking program. This is no different from our use of READLN or any of Pascal's other standard procedures.

Details of the procedure's activities are described in its definition [Figure 10.1(b)], and the entire program is seen in Figure 10.1(c). Since

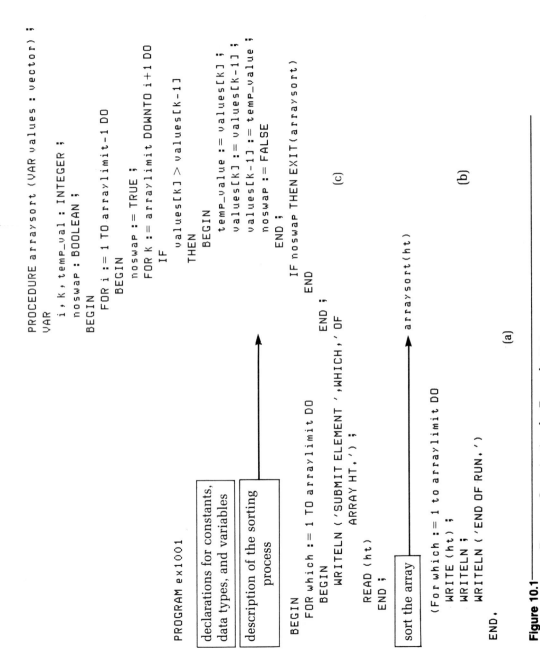

```
PROGRAM ex1001

[ declarations for constants,
  data types, and variables ]

[ description of the sorting
  process ]

BEGIN
FOR which := 1 TO arraylimit DO
  BEGIN
    WRITELN ('SUBMIT ELEMENT ','WHICH,' OF
             ARRAY HT,') ;

    READ (ht)
  END ;

[ sort the array ] ───→ arraysort(ht)

  (For which := 1 to arraylimit DO
    WRITE (ht) ;
    WRITELN ;
    WRITELN ('END OF RUN,')

END.
```

(a)

```
PROCEDURE arraysort (VAR values : vector) ;
VAR
   i, k, temp_val : INTEGER ;
   noswap : BOOLEAN ;
BEGIN
  FOR i := 1 TO arraylimit-1 DO
    BEGIN
      noswap := TRUE ;
      FOR k := arraylimit DOWNTO i+1 DO
        IF
          values[k] > values[k-1]
        THEN
          BEGIN
            temp_value := values[k] ;
            values[k] := values[k-1] ;
            values[k-1] := temp_value ;
            noswap := FALSE
          END ;
      IF noswap THEN EXIT(arraysort)
    END
END ;
```

(c)   (b)

Figure 10.1———— Program Organization for Example 10.1

```
{*******************************************************************}
{                          EXAMPLE 10.1                             }
{*******************************************************************}
{   THIS PROGRAM SORTS A 6-ELEMENT INTEGER ARRAY IN DESCENDING ORDER }
{   USING A BUBBLE SORT TECHNIQUE. SUDDEN DEPARTURE FROM THE SORTING }
{   LOOP IS ACHIEVED BY A GOTO STATEMENT AS WAS DONE PREVIOUSLY. THE }
{   DIFFERENCE HERE IS THAT WHEN WE LEAVE THE LOOP, WE WANT TO RETURN}
{   TO THE INVOKING PROGRAM. SINCE THE RETURN IS AUTOMATIC (THAT IS, }
{   WE DO NOT HAVE TO SAY ANYTHING EXPLICIT TO PERFORM THE RETURN,   }
{   THE GOTO STATEMENT BRINGS THE PROGRAM TO AN EMPTY STATEMENT. THIS}
{   CONSISTS OF A LABEL AND A SEMICOLON.                             }
{   FOR CONVENIENCE, THE 6-ELEMENT ARRAY IS SET UP AS A SEPARATE DATA}
{   TYPE. THIS SIMPLIFIES THE INVOCATION.                            }
{*******************************************************************}
PROGRAM   ex1001 (INPUT, OUTPUT)  ;
LABEL
   99 ;
CONST
   arraylimit = 6  ;
TYPE
   vector  :   ARRAY[1..arraylimit] OF INTEGER  ;
VAR
   ht  :   vector ;
   which   :   INTEGER  ;

   PROCEDURE   arraysort(VAR values  :   vector)  ;
   VAR
     i, k, tempval  :   INTEGER  ;
     noswap  :   BOOLEAN  ;
BEGIN
   FOR i  := 1 TO arraylimit-1  DO
     BEGIN
       noswap := TRUE  ;
       FOR  k := arraylimit DOWNTO i+1  DO
         IF
           values[k] > values[k-1]
         THEN
           BEGIN
             tempvalue := values[k] ;
             values[k] := values[k-1] ;
             values[k-1] := tempvalue ;
             noswap := FALSE
           END  ;
       IF   noswap  THEN GOTO 99
     END
99:  ;
END  ;
```

Figure 10.1

(d) Program for Example 10.1

```
{  HERE IS THE MAIN PROGRAM.  }
BEGIN
  FOR  which := 1 TO arraylimit  DO
    READ (ht[which]) ;
  arraysort (ht)  ;
  WRITELN ('SORTED ARRAY:')  ;
  FOR  which := 1 TO arraylimit  DO
    WRITE (ht[which]:8)  ;
  WRITELN  ;
  WRITELN ('END OF RUN.')
END.
```

(d)

Figure 10.1

(d) Program for Example 10.1 (continued)

arraysort appears as part of the program's declaration section, its position in the program is totally unrelated to its usage. The only way any
subprogram's activity gets to be performed is by invocation from some
point in the program's procedure section. Subprograms may be invoked
any number of times from many different places in the procedure section.

Having introduced the basic relationship between subprograms and
their use in a program, we can turn our attention to their properties and
construction. These issues are the subject of this chapter.

10.1 STRUCTURE OF SUBPROGRAMS

Pascal recognizes two kinds of subprograms: the function and the procedure. The function enables the programmer to treat a process as if it were a
single operation. This characterization is supported by the function's
structural properties:

1. A function operates in a predefined way on an appropriate number of
values (*arguments*) to produce a single result.
2. A function is invoked in an expression, and the result is returned to
that expression for further processing within the same statement.

A procedure (traditionally called a *subroutine*) is a more general type of
subprogram that enables the programmer to treat a process as if it were a
single Pascal statement. This is reflected in the following properties:

1. A procedure operates in a predefined way on an appropriate number of
arguments with no limit being imposed on the number of values
produced. (In Example 10.1, the procedure arraysort operates on
six numbers, even though we referred to them collectively with a
single argument.)

2. A procedure is invoked as a separate statement. Regardless of the complexity of the underlying process, the procedure's mechanism makes sure that when the procedure is completed, the program continues right after the statement that invoked *(called)* the procedure.

Because of the differences between functions and procedures, any function also can be expressed as a procedure, but the reverse is not true for all procedures.

The syntax diagrams for functions and procedures [Figures 10.2(a) and 10.2(b), respectively] describe similar constructions. Each subprogram has two major components:

1. The subprogram's identification appears at the beginning of the description and defines exactly how the subprogram is used.
2. The body is a block containing the processing statements and the supporting data definitions.

These components are identified in Figure 10.1(b) for the `arraysort` procedure.

The identification component for either type of subprogram includes a *parameter list* (Figure 10.3) that specifies the number of data items (and their respective types) to be supplied to the subprogram when it is invoked. The parameter list for a given subprogram may be empty. Each of these specifications is expressed as a *formal parameter*. This is not an actual value or a reference to an actual value. Instead, it is a piece of bookkeeping that helps define the way the subprogram works. The role of each formal parameter is described in the body of the subprogram by that parameter's appearance(s) in the computational statements. As pointed out earlier,

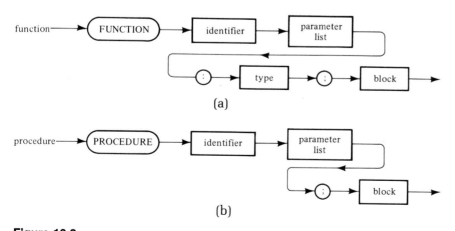

(a)

(b)

Figure 10.2

Organization of Pascal Subprograms

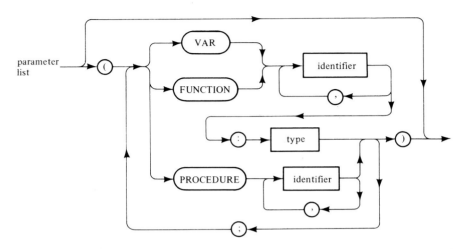

Figure 10.3

Syntax of a Parameter List

these computations do not take place until the subprogram is invoked. At that time, the arguments (or *actual parameters*) supplied by the invocation are used, guided by the association that the program establishes between these values and the corresponding formal parameters. In Example 10.1, values is a formal parameter. The VAR indicates that the parameter's value is likely to change as a result of the subprogram's activity. When the function is invoked [Figure 10.1(a)], the program uses the actual parameter (ht) wherever values appears in the computations.

Since formal parameters do not represent variables in storage, they are not declared. Their appearance in the parameter list establishes their purpose. Note, however, that the arraysort procedure in Figure 10.1(b) does have declarations (i, k, temp_val, and noswap) that do not appear in the parameter list. These variables have no purpose outside the subprogram. Consequently, they have been removed from the main program's declaration section, and their existence is limited to the activities within the procedure. Such variables are called *local variables*.

10.1.1 Construction of Functions

The requirements for a function's description [Figure 10.2(a)] underscore Pascal's intent with regard to a function's uses: The function performs some type of process that produces exactly one resulting value. This value is delivered in a variable carrying the function's name, and its data type is defined by the specification following the formal parameter list.

As seen in Figure 10.3, there are several kinds of formal parameters.

The simplest merely specifies a name and a data type. During invocation, the value of the corresponding actual parameter will be used, but not changed, during the processing. When the word VAR is placed in front of a parameter's name (as it was in Example 10.1), it identifies that parameter as one whose corresponding actual value can be expected to change as a result of the processing. Either form of parameter can be used in a function's parameter list. However, we shall impose an additional constraint by avoiding the use of VAR. This restriction brings a Pascal function closer in concept to a mathematical function. As a result, we shall characterize a function more specifically as a process that produces a single result without changing the values of any of its parameters.

Pascal places no restriction on the type(s) of data that a function may process or on the type produced as the single result. Consequently, a function can be built to operate on and/or produce programmer-defined data as long as such values do not take part in input/output operations.

10.1.2 Construction of Procedures

As Figure 10.2 indicates, the procedure is structurally similar to the function: It has an identifying portion that defines its requirements and a body that describes its processing. The detailed differences reflect the procedure's complete generality, placing no limitations on the number of returned results. Because of this, there is no point in assigning a specific data type to the procedure's name. Instead, the parameter list includes formal parameters representing all the items returned by the procedure as well as those brought to the procedure.

10.2 INVOCATION OF SUBPROGRAMS

Inclusion of a subprogram's definition enables us to use that subprogram as often as we need it from any number of different places in our program with arbitrarily different lists of actual parameters. Invocation itself simply is patterned after the example given in the subprogram's FUNCTION or PROCEDURE statement.

10.2.1 Invocation of Functions

When we invoke a function, we arrange to present it with the required number and types of values on which it is to operate. The function is not "aware" of how these values originally appear in the invocation. Consequently (as Figure 10.2 indicates), an actual parameter can be presented in a variety of forms, as long as the resulting data type matches that specified by the corresponding formal parameter.

Example 10.2

As an example, consider the simple function integerpower defined in Figure 10.4(a). When invoked, this function computes the value of the first parameter raised to the positive integer power specified by the second

```
FUNCTION  integerpower (value  :  REAL ;  power : INTEGER) : REAL  ;
VAR
    tracker : INTEGER  ;
BEGIN
   IF   power = 0   THEN
      integerpower := 1.0
   ELSE IF   power = 1   THEN
      integerpower := value
       ELSE
          BEGIN
              integerpower := value  ;
              FOR  tracker := 1 TO power-1   DO
                 integerpower := integerpower * value
          END
END
```

(a) Definition of the function integerpower

```
                . . . . . . . . . . . . . . . . .
VAR
    xcat, yval, zval, relwt, in4   :   REAL  ;
    uplim, lowlim, n1, acct        :   INTEGER
                . . . . . . . . . . . . . . . . .
    relwt := 3.5   ;
    in4 := 2.61    ;
    uplim := 6     ;
    lowlim := 2    ;
    n1 := 4        ;
    acct := 5
                . . . . . . . . . . . . . . . . .
xcat := integerpower (3.56,3)
                . . . . . . . . . . . . . . . .
yval := relwt + integerpower (in4,uplim)
                . . . . . . . . . . . . . . . .
zval := integerpower (SQRT(relwt),uplim-lowlim-1)
        + 3.1 * integerpower (integerpower(in4,3),acct-n1)
                . . . . . . . . . . . . . . . .
```

(b) Invocation of the function integerpower

Figure 10.4

Multiple Uses of a Function in a Main Program

parameter. Figure 10.4(b) shows a fragment of a main program in which integerpower is invoked from several different places.

In the first invocation, the function computes

$$3.56^3$$

and stores the result in the variable xcat. Both actual parameters are constant values requiring no further processing prior to their delivery to integerpower. In the second invocation, the values used by integerpower are taken from the two locations associated with in4 and uplim. The result thus produced, namely,

$$2.61^6$$

represents only an intermediate step in the computations requested by the expression in which the invocation appears. Once integerpower completes its work, the main program resumes processing at the point it left off. Accordingly, the value delivered by integerpower is added to relwt's value, and that sum is then assigned to yval. (For reference, the result is 319.613.)

The last statement in Figure 10.4(b) contains three separate invocations of integerpower. First, the function is called upon to raise to a power a value (SQRT(relwt)) that itself must be computed before the integerpower can use it. That computation involves the invocation of another function, SQRT. Similarly, the power to which the first actual parameter is to be raised (i.e., uplim-lowlim-1) also has to be computed. Thus, when the main program turns control over to integerpower, all this preparatory work will have been done, and what the function "sees" as its actual parameters are the values 1.87083 and 3. The result, 6.54688, is delivered back to the main program where it will be a term in the larger expression for zval. A second invocation asks integerpower to use as its first actual parameter a value (integerpower(in4,3)) whose computation involves another invocation of that same function. Pascal takes the request in stride by invoking integerpower again. The function, using the values 2.61 (i.e., in4) and 3 as its actual parameters, delivers a result of 17.7796 back to the point of the most recent invocation. At that point, the 17.7796, together with a value of 1 (acct-n1), provide the actual parameters for integerpower's previous invocation. Consequently, the function now delivers a value of 17.7796 (more precisely, 17.7796 to the first power) to the expression, where this result is multiplied by 3.1, added to the first term (6.54688), and the final result (61.6636) is assigned to zval.

To summarize, the computation of zval can be considered to take place as follows:

1. Compute $SQRT(relwt)$ (1.87083) and store in $t1$.
2. Compute $uplim - lowlim - 1$ (3) and store in $t2$.
3. Compute $t1$ (6.54688) and store in $t3$.
4. Compute $in4$ (17.7796) and store in $t4$.
5. Compute $acct - n1$ (1) and store in $t5$.
6. Compute $t4$ (17.7796) and store in $t6$.
7. Multiply $t6$ by 3.1 (55.1168) and store in $t7$.
8. Add $t3$ and $t7$.
9. Store the result (61.6636) in $zval$.

10.2.2 Invocation of Procedures

As we have seen in Section 10.1 and Example 10.1, the invocation of a procedure forms a complete statement. To illustrate this further, we shall construct a procedure that produces several values: If we locate two points on a set of X-Y coordinates by defining their respective horizontal and vertical positions as X1, Y1 and X2, Y2, a straight line connecting these points will have a slope A of

$$\frac{Y2 - Y1}{X2 - X1}$$

and an intercept B of

$$Y1 - A(x1)$$

Our procedure, to be named $strline$, will operate on four real values (represented by formal parameters $x1$, $y1$, $x2$, and $y2$), submitted in that order, to produce the slope a, the intercept b, and the length $linelgth$ of the segment between the two points.

Figure 10.5(a) shows $strline$'s definition, and its use is illustrated by two invoking statements in the main program fragment of Figure 10.5(b). The first invocation provides $strline$ with four actual parameters expressed as constants. In response, the procedure will deliver the values

$$\frac{13.7 - 6.8}{5.4 - 3.7} \qquad 6.8 - \left(\frac{13.7 - 6.8}{5.4 - 3.7}\right)(3.7)$$

and

$$\sqrt{(13.7 - 6.8)^2 + (5.4 - 3.7)^2}$$

to $slope$ $intercept$, and $dist$, respectively. A second invocation specifies the two vertical coordinates as expressions. These are evaluated automatically by the program, and the resulting values are delivered to the procedure: Thus, the second and fourth actual parameters for this invocation will be $3.6 * 8.0$ and $2.1 * 12.5 + 10.0 * SQR(12.5)$, respectively.

```
PROCEDURE strline (x1, y1, x2, y2 : REAL ;
                   VAR a, VAR b, VAR linelgth : REAL)  ;
BEGIN
  a := (y2 - y1)/(x2 - x1)  ;
  b := y1 - a * x1  ;
  linelgth := SQRT (SQR(y2-y1) + SQR(x2-x1))
END
```

(a) Description of the procedure strline

```
       ................

VAR
  veloc, time1, time2, accel, slope, intercept, dist  :   REAL

       ................

              description of the strline procedure

       ................

  strline (3.7, 6.8, 5.4, 13.7, slope, intercept, dist)  ;
  WRITELN ('SLOPE:  ',slope,'  INTERCEPT:  ',intercept,'  DIST:   ',dist)
  veloc := 2.1  ;
  time1 := 8.0  ;
  time2 := 12.0  ;
  accel := 10.0  ;
  strline (0.0, 3.6 * time1, 1.2, veloc * time2 + 0.5 * accel * SQR(time2),
           slope, intercept, dist)  ;
  WRITELN ('SLOPE:  ',slope,'  INTERCEPT:   ',intercept,'  DIST:   ',dist)

       ................
```

(b) Invocation of the procedure strline

Figure 10.5 ———— Multiple Uses of a Procedure in a Main Program

217

10.3 NESTED CONSTRUCTION OF SUBPROGRAMS

Hidden within the innocent appearance of Figure 10.2 are opportunities to construct intricate, multilayered subprograms. Since the body of a subprogram is (organizationally) a block, its declaration section may contain any number of complete subprogram definitions. This type of *nested construction* is helpful when the processing in a subprogram can be classified by representing some of its multistep activities as single operations or statements.

Example 10.3

Triad County is a peculiar place in that it is dotted with dozens of triangular lakes. Geologists say this cannot happen, but there they are. The Water Authority would like to know the total area covered by these lakes. For this purpose they have hired flying ace Louppe de Loupe to take a series of aerial photographs which were combined to form a county map. Onto this map the county surveyor superimposed a set of X-Y coordinates with the origin beyond the southwest corner of the county. This gave every point in the county a positive set of X and Y coordinates (Figure 10.6), and each lake could be described by specifying three points.

    At its highest level, the program for computing the total area is straight-

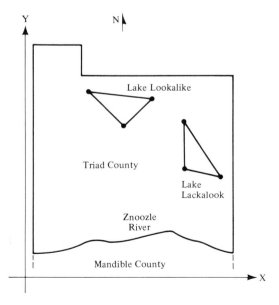

Figure 10.6

Triad County Set in X-Y Coordinates

forward: A set of input consists of a lake's name (20 characters) followed by the six real values $(x1, y1)$, $(x2, y2)$, and $(x3, y3)$ describing that lake's position. For each set read, the program computes the area, adds it to a running total, and displays a line showing the name, the three points, and the area. This processing is reflected in the pseudocode description of Figure 10.7(a), where the computation of the area is represented as a single step.

To promote the single-step representation mentioned above, the area's

Define `lakename, point1, point2, point3, numoflakes,`
        `area, totalarea.`
Initialize `numoflakes, totalarea.`
Read the first set of input.
WHILE there are data values to process, DO:
    Compute the triangle's area from `point1, point2, and`
        `point3.` (*)
    Add the area to `totalarea.`
    Display the input data and the triangle's area.
    Read the next set of input data (if there are any).
ENDWHILE
Display summary information (`numoflakes` and `totalarea`).
Stop.

      (a) Overall pseudocode description for Example 10.3

(*)   Define `base, side[1], side[2]`, and `side[3]`.
     Compute each side's length from two points(**).
     Compute `base = 0.5 * (side[3]+side[2]+side[3])`.
     Compute `area = base * (base-side[1]) * (base-`
     `side[2]) * (base-side[3])`.

     (b) Expanded pseudocode for triangular area computation

(**)   Given points (X1,Y1) and (X2,Y2):
      length = (Y2-Y1) * (Y2-Y1)+(X2-X1) * (X2-X1)

     (c) Expanded pseudocode for computation of a side's length

Figure 10.7————————————————————————————————
            Pseudocode for Example 10.3

computation will be organized as a separate procedure l a k e a r e a that operates on the three points to produce the area. The pertinent formula for the area is

$$\text{base} = \tfrac{1}{2}\,(\text{side 1} + \text{side 2} + \text{side 3})$$

$$\text{area} = \sqrt{\text{base}(\text{base} - \text{side 1})(\text{base} - \text{side 2})(\text{base} - \text{side 3})}$$

$$\text{side 1} = \sqrt{(X2 - X1)^2 + (Y2 - Y1)^2}$$

where

$$\text{side 2} = \sqrt{(X3 - X1)^2 + (Y3 - Y1)^2}$$

$$\text{side 3} = \sqrt{(X3 - X2)^2 + (Y3 - Y2)^2}$$

This closer look at the area computation is reflected in the expanded pseudocode description of Figure 10.7(b).

One of the activities listed in Figure 10.7(b) calls for the procedure to compute the lengths of the lake's three sides. More precisely, it requires the same computation to be applied three times, each time to a different pair of points. There is a clear opportunity here for another procedure (which we shall call s i d e l g t h), this one designed to compute the length between two given points on an X-Y coordinate system. (We have already used this computation in the previous section.) Since this computational service is something needed specifically by the l a k e a r e a procedure, we shall place its definition inside l a k e a r e a so that the entire process appears as a single structural entity. As a result, we can bring the simplicity of the specifications in Figure 10.7(a) directly to the corresponding main program (Figure 10.8). The processing details are submerged within the l a k e a r e a procedure, and some of *its* details are submerged further within s i d e l g t h.

10.4 DEVELOPMENT OF SUBPROGRAMS

Besides the enhancements to program clarity mentioned earlier, the use of a subprogram offers an additional advantage: Since a subprogram is a distinct structural entity, it can be developed and tested by itself, outside the context of any main program into which it ultimately might be integrated. Once the developer is satisfied that the subprogram operates properly, it can be installed as a "prefabricated" component in any program that has a use for it.

A subprogram, by its nature, cannot operate by itself. Consequently, its independent development requires a main program that will invoke it. Such a program, called a *driver*, is constructed to provide just enough support so that the subprogram can be invoked in the same way as it would be in actual usage. When the subprogram's development has been completed, the driver can be thrown away without remorse in the same way that scaffolding is torn down when a building is finished.

To illustrate the use of a driver, we shall write one for the s t r l i n e procedure of Figure 10.5(a). Bear in mind that we want to focus our attention on the procedure and not on the main program. Consequently, the

```
(****************************************************************************)
(                              EXAMPLE 10.3                              **)
(****************************************************************************)
(** THIS PROGRAM CONSISTS OF A MAIN PROGRAM AND TWO SUBPROGRAMS, ONE     **)
(** NESTED INSIDE THE OTHER. THE MAIN PROGRAM PRODUCES AND DISPLAYS      **)
(** A SERIES OF AREAS, EACH COMPUTED FROM A SET OF THREE INPUT POINTS.   **)
(** EACH TRIANGULAR AREA IS COMPUTED BY A SUBPROGRAM FROM THE THREE      **)
(** SIDES, EACH OF WHICH, IN TURN, IS COMPUTED FROM A PAIR OF POINTS     **)
(** BY A SECOND SUBPROGRAM INVOKED BY THE ONE THAT COMPUTES THE AREAS.   **)
(****************************************************************************)
PROGRAM ex1003 (INPUT,OUTPUT) ;
CONST
    blank5 = '     '  ;
    blank2 = '  '  ;
TYPE
    coordinate = (horizontal, vertical) ;
    lakepoint = ARRAY [coordinate] OF REAL  ;
VAR
    point1, point2, point3  :  lakepoint  ;
    lakename :  ARRAY [1..20] OF CHAR  ;
    area, totalarea :  REAL  :
    i, numoflakes :  INTEGER  ;
    sw :  BOOLEAN  ;

    PROCEDURE  lakearea (p1, p2, p3  :  lakepoint ; VAR a : REAL)  ;
    VAR
        side : ARRAY [1..3] OF REAL  ;
        base : REAL  ;

        PROCEDURE  sidelgth (pta, ptb : lakepoint ; VAR dist : REAL)  ;
        BEGIN
            dist := SQRT(SQR(pta[horizontal] - ptb[horizontal])
                    + SQR(pta[vertical] - ptb[vertical]))
        END  ;
    BEGIN
        sidelgth (p1, p2, side[1])  ;
        sidelgth (p1, p3, side[2])  ;
        sidelgth (p2, p3, side[3])  ;
        base := 0.5 * (side[1] + side[2] + side[3])  ;
        a := SQRT(base * (base-side[1]) * (base-side[2]) * (base-side[3]))
    END  ;
```

Figure 10.8

Program for Example 10.3

```
(******************************************************************)
(**                      THE MAIN PROGRAM                       **)
(******************************************************************)
BEGIN
    WRITELN  ;    WRITELN   ;
    sw := TRUE  ;
    numoflakes := 0  ;
    totalarea := 0.0  ;
    WHILE   sw   DO
        BEGIN
            FOR   i := 1 TO 20  DO
                READ (lakename[i])  ;
            READ (point1[horizontal],point1[vertical]),
                 (point2[horizontal],point2[vertical]),
                 (point3[horizontal],point3[vertical])  ;
            numoflakes := numoflakes + 1  ;
            lakearea (point1, point2, point3, area)  ;
            totalarea := totalarea + area  ;
            WRITELN  ;
            WRITE (blank2) ;
            FOR   i := 1 TO 20  DO
                WRITE (lakename[i])  ;
            WRITE (blank2,'(',point1[horizontal]:5:1,',',
                            point1[vertical]:5:1,')',
                  blank2,'(',point2[horizontal]:5:1,',',
                            point2[vertical]:5:1,')',
                  blank2,'(',point3[horizontal]:5:1,',',
                            point3[vertical]:5:1,')',
                  blank5,area:8:2)  ;
            WRITELN  ;
            READLN  ;
            IF   FOR   THEN sw := FALSE
        END  ;
    WRITELN  ;
    WRITELN  ;
    WRITELN ('NUMBER OF LAKES:   ',numoflakes)  ;
    WRITELN ('TOTAL LAKE AREA:   ',totalarea:12:2)  ;
    WRITELN ('END OF RUN.')
END.
```

Figure 10.8

Program for Example 10.3 (continued)

driver will have no unnecessary complications. For instance, the four values on which strline will operate simply will be assigned in the driver. The driver is shown in Figure 10.9 Note also that the driver includes simple statements for displaying the results. Thus, the procedure's behavior is revealed in a convenient, straightforward fashion.

```
PROGRAM   strdriv (INPUT, OUTPUT)   ;
VAR
    h1, h2, v1, v2, slope, intercept, seglength  :  REAL  ;

              strline procedure

BEGIN
    h1 := 1.0  ;
    v1 := 6.0  ;
    h2 := 2.0  ;
    v2 := 10.0  ;
    strline (h1, v1, h2, v2, slope, intercept, seglength)  ;
    WRITELN ('INPUT VALUES:')  ;
    WRITELN ('(H1,V1):   ', h1, v1)  ;
    WRITELN ('(H2,V2):   ', h2, v2)  ;
    WRITELN ('SLOPE:   ',slope,'INTERCEPT:   ',intercept)  ;
    WRITELN ('LINE LENGTH:   ',seglength)
END.
```

Figure 10.9

strline Procedure for Figure 10.7(a) with its Driver

Problems

1. Each of the following statements is a legal or illegal attempt to identify some kind of Pascal subprogram. For each one that is legal, indicate the number of required parameters and their respective data types. In addition, indicate the data type of the result of each FUNCTION statement. Show what is wrong with the illegal statements:

    (a) FUNCTION physmark(veloc : REAL ; n1, n2 : INTEGER) : REAL

    (b) FUNCTION findout(visc, diam, dens, veloc : REAL) : BOOLEAN

    (c) PROCEDURE trichar (c1, c2, c3 : CHAR ; n1 : INTEGER) : REAL

    (d) FUNCTION last3 (c1 : CHAR ; r1 : REAL ; n1 : INTEGER)

    (e) PROCEDURE farwt (r1, r2 : REAL ; VAR r3, VAR r4, VAR r5 : REAL)

2. Consider the following declaration section:

```
. . . . . . . . . . . . . . . . . .
VAR
    hival, lowval, range : INTEGER  ;
```

```
FUNCTION produce (value, limit : INTEGER)  :  INTEGER  ;
CONST
   factor := 3 ;
VAR
   i : INTEGER ;
BEGIN
   produce := 0 ;
   FOR  i := 1 TO limit  DO
      produce := produce + factor * (value-i)
END
. . . . . . . . . . . . . . . . . .
```

(a) What assumption does the function make about limit? Show the result(s) displayed by each of the independent sequences given below:

(b)   `range := produce (3,6) ;`
    `WRITELN (range)`

(c)   `lowval := 5 ;`
    `range := 8 + produce (lowval, hival) ;`
    `WRITELN (range)`

(d)   `lowval := 5 ;`
    `hival := 8 ;`
    `lowval := lowval - highval * produce (highval, lowval) ;`
    `WRITELN (lowval)`

(e)   `lowval := 2 ;`
    `hival := lowval + produce (lowval, 2) ;`
    `range := produce (hival, lowval) - produce (lowval, hival) ;`
    `WRITELN ('LOWVAL: ',lowval) ;`
    `WRITELN ('HIVAL: ',hival) ;`
    `WRITELN ('RANGE: ',range)`

3. Consider the following function:

```
FUNCTION vcomp (pr1, pr2, pr3 : REAL)  :  REAL;
CONST
   critval = 230.0  ;
BEGIN
   vcomp := SQRT ((SQR(pr1)-SQR(pr2)+SQR(pr3))  ;
    IF vcomp >= critval  THEN  vcomp := critval
END
```

Assuming values of 3.6 for trn, 8.0 for bks, 1.0 for adl, and 10.5 for spl, show the output values (if output is possible) resulting from each of the following independent fragments:

(a) `adl := adl * vcomp(trn, trn, trn) ;`
     `WRITELN (adl)`

(b) `adl := adl + adl * 2 * vcomp(trn+bKs+spl) ;`
     `WRITELN (adl)`

(c) `adl := trn * vcomp(4.1 * trn, adl, bsK) ;`
     `WRITELN (adl)`

(d) `bKs := bKs - vcomp(38.7, 6.6-trn, spl+1) ;`
     `WRITELN (bKs)`

(e) `adl := SQR(vcomp(1.0, trn, spl)) ;`
     `WRITELN (adl)`

(f) `vcomp(bKs, 3.3, -trn, adl) ;`
     `WRITELN (vcomp)`

(g) `adl := vcomp(bKs, -trn, 3.2) + 1.1 * vcomp(3.2,`
     `- trn, bKs) ;`
     `WRITELN (adl)`

(h) `spl := adl + 2.0 * vcomp ;`
     `WRITELN (spl)`

(i) `spl := vcomp(bKs, vcomp(2.0, spl, bKs), trn) ;`
     `WRITELN (spl)`

4. Write a function named `extremes` that operates on two integer values to produce the ratio of the larger to the smaller value, rounded to the nearest integer.

5. Rewrite the function in Problem 4 as a procedure. In addition to the result specified in that problem, the procedure is to produce the ratio of the smaller to the larger value, expressed as a percentage to the nearest tenth of a percent.

6. Generalize the function in Figure 10.4(a) so that it handles integer exponents that are either positive or negative.

7. Write a simple driver suitable for developing and testing the function prepared in Problem 6.

8. Generalize the function in Problem 6 so that it handles real as well as integer exponents.

9. Write a program that reads and processes an arbitrary number of input sets. Each input set consists of six real values: $x1$, $y1$, $x2$, $y2$, $x3$, and $y3$. Each pair of values represents a point on a rectangular coordinate system (as described in Section 10.2.2). The three points are to be processed as follows: After displaying the first two points (i.e., the first four input values) on an output line, the program is to display another line showing the slope and intercept of the straight line formed by these two points. This is followed by a third line that shows the third point and one of these three messages:

LIES ON THE LINE BETWEEN THE FIRST TWO POINTS
LIES ON THE LINE OUTSIDE THE FIRST TWO POINTS
DOES NOT LIE ON THE LINE FORMED BY THE FIRST TWO POINTS

Leave two blank lines between output sets. (*Caution:* It will be up to you to decide when a point is on the line and when it is "not quite" on the line.)

10. Modify the program in Problem 9 so that each input set now consists of the first two points (i.e., the ones defining the straight line) followed by *one or more* points, each of which is to be tested against the line. There is no indication as to how many points are to be tested against a given line, but there will be at least one. Thus, the output for each line (i.e., for each input set) will consist of the two points defining that line, a second output line showing the slope and intercept (as before) and one or more additional output lines showing each additional point along with the appropriate message. As in the previous problem, leave two blank lines between the output sets.

11. In Example 10.3, we prepared a subprogram for computing the area of a triangle from three (X,Y) points (Figure 10.8). Implied in that subprogram is the assumption that the points do not lie on the same straight line, so that there is a triangle there with some area to it. For this problem, generalize that subprogram so that, if the three points do not lie on a single line, the subprogram delivers the area. If not, the subprogram delivers an area of 0.0.

12. Write a program in which an input set consists of four real (X,Y) points (i.e., eight values). This time, the program is to use the first three points to form a triangle. (There is no guarantee that these points do not lie on a single line.) The first line of output (for each input set) is to show the three points and the area formed by the triangle (or zero if there is only a single straight line). This is followed by a second output line that shows the fourth point and one of the following messages:

LIES INSIDE THE TRIANGLE FORMED BY THE ABOVE THREE POINTS
LIES OUTSIDE THE TRIANGLE FORMED BY THE ABOVE THREE POINTS
LIES ON THE SINGLE LINE FORMED BY THE ABOVE THREE POINTS
LIES OFF THE SINGLE LINE FORMED BY THE ABOVE THREE POINTS

13. Simplify the main program in Example 10.3 (Figure 10.8) to whatever extent seems reasonable to you by converting appropriate parts of the input and output activities to separate subprograms.

14. Reorganize the program for Example 7.1 (Figure 7.2) so that the following (simpler) main program will produce the same results as the original version:

```
BEGIN
   FOR pianosize := upright TO mislabel  DO
      numsold[pianosize] := 0  ;
```

```
READLN (startyr, endyr)  ;
WHILE  NOT EOF(INPUT)  DO
   BEGIN
      READLN (serial, piano, pianowt, price,
              yrofsale, custloc[1], custloc[2])  ;
      IF  (yrofsale >= startyr) AND
          (yrofsale <= endyr)  THEN
         BEGIN
            pianosize := findit (piano)  ;
            numsold[pianosize] :=
            numsold[pianosize] + 1
         END
   END  ;
   display (startyr, endyr, numsold)  ;
   WRITELN ('END OF RUN.')
END.
```

15. Ivan's Candies, Ltd. ("candy-makers for the Czars") has two kinds of candies: Supreme, priced at $8.80 the kilo, and Oboy, priced at $12.40 the kilo. The manufacturer has agreed to mix these in any proportion so that a range of prices may be obtained. Write a subprogram named mixem that takes values for a desired weight (in kilograms) and a desired price (in dollars per kilogram) and computes the number of kilograms of each type required to achieve the specified price. An additional result, status, reports the outcome: status is 0 if the specified requirements are met; it is −1 if the desired price is impossibly low, in which case all of the weight is assigned to the Supreme type; status is 1 if the desired price is impossibly high, in which case all of the weight is assigned to the Oboy type.

16. Prepare a driver for the subprogram in Problem 15. Equip your driver with appropriate values to produce results for an inexpensive mixture, an expensive mixture, an impossibly inexpensive request, and an impossibly expensive request.

17. Under ideal conditions, the gas velocity at the exhaust end of a nozzle can be obtained as a function of the inlet conditions from the equation

$$v2 = \sqrt{\left(\frac{2gk}{k-1}\right)RT\left[1-\left(\frac{p2}{p1}\right)^{\frac{k-1}{k}}\right]+v1^2}$$

where v1 and v2 are velocities at the inlet and exit, respectively, g is the gravitational constant, k is a dimensionless thermodynamic ratio, T is the inlet temperature in degrees Rankine, p1 and p2 are inlet and outlet pressures, respectively (the units are immaterial as long as they are the same for both pressures), R is 1544/29 for air. Write a program that reads in sets of values consisting of v1, p1, p2, T, and k, and produces $v1$, T, $p2/p1$, and $v2$, with the latter expressed in both feet per second and miles per hour. The input value of $v1$ is always in miles per hour. Assume that the gas under consideration is always air, and so R need not change. T is submitted in degrees Fahrenheit.

(a) Prepare a general pseudocode description of your program. Indicate clearly those activities to be handled by subprograms.

(b) Prepare a driver for each of the subprograms defined in (a).

18. Referring to Problem 17, assume that the value for k can be determined from the formula

$$k = a0 + a1\,T + a2\,T^2$$

where $a0$ is 1.4, $a1$ is -0.00014, and $a2$ is 0.0000000032 for air. Accordingly, rewrite the program so that input consists only of $v1$, $p1$, $p2$, and T. Everything else is unchanged. How does this affect the structure of your program?

19. Write a function named numofdays that computes the number of days between two twentieth century dates submitted as month1, day1, year1 and month2, day2, year2. Remember to take leap year into account.

20. Write a suitable driver for the subprogram prepared for Problem 19.

21. The public library at Fenwick's Foothold just purchased a computer, and they are ready to automate everything. As a start, they would like a program that computes (and displays) the fines charged for overdue books. For each book, a line of input is submitted consisting of:

cardnum, the cardholder's number (a six-digit integer);
booknum, the book's identification (two letters followed by four digits, followed by a period, followed by two digits. For example: HJ0587.31)
bmnth, the month the book was borrowed (1–12)
bday, the day the book was borrowed (1–31)
byr, the year the book was borrowed (1900–2200)

After reading today's date, the program is to read and process the input of the books being returned that day. Any number of books may be returned on a given day, and any number of them may be overdue. There is no limit to the number of books that an individual may borrow, and any book in the Fenwick's Foothold library may be borrowed for 18 days. The library promises to submit all of the information about a particular borrower on consecutive lines, so that once the program has completed processing the data for a borrower, it is done with that individual. A fine of 4 cents for each extra day is imposed on an overdue book. The library is open every day of the year.

After producing a suitable set of headings, your program is to print a line for each borrower showing the borrower's identification, the number of books returned, the number overdue, and the total amount of the fine. (If none of a borrower's books were overdue, there is no need to show any output for that borrower.) After the last borrower's input has been processed, the program is to leave two blank lines, and then it is to display the number of borrowers returning overdue books that day, the number of overdue books returned, and the total amount of fines collected.

22. Now that Fenwick's Foothold is computerizing their library, they have found that other libraries are interested in buying their overdue fines program (the one specified in Problem 21). There is a chance to sell the program to the nearby village of Stodgy Swope, but a change is needed. Stodgy Swope closes their library on Christmas, July Fourth, and National Small-But-Well-Run Library Day (March Ninth). There is no fine connected with any of these days. Modify the program in Problem 21 to accommodate this change.

23. Good news travels at amazing speeds. Now, the town of Dubious Dunes wants Fenwick Foothold's program too. Again, there are differences. First of all, books whose identifications begin with the letters A through M can be taken out for 16 days, and the others go for 19 days. Second, although every overdue day counts, holiday or not, the fines are imposed differently from those in the two hamlets mentioned in the previous two problems: It is 5 cents a day for the first 10 days, 4 cents a day for the next 20 days, and 3 cents a day thereafter. Modify the program specified in either Problem 21 or 22 to accommodate these requirements.

Chapter Eleven

Behavior of Subprograms

The concepts developed and illustrated in the previous chapter enabled us to construct subprograms and use them as if they were single statements or operations. With this background we are ready to look more closely at the way a subprogram operates in Pascal's environment.

11.1 TRANSFER OF INFORMATION AMONG SUBPROGRAMS

When we set up our subprogram definitions, we included parameter lists. Then, when those subprograms were invoked, the calling expressions or statements contained corresponding lists of actual parameters consisting of constants, variables, or expressions. In this section we shall concentrate on these invoking mechanisms and on the ways in which a Pascal program and its subprograms communicate with each other.

11.1.1 Transfer by Value

When we specify an actual parameter, we activate a mechanism by which Pascal transfers that actual parameter's value to the invoked subprogram. This mechanism is known as *passing by value* or *transfer by value*. To understand this type of data transfer, it is helpful to think of it as follows: Suppose we specify a variable name as an actual parameter. That name is associated with a location containing a value, and it is this value that is copied and sent to the invoked subprogram. The location from which the value was copied is not part of the information sent. As a result, the invoked subprogram cannot change the contents of that location because it does not "know" the address.

The same mechanism applies to the use of constant values for actual parameters. Since the transfer of actual values is completely detached from the production of those values, Pascal does not "care" where such a value comes from or how it was produced. Thus, when we specify a constant as an actual parameter, it makes no difference (to the program) that the value is produced "on the spot," so to speak. For instance, if we were to invoke the SQRT function by writing a statement such as

```
freeval := SQRT (325.87)
```

the value 325.87 would be generated and passed to SQRT for processing. As expected, the function would return a value equal to the square root of 325.87, and that value would be stored in freeval.

A more extensive expression is handled no differently. Thus, if we invoke the SQR function in the statement

```
magnif := SQR(x-2.2 * y)
```

the values are copied from locations x and y and used to produce a single number, and *that* value, in turn, is delivered to SQR. The function, as before, has no access to the variables' locations. Consequently, if we write a subprogram in which we attempt to change an actual parameter passed by value, the Pascal compiler will reject the statement in which the attempt appears.

11.1.2 Transfer by Reference

When we attach the VAR specification to a formal parameter, Pascal associates that parameter with its *pass-by-reference* or *transfer-by-reference* mechanism. This means that when a corresponding actual parameter is named during a subprogram's invocation, Pascal supplies the *location* of that parameter to the invoked subprogram. Since the subprogram now "knows" where the value is stored, it can obtain the value from its source. More importantly, *it can change that value* simply by assigning a new one.

The conceptual difference between the pass-by-value and pass-by-reference mechanisms makes it easier to clarify the intended use of the parameters in our subprograms: *Generally, input items are passed by value, and output destinations are passed by reference.* (We have already seen that grouping the input items next to each other in the parameter list also helps clarify the subprogram's description.)

Although the guideline just stated for the transfer of information sounds straightforward enough, there may be exceptions because the pass-by-value mechanism requires more storage than the pass-by-reference mechanism. Delivery of a variable's value (rather than its location) means that the value has to be copied and put someplace so that the subprogram can work with it. This is no big deal when a small number of values are involved. However, if a subprogram is designed to process a large input array or any other appreciable data collection, the additional storage may make the resulting program too large for the processor. Thus, there are times when the programmer might attach the VAR specification to an input parameter, even though there is no intent to change its value in the subprogram. This practice should be considered an emergency measure. If it is followed, the programmer must make sure that the input data, in fact, are not changed. Pascal gives up this responsibility when the programmer uses the pass-by-reference mechanism.

Example 11.1

First Class Science, Ltd. wants to conduct a series of tests on a new chemical. In each test, acidity readings are to be taken on 21 samples of liquid. For this initial investigation, they want a program that prepares the median, mean, and standard deviation for each group of 21 readings. (The median is the value such that there is an equal number of values above and below that value.) There may be any number of tests in a run. Input for a test consists of an integer representing the test number, followed by 21 readings. (A typical reading is 7.84.) Output for each test is to consist of two lines, the first of which gives the test number and the second shows the median, mean, and standard deviation. There will be two blank lines between adjacent test results. After the last test has been processed, the program will leave three blank lines and display a summary giving the number of tests processed, the highest median value, the highest mean value, the lowest median value, the lowest mean value, and their respective test numbers. First Class Science assures us that the median and mean values will be unique.

If *acidity* is an individual reading ($i = 1, 2, ..., 21$), the mean, *avgacidity*, is computed as

$$avgacidity = \frac{\sum_{i=1}^{21} acidity_i}{21}$$

and *stdevacid*, the standard deviation, is computed as

$$stdevacid = \sqrt{\frac{\sum_{i=1}^{21} (acidity_i - avgacidity)^2}{21 - 1}}$$

[This formula for standard deviation requires all 21 readings to be available at the same time. We need all 21 in any case so we can compute the median. The median will be found simply by sorting the 21 values in ascending order and then taking the middle value (i.e., `acidity[11]`).]

We shall organize the processing as shown in Figure 11.1. The overall activity is a loop that cycles once for each test. During that cycle:

1. The test number and the 21 readings are brought in.
2. The 21 acidity readings are sorted in ascending order.
3. Values for the mean and standard deviation are computed and the median value is assigned.
4. The output for that test is displayed.
5. The overall run is updated by adding 1 to the number of tests processed and replacing the highest or lowest median and/or mean values as appropriate.

The summary information is displayed after this loop has gone through the necessary cycles (controlled by the end-of-file condition).

Activities 2 to 4 will be implemented as separate subprograms to keep the main program simple. These are shown in Figure 11.2 as parts of the overall program. The transfer of the 21 readings is set up conveniently by defining a data type named testgroup and then specifying that type to be one of the formal parameters for sortrdg and mstdev, the procedures for sorting the readings and computing the mean and standard deviation, respectively. Note (Figure 11.2) that the mean value and test numbers for

Define variables for test number, test readings, median, mean, standard deviation, test counter, and maximum and minimum values and respective test numbers for median and mean.
　　Description of sorting procedure.
　　Description of computations for mean and standard deviation.
　　Description of computations for updating the maximum and/or minimum median and mean values.
WHILE there is input to process:
　　Read the test number.
　　Read the 21 test results.
　　Sort the test results in ascending order.
　　Compute the mean and standard deviation for the test results.
　　Determine the median value.
　　Replace the minimum or maximum values if appropriate.
　　Increment the test counter.
　　Display the median, mean, and standard deviation for this test.
ENDWHILE
Display the number of tests, maximum and minimum median values and corresponding test numbers, and maximum and minimum mean values and corresponding test numbers.
Stop.

Figure 11.1

Organization of the Program for Example 11.1

the current test (named thismean and thistest, respectively) in up-date's formal parameter list are passed by value because they are used by update as input. These same items are passed by reference in mstdev

```
PROGRAM ex1101 (INPUT, OUTPUT)    ;
CONST
   numofreads = 21 ;
TYPE
   testgroup = ARRAY [1..numofreads] OF REAL ;
VAR
   acidity : testgroup ;
   median, avgacidity, stdevacid, maxmed, maxmean,
                                minmed, minmean : REAL ;
   testid, numoftests, maxmedtest, minmedtest,
                    i, minmedtest, minmntest ; INTEGER ;
   sw : BOOLEAN ;

PROCEDURE  sortrd (VAR rds : testgroup) ;
VAR
   track1, track2 : INTEGER ;
   temp : REAL ;
   keepsorting : BOOLEAN ;
BEGIN
   track1 := numofreads ;
   keepsorting := TRUE ;
   WHILE (track1 >= 2) AND (keepsorting = TRUE) DO
      BEGIN
         keepsorting := FALSE ;
         FOR  track2 := 1 TO track1-1   DO
            IF  rds[track2] > rds[track2+1]   THEN
               BEGIN
                  temp := rds[track2+1] ;
                  rds[track2+1] := rds[track2] ;
                  rds[track2] := temp ;
                  keepsorting := TRUE
               END ;
         track1 := track 1 - 1
      END
   END ;

PROCEDURE mstdev (rds : testgroup ; VAR thismean : REAL ;
                                    VAR thisdev : REAL) ;
VAR
   index : INTEGER ;
   sumrd, sumsqr : REAL ;
```

Figure 11.2

Program for Example 11.1

```
BEGIN
   sumrd := 0.0 ;
   sumsqr := 0.0 ;
   FOR  index := 1 TO numofreads  DO
       sumrd := sumrd + rds[index] ;
   thismean := sumrd/numofreads  ;
   FOR  index := 1 TO numofreads  DO
       sumsqr := sumsqr + SQR(rds[index]-thismean) ;
   thisdev := SQRT(sumsqr/(numofreads-1))
END  ;


PROCEDURE update (thismed, thismean: REAL ; thistest : INTEGER;
                  VAR hmd : REAL ; VAR hmn : REAL; VAR lmd : REAL ;
                  VAR lmn : REAL ; VAR himedtest : INTEGER ;
                  VAR himeantest : INTEGER ; VAR lowmedtest : INTEGER ;
                  VAR lowmeantest : INTEGER) ;
BEGIN
   IF   thismed > hmd  THEN
       BEGIN
          hmd := thismed ;
          himedtest := thistest
       END ;
   IF   thismean > hmn  THEN
       BEGIN
          hmn := thismean ;
          himeantest := thistest
       END ;
   IF   thismed < lmd  THEN
       BEGIN
          lmd := thismed ;
          lowmedtest := thistest
       END ;
   IF   thismean < lmn  THEN
       BEGIN
          lmn := thismean ;
          lowmeantest := thistest
       END
   END  ;



(                    THE MAIN PROGRAM
BEGIN
   numoftest := 0 ;     maxmed := -200.0 ;   minmed := 200.0 ; sw := TRUE ;
   maxmean := -200.0 ;   minmean := 200.0 ;
   WHILE  sw  DO
```

Figure 11.2

Program for Example 11.1 (continued)

```
BEGIN
   READLN (testid) ;
   FOR i := 1 TO numofreads DO
     READ (acidity[i])   ;
   READLN ;
   sortrds(acidity) ;
   mstdev (acidity, avgacidity, stdevacid) ;
   median := acidity[11] ;
   update (median, avgacidity, testid, maxmed, maxmean, minmed,
           minmean, maxmedtest, maxmeantest, minmedtest, minmeantest) ;
   numoftests := numoftests + 1 ;
   WRITELN ;
   WRITELN ('TEST NO.: ',testid) ;
   WRITELN ('MEDIAN ACIDITY; ',median:7:3,'MEAN ACIDITY: ',
            avgacidity:7:3,' STD DEV.: ', stdevacid:7:3) ;
   WRITELN ;
   IF  EOF  THEN sw := FALSE
   END ;
 WRITELN ;  WRITELN ;
 WRITELN ('SUMMARY:') ;
 WRITELN ('NO. OF TESTS THIS RUN: ',numoftests) ;
 WRITELN ('TEST NUMBER ',maxmedtest,'HAD A HIGH MEDIAN OF ',maxmed:7:3) ;
 WRITELN ('TEST NUMBER ',maxmeantest,'HAD A HIGH MEAN OF ',maxmean:7:3) ;
 WRITELN ('TEST NUMBER ',minmedtest,'HAD A LOW MEDIAN OF ',minmed:7:3) ;
 WRITELN ('TEST NUMBER ',minmeantest,'HAD A LOW MEAN OF ',minmean:7:3) ;
 WRITELN ('END OF RUN.')
END.
```

Figure 11.2

Program for Example 11.1 (continued)

because that is where their values are computed and assigned. maxmed, minmed, maxmean, minmean, maxmedtest, minmedtest, maxmntest, and minmntest are set up for passing by reference because they are subject to change. (Of course, no more than four of these values may change during any invocation, but we do not know which four, if any, will change.)

Since acidity is passed by value, all 21 readings are duplicated for sortrds's use and again for mstdev's use. The same would be true if acidity were to consist of 14, 232 or 10,000 readings. This duplication can be avoided by changing the formal parameter rds in the procedure mstdev to a VAR parameter:

```
. . . . . . . . . . . . . . . . . . . . . . . . . . . . .
PROCEDURE mstdev (VAR rds : testgroup ; VAR thismean :
                  REAL ;VAR thisdev : REAL)
. . . . . . . . . . . . . . . . . . . . . . . . . . . . .
```

A similar change is introduced in the `sortrds` procedure:

```
· · · · · · · · · · · · · · · · · · · · · · · ·
PROCEDURE   sortrds (VAR rds : testgroup)
· · · · · · · · · · · · · · · · · · · · · · · ·
```

Now, invocation of `sortrds` or `mstdev` will deliver `acidity`'s location. There is no change in the output. (As far as the observer is concerned, there is no apparent change in the program's behavior either.)

11.1.3 Subprograms as Parameters

We have already seen that a subprogram can invoke other subprograms. In Figure 1.6(a), for instance, the procedure `strline` uses `SQR` and `SQRT` to prepare its results. Every time `strline` is invoked, it invokes the same functions as part of its processing.

There are occasions, however, when a subprogram needs to use one of several other subprograms, but we cannot know which one it is until the first subprogram is invoked. Pascal provides this flexibility by accepting subprogram names as parameters. This feature offers a convenience in certain special situations. These occur relatively rarely, so that we shall restrict ourselves to a brief discussion of the basic syntax.

Functions as Parameters   Figure 10.3 showed us that one type of formal parameter can be built by attaching the word `FUNCTION` to the parameter's name. (The syntax is repeated for convenience in Figure 11.3.) This identifies the parameter as a function parameter. When used inside the subprogram, the parameter indicates that some function will be invoked when that subprogram executes. The specific function, of course, is not known until its name is suppled as an actual parameter. Note that we need to specify the data type returned by the function as part of the formal parameter's description.

For example, consider the function described in Figure 11.4. `adjust` uses its two value parameters to build an expression which, in turn, provides a value for another function as yet unnamed. The function parameter is represented by the name `fsub`. Pascal "knows" that `fsub` is not an actual function because the `FUNCTION` designator in `adjust`'s first statement defines it as a formal parameter. Now, suppose `r`, `p`, and `q` are `REAL` variables with values in them. The statement

```
r := r + adjust(SQRT, p, q)
```

invokes `adjust` with `SQRT`, `p`, and `q` as the three actual parameters. Accordingly, `adjust` assigns the appropriate values to `minv` and `maxv`, after which it computes `r` as

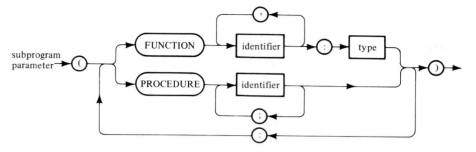

Figure 11.3

Syntax for Subprogram Parameters

```
r + 2.207/SQRT(minv+0.5 * maxv)
```

and the result is assigned to r. Another invocation, say,

```
r := r + adjust(LN, p, q)
```

forces adjust to invoke the function LN this time, so that the value assigned to r is computed as

```
r + 2.207/LN(minv + 0.5 * maxv)
```

Of course, programmer-defined functions also may be used as actual function parameters.

Procedures as Parameters   When we attach the word PROCEDURE to a formal parameter's name (as is shown in Figure 11.5), we define it as being

```
FUNCTION   adjust   (FUNCTION fsub : REAL ; pval, qval : REAL) : REAL ;
VAR
    minv, maxv : REAL ;
    minv := pval  ;
    maxv := qval  ;
BEGIN
    IF   pval > qval   THEN
        BEGIN
            maxv := qval ;
            minv := pval
        END   ;
    adjust := 2.207/fsub(minv+0.5 * maxv)
END
```

Figure 11.4

Use of a Function Parameter in a Subprogram

a procedure parameter. This indicates that when the subprogram executes, it, in turn, will call a procedure that is named as an actual parameter by the invoking program.

To illustrate, consider the program skeleton shown in Figure 11.5. As part of the main program's declaration section we see three subprogram

```
PROGRAM  procparam (INPUT,OUTPUT) ;
VAR
    y, in1, in2, meas1, meas2, rslt  :   REAL  ;

    PROCEDURE   fixup (PROCEDURE eval ; v1, v2 : REAL ;
                       VAR v3, VAR v4, VAR v5 : REAL)  ;
    BEGIN
        IF   v1 > 1.5 * v2   THEN
            eval (v1, v2, v3, v4)
        ELSE
            eval (v2, v1, v3, v4)  ;
        v5 := SQRT(SQR(v3) + SQR(v4))
        END ;

    PROCEDURE  adj1(p1, p2 : REAL ; VAR p3, VAR p4 : REAL)  ;
    BEGIN
        p3 := LN(SIN(p1) + 2 * COS(p2))  ;
        p4 := EXP(SQRT(p1) + 1.3 * SQRT(p2))
        END  ;

    PROCEDURE  adj2(q1, q2 : REAL ; VAR q3, VAR q4 : REAL)  ;
    BEGIN
        q3 := 0.87 * LN(SIN(0.94 * q1) - 1.76 * COS(1.08 * q2))  ;
        q4 := LN(SQRT(EXP(q1+q2) + SQR(q1-q2)))
        END
            . . . . . . . . . . . . . . . . . . . . . .
            . . . . . . . . . . . . . . . . . . . . . .
    BEGIN
            . . . . . . . . . . . . . . . . . . .
            . . . . . . . . . . . . . . . . . . .
        IF  in1+in2 < y   THEN
            fixup(adj1,in1,in2,meas1,meas2,rslt)
        ELSE
            fixup(adj2,in1,in2,meas1,meas2,rslt)
            . . . . . . . . . . . . . . . . . . .
        WRITELN (rslt)
            . . . . . . . . . . . . .
    END.
```

Figure 11.5

Use of Procedure Parameters in a Subprogram

definitions. The two procedures adj1 and adj2 are straightforward enough. fixup is a procedure whose first formal parameter, eval, is a procedure parameter. Thus, when fixup is invoked, the first member of the actual parameter list will name a specific procedure that fixup will invoke. An example of such an invocation is seen further down, in the main program. Each alternative activity in the IF statement is a call to fixup: In one case, fixup is directed to call the procedure adj as part of its processing; on the other hand, if the outcome of the test is FALSE, the procedure fixup still is invoked, but this time it is directed to use the procedure adj2.

11.2 RECOGNITION OF NAMES IN PROGRAMS

When we declare a variable in a Pascal program, we make that variable available to different parts of the program. Thus far, our movement of variable values (or their addresses) between blocks might leave the impression that once a variable is declared, we can refer to it anywhere in the program and it will be recognized. This is true only under certain organizational conditions. When these conditions are not met, Pascal restricts a variable's availability to carefully defined parts of the program. The next two sections discuss these rules and their application.

11.2.1 Scope of Variables

Declaration of a variable establishes a range of statements over which that variable's name is recognized. This is known as the variable's *scope*. The general rule that defines the scope of a Pascal variable can be stated simply: *A variable is recognized throughout the entire block in which it is declared.* This is true regardless of the number of blocks that may be contained in the block in which the variable is declared. To illustrate, consider the program outline shown in Figure 11.6. Organizationally, the program consists of an outer block (associated with the name P1) containing a block named P11. Note that the REAL variable bfac declared in the outer block does not appear as a formal parameter in P11's list, nor does it appear as an actual parameter in P1's invocation statement. Yet, its appearance in assignment statements in both blocks is legal. Since P11 is contained in P1, the program has no trouble finding the location associated with the name bfac and changing the value there. The same rule, when applied to the variable stnd, makes that variable available throughout P11 but nowhere else. stnd is said to be *local* to P11, and bfac is said to be *global*.

The same is true for the more complicated organization outlined in Figure 11.7: The nesting is more extensive here in that outer block P2 contains block P21 which, in turn, contains another block P211. By taking a look at the declarations and applying the rule stated earlier, we can determine each variable's scope:

```
PROGRAM  P1 (INPUT,OUTPUT)
    ...................
VAR
    asx, trn, stc, frb, bfac : REAL
    .....................
    PROCEDURE P11 (v1, v2 : REAL ; VAR v3, VAR v4 : REAL) ;
    VAR
        stnd : REAL
        ................
    BEGIN
        ................
        bfac := bfac + 2.5
        ................
    END

    ...................
BEGIN
    ....................
    bfac := 17.0
    ...................
    P11 (asx, trn, stc, frb)
    ...................
END.
```

Figure 11.6 A Program with Global and Local Declarations

1. Since ꟼvar is delcared in the outer block, its scope extends over the entire program. Thus, it is legal (as Figure 11.7 shows) to read ꟼvar's value in the main program and then to use it as a term in blocks P21 and P211.

2. Variables b1 and b2 are declared in block P21, thereby defining their scope as being that entire block, including the block P211 contained in it. Consequently, we can read values for b1 and b2 in block P1 and then use those values in P211. Note that we *cannot* use them in that part of the main program that is not inside P21.

3. Variables w1 and w2, having been declared in P211, are local to P211 and cannot appear outside of it. In fact, w1 and w2 exist only when P211 is invoked. As soon as P211 completes its processing, w1 and w2 disappear, to be re-created only when P211 is invoked again.

4. The variable named emuk is introduced in Figure 11.7 to emphasize the difference between global and local variables. Note that emuk is declared in P2 and in P211. These are two different emuks. The one declared in P2 is recognized in all of P2 and P21 except for the block P211. The one declared in P211 is recognized only in P211 and nowhere else. Thus, the assignment

```
PROGRAM   P2 (INPUT,OUTPUT)
    ................
VAR
    qvar, ctr, mvb, cvac, Pmtr, emuK  :   REAL
    ................
    PROCEDURE   P21 (r1, r2 : REAL ; VAR r3, VAR r4 : REAL) ;
    VAR
        b1, b2 : REAL
        ................
        PROCEDURE   P211 (t1 : REAL ; VAR t2, VAR t3 : REAL)   ;
        VAR
            w1, w2, emuK : REAL
            ...............
        BEGIN
            READLN (w1, w2)
            ...............
            emuK := 0.0  ;
            t3 := w1 + b1 - qvar
            ...............
        END
        ...............
    BEGIN
        ...............
        READLN (b1, b2)
        ...............
        r3 := b1 + SQRT(qvar)   ;
        P211 (b2, r3, r4)
        ...............
    END
    ...............
BEGIN
    emuK := 24.0  ;
    READLN (qvar, ctr, mvb)
    ...............
    P21, (ctr, mvb, cvac, Pmtr)
    ...............
    WRITELN (qvar, ctr, mvb, cvac, Pmtr)
    ...............
END.
```

Figure 11.7 ——————————————————————————

Program Organization with Nested Subprograms

```
emuK := 0.0
```

in block P211 refers inevitably to the local emuK and has no effect on the global emuK, whose value remains 24.0. No sensible programmer would use the same name for two different items. However, it is helpful to know and understand the rule governing the scope of such duplicate names for the following reason: There are cases where we may be building a program in which we wish to incorporate a subprogram obtained from some external source. Since the names used in that subprogram are generally not within our control, we could end up with the kind of name duplication seen for emuk in Figure 11.7. Pascal's mechanisms for protecting local names makes it possible for such situations to be handled consistently.

Another simple organizational rule governs the relationships among the blocks in a program: Although blocks can be nested to any level, a block may invoke only those blocks immediately "below" it. In Figure 11.7, for example, the main program may invoke P21 but not P211. Block P21 may invoke only P211, and P211, sad to say, may invoke no one.

11.2.2 Why Use Parameters?

Take a look at the two little programs in Figure 11.8. It is obvious that they both perform the same computations. It is also clear (now that we have discussed the scope of variables) that both programs will produce the same results when given the same input values. Since that is the case, why complicate the subprogram definition by including a formal parameter list? All that seems to do is to obligate us to include an actual parameter list when we invoke the subprogram. Why not simplify things and write our programs as in Figure 11.8's second version, without a parameter list?

The advantages of one organizational approach versus the other depend on the particular circumstances. Use of a parameter list admittedly tends to complicate both the definition and invocation of a subprogram. However, it makes that subprogram more flexible since we can invoke it with different actual parameters each time. Moreover, the use of a parameter list gives the programmer direct control over those variables whose values can or cannot be changed by an invoked subprogram. (Recall that a variable whose value is to be used but not changed by a subprogram is easily protected by specifying it as a value parameter.) Such protection is not available from Pascal without the parameter mechanism. When we eliminate the parameter list, we simplify the statements in exchange for a more rigid subprogram which will operate only on the global variables named in its processing statements. Thus, in Figure 11.8's second version, vctradd will compute the vector sum only of the two variables vside1 and vside2.

If the computations performed by a subprogram are extensive and/or complicated, and the processing is expected to be useful above and beyond

```
PROGRAM   h1  (INPUT,OUTPUT)   ;
VAR
    vside1,  vside2,  vsum : REAL ;

    PROCEDURE   vctradd (v1,  v2 : REAL ;  VAR rslt : REAL)   ;
    BEGIN
        rslt := SQRT(SQR(v1)+SQR(v2))
    END  ;

BEGIN
    READLN (vsdie1,  vside2)   ;
    WHILE   NOT EOF(INPUT)  DO
    BEGIN
        vctradd(vside1,  vside2,  vsum)   ;
        WRITELN (vside1,  vside2,  vsum)   ;
        READLN (vside1,  vside2)
    END  ;
    WRITELN (`END OF RUN.')
END.
```

(a) Subprogram organization with a parameter list

```
PROGRAM   h2  (INPUT,OUTPUT)   ;
VAR
    vside1,  vside2,  vsum : REAL ;

    PROCEDURE   vctradd   ;
    BEGIN
        vsum := SQRT(SQR(vside1) + SQR(vside2))
    END  ;

BEGIN
    READLN (vside1,  vside2)   ;
    WHILE   NOT EOF(INPUT)  DO
        BEGIN
            vctradd
            WRITELN (vside1,  vside2,  vsum)   ;
            READLN (vside1,  vside2)
        END  ;
    WRITELN (`END OF RUN.')
    END.
```

(b) Subprogram organization without a parameter list

Figure 11.8

Alternative Subprogram Organizations

the context of a single program or application, there is good reason to design that subprogram with a parameter list. Then the statements can be lifted and placed in any program that needs them without having to change anything. (Pascal's extensive collection of built-in functions and procedures is an obvious example in which this policy is applied.) On the other hand, processing that is specific to a particular collection of variables in a particular program lends itself to organization as a subprogram without a parameter list. For example, if we have a program that repeatedly reads and processes sets of values for the same variables, the input and initial examination of the data are likely activities for a subprogram without parameters.

The criteria for using or avoiding a parameter list are not clear-cut. Consequently, it is impossible to draw up a set of well-defined rules for all occasions. Instead, the programmer is well advised to examine each situation and make his or her choice accordingly.

11.3 RECURSIVE SUBPROGRAMS

When we set up syntax diagrams for Pascal's language components, we found it convenient, on occasion, to use recursive definitions. The consistency of such definitions was established in Chapter 2, where we saw that we can construct a recursive definition as long as we have a way of describing the object without using that same object in the description.

Recursion also can be applied to certain computational processes. A recursive process is one that uses itself to carry out the intended activities. For example, let us look at the process for computing n!, the factorial value for the positive integer n. One way to describe this computation is to say

$$n! = n(n-1)(n-2)(n-3) \ldots (3)(2)(1)$$

Another way to specify this computation is to describe it recursively:

$$n! = n(n-1)!$$
$$1! = 1$$

This says that we can compute n! by first computing $(n-1)!$. More significantly for our discussion here, it implies further that we can compute $(n-1)!$ by first computing $(n-2)!$. $(n-2)!$, in turn, can be produced from $(n-3)!$, and so on, until we have reached a number small enough (i.e., 1) so that further reduction is not needed. Then, we can work our way back up again through the values until we obtain the result we want.

For example, suppose n is 5. Then,

$$5! = 5(4!)$$
$$4! = 4(3!)$$
$$3! = 3(2!)$$
$$2! = 2(1!) = 2(1) = 2$$

Now, having reached a stopping point and obtained a factorial value, we can use that value as a basis for completing the computations:

$$3! = 3(2) = 6$$
$$4! = 4(6) = 24$$
$$5! = 5(24) = 120$$

Why go through all this intricacy? It is good that you asked. There are many instances where the representation of a process in recursive form is simpler or more "natural" than an alternative expression. (The recursive form for factorials does not offer a particularly dramatic simplification; however, it is a useful vehicle for introducing recursive forms and their implementation.)

11.3.1 Recursive Processes as Subprograms

Just as a recursive syntax definition must include a logical "escape hatch," it is necessary for a recursive algorithm to include a control mechanism that limits the level of recursion in some orderly way. In our factorial example, this "logical brake," so to speak, is applied by preventing a factorial calculation of any number less than 1. Consequently, when the algorithm is represented as a subprogram, the control mechanism must be stated explicitly so that every situation is handled properly.

We can see how this looks by implementing the recursive factorial algorithm as a Pascal function [Figure 11.9(a)]. [A nonrecursive version is included in Figure 11.9(b).] There are two controls at work here: The first of these prevents any factorial computations at all if the argument's value is negative. Should such a situation occur, the computations are bypassed and the function returns a value of zero to indicate an erroneous (i.e., meaningless) invocation. Incidentally, the need for this mechanism can be avoided if we were to define a data type (let us name it positiveinteger) as follows:

```
TYPE
    positiveinteger = 0..MAXINT
```

Then, if the FUNCTION statement were to say

```
FUNCTION  factr (num : INTEGER) : INTEGER ;
BEGIN
   IF  num < 0  THEN
      factr := 0
   ELSE
      BEGIN
         factr := 1 ;
         IF  num >= 2  THEN
            factr := num * factr(num-1)
      END
END
```

(a) Recursive subprogram for factorial computation

```
FUNCTION  factr  (num : INTEGER) : INTEGER ;
VAR
   i : INTEGER ;
BEGIN
   IF  num < 0  THEN
      factr := 0
   ELSE
      BEGIN
         factr := 1 ;
         IF  num >= 2  THEN
            factr := i * factr
      END
END
```

(b) Conventional (nonrecursive) subprogram for factorial computation

Figure 11.9

Subprograms for Factorial Computation

```
FUNCTION factr (num : positiveinteger) : positiveinteger
```

the check for an appropriate value would be built in automatically.

The second control mechanism limits the recursive computation to a minimum value of 2: After initializing the function value to 1 (which is the value for 0! or 1!), further processing is allowed only as long as the argument exceeds 1.

Strictly speaking, there is another problem that the function in Figure 11.9 does not address: In standard Pascal implementations, MAXINT is determined by the inherent capacity of the specific processor being used. The ceiling thus imposed on the value of factr limits num to 7 for 16-bit processors and 12 for 32-bit machines. (Some Pascal implementations, such as UCSD Pascal, include extended integer capabilities, in which case the factorial computation actually may be useful.)

11.3.2. Operation of Recursive Subprograms

The concept described earlier, i.e., working down through a series of recursive invocations and then working back up in reverse order, applies directly in recursive subprograms. Its success is based on the idea that each time a subprogram invokes itself, that subprogram is activated anew. This means that, at any time, there may be several such activations for a subprogram, each with its own set of argument values and data areas for computed results. Each activation is temporarily suspended, somewhere between its beginning and its conclusion. The only activation that is running is the one triggered by the most recent invocation. If it invokes itself again, a new activation is triggered, and the invoking one is suspended. Sooner or later (if the process is implemented properly), a subprogram will invoke itself, and this last invocation will run to its conclusion. As a result, it will be deactivated (not suspended), its designated storage areas will "disappear," and its result(s) will be delivered to the activation that invoked it. That activation now can continue and, when it concludes, the same type of deactivation/return will occur, thereby allowing the previous invocation to conclude. In this way, the cycle eventually reaches the top level (i.e., the invocation from the main program that started the recursion in the first place) and the process is completed.

Now we shall apply this mechanism to our factorial example by following the course of events for an argument of 5. Let us say that v n u m is suitably declared and the initial invocation of f a c t r occurs in the statement

```
vnum := factr(5)
```

As a result, f a c t r is activated. Let us call this activation level 1. Looking at the subprogram in Figure 11.9(a), we see that the initial I F test fails, so that f a c t r is initialized to 1. Since the argument given to this activation is >=2 (it is 5), the second I F test passes, and f a c t r invokes itself. This means that activation level 1 is suspended and a new activation level 2 is running. This new activation has been given an argument of 4 (i.e., one less than the previous argument). Note that activation level 1 has been suspended in the midst of a computation. When it resumes control later on, it will receive a value which will then be multiplied by 5 and the result will be assigned to v n u m.

Now activation level 2 starts, fails the first I F test, initializes its function value (a separate one, remember), passes the second I F test, and proceeds. In doing so, *it* invokes itself, so now we have activation 3, operating on an argument of 3 (one less than the argument given to the previous invocation). The same thing happens again: Activation 3 invokes itself, triggering activation 4 with an argument of 2. This activation invokes itself, so that it is activation 5 that is running (with an argument of 1), and the previous four activations are suspended, each waiting to receive a value so that it can conclude.

Activation 5, because of its argument, will not pass the second IF test. Consequently, it will *not* produce another invocation; instead, it concludes, reactivating level 4 and returning a value of 1 to it. This allows level 4 to conclude by performing the multiplication and producing a function value (2) which is delivered to the newly rekindled activation 3. This level now can conclude and, in doing so, delivers a value of 6 to the level that invoked it, and so on, until level 1 is the only one left. It takes the 24 given to it by the recently departed level 2, multiplies it by 5, assigns the result to vnum, and that is that.

11.3.3 Pascal's Support of Recursion

Another look at Figure 11.9(a) shows that, aside from the fact that factr invokes itself, there is nothing special in the statement to earmark the subprogram as being recursive. Nothing was omitted; as far as Pascal is concerned, *all subprograms are inherently recursive*. If the programmer chooses not to write a recursive subprogram, fine. However, if recursion is used, it is up to the programmer to make sure that the subprogram can stop chasing itself when it is time for it to stop chasing itself.

Problems ————————————————

1.   Consider the following program skeleton:

```
PROGRAM c11p1 (INPUT,OUTPUT) ;
CONST
   octo = 8 ;
VAR
   c , x , y , z : INTEGER ;
      . . . . . . . . . . .
   FUNCTION  zmake (a1 , a2 , a3 : INTEGER) : INTEGER;
   VAR
      pr : INTEGER ;
   BEGIN
      pr := SQR (a2-a3) ;
      zmake := a1 * pr
   END ;
```

```
BEGIN
    READLN (c, x, y) ;
        ...............
```

statement including invocation(s) of zmake

```
    WRITELN (z) ;
        .............
END.
```

Show the value produced by the WRITELN statement for each of the following:

- (a) input: 3 − 4 7
       statement: z := octo * zmake(c, x, y)
- (b) input: 3 − 4 7
       statement: z := 6 + zmake (c-5, 2 * x, y)
- (c) input: 4 8 2
       statement: z := 2 * zmake(x-octo, c-2 * x, 5)
- (d) input: 4 2 8
       statement: z := zmake(6, 4) + 12
- (d) input: −3 0 4
       statement: z := zmake (c, octo, x) + zmake (y, c, zmake(x, y, c))

2. Here is another program skeleton:

```
PROGRAM c11p2 (INPUT, OUTPUT) ;
CONST
    quatro = 4 ;
VAR
    p, u, r, s, t, z, : INTEGER ;
        .............
    PROCEDURE cp1 (i1, i2, i3, VAR o1, VAR o2, VAR o3 : INTEGER) ;
    VAR
      t1 : INTEGER ;
    FUNCTION zmake (i1, i2, i3) INTEGER) : INTEGER;
    VAR
        b : INTEGER ;
    BEGIN
        b := SQR(i2-i3) ;
        zmake := i1 * b
        END ;
```

```
    BEGIN
        t1  :=  zmake (i1, i2, i3) ;
        o1  :=  i1 + t1 ;
        o2  :=  i1 - t1 ;
        o3  :=  SQRT(SQR(o1) + SQR(o2))
    END ;
BEGIN
    READLN (r, s, t) ;
      . . . . . . . . .

            statement invoking cp1

            . . . . . . . . . .
            WRITELN (p, v, z)
        END.
```

Show the results displayed by the WRITELN statement in each of the following situations:

(a) input: 10 −2 4
   statement: cp1 (r, s, t, p, v, z)

(b) input: 2 2 2
   statement: cp1 (r, t, s, v, p, z)

(c) input: 2 0 −4
   statement: cp1 (r−quatro, s−t, t−r, z, v, p)

(d) input: 8 10 4
   statement: cp1 (quatro, r−s, (r−s) * p, 6, t, quatro)

(e) input: 16 8 4
   statement: cp1 (3 * quatro−r, p, s, p, v, z−4)

3. A program consists of the procedures shown in the box on p. 253.

   Write the appropriate declaration sections to produce each of the following situations:

   (a) x is an integer variable recognized everywhere;
       y is a real variable recognized only in p12;
       z is a real variable recognized only in p2.

   (b) x is a real variable recognized everywhere but p12;
       y is a real variable recognized everywhere but p11 and p12;
       num is an integer recognized in mp but not in p1 or p2.

   (c) x is a real variable recognized in p11;
       x is a (separate) real variable recognized in p1 but not in p11 or p12;
       1tr is a character variable recognized in p2;
       1tr is a boolean variable recognized in p1 but not in p11;
       1tr is a character variable recognized wherever the other two variables named 1tr are not recognized.

```
PROGRAM  mP (INPUT,OUTPUT)
              declarations
     PROCEDURE  P1...................
                 declarations
          PROCEDURE  P11.............
                      declarations
          BEGIN
       processing
          END ;

          PROCEDURE  P12...........
                      declarations
          BEGIN
                    processing
          END ;

          BEGIN

                 processing

          END ;

          PROCEDURE  P2...........
                   declarations
          BEGIN
                    processing
          END ;

 BEGIN

    processing

 END .
```

4. If we write the formula for the polynomial P(x) in the following form:

$$P(x) = A_0 x^n + A_1 x^{n-1} + A_2 x^{n-2} + \ldots + A_{n-1} x + A^n$$

We can conveniently isolate and factor out an x from the remaining terms, giving us

$$P(x) = A_n + x(A_0 x^{n-1} + A^1 x^{n-2} + \ldots + A^{n-1})$$

Note that the expression inside the parentheses is another polynomial having one term less (and being one degree lower) than the original one. Given this fine start, write a recursive function named poly with degree, xvar, and coefficients as the formal parameters. Limit the maximum value of degree to 8. Support poly with a suitable main program.

5. If n is an integer, and a and b are real numbers, the expansion of $(a + b)^n$ can be written as

$$(a + b)^n = a^n + na^{n-1}b + \frac{n\,(n-1)a^{n-1}b^2}{2!} + \frac{n(n-1\,(n-L)}{3!}\,a^{n-3}b^3 + \cdots + b^n$$

$$= C_1 a^n + C_2 a^{n-1}b + C_3 a^{n-L}b^2 + C_4 a^{n-3}b^3 + \cdots + C_n ab^{n-1} + C_{n+1}b^n$$

where $C_1 = 1$

$C_2 = n$

$C_3 = \dfrac{n(n-1)}{2!}$

$C_4 = \dfrac{n(n-1)(n-2)}{3!}$

etc.

(a) Write a formula for the *i*th term in a binomial expansion given *i* and *n*.

(b) Express the formula in (a) in recursive form.

(c) Implement a recursive function named binum from (b). Support it with a suitable main program.

6. Using the function from Problem 5 as a basis, write a program that reads integers *n* and *i* and computes and displays the first *i* coefficients of the binomial expansion.

7. Write an interactive version of the program for Problem 6.

Chapter Twelve

Arrays

Organization of data into arrays (introduced in Chapter 4) provides certain advantages for a variety of information-handling processes. This chapter looks at some of these processes and discusses Pascal's facilities for supporting them.

12.1 DECLARATION OF ARRAYS

The description of an array includes a considerable amount of information:

1. The array's name
2. The number of elements in the array
3. The type of data to be stored in the array
4. The way the elements are organized
5. The method for referring to an individual element (i.e., the way an element is indexed)

All these specifications are contained within the concise declaration whose form is defined in Figure 12.1. (Figure 4.7 places this syntax in context with the other variable declarations.)

For example,

```
VAR
    total : ARRAY[1..24] OF INTEGER
```

allocates storage under the collective name total for an array of 24 INTEGER values indexed by the subrange of integers from 1 through 24. That is, the first of total's 24 elements is designated as total[1], the second as total[2], and so on. Similarly, the declaration of numsold in Example 7.1 defined a 7-element array of integers in which the elements were indexed by an enumerative variable of the type pianotype. Although numsold's declaration does not say explicitly that there are seven elements, the designation of pianotype as the data type for the

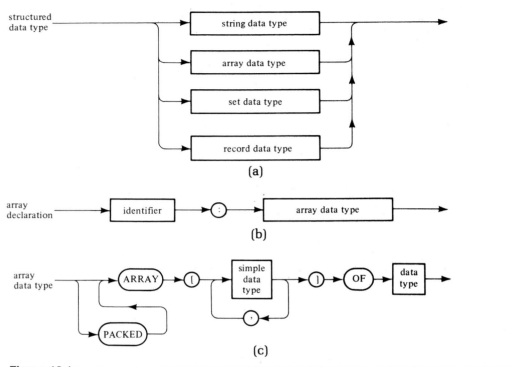

Figure 12.1

Syntax for an Array Declaration

index refers back to the seven eligible values associated with ᴘⁱᵃⁿᵒᵗʸᴘᵉ in its TYPE definition.

12.1.1 Dimensionality of Arrays

Implied in these declarations is the fact that numsold and total are *one-dimensional* arrays. This means that only one distinguishing characteristic (i.e., one *subscript*) is needed to isolate any element in the array. In the case of total, that subscript is an integer not less than one and not greater than 24; in the case of numsold, the subscript is one of the seven values upright, spinet, . . ., mislabel.

The *dimensionality* of an array reflects the number of subscripts required to isolate an element. For example,

```
VAR
    abrev : ARRAY[1..3,1..4] OF CHAR
```

defines an array of characters. There are 12 elements organized into three *rows* and four *columns* as shown in Figure 12.2. Thus, the statement

```
abrev[2,3] := 'T'
```

places the character T in the element occupying the second row and third column of abrev. The fact that this is the seventh of abrev's elements does not mean that we could refer to it by the alternative designation abrev[7]. Conditions defined by our declaration compel us to use two subscripts, each within the respective range defined for it.

Note that each of the following arrays

```
VAR
    vocabule : ARRAY[1..12] OF CHAR ;
       utter : ARRAY[1..4,1..3] OF CHAR ;
        noun : ARRAY[0..2,7..10] OF CHAR ;
       scrab : ARRAY[1..2,1..3,1..2] OF CHAR
```

occupies the same amount of storage for the same number of elements of the same type as does abrev. The differences, therefore, are organizational, and the implications are worth noting:

1. vocabule is a one-dimensional array. Consequently, a reference to vocabule[2,6] would be illegal, just as a reference to abrev[5] would be.
2. utter, like abrev, is a two-dimensional array, but its organization into four rows and three columns makes it structurally different from abrev. A reference to abrev[2,4] would be legal, but the compiler would reject a reference to utter[2,4]. On the other hand, utter[4,1] identifies one of its elements while a reference to abrev[4,1] falls on unsympathetic ears.

Column 1	Column 2	Column 3	Column 4	
abrev[1,1]	abrev[1,2]	abrev[1,3]	abrev[1,4]	row 1
abrev[2,1]	abrev[2,2]	abrev[2,3]	abrev[2,4]	row 2
abrev[3,1]	abrev[3,2]	abrev[3,3]	abrev[3,4]	row 3

Figure 12.2

Structure of the 3 × 4 Array abrev

3. `noun` is disturbingly similar to `abrev`. Both are two-dimensional `CHAR` arrays, and each is organized with three rows and four columns. The difference lies in the way the subscripts are defined: `noun`'s rows are designated 0, 1, and 2, and its four columns are identified as 7, 8, 9, and 10. Thus, `noun[2,8]` isolates the second element in `noun`'s third row. The element in `abrev` with the same *organizational* position is `abrev[3,2]`.

Who wants such a thing? Different people. Sometimes the use of a desired subscript range improves clarity. For example, suppose the Achilles Shoe Company makes runners' shoes in three models (Galumpho, Callousthenics, and Supercorn). Although each model is changed slightly every year, there is enough demand for earlier models to enable Achilles to keep producing previous years' models. If we wanted to build an array for the process of each model over the years 1976 through 1983, we could set up the following declarations:

```
TYPE
     shoemodel = (galumpho, callousthenics, supercorn) ;
VAR
     shoeprice : ARRAY[shoemodel, 1976..1983] OF REAL
```

Now, if we were to refer to the element `shoeprice[galumpho,1978]`, for instance, we know immediately that its value represents the price for a pair of 1978 Galumphos (beautiful shoes; wings on the feet).

4. `scrab` gives us an array with 12 character elements (like `abrev`) but with a more intricate structure. Now we have a three-dimensional array organized into two *rows*, three *columns*, and two *blocks* (Figure 12.3). The first element is designated `scrab[1,1,1]`, the second one is `scrab[1,1,2]`, the third is `scrab[1,2,1]`, and the last one is `scrab[2,3,2]`. (The form `scrab[2],[3],[2]` also is accepted, but we shall use a single set of brackets to enclose all the subscripts.)

Internally, Pascal deals only with one-dimensional arrays. A two-dimensional array actually is treated as an array of one-dimensional arrays. We can see this by noting that the array `noun` discussed above, for instance, also can be declared as

```
noun : ARRAY[0..2] OF ARRAY[7..10] OF CHAR
```

Thus, while we think of `noun` as having three rows and four columns, Pascal treats it as a 3-element array in which each "element," in turn,

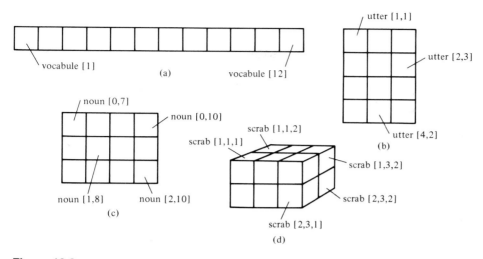

Figure 12.3

Alternative Organization for 12-Element Arrays

consists of an array of 4 elements. As a result, there is no limit on the number of dimensions an array may have. Such limitations must be imposed by the programmer in line with the array's usefulness and the programmer's ability to keep track of its elements.

12.1.2 Packed Arrays

You will notice that Figure 12.1(c) shows the Pascal word PACKED as an optional part of an array declaration. This relates primarily to character arrays, in which case it gives the programmer the opportunity to conserve storage. Ordinarily, Pascal places each element of a character array in the rightmost byte of a word of storage. If the underlying processor is organized to use 32-bit (i.e., 4-byte) words (as is the case with the IBM 370/43XX/303X series or the DEC VAX series), this means that three of the four bytes in each word of a character array are unused. However, when PACKED is specified, all the bytes are used. Thus, assuming a machine with its storage organized into 4-byte words, the following declarations

```
VAR
    banner : ARRAY [1..20] OF CHAR ;
    squeeze : PACKED ARRAY [1..20] OF CHAR ;
    acronym : ARRAY [1..9] OF CHAR ;
    acrnm : PACKED ARRAY [1..9] OF CHAR
```

Pascal will allocate 20 words, 5 words, 9 words, and 2 words, respectively, for banner, squeeze, acronym, and acrnm. For a machine with 2-byte words (such as the Hewlett-Packard 1000 Series or DEC and IBM Personal Computers), the same declarations would produce allocations of 20 words, 10 words, 9 words, and 5 words, respectively.

Analogous savings also may be realized by packing arrays of subrange and enumerative data types. For instance, we know (from Chapter 4) that Pascal associates an internal integer value with each value defined for an enumerative data type. Thus, when we declare

```
TYPE
    shoemodel = (Galumpho, Callousthenics, Supercorn) ;
VAR
    shoes : ARRAY [1..8] OF shoemodel
```

Pascal associates internal values of 0, 1, and 2 with the three respective values for the showmodel data type. Consequently, it allocates a word of storage for each of the 8 elements of shoes. If we make shoes a packed array, i.e.,

```
VAR
    shoes : PACKED ARRAY [1..8] OF shoemodel
```

Pascal allocates only one word for the whole thing: Each element, which can have an internal value of only 0, 1, or 2, needs no more than 2 bits for its representation. Consequently, a 32-bit or 16-bit word accommodates all 8 elements. [If we had declared shoes as a packed array of 9 elements, Pascal would allocate two words in a 16-bit machine but only one word in a 32-bit machine. That same amount of storage still would be sufficient for 10, 11, 12, or even 16 elements. (Do you know why?)]

Now that we see what the packing mechanism does with enumerative variables, we can apply it easily to subrange data. The declaration

```
VAR
    lengths : ARRAY [1..24] OF INTEGER
```

reserves 24 words. Alternatively,

```
VAR
    lengths : PACKED ARRAY [1..24] OF 0..3
```

obtains the same capacity with three 16-bit words or two 32-bit words (two bits per element, 8 elements per word for the 16-bit machine, 16 elements per word for the 32-bit machine). Since Pascal (sensibly) will not split a value across words, the declaration

```
VAR
    lengths : PACKED ARRAY [1..24] OF 0..6
```

reserves five 16-bit words or two 32-bit words.

Pascal, like many other things in life, is devoid of free lunches. Consequently, there is a price for using packed arrays:

1. Packed arrays cannot be compared with regular (unpacked) values, even if they are the same data type.
2. Packed elements can only be passed as value parameters.
3. Character arrays are the only kind of packed arrays that can be read or written.

Just how steep this price is depends on the individual situation.

12.1.3 Arrays as Data Types

The syntax of Pascal's TYPE declaration is flexible enough to allow definition of programmer-defined types consisting of arrays. To illustrate, let us use the little 3 × 4 array we examined in the first section. This time we shall describe that data structure in a data type named wordtable:

```
TYPE
    wordtable = ARRAY [1..3,1..4] OF CHAR
```

Now, we can say

```
VAR
    noun, verb, adjective : wordtable
```

in which case we have allocated 3 two-dimensional arrays of character elements.

We shall carry the idea one step further so that you see what the possibilities are: By expanding our TYPE definition as follows:

```
TYPE
    wordstrength = (weak, neutral, intense) ;
    wordtable = ARRAY [wordstrength,1..4] OF CHAR
```

and declaring noun, verb, and adjective as before, we define data structures for which we can write statements such as

```
adjective [neutral,2] := 'F'
```

or

```
noun[intense,3] := 'S'
```

12.2 ARRAY PROCESSING

A basic reason for setting up an array is that there are certain processes that we wish to apply in common to all or some of its elements. Pascal, being acutely aware of this, makes it convenient to describe such processes. Much of what we shall do requires no special features. Rather, we shall make good use of simple techniques based on familiar language components.

12.2.1 Assignment of Values to Array Elements

There is only one operation that applies to an entire array: Pascal allows assignment of an array's values to another array of the same data type and organization. For example, if we say

```
VAR
    oldtotal, newtotal : ARRAY [1..18] OF INTEGER
```

and `oldtotal` has values in its elements, the statement

```
newtotal := oldtotal
```

will copy `oldtotal[1]` into `newtotal[1]`, and so on. Any other operations on arrays must be specified for each of the elements, one at a time. Once an array element is identified by an appropriate subscript, it can be treated like any single-valued variable. We have done this numerous times (recall Examples 7.1 and 9.1, for instance) so that we need not press the issue further.

12.2.2 Loops for Processing Groups of Elements

When a computing activity is to be applied to a series of array elements, the process is described most conveniently as a loop controlled by a `FOR` statement. To illustrate, let us assume the following situation:

```
VAR
    limit, which, leftover : INTEGER ;
    newtotal : ARRAY [1..18] OF INTEGER
        . . . . . . . . . . . . . . . . . .
        . . . . . . . . . . . . . . . . . .
    READLN (limit, leftover)
```

The `INTEGER` variable `which` will be used as an index whose changing value will enable the loop to process a different element of `newtotal` each time around. `leftover` and `limit` are additional `INTEGER` variables whose values are available to us.

First let us review the processing of an entire array by setting all of `newtotal`'s elements to a common value (we shall use `leftover`):

```
FOR  which := 1 TO 18  DO
   newtotal[which] := leftover
```

Now, going back to the declarations and READLN, and assuming no prior value assignments to newtotal, we shall assign zero to newtotal's first 11 elements and leftover's values to the other 7 elements:

```
FOR which := 1 TO 11  DO
   IF which <= 12
      THEN
         newtotal[which] := 0
      ELSE
         newtotal[which] := leftover
```

As a third example (again assuming no prior processing for newtotal), we shall set the first limit elements (i.e., newtotal[1] through newtotal[limit]) to leftover and the rest to zero. To add a little suspense, we shall recognize (and account for) the possibility that limit, which must have a value between 1 and 18 to make any sense, may not meet that requirement. If that happens, we shall set all of newtotal's elements to −1. Here is a reasonably simple way to specify the processing:

```
IF  (limit < 1) OR (limit > 18)
   THEN
      FOR  which := 1 TO 18  DO
         newtotal[which] := -1
   ELSE
      FOR  which := 1 TO 18  DO
         IF  which <= limit
            THEN
               newtotal[which] := leftover
            ELSE
               newtotal[which] := 0
```

Just to complete the picture, we shall rewrite the activity using two separate loops to fill newtotal's elements as we did before:

```
IF  (limit < 1) OR (limit > 18)
   THEN
      FOR  which := 1 TO 18  DO
         newtotal[which] := -1
   ELSE
      BEGIN
         FOR  which := 1 TO limit  DO
            newtotal[which] := leftover ;
         FOR  which := limit+1 TO 18  DO
            newtotal[which] := 0
      END
```

This last version looks innocent enough. In fact, it will perform properly, even when limit is 18. (Try it.) However, this approach is the less desirable one because its behavior is not apparent from the code itself.

Incidentally, we could have made Pascal responsible for testing limit's value by declaring limit as a subrange variable, i.e.,

```
VAR
    limit : 1..18
```

However, if we did that, the program would intercept an attempt to read an out-of-range value for limit, and we would have had a more difficult time setting newtotal's elements to their proper values and continuing with whatever processing might follow.

Series of elements in two-dimensional arrays are handled with nested loops. Since it takes two subscripts to identify an element uniquely in a two-dimensional array, we need a separate index for each subscript. To illustrate, we shall go back to the 3 × 4 array of characters named word and make the following declarations:

```
CONST
    blank = ' ' ;   stars = '*' ;
VAR
    word : ARRAY[1..3,1..4] OF CHAR ;
    rownum : 1..3 ;   colnum : 1..4
```

Now, if we want to set all 12 elements to blanks, we can say

```
FOR rownum := 1 TO 3  DO
    FOR  colnum := 1 TO 4  DO
        word[rownum,colnum] := blank
```

To set the second row to asterisks while setting the others to blanks, we can construct the following loops:

```
FOR  rownum := 1 TO 3  DO
    FOR  colnum := 1 TO 4  DO
        IF  rownum = 2
            THEN  word[rownum,colnum] := star
            ELSE  word[rownum,colnum] := blank
```

Problems

1. Each part of this problem refers to the array in Figure 12.4. Assuming the array is declared as follows:

```
VAR
    level : ARRAY[1..4,1..5] OF INTEGER
```

16	−3	212	72	−81
26	27	704	36	7
41	−28	8	801	84
−5	73	−7	50	62

Figure 12.4

Array for Problems 1, 2, and 3

(a) Give the respective subscripts of the largest and smallest elements.

(b) Which column has the greatest number of negative values?

(c) What is the value of level[2,4] + level[4,3]?

(d) Show what is displayed by the following:

```
IF  level[2,4] <= level[4,2]-level[3,4]
    THEN  WRITE('CHOICE IS:  ',level[2,3])
    ELSE  WRITE('CHOICE IS:  ',level[3,2])
```

(e) What is the value of the ninth element in level?

(f) Assuming partsum to be declared as an INTEGER variable, write the necessary statement(s) to compute (and assign to partsum) the sum of the first three rows of level.

(g) Given partsum as in part (f), write the necessary statement(s) to compute (and store in partsum) the sum of the last three columns of level.

(h) Using partsum as before, write the statement(s) to compute (and store in partsum) the sum of level's elements having odd values.

(i) Using partsum again, write the statement(s) to compute (and store in partsum) the sum of all of level's elements having odd row numbers and even column numbers.

(j) Using partsum one more time, write the statement(s) to compute (and store in partsum) the sum of each of the largest value in each of level's columns.

2. Using the same array as in Figure 12.4, repeat Problem 1 based on the declaration:

```
VAR
    shift : ARRAY[0..3,-2..2] OF INTEGER
```

3. Using Figure 12.4 again, assume the following declarations:

```
TYPE
    season = (fall, winter, spring, summer) ;
    model = (standard, special, custom, deluxe, hooboy) ;
VAR
    adjust : ARRAY[season,model] OF INTEGER ;
    partsum : INTEGER ;
    result : REAL ;
    when : season ;
    status : model
```

(a) Repeat Problem 1(a).

(b) Repeat Problem 1(b).

(c) Write the statement(s) to compute and store in partsum the sum of all winter values in adjust.

(d) Write the statement(s) to compute and store in result the average deluxe value rounded to two decimal places.

(e) Repeat Problem 1(f).

(f) Repeat Problem 1(g).

(g) Repeat Problem 1(h).

(h) Repeat Problem 1(i).

(i) Repeat Problem 1(j).

(j) Write the statement(s) to compute and store in result the average ratio of winter values to summer values.

4. Each part of this problem applies to a 12-element one-dimensional INTEGER array named numbers and an INTEGER variable named j:

(a) Write the statement(s) to store the first 12 positive integers in numbers.

(b) Write the statement(s) to store the first 12 multiples of 14 in numbers.

(c) Write the statement(s) to store the first six multiples of 17 in numbers[1], numbers[3], numbers[5], etc. and the squares of those values in numbers[2], numbers[4], numbers[6], etc.

(d) Write the statement(s) to store -5 in numbers[1], −7 in numbers[2], −9 in numbers[3], etc.

(e) Write the statement(s) to store the same values as in (d), but in reverse order.

(f) Write the statement(s) to store 17, 19, . . . , 27 in numbers[1] through numbers[6], respectively, and 27, 25, . . . , 17 in numbers[7] through numbers[12], respectively.

(g) Given the following statements:

```
numbers[1] := 8;
```

```
FOR  j := 2 TO 12  DO
   numbers{j} := (j-1) * numbers[j-1] DIV j-1
```

show the resulting contents of numbers.

5. Write a procedure named facts that operates on a 50-element one-dimensional array of integers to find the maximum value and its position in the array, the minimum value and its position, and the difference between the two extreme values. Test your procedure with a suitable driver and the data given below:

32 31 54 67 −8 96 43 −20 9 10 21 19 6 44 57 78 11 −9 46 101
−77 42 59 33 65 76 87 98 109 −109 28 41 52 63 74 85 7 18 12 20
4 51 62 73 84 15 100 71 −4 101

6. Write a procedure named second that operates on a 50-element one-dimensional array of integers to find the second largest value and its position in the array. Test your procedure with a suitable driver using the data given in the previous problem.

7. Write a procedure that examines a 50-element one-dimensional array of integer values. If there are more odd values than even values, produce a second array with the original values sorted in descending order. If there are more even values than odd values, the second array's elements should be sorted in ascending order. If the original array contains the same number of odd and even values, the second array's elements should be in reverse order from those in the original array. Here are three arrays with which to test your procedure:

11 99 13 97 15 95 17 93 19 91 21 89 23 87 25 85 27 83 29 81
31 79 33 77 35 75 37 73 39 71 41 69 43 67 45 65 66 68 70 72
−74 76 −78 80 82 84 86 88 90 92

2 98 4 96 6 94 8 92 10 90 12 88 14 86 16 84 18 82 20 80
3 5 7 9 11 23 25 27 29 31 33 35 37 39 41 −43 −45 −47 49 −51
−8 42 44 46 48 −50 52 54 56 58

11 13 15 17 19 21 23 25 27 29 99 97 95 93 91 89 87 85 83 81
66 64 62 60 58 56 54 52 50 48 46 44 42 40 38 36 28 30 32 34
101 102 103 104 105 208 207 206 205 204

8. Modify the procedure in Problem 5 so that it treats the 50 elements as a 5 × 10 array. Use the same data.

9. Modify the procedure in Problem 6 so that it treats the 50 elements as a 5 × 2 × 5 array. Use Problem 5's data to test your procedure.

10. Data smoothing, a process frequently used in data analysis, seeks to

reduce the effect of incidental local disturbances in data values by replacing those values with numbers that emphasize the trend rather than the individual reading. A common type of data smoothing involves the computation of *moving averages*. When we take a series of readings at fixed time intervals over an extended period, we report the results by replacing each reading with the average value of that reading and some number of subsequent readings. For instance, suppose we were interested in stock market trends as measured by the Dow Jones Industrial Average. On the basis that daily fluctuations are less important than the overall direction, we could compute, say, a 10-day moving average. As a result, each day's (adjusted) value would be reported as an average of the values for 10 consecutive days beginning with that day. Thus, for day 1, the reported figure would be the average of days 1 through 10, for day 2 it would be the average of days 2 through 11, and so on. The same could be done for an individual stock, the day's high temperature reading, or anything else that is believed to be subject to local fluctuations. Now that all of that has been said, write a procedure that processes a series of real values and reports the 10-day moving averages rounded to two decimal places. There is no information as to how many individual values are to be processed for a given input set, but the procedure must be ready to process any number. For a given run, there also is a possibility that there may not be enough input values to prepare even one 10-day moving average. Here are three sets of input on which to test your procedure:

```
5.5 5.6 5.5 5.4 5.6 5.5 5.7 5.9 5.9 5.9 5.9 6.0 5.6 5.4 5.5 5.8
5.8 5.9 5.9 6.0 6.3 6.2 6.1 6.0 6.0 6.4 6.3 6.3 6.2 6.6 6.3 6.1
6.2 6.7 6.4 6.5 6.4 6.5 6.4 6.5 6.8 6.9 6.8 6.7 6.7 6.8 6.5 6.6
6.4 6.8 6.8 6.8 6.7 6.9 6.9 7.0 6.8 6.9 6.8 6.9 7.0 7.1 6.9 6.8

3.8 3.9 4.1 4.4 4.5 4.6 3.9 4.2 4.4 4.5 4.5 4.5 5.3 4.9 4.8 4.9
5.2 5.4 5.4 5.5 5.7 5.8 5.8 5.3 5.4 5.6 5.9 6.3 6.3 6.2 6.1 6.4
6.3 6.6 6.6 6.5 6.4 6.5 6.7 6.7 6.5 6.8 6.9 6.8 6.4 7.2 7.0 7.1
7.3 7.4 7.4 7.3 7.7 7.6 7.8 7.6 7.8 7.6 7.4 7.6 7.8 7.8 7.9 7.9
8.1 8.1 8.2 8.0 8.1 7.8 7.6 7.7 7.7 7.4 7.1 7.2 7.0 7.1 6.9 7.0

4.5 6.6 4.4 6.7 4.4 6.5 4.6 6.6 4.8 6.6 4.9 6.5 4.8 6.7 4.9 6.6
4.9 6.6 5.1 6.8 5.3 6.6 5.2 6.7 5.2 7.0 6.3 7.0 7.0 6.1 7.3 6.1
7.2 5.8 7.2 5.7 7.1 5.8 7.1 5.7 6.6 5.7 6.7 5.6 6.6 5.6 6.6 5.5
6.4 5.5 6.4 5.3 6.1 5.3 6.1 5.4 6.0 5.3 5.3 5.8 5.4 5.7 5.3 5.3
```

11. Generalize the program in the previous problem so that it prepares and displays moving averages as before. However, the number of readings included in the averages now will be a variable that the user

submits interactively for each input set in response to the program's request. Thus, for example, the user might request 10-day moving averages for the first input set, 12-day moving averages for the second set, 5-day moving averages for the third set, and so on. Use the test data from the previous problem.

12. Here is a slightly more intricate version of the previous problem: Before each collection of input data is read, the program asks for the period over which the averages are to be computed (as before). The difference is that there is a built-in default of 10 days (readings). Thus, if the user specifies some value other than 10, the program will use it. If not, the program will use the 10-reading default. Of course, if the user specifies 10 readings anyway, no harm is done. Test your program with the data from Problem 10.

13. Now we shall complicate the previous problem just a bit more: The program asks for a time period, and it has a built-in default of 10 as in the previous problem. The user now has a third option in addition to specifying a new time period or directing the program to use the default. As a third possibility, the user can direct the program to use the time period it used for the previous collection of input values. If the user specifies the "use what you used the last time" option, and there was no last time (i.e., the first set of input values is about to be read and processed), the program is to display a message to that effect and give the user another chance. As before, use Problem 10's test data.

14. (Small fanfare for the *Special Challenge*) In this deluxe version of the moving averages problem, we want to work with only a single collection of input values (we can use the first collection from Problem 10). This time, using that single collection, we are interested in seeing the effect of the time period on the computed results. Accordingly, design a moving averages program that asks the user for a time period (there is no default value) and produces the moving averages with that time period. Then, it asks the user for another time period, rereads the data, and produces the averages with *that* time period. This goes on until the user (by some signal) stops the run.

15. One more wrinkle and we shall drop the issue. Design and prepare the program described in the previous problem with one difference: Instead of allowing the user to specify as many time periods as he or she wants, the program will limit the number of examinations to 10. [If the user specifies an impossible time period (for instance, the user wants a time period of 70 and there are only 54 readings), the program, of course, must reject the request, but it counts as an examination.] Anyway, the program keeps track of which periods have been requested so that it can prevent the user from requesting the same period more than once. As before, use the first set of input values from Problem 10.

Chapter Thirteen

Nonnumeric Data Handling

The rapid growth of word processing, electronic mail, and other text-based computer applications has focused renewed attention on the importance of nonnumeric data processing. Pascal acknowledges this importance by supporting character data and enumerative data. This chapter examines these features and illustrates their use.

Pascal's approach to character string processing is to support a collection of simple operations performed on individual characters and strings constructed as character arrays. With these as a basis, the programmer can construct more extensive processes in accordance with the application's requirements. (Some implementations extend this standard approach by recognizing a STRING data type and supporting it with a collection of string-processing subprograms. However, since these facilities may vary from one dialect to another, we shall concentrate on the standard character-handling features.)

13.1 PROCESSING OF CHARACTER DATA

We shall build a repertoire of string-processing capabilities by starting with individual characters, i.e., Pascal's standard CHAR data type. Then, with the character array as a basic data structure, we shall devise subprograms for a variety of operations on character strings. These processes are not intended to be complete, nor is their construction meant to be ideal. Rather, they are designed to introduce some useful operations for string manipulations.

13.1.1 Declaration of Character Variables

The declaration

```
VAR
    letter : CHAR
```

sets up a variable with a capacity of one character. If we want to use the CHAR type for a string of several characters, we must set up an array. Thus,

```
VAR
   ltrstring : ARRAY[1..20] OF CHAR
```

gives us the equivalent of a 20-character string in which each character can be isolated by attaching an appropriate subscript. The alternative declaration

```
VAR
   ltrstring : PACKED ARRAY[1..20] OF CHAR
```

produces functionally the same result, but the array requires less storage. The advantages and disadvantages of packed character arrays are discussed in Section 13.2.

Since our major focus will be on character strings rather than individual characters, we shall define a data type named stringofchar. The crucial component will be an 80-character array, but its array properties will be hidden so that we can treat it as a string. This will be the data type around which we shall organize our processing activities. The array size of 80 is used as a matter of convenience. (It coincides with the typical line length.) However, the ensuing material applies just as easily to any size.

13.1.2 Character Manipulation

There are no special operations for CHAR data. Assignment is really the only available activity, "operations," each expressed as a subprogram. The data type of interest, i.e., stringofchar, is defined in the next section.

The stringofchar Data Structure Although Pascal must deal with an array of fixed size, we would like to operate as if our character string expanded or contracted in accordance with each situation. To support this illusion, we shall equip our string with an indicator that tells us how long the string is at any time. We can establish an inseparable relationship between the string and its size indicator by combining them in a RECORD data structure (see Section 4.3.2). Accordingly, our declaration might appear as follows:

```
CONST
   strmax = 80 ;
```

```
TYPE
   stringofchar = RECORD
                     chrstring : PACKED ARRAY[1..strmax]
                     OF CHAR ; strlength : 1..strmax
                  END
```

Then, if we were to declare a variable named message of type string-ofchar, the string itself (message.chrstring) automatically would be accompanied by its own length indicator (message.strlength). A string length of zero would indicate an empty string.

Assignment of Individual Characters in Strings Although standard Pascal allows us to define string constants and specify them as literal output values, there are no facilities for processing strings as such. Unless we are using a particular implementation of Pascal that supports string handling as an extension to the standard language, we cannot write something like

```
message := 'DATA RECEIVED, THANK YOU,'
```

regardless of the kind of variable message is or how it was declared. Consequently, the basic operation of string assignment must be handled one character at a time. This process is straightforward, as the next example illustrates.

Example 13.1 In the faraway Kingdom of Funfeh (where everyone speaks through his nose) there is great intrigue. Coded messages travel hither and yon in great profusion. The Royal Palace has become such a giant hatchery for plots and counterplots that playwrights lurk in every dark corner (and a few that are well lit) hoping to steal ideas. Especially active in these goings on is the Princess Adenoida, third-from-youngest daughter of King Znehvn by his second-favorite concubine Unnhnye. Noida (as she is known to her many friends and acquaintances) sends secret notes to her lover Vnm (the Gorgeous Goatherd) by hiding the messages in innocent-looking news reports. The way she does it is to construct the message from individual characters in the news story. Directions for finding the appropriate characters consist of a series of integers, each specifying the position to be used next. For instance, suppose there was the following news report:

```
'SOURCES CLAIM A VINTAGE YEAR FOR FUNFEH'S GRAPES!'
```

and Noida wanted to tell her friend:

'I LOVE MY VNM!'

She would send the news release as is, and hidden in the ear of Vnm's pet goat Mehmeh would be the sequence

12 8 10 2 17 6 24 13 25 14 17 19 13 49 −1

(The −1 is Noida's special end-of-message indicator.) News stories never exceed 240 characters, and Noida's secret messages never exceed 80 characters. Vnm has won a personal computer in the Annual Goatherds Drawing, but he has no program to find the hidden messages. In the interest of good causes we shall write Vnm's program. To focus attention on the string-handling aspects, we shall simplify matters by saying that the input consists of the position numbers, concluded by a −1. The −1, in turn, is followed by the text containing the news story.

The program (Figure 13.1) is organized so that the decoding directions

```
{*******************************************************************}
{                        EXAMPLE 13.1                               }
{*******************************************************************}
{   THIS PROGRAM USES A SERIES OF INTEGER VALUES TO FIND AND EXTRACT   }
{   CHARACTERS FROM A STRING TO FORM A MESSAGE. THE SOURCE STRING MAY  }
{   BE UP TO 240 CHARACTERS LONG, AND THE MESSAGE EXTRACTED FROM IT MAY}
{   BE UP TO 80 CHARACTERS LONG.                                      }
{*******************************************************************}
{   announcement: the source string;                                }
{   lovenote: the message extracted from announcement;              }
{   howlong: the length of the message;                             }
{   key: the series of position indicators for the message's characters}
{*******************************************************************}
PROGRAM  ex1301 (INPUT, OUTPUT) ;
CONST
  blank := ' ' ;
  strmax = 240 ;
TYPE
  news = RECORD
           chrstring : ARRAY[1..strmax] OF CHAR ;
           strlength : 0..strmax
         END ;
  message = RECORD
              chrstring : ARRAY[1..80] OF CHAR;
              strlength : 1..80
            END ;
```

Figure 13.1

Program for Example 13.1

```
VAR
  Key : ARRAY[1..80] OF INTEGER ;
  i, howlong, next : INTEGER ;
  announcement : news ;
  lovenote : message ;
PROCEDURE  readKey ;
VAR
  sw : BOOLEAN ;
BEGIN
  howlong := 0 ;
  sw := TRUE ;
  WHILE  sw  DO
    BEGIN
      READ (Key[howlong+1]) ;
      howlong := howlong + 1 ;
      IF  Key[howlong] = -1
        THEN
          BEGIN
            howlong := howlong-1 ;
            READLN ;
            sw := FALSE
          END
      END
  END ;

PROCEDURE  readnews ;
  VAR
    flag : BOOLEAN ;
    j : INTEGER ;
  BEGIN
    flag := TRUE ;
    j := 0  ;
    WHILE  flag  DO
      BEGIN
        READ (announcement.chrstring[j+1]) ;
        IF  EOF  THEN
          BEGIN
            announcement.strlength := j ;
            flag := FALSE
          END
        ELSE
          j := j + 1
      END
  END ;
```

Figure 13.1
Program for Example 13.1 (continued)

```
{                THE MAIN PROGRAM'S PROCESSING SECTION                    }
BEGIN
   readKey ;
   readnews ;
   FOR  i := 1 TO 80  DO
     lovenote.chrstring[i] := blank ;
   FOR i := 1 TO howlong  DO
     BEGIN
        lovenote.strlength := howlong ;
        next := Key[i]
        lovenote.chrstring[i] := announcement.chrstring[next]
     END ;
   WRITELN ('HERE IS THE MESSAGE';) ;
   WRITELN ;
   FOR i :+ 1 TO howlong  DO
     WRITE (lovenote.chrstring[i]) ;
   WRITELN (message) ;
   WRITELN ('THANK YOU, CALL AGAIN.')
END.
```

Figure 13.1

Program for Example 13.1 (continued)

and the news report are read by separate procedures. By the time the main program is ready to extract the message, its length (howlong) is already known. lovenote, the string from which the final message will be displayed, is initialized to blanks, and the characters are assigned to it, one by one.

Assignment of Character Strings   The character-by-character process of string assignment can be hidden by setting up a procedure to produce the desired effect: Each element of the *source* string is assigned to the corresponding element of the *destination* string, and the destination string's length is set to that of the source string. The procedure's definition is shown in Figure 13.2. Both the source and destination are shown with the VAR specification since there is nothing to be gained with the transfer by value mechanism. (This also precludes any temptation to attempt the use of a string constant as an argument.)

Isolating Part of a String   Many string-processing activities depend on the ability to isolate and manipulate part of a string (i.e., a *substring*). substr, shown in Figure 13.3, copies a designated portion of the source string into the destination string. The entire destination string is replaced, and a new length is stored in its length indicator. As is the case with strassign, the contents of the source string are unaffected. The sub-

```
(*******************************************************************)
(**                       STRASSIGN                            **)
(*******************************************************************)
(** THIS PROCEDURE REQUIRES TWO ARGUMENTS OF THE stringofchar TYPE. **)
(** THE FIRST ARGUMENT IS ASSIGNED TO (COPIED INTO) THE SECOND, RE- **)
(** PLACING ITS ENTIRE PREVIOUS CONTENTS. THE LENGTH IS ADJUSTED AS **)
(** NECESSARY. strmax IS ASSUMED TO BE DEFINED EXTERNALLY.          **)
(*******************************************************************)
PROCEDURE  strassign (VAR sourcestr, VAR deststr : stringofchar) ;
VAR
    strindex : 0..strmax ;
BEGIN
    FOR strindex := 1 TO sourcestr.strlength  DO
        deststr.chrstring[strindex] := sourcestr.chrstring[strindex] ;
        deststr.strlength := sourcestr.strlength
END
```

Figure 13.2

Procedure for Character String Assignment

string to be copied is described by a starting position and an ending position. substr also reports any failed attempts due to an improper description of the desired substring.

Extracting Part of a String   This operation is similar to substr except that the designated substring is removed from the source string after being copied to a new destination. Consequently, the source string's length is reduced and its length indicator is adjusted accordingly The procedure, named remove, is shown in Figure 13.4. Examination of the statements makes it clear that much of the code is a duplicate of that used for substr. In one of the problems at the end of the chapter, you are asked to exploit this similarity by writing a general subprogram for substring isolation and/or removal.

Extending a String   One of the fundamental string handling processes is that of *concatenation*—creation of a new string by combining two strings end to end. The procedure strextend performs this activity (Figure 13.5). As is the case in the previous two procedures, we shall include an argument that reports on the procedure's conduct.

Copying a String   We can generalize the operation of strextend by providing a duplicating operation in which a designated substring is copied into a destination string at some specified position. This is done in a procedure named strcopy, shown in Figure 13.6.

```
(**********************************************************************)
(**                          SUBSTR                                **)
(**********************************************************************)
(** THIS PROCEDURE COPIES A DESIGNATED PORTION (SUBSTRING) OF THE   **)
(** THIRD ARGUMENT INTO THE FOURTH ARGUMENT, REPLACING ITS ENTIRE   **)
(** CONTENTS.  THE FIRST TWO ARGUMENTS GIVE THE STARTING AND ENDING **)
(** POSITIONS OF THE SUBSTRING.  THE FIRST POSITION IS 1.           **)
(** THE FIFTH ARGUMENT IS USED TO RETURN AN INTEGER VALUE THAT      **)
(** INDICATES THE RESULT OF THE PROCEDURE'S ACTIVITIES: 0 MEANS     **)
(** THAT PROCESSING WAS NORMAL: 1 MEANS THAT THE STARTING POSITION  **)
(** EXCEEDED THE END POSITION: 2 MEANS THAT THE STARTING POSITION   **)
(** WAS MEANINGLESS; 3 MEANS THAT THE END POSITION WAS MEANINGLESS. **)
(** strmax IS ASSUMED TO BE DEFINED EXTERNALLY.                    **)
(**********************************************************************)
PROCEDURE substr (startpos, endpos : INTEGER ;
                  VAR sourcestr : stringofchar ;
                  VAR deststr : stringofchar ;
                  VAR report : INTEGER) ;
VAR
  destindex, s : 0..strmax ;
BEGIN
   IF startpos >= endpos   THEN
      report := 1
   ELSE IF startpos < 1   THEN
           report := 2
        ELSE IF endpos > strmax   THEN
                report := 3
             ELSE
                BEGIN
                   report := 0 ;
                   deststr.strlength := endpos - startpos + 1 ;
                   s := startpos - 1 ;
                   FOR  destindex := 1 TO deststr.strlength+1   DO
                       deststr.chrstring[destindex] :=
                       sourcestr.chrstring[destindex+s]
                END
END.
```

Figure 13.3————— Procedure for Isolating and Assigning Substrings

13.1.3 String Comparisons

Individual characters may be compared with each other using Pascal's regular relational operators. The basis for comparison is the internal collating sequence of the character set used by a particular computer. Such comparisons are called *lexicographic comparisons*. In the American Stan-

```
(**********************************************************************)
(**                            REMOVE                               **)
(**********************************************************************)
(** THIS PROCEDURE REMOVES A DESIGNATED SUBSTRING FROM THE SOURCE   **)
(** STRING (THE THIRD ARGUMENT) AND ASSIGNS IT TO THE DESTINATION   **)
(** STRING (THE FOURTH ARGUMENT). THE FIRST, SECOND, AND FIFTH      **)
(** ARGUMENTS HAVE THE SAME MEANINGS AS IN substr.                  **)
(** strmax IS ASSUMED TO BE DEFINED EXTERNALLY.                     **)
(**********************************************************************)
PROCEDURE remove (startpos, endpos : INTEGER ;
                  VAR sourcestr : stringofchar ;
                  VAR deststr : stringofchar ;
                  VAR report : INTEGER) ;
VAR
    useindex, s : 0..strmax ;
BEGIN
    IF startpos > endpos  THEN
      report := 1
    ELSE IF  startpos < 1  THEN
            report := 2
        ELSE IF  endpos > strmax  THEN
                report := 3
            ELSE
              BEGIN
                report := 0 ;
                deststr.strlength := endpos - startpos + 1 ;
                s := startpos -1 ;
                FOR  useindex := 1 TO deststr.strlength  DO
                    deststr.chrstring[useindex]:= ;
                    sourcestr.chrstring[useindex+s] ;
                    s := deststr.strlength ;
                FOR useindex := endpos + 1 TO sourcestr.strlength  DO
                    sourcestr.chrstring[useindex] :=
                    sourcestr.chrstring[useindex-s] ;
                    sourcestr.strlength := sourcestr.strlength
                                           - desstr.strlength
              END
END
```

Figure 13.4

Procedure for Removing a Substring from a String

dard Code for Information Interchange (ASCII), '1' is earlier than ("less than") '2', '9' is earlier than 'A', and 'Z' is earlier than 'a'. In other words, the numeric characters precede the uppercase letters which, in turn, precede the lowercase letters in lexicographic order. In the Extended Binary coded Decimal Information code (EBCDIC), 'a' is earlier than 'b', 'z' is earlier than

```
(********************************************************************)
(**                        STREXTEND                             **)
(********************************************************************)
(** THIS PROCEDURE PERFORMS CONCATENATION--ATTACHING THE SOURCE  **)
(** STRING TO THE END OF THE DESTINATION STRING, THEREBY LENGTHENING **)
(** IT. A VALUE OF 0 IS RETURNED IN THE FINAL ARGUMENT IF ALL GOES **)
(** WELL; A VALUE OF 1 INDICATES THAT THE RESULTING STRING WOULD BE **)
(** TOO LONG, AND A VALUE OF 2 INDICATES AN EMPTY SOURCE STRING.  **)
(** strmax IS ASSUMED TO BE DEFINED EXTERNALLY.                  **)
(********************************************************************)
PROCEDURE strextend (VAR sourcestr : stringofchar ;
                     VAR deststr : stringofchar ;
                     VAR report : INTEGER ) ;
VAR
    sourceindex : 0..strmax ;
BEGIN
    IF sourcestr.strlength + deststr.strlength > strmax   THEN
        report := 1
    ELSE
        BEGIN
            report := 0 ;
            FOR  sourceindex := 1 TO sourcestr.strlength  DO
                deststr.chrstring[sourcestr.strlength+sourceindex] :=
                sourcestr.chrstring[sourceindex] ;
            deststr.strlength := deststr.strlength + sourcestr.strlength
        END
END
```

Figure 13.5───────────────────────────────────

Procedure for String Concatenation

'A', and 'Z' is earlier than '0', the lowest of the 10 numeric characters. That is, the lowercase letters precede the uppercase letters which, in turn, precede the numeric characters. The blank is lexicographically ahead of numbers and letters in both systems (Appendix B). Consequently, when we say (in a program) that an uppercase letter is less than another uppercase letter, it is the same as saying that the first letter would be ahead of the second letter in an alphabetized list.

The same rule can be applied to arrays of characters by testing pairs of corresponding elements in succession. Thus, the string 'BASH' would be "less than" the string 'BATH'. [The 'S' in 'BASH' puts it alphabetically (i.e., lexicographically) ahead of 'BATH'.] The outcome of a comparison between 'BATH' and 'bath' will depend on whether the computer being used is designed for the ASCII or EBCDIC character system.

Using the same general approach as we did for character-array processing, we can write a simple subprogram that will enable us to compare two arrays. The two strings to be compared will be provided as parts of

```
(**********************************************************************)
(**                            STRCOPY                            **)
(**********************************************************************)
(** THIS PROCEDURE INSERTS A DESIGNATED SUBSTRING FROM sourcestr INTO **)
(** deststr STARTING AT POSITION sstart AND PROCEEDING FOR slength  **)
(** CHARACTERS. strmax, THE MAXIMUM ALLOWABLE STRING LENGTH, IS     **)
(** ASSUMED TO BE DEFINED EXTERNALLY AND AVAILABLE HERE.           **)
(**********************************************************************)
PROCEDURE strcopy (VAR sourcestr : stringofchar ; sstart, slength : INTEGER ;
                   VAR deststr : stringofchar ; dstart : INTEGER ;
                   VAR report : INTEGER) ;
VAR
   newlength, i : 0..strmax ;
BEGIN
   newlength := deststr.strlength + slength ;
   IF  newlength > strmax  THEN
      report := 1
   ELSE IF  (sstart < 1) OR (sstart+slength > source.strlength) OR
            (dstart < 1) OR (slength <= 0)  THEN
         report := 2
      ELSE
         BEGIN
            FOR i := deststr.strlength DOWNTO dstart  DO
               deststr.chrstring[i+slength] := deststr.chrstring[i] ;
            FOR  i := 0 TO slength  DO
               deststr.chrstring[dstart+i] := sourcestr.chrstring[sstart+i];
            deststr.strlength := newlength ;
            report := 0
         END
END
```

Figure 13.6

Procedure for Copying Strings

stringofchar data structures defined earlier. (Thus, their corresponding "lengths" also will be available.) We shall report the outcome of the
comparison in a single character whose value will be set to 'E' if the strings
are identical (i.e., "equal"), 'L' if the first string is lexicographically ahead
of ("less than") the second, 'G' if the reverse is true, and 'X' if the comparison cannot be performed. When the two strings are of unequal "lengths,"
the longer string automatically is "greater." The procedure, named
strcompare, is shown in Figure 13.7.

13.1.4 Searching Character Strings

The ability to compare two character strings and direct a course of action
based on the outcome forms the basis for a more general search operation

that has many uses in text processing work. It often is helpful to be able to look for a particular character string inside another, larger one. When such a capability is provided, it usually tells us where the match is (i.e., the

```
(**********************************************************************)
(**                            STRCOMPARE                          **)
(**********************************************************************)
(** str1 AND str2 ARE VARIABLES OF THE stringofchar DATA TYPE DEFINED **)
(** EARLIER.  WHEN THE STRINGS ARE OF EQUAL LENGTH, THE PROCEDURE RE- **)
(** TURNS A VALUE OF 'C' IF THE STRINGS ARE IDENTICAL, 'L' IF str1 IS **)
(** LEXICOGRAPHICALLY AHEAD OF sr2, OR 'G' IF THE REVERSE IS TRUE. A  **)
(** VALUE OF 'X' IS RETURNED IF EITHER OF THE LENGTHS IS MEANINGLESS. **)
(** THE LONGER STRING AUTOMATICALLY IS GREATER THAN THE SHORTER ONE.  **)
(**********************************************************************)
PROCEDURE strcompare (VAR str1 : stringofchar ; VAR str2 : stringofchar ;
                          outcome : CHAR) ;
VAR
  i : INTEGER ;
  sw : BOOLEAN ;
BEGIN
  IF  (str1.strlength <= 0) OR (str2.strlength <= 0)   THEN
    outcome := 'X'
ELSE IF  str1.strlength < str2.strlength   THEN
      outcome := 'L'
    ELSE IF  str1.strlength > str2.strlength   THEN
      outcome := 'G'
          ELSE
            BEGIN
              i := 1 ;
              sw := TRUE ;
              WHILE  (sw) AND (i <= str1.strlength)  DO
                BEGIN
                  IF  str1.chrstring[i] = str2.chrstring[i]   THEN
                    i := i + 1
                  ELSE
                    BEGIN
                      sw := FALSE ;
                      IF  str1.chrstring[i] < str2.chrstring[i]   THEN
                        outcome := 'L'
                      ELSE
                        outcome := 'G'
                    END
                END ;
              IF  sw  THEN
                outcome := 'C'
END
```

Figure 13.7

Procedure for Comparing Two Character Strings

starting position of the matching string) or it delivers an explicit signal (e.g., a positional value of 0) to indicate that the search was unsuccessful. If a string contains several occurrences of the pattern being sought, the operation locates only the first one, so that the programmer usually has to make his or her own arrangements to find additional matches.

This type of search operation is implemented as a procedure named strsearch (Figure 13.8.). Here again we use the stringofchar data type for both strings—the one to be searched and the one to be matched.

```
(****************************************************************************)
(**                            STRSEARCH                                  **)
(****************************************************************************)
(** THIS PROCEDURE SEARCHES bigstr FOR AN OCCURRENCE OF smallstr. IF       *)
(** THERE IS ONE, IT REPORTS THE POSITION WHERE THE MATCH STARTS. IF THE   *)
(** SEARCH FAILS, A POSITION OF 0 IS REPORTED. A POSITION OF -1 MEANS      *)
(** THAT smallstr WAS LARGER THAN bigstr.                                  *)
(****************************************************************************)
PROCEDURE strsearch (VAR bigstr : stringofchar ; VAR smallstr : stringofchar ;
                     VAR position : INTEGER ;
VAR
  bigpos, smallpos, extent, j : INTEGER ;
  stillamatch, stillmorepositions : BOOLEAN ;
BEGIN
  position := 0 ;
  IF  (smallstr.strlength > bigstr.strlength) OR (smallstr.strlength <= 0)
  THEN
    position := -1 ;
  ELSE
    BEGIN
      bigpos := 1 ;
      stillmorepositions := TRUE ;
      WHILE stillmorepositions  DO
        BEGIN
          extent := bigpos + smallstr.strlength - 1 ;
          smallpos := 1 ;
          position := bigpos ;
          j := 0 ;
          stillamatch := TRUE ;
          WHILE (stillamatch) AND (smallpos <= smallstr.strlength)  DO
            BEGIN
              IF smallstr.chrstring[smallpos] = bigstr.chrstring[bigpos+j]
              THEN
                BEGIN
                  smallpos := smallpos + 1 ;
                  j := j + 1
                END
```

Figure 13.8

Procedure for Searching a String for Another String

```
            ELSE
              BEGIN
                Position := 0 ;
                stillamatch := FALSE
              END
          END ;
        IF  Position > 0  THEN
          stillmorePositions := FALSe
        ELSE
          IF  extent = bigstr.strlength  THEN
            stillmorePositions := FALSE
          ELSE
            bigPos := bigPos + 1
      END
    END
END ;
```

Figure 13.8

Procedure for Searching a String for Another String (continued)

Example 13.2

Dr. Nasal B. Flatte, the famous paleosocioanthropsychomusicologist, feels she is close to an important breakthrough. Her theory is that, hidden in the titles of ancient hunting and gathering songs (and perhaps in some more recent ones, too) are characteristic syllables and fragments that can reveal hitherto hidden insights about the people who sang (sing) those songs. To facilitate her data analyses, she would like a program that reads a song title and a string for which that title should be searched. In response, the program is to display the position(s) in which the specified substring appears.

The heart of the program (Figure 13.9) is a loop that sets a new starting position for the substring to be searched based on the position of the last successful match. Note that the starting point is one position removed from the previous successful match, even though the program is designed to look for strings that are more than one character long. This takes care of situations like the one where we might be looking for the string 'eee' and the source string contains 'teeeeef'. There are three occurrences of 'eee' there, and the only way to find all of them is to advance through the string one position at a time.

13.1.5 Input/Output of Character Data

Character data can be transmitted using READ, READLN, WRITE, and WRITELN. Since each character variable holds exactly one character, a READ or READLN reads exactly one character, and it is the next one available. Consequently, the programmer must be careful about which character is being read. One of the most common difficulties occurs when the programmer forgets about this and prepares an input line in which a numerical value is followed by a separating blank which, in turn, is fol-

```
(****************************************************************)
(**                        EXAMPLE 13.2                       **)
(****************************************************************)
(** THIS PROGRAM READS A SONG TITLE FOLLOWED BY A SUCCESSION OF STRINGS *)
(** CALLED CLUES.  FOR EACH CLUE, THE PROGRAM SEARCHES THE SONG TITLE AND*)
(** DISPLAYS THE POSITION OF EACH OCCURRENCE OF THAT CLUE IN THAT SONG. *)
(****************************************************************)
PROGRAM   ex1302 (INPUT,OUTPUT) ;
CONST
  strmax = 80 ;
TYPE
  stringofchar = RECORD
                   chrstring : ARRAY [1..80] OF CHAR ;
                   strlength : 0..strmax
                 END
VAR
  song, clue, temp, temp2 : stringofchar ;
  i, mark, where, outcome : INTEGER ;


(****************************************************)
(* THIS IS WHERE THE DESCRIPTION OF strsearch WOULD BE. *)
(****************************************************)
(***************************)
(* HERE IS THE MAIN PROGRAM *)
(***************************)
BEGIN
  song.strlength := 0 ;
  REPEAT
    song.strlength := song.strlength + 1 ;
    READ (song.chrstring[song.strlength]
  UNTIL  EOLN ;
  song.strlength := song.srlength - 1 ;
  WRITELN ('HERE IS THE SONG:') ;   WRITELN ;
  FOR  i := 1 TO song.strlength  DO
    WRITE (song.chrstring[i]) ;
  REPEAT
    clue.strlength := 0 ;
    REPEAT
      clue.strlength := clue.strlength + 1 ;
      READ (clue.chrstring[clue.strlength]
    UNTI1  EOLN ;
    clue.strlength := clue.strlength - 1 ;
```

Figure 13.9

Program for Example 13.2

```
    WRITELN ('THIS CLUE: ') ;
    FOR i := 1 TO clue.strlength  DO
      WRITE (clue.chrstring[i] ;  WRITELN ;
    FOR  i := 1 TO clue.strlength  DO
      temp.chrstring[i] := song.chrstring[i] ;
    temp.strlength := song.strlength ;
    where := MAXINT ;
    mark := 0 ;
    WHILE  where > 0  DO
      BEGIN
        strsearch (temp, clue, where) ;
        IF  where > 0  THEN
          BEGIN
            mark := mark + where ;
            WRITELN ('CLUE IS FOUND IN POSITION ',mark) ;
            remove (1, where, temp, temp2, oputcome)
          END
        ELSE
          WRITELN ('THIS CLUE IS NOT IN THE SONG.')
      END ;
      WRITELN ;  WRITELN
  UNTIL  EOF ;
  WRITELN ;
  WRITELN ('END OF RUN.')
END.
```

Figure 13.9

Program for Example 13.2 (continued)

lowed by the character to be read. Instead of picking up the character, the READ brings in and stores the blank instead.

There are no special statements for transmission of character arrays. As we have seen in past experience, character arrays must be read or written one element at a time.

13.2 PACKED CHARACTER ARRAYS

When we declare a character array, Pascal reserves a word of storage for each element (i.e., each character). In many types of processors, this results in only partial occupancy of each unit of storage. For example, each word in the IBM and DEC personal computers can hold 2 characters; other systems have word capacities of 4, 6, or even more characters. When we deal with large arrays, this wasted storage may be substantial and, in some cases, may be sufficient to compromise a program's effectiveness. Consequently, Pascal provides the PACKED specification, a feature that forces the compiler to fill each word with as many characters as it can hold. For instance, suppose we were using a DEC VAX computer or an IBM 370/43XX/30XX type of system and we declared message as follows:

```
VAR
   message : ARRAY [1..10] OF CHAR
```

Since a single word in each of these types of computers can hold 4 characters, the result would be an allocation of 10 words with only one-fourth of each word in actual use. Changing the declaration to

```
VAR
   message : PACKED ARRAY[1..10] OF CHAR
```

allocates only three words. (The first two words would be fully occupied, and the last half of the third word would be unused.)

In most respects, packed character arrays can be manipulated like ordinary (unpacked) arrays. This would seem to make the use of such arrays an obvious choice. However, the advantages of reduced storage requirements may be neutralized by the fact that such arrays take longer to process because additional operations have to be performed to extract the individual characters from the words into which they are packed. Consequently, as we examine the facilities for handling packed character arrays, bear in mind that the choice is likely to depend on the conditions existing in each individual situation.

13.2.1 Assignment of Values in Packed Character Arrays

Under certain specific conditions, it is possible to assign a string to an entire packed array with a single "operation." While the string to be assigned is a constant, it must be exactly the same length as the packed array that will receive the value. Thus,

```
VAR
   vwd : PACKED ARRAY[1..8] OF CHAR
         .................
   vwd := 'BINDINGb'
```

is acceptable. [It would be rejected if vwd were not PACKED. Moreover, it would be rejected if vwd were PACKED but the string constant were specified as 'BINDING' (i.e., without the blank).]

The contents of a packed array can be assigned to another identically organized array. Thus, if vwd and wstr both are declared as PACKED ARRAY[1..14] OF CHAR, the sequence

```
vwd := 'LARGE AND BLUE' ;
wstr := vwd
```

is legal.

13.2.2 Comparisons with Packed Arrays

Two identically organized packed character arrays of equal length can be compared lexicographically with a single IF statement. Any of the six relational operators may be used to define the comparison, and the collating sequence applies as it does for unpacked character arrays. For instance, if wd1 contains "BATH' and wd2 contains "BOTH', the test

```
IF   wd1 <= wd2   THEN....
```

will have an outcome of TRUE.

13.2.3 Input/Output of Packed Arrays

A single WRITE or WRITELN call can be used to display an entire packed array of characters. Thus, if the 4-element packed array wd2 contains the string "BOTH', then

```
WRITELN (wd2)      and      WRITELN('BOTH')
```

produce the same output.

There is no corresponding facility for reading entire arrays, packed or otherwise. Each element must be read individually.

13.2.4 Conversion Between Packed and Unpacked Character Arrays

We have already noted that the storage savings and string-handling conveniences provided by packed character arrays may be less attractive when weighed against the additional time required to manipulate individual packed array elements. To help exploit some of the advantages of packing, Pascal's subprogram library includes two procedures that facilitate conversion between packed and unpacked arrays.

The PACK Procedure   As its name implies, the PACK procedure compresses an unpacked array into a packed destination. The general form is

PACK *(sourcearray, startpos, destinationarray)*

where *sourcearray* is the unpacked array supplying the string and *destinationarray* is the packed array receiving the string. The second argument specifies the position of the first element in *sourcearray* to be packed. There is no need to specify a starting position for *destinationarray* because it always is 1. Thus, assuming the declarations

```
VAR
    xpnd : ARRAY[1..10] OF CHAR ;
    cntrct : PACKED ARRAY[1..10] OF CHAR
```

the call

```
PACK (xpnd, 1, cntrct)
```

places xpnd[1] in cntrct[1], xpnd[2] in cntrct[2], and so on.

It is also possible to pack part of an unpacked array as long as the destination array is sized to accommodate the characters. For instance, if sparse is a 10-character unpacked array and dense is a 6-character packed array, then any of the invocations

```
PACK (sparse, 1, dense)
```

or

```
PACK (sparse, 2, dense)
```

or

```
PACK (sparse, 5, dense)
```

will store six of sparse's elements in dense, but

```
PACK (sparse, 8, dense)
```

will be rejected.

Since PACK is a relatively efficient process, it often helps to read the string (character by character) into an unpacked array (this takes considerably less time than it would to read the characters into a packed array) and then transfer it (using PACK) into a packed array. (Of course, we pay in this case by using extra storage for both forms of the array.)

The UNPACK **Procedure** UNPACK converts in the opposite direction. Thus, using sparse and dense as defined in the previous paragraph,

```
UNPACK (dense, sparse, 4)
```

unpacks dense's 6 characters into spase[4] through sparse[9].

13.3 CHARACTERS AND INTEGERS

There are several functions which, when applied to character data, give the programmer convenient access to the collating sequence. We shall just describe their characteristics briefly, leaving it to you to find a use for them.

13.3.1 CHR and ORD

The ORD function relates each character to the numerical equivalent of its internal representation. For instance, if whatnum is declared as an INTE-GER variable and we are using the ASCII system, the assignment

```
whatnum := ORD('W')
```

stores a value of 87 in whatnum because the bit pattern used to represent a W is equivalent to an integer value of 87.

The function CHR works in the opposite direction. If quan is declared as INTEGER and is given a value of 116, and syll is declared as CHAR, the assignment

```
syll := CHR(quan)
```

will place the character 'm' in syll. To cement things down once and for all, the assignment

```
quan := ORD(CHR(110))
```

will place the integer value 110 in quan, and

```
word := CHR(ORD('S'))
```

will place the character 'S' in word. There are other ways to get nowhere but they are beyond the scope of this book.

The ORD function does not translate a character into an integer. ORD('7') is not 7. (It happens to be 55 in the ASCII collating sequence.) If we want to translate a numerical character string into an integer, we have to write a sequence of statements to do it. Here is one simple way: The technique is based on the fact that the 10 numeric characters occupy consecutive positions in the collating sequence. That being the case, the integer value for any numeric character is the difference between its internal representation and that of '0'. For instance, ORD('7') - ORD('0') will produce a 7.

We shall use this idea as the nucleus of a loop for converting a string consisting of 4 numerical characters to a four-digit integer. Remember that the leftmost digit of a four-digit integer has to be multiplied by 1000 to obtain its actual magnitude, the next one has to be multiplied by 100, and so on:

```
CONST
    reference = ORD('0') ;
VAR
    digit, i, convert : INTEGER ;
    numstring : ARRAY [1..4] OF CHAR
    . . . . . . . . . . . . . .
    convert := 0 ;
    FOR i := 1 TO 4  DO
      READ (numstring[i]
    . . . . . . . . . . . . .
    FOR  i := 1 TO 4  DO
      convert := 10 * convert + ORD(numstring[i] - reference
    . . . . . . . . . . . . . . . . . . . .
```

13.3.2 Pred and succ

The ability to find a character's position in the collating sequence is complemented by two functions that identify the characters on either side. PRED('W') returns W's predecessor (i.e., 'V'), PRED('3') returns '2', and so on. Similarly, SUCC('W') return's W's successor (i.e., 'X'), and SUCC('3') returns '4'. For those with a continuing interest in going nowhere at electronic speed, SUCC(PRED('3')) returns '3', but with a flourish and a cloud of smoke.

Incidentally, PRED and SUCC can be applied to any simple data type except REAL. Thus, PRED(3297) is 3296, and SUCC(-81) is −80.

13.4 PROCESSING BOOLEAN DATA

Boolean data (with values of TRUE or FALSE) may be stored as single-valued variables or BOOLEAN arrays declared via the usual VAR mechanism. The declarations

```
VAR
    switch : BOOLEAN ;
    selector : ARRAY[1..8] OF BOOLEAN
```

are typical examples.

Pascal recognizes three fundamental BOOLEAN operations: AND, OR, and NOT, from which boolean expressions may be cnstructed. We have used these in setting up IF-THEN-ELSE decisions, so that their properties are familiar to us.

13.4.1 Evaluation of Boolean Expressions

A boolean expression can be built by combining boolean terms and factors just as we would construct an arithmetic expression. For instance, assuming sw1, sw2, sw3, and sw4 to be declared as single-valued BOOLEAN variables, we can write assignment statements such as

```
sw4 := sw1 AND sw2 OR NOT sw3
```

These expressions may be as complex as necessary, but the final result inevitably must be TRUE or FALSE. Further insight into the behavior of boolean expressions can be gained by knowing that Pascal uses the following priority ranking for performing boolean computations:

1. NOT
2. AND
3. OR

Thus, using sw1, sw2, and sw3, the expression

```
NOT sw1 AND sw2
```

is equivalent to

```
(NOT sw1) AND sw2
```

and

```
sw2 OR sw1 AND sw3
```

is equivalent to

```
sw2 OR (sw1 AND sw3)
```

Here, as in arithmetic expressions, the programmer is well-advised to use parentheses to be sure that the boolean processing conveys his or her exact intent.

13.4.2 Relational Operators in Boolean Expressions

We already know that Pascal's relational operators can be used to construct comparisons between expressions so that the outcome is either TRUE or FALSE. In addition, these same relational operators (=, <>, <=, >=, <, >) are accepted as Boolean operators. This is based on Pascal's internal use of 0 for FALSE and 1 for TRUE. The obvious consequences (by definition) are that:

1. FALSE is "less than" TRUE.
2. SUCC(FALSE) is TRUE.
3. PRED(TRUE) is FALSE.

This means that we can apply any type of comparison to Boolean express-ions and expect the resulting processing to follow a set of rules consistent with the foregoing relationships. These rules can be summarized conve-niently by constructing a *truth table* in which the outcome of each compari-son is shown for all possible combinations of Boolean values. (Since two Boolean values are being compared, the truth table needs to show only four combinations.) This information is given in Table 13.1 (with AND, OR, and NOT thrown in for good measure).

13.4.3 Input/Output of Boolean Data

Our use of Boolean constants and variables typifies the roles such data play in most programs: They often serve as switches or flags to help guide a program's internal actions. Transmission of Boolean data to or from the processor is considered to be less important than input/output of other data types. Consequently, many Pascal implementations cannot read or write Boolean data.

Standard Pascal allows Boolean output but prohibits Boolean input. When a Boolean variable is specified with WRITE or WRITELN, Pascal displays TRUE or FALSE preceded by some number of blanks. This num-ber may be controlled by explicit specification or the programmer can leave it to Pascal's default. A typical default is 10 characters, so that the output for Boolean variable wflag produced by

Table 13.1 Boolean Operations

sw1, sw2, and sw3 are delcared as BOOLEAN

sw1	sw2	AND	OR	=	<> (Exclusive OR)	<= (Implies)	>= (Is implied by)	> (Does not imply)	< (Is not implied by)
					sw3 resulting from sw3 := sw1 *operation* sw2				
T	T	T	T	T	F	T	T	F	F
T	F	F	T	F	T	F	T	T	F
F	T	F	T	F	T	T	F	F	T
F	F	F	F	T	F	T	T	F	F

sw1	swL := NOT sw1
T	F
F	T

```
WRITELN (wflag)
```

would be either bbbbbbTRUE or bbbbbFALSE. If we were to say

```
WRITELN (wflag:8)
```

the result would be either

```
    bbbbTRUE bbbFALSE
```

13.5 PROCESSING OF ENUMERATIVE DATA

Although programmer-defined enumerative data types cannot be read or written, Pascal provides limited facilities for their internal manipulation.

13.5.1 Assignment of Enumerative Values

Given the nature of programmer-defined enumerative data types, it would not make sense to support such data with extensive arithmetic or character-handling capabilities. Accordingly, the manipulative facilities are limited to simple assignment, examples of which we have already seen in previous chapters. We shall complete the story here by defining a couple of data types, declaring appropriate variables, and exercising Pascal's facilities on them:

```
TYPE
    eyecolor = (blue, brown, gray, green, hazel) ;
    ocean = (Atlantic, Pacific, Indian, Arctic,
            Antarctic) ;
VAR
    peepers, orbs : eyecolor ;
    waterbody, vastness : ocean
```

Given these declarations, assignments such as

```
waterbody := Pacific ;
vastness := waterbody
```

and

```
peepers := blue ;
orbs := SUCC(peepers)
```

are legitimate. In the latter case, the variable orbs will receive a value of brown. Similarly, PRED(Indian) is Pacific, and SUCCSUCC-(brown) is green.

13.5.2 Enumerative Data and Integers

Since enumerative values are represented internally as integers (see Table 4.1), it is consistent for Pascal to provide a pathway from an enumerative value to the corresponding (internal) integer representation. This is done by means of the ORD function. The integer value returned by the function can be used like any other integer. Thus, ORD(Pacific) returns a value of 1, and the expression

```
ORD(peepers) + ORD(orbs)
```

is legal. Whether it makes any sense or not depends on the particular situation. Since these enumerative values are *not* character strings, the CHR function is irrelevant here and cannot be used.

Problems

1. Write a subprogram named reverse that will return a string's characters in reverse order. reverse is to handle strings up to 80 characters long.

2. Write a subprogram named squeeze that operates on strings of 80 characters or less and removes excess blanks between words. The length is adjusted accordingly. Test your subprogram with a suitable driver using the following data (each line starts a new string):

Seers   Find a Ready   Market   For   Predictions   in   Users
But   few corporations in   any   field   are more   close-mouthed
Tourists   Hail   Their   Courtesy; Foreigners   Residing   There   disagree.

(*Note:* You may find it helpful to write a little subprogram that finds the next word in the string.)

3. Write a subprogram named replace whose invocation looks like this:

```
replace(VAR whichstring : stringofchar ;
        VAR oldstring : stringofchar ;
        VAR newstring : stringofchar)
```

replace is to go to the string specified by the first argument and replace the string indicated by the second argument with the string given by the third argument. The strings in the last two arguments are not necessarily the same size, nor is it guaranteed that the string to be replaced actually appears in the string on which replace is to operate. It is up to you to figure out what r e p l a c e should report and how it should report it.

4. Generalize the subprogram from the previous problem so that it does the replacement for all occurrences of o l d s t r i n g in w h i c h - s t r i n g.

5. Write a program that will read and process a succession of strings having a length of 15 characters or less. For each string read, the program is to display the string with all vowels replaced by dollar signs.

6. Write a program that processes strings as in the previous problem. This time, the program is to produce an output string consisting of all the vowels in the input string.

7. Write a program similar to the one for Problem 6. This time, the output string is to be the same length of the input string, and it is to consist of the vowels from the input string, placed in the rightmost positions of the output string and padded on the left with asterisks.

8. Take a look at the subprogram s t r c o p y (Figure 13.6). Is it possible to invoke that subprogram so that it copies a part of a string into another part of the same string? If it is, explain why it is. If it is not, explain why not and modify it so that this capability is included.

9. The H. P. Middleman Company is a wholesale distributor dealing in a wide variety of manufactured parts and components. For years they managed their business in a haphazard way, but now the competition is killing them with computers: Everything is systematized and Middleman must mend their ways. One of the areas that needs tightening stems from the fact that the various parts are identified using a scheme invented decades ago by the founder's brother-in-law William E. Nilley, Jr. Some parts were identified by numbers, some by names containing only letters, others by combinations of letters and numbers—all in all a mess. This is to be straightened out by a simple system that assigns an all-numerical identifier to each part:

1. Identifiers containing only numbers are left alone.

2. Identifiers containing only letters are converted with each letter being replaced by a number corresponding to that letter's position in the alphabet. For instance, A is replaced by 1, E by 5, X by 24, and so on.

3. Identifiers containing letters and numbers are handled by leaving the numbers alone and converting the letters as described for all-letter identifiers. In addition, a 0 (zero) is placed at the beginning of the converted identifier. (It was found that there are no part identifiers beginning with zero in the current system.)

A few examples will clarify this: A part identifier of 62505 remains 62505, an identifier of GUZZLR would be converted to 72126261218, an identifier of 21GJ7B would convert to 02171072. Careful examination of the inventory assured one and all that this conversion would guarantee against producing the same identifier for more than one type of item.

Write a program that reads a succession of old identifiers (one to a line) interactively and displays that identifier, along with its new version. An old identifier is never more than 6 characters long, no matter what type it is. (Of course, some new ones will have to be longer.) Stop the run with end of file. Each line of output is to look like this:

PART NAME   GUZZLR   CHANGES TO   72126261218

After all the input has been processed, the program is to display four additional lines showing how many all-digit part identifiers were processed, how many all-letter identifiers were processed, how many mixed identifiers were processed, and the total number of identifiers processed. One more thing: Old identifiers consist only of letters and numbers.

10. Write a batch version of the program specified for the previous problem and use the following input values when you run the program:

        FOOZIK
        304665
        G569J
        PLEVVL
        P6K45H
        (*HC77 (it is up to you to decide how to handle this)
        400400
        400400
        −20476
        BENDL

11. Sir Sedgewick Thruncklestrop left a peculiar will. He was sure that the hamlet of Threckfordshirehamburghville-on-the-Grobe was the cradle of his family, and that many of his distant relatives still lived there. The villagers didn't know they were descended from the famous Duke of Thruncklestrop, but Sir Sedgewick had a theory. He believed that his family could be traced through their names. If the last name had a TH in it, followed anywhere by a CK, that family (or so Sir Sedgewick believed) was related. Accordingly, the will set up a fund that would pay for a crack team of genealogists to travel to Threckfordshirehamburghville-on-the-Grobe and check the popula-

tion. Every family with the appropriate type of last name would then receive a handsome simulated vinyl wall sculpture of the Thruncklestrop coat of arms (at no charge) and a fine certificate attesting to the fact that the family had indeed received a handsome simulated vinyl wall sculpture, etc. The sleepy village of (oh no, we are not going to go through that again) will never be the same after that.

Luckily, the village is considerably more modernized than was first thought. For each household, the genealogists were amazed to find that there existed a line of computer-compatible data showing a six-digit identification number and a last name (up to 25 letters). Now, they need a program to process the data and display the name and i.d. number for each family eligible to receive a handsome, simulated, etc. After the last household has been processed, the program is to show a line indicating the total number of households processed and the total number of eligible households. (Note that a name like THROCKLEY is eligible while a name like BRACKTHISTLE is not; reread the problem if you are not sure why this should be so.) Run the program interactively using the following data:

```
334068THROCKMORTON
109877SNAPTHICKET
207654BILGEWEATHER
886002CROCKTHRESHER
797634TRICKLETHORPER
453231THIMBLEDERRICK
795112HIPTHWACKER
603114THWEBWYTHE
842331CRAZZWOCKER
785409BICKTHWICKMORESHAM
```

12. Write a batch version of the program described in the previous problem, and test the program with the same data.

13. Just as the genealogical program was being written, somebody discovered that the team had been misinformed. The household data are available, sure enough, but the order actually is reversed: The i.d. number follows the name. Rewrite the program so that it will handle these values.

14. Prepare a version of the program described in Example 13.2. Instead of reading a song title and a string for which that title is to be searched, arrange for the program to read the string to be matched first. Then this may be followed by any number of song titles to be searched for that same string. After all the titles have been processed, the program is to display the number of titles searched and the maximum number of matches in any one title.

15. Write a subprogram named `strcenter` that positions a string of a specified length in the center of a line of a specified length. The two lengths are not necessarily the same. In fact, there is no guarantee that the line length will be sufficient to accommodate the string.

16. Write a program that reads in a line length followed by a succession of strings. Each of these strings is to be centered and displayed on a separate line.

17. Write a truth table for each of the following expressions or statements. Assume that all of the variables have been declared as `BOOLEAN`, but do not assume that all of the expressions or statements are written correctly.
    - (a)   `m1 OR TRUE`
    - (b)   `m2 OR NOT TRUE`
    - (c)   `m3 := m1 OR NOT m2`
    - (d)   `m3 := m1 AND (NOT m2 AND NOT m3)`
    - (e)   `m1 <> (m2 AND m3)`
    - (f)   `m4 := m4 <= (m3 > m2)`
    - (g)   `m3 := m1 = m2`
    - (h)   `m3 := NOT m1 AND NOT (m2 <= NOT m4)`

18. Indicate what the final value will be for each of the following independent statements. Assume that all variables are declared as `BOO-LEAN`, and that they have the following values just before the statement is executed:
    - (a)   `m3 := m3 AND TRUE`
    - (b)   `m5 := m1 AND m2 AND m3 AND m4`
    - (c)   `m4 := (m4 <= m1) >= (m3 AND m2) OR m1`
    - (d)   `m5 := (m1 > m2) OR NOT (m2 <> m3) AND (m3 AND m4)`

19. Write a function named `numones` that processes a 20-element one-dimensional `BOOLEAN` array and returns an integer indicating the number of elements that have values of `TRUE`.

20. Write a function named `numzeros` that processes a 20-element one-dimensional `BOOLEAN` array and returns an integer indicating the number of elements that have values of `FALSE`.

21. Combine the processing for the previous two problems by developing a subprogram that allows the invoking program (or subprogram) to specify whether it wants the number of `TRUE`s or `FALSE`s reported. The subprogram returns the number, along with some kind of signal that indicates what is being reported.

22. Write a function named `howtrue` whose arguments are a 24-element `BOOLEAN` array, two integers defining which part of the array is of interest, and another integer indicating how many `TRUE` values we are seeking. For example, the expression

```
how true(switches,12,22,8)
```

asks the function to examine elements switches[12] through switches[22]. If it finds at least eight values of TRUE, it is to return a value of TRUE; if not, the returned value is FALSE. Test your function with a suitable driver.

Chapter Fourteen

Files

There are many circumstances where there is no particular advantage in processing information interactively. Instead, it would be more desirable to set up a program whose design enables us to prepare input ahead of time so that it can be read and processed automatically, without the user's intervention. Similarly, we may want to produce output that can be retained in machine-readable form for use as input later on.

To equip programs with these capabilities, we shall use Pascal's facilities for defining and handling files other than the standard ones (such as INPUT and OUTPUT) that the system defines automatically. This chapter discusses the properties of such user-defined files and techniques for manipulating them.

14.1 FILE ORGANIZATION

In Chapter 7 we saw that the use of READLN in the form

```
READLN (item,item,...,item)
```

persuaded Pascal to treat it as if we had said

```
READLN (INPUT,item,item,...,item)
```

INPUT, we learned, is one of several predefined textfiles. Since we have accumulated some experience with such textfiles, we shall start expanding our processing capabilities with programmer-defined textfiles.

14.1.1 Internal and External Files

INPUT and OUTPUT are examples of *internal files* defined within Pascal by Pascal itself. Other internal files may be defined by the programmer. We distinquish these files from *external files*. An external file, in this context, is a collection of data organized under (and managed by) the operating system's file-handling software. For example, each Pascal source program typically is stored on a secondary medium (such as a magnetic disk) as an external textfile, independent from any meaning or intended use by Pascal. Of course, such files were prepared for eventual use within Pascal's environment, but there is no apparent hint of that intention in the file's construction. Other external files, prepared under the same system, may be programs written in other languages or collections of data. The connection between an external file and Pascal is established by associating the external file with an internal file. The exact mechanism for doing this varies from one system to another. Regardless of the mechanism, standard Pascal itself deals with internal files; the assumption is that the connection to any external file is handled elsewhere in the system. (Some nonstandard implementations establish such connections within Pascal.)

14.1.2 Declaration of Internal Files

As far as Pascal is concerned, an internal file is a named data structure like an array. Specifically, a file consists of a series of data values, one after the other. There is no inherent limit to the size of a file; it may change as the file is processed. (Many people find it convenient to think of a file as a stream of data.) The organizational integrity of a file is unrelated to its size. In fact, it is possible to have an empty file whose name is recognized by the program.

A file is declared as part of Pascal's VAR declaration. Figure 14.1 shows the syntax, relating it back to the general categorization of Figure 4.7. Of specific concern to us right now is the FILE OF CHAR declaration because this is the way to describe a textfile. For example, if we wanted to declare an internal textfile named chemfile, we could say

```
VAR
   chemfile  :  FILE OF CHAR
```

In fact, the many uses of textfiles prompted the inclusion of a separate form for declaring them. The declaration

```
VAR
   chemfile  :  TEXT
```

has the same effect as the previous ones. In either case, Pascal is "made aware" of the existence of a textfile named chemfile.

14.2 PROCESSING OF TEXTFILES

Since programmer-defined textfiles have the same organizational characteristics as standard ones, the READ, READLN, WRITE, and WRITELN procedures are applicable in much the same way as before. However, it is

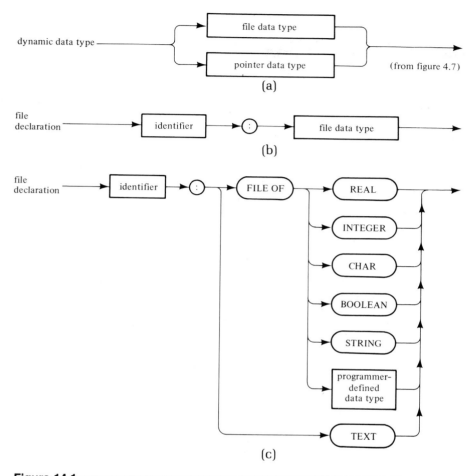

Figure 14.1

File Declaration Syntax

up to the programmer to inform Pascal of the files' existence. This is done by declaring the files and including their names in the PROGRAM statement. For example, if we say

```
VAR
   oldtext, newtext  :  FILE OF CHAR
```

and we expect to use the standard INPUT and OUTPUT files as well, our program would begin with

```
PROGRAM  programname (INPUT, OUTPUT, oldtext, newtext)
```

14.2.1 Opening a Textfile

Opening a file makes that file available for use by setting the file at its beginning. (We can think of this activity as being roughly analogous to placing the tone arm of a phonograph at the beginning of a record.) Only a certain part of the file is available to the program at any given time. Access to that part of the file is said to be provided by a *window*, and the information thus available is said to be the *window variable*. (The window variable has the same name as the internal file.) The amount of information in the window depends on the way the file is organized; this is a concern when handling files other than textfiles. If the program is to work on any information from the file, that information must appear in the window first. Moreover, textfiles are *sequential in that information is available in the window only in the order in which it is stored.* Consequently, it is necessary to provide a starting point for many file-related processes by setting the window at the beginning of the file and placing the file's initial data in the window variable. This is performed by Pascal's RESET procedure:

```
RESET (filename)
```

In a way, RESET performs an initialization, so that it is best placed at the beginning of a program's block, together with the other initializations.

14.2.2 Reading Programmer-Defined Textfiles

As pointed out earlier, READ and READLIN are used for all textfiles, interactive or otherwise, and we can apply them to programmer-defined textfiles without difficulty. The only major difference stems from the fact that the data in noninteractive files are available at the time the input operation is executed. This affects the way end of file is handled: For noninteractive files, a READ or READLN transfers data values to their respective destinations from the window. Then the window "moves" on to new data. This means that the value of EOF *(filename)* is FALSE until the window "moves" *beyond* the end of file. For interactive files, there are no values in the window variable because the user has to supply them on the spot. Consequently the process is reversed: A READ or READLN "moves" the window to pick up new input, and *then* the values are transferred to their destinations. As a result, the value of EOF *(filename)* becomes true as soon as the end of file is read. This means that if a line in an interactive file is followed by an end-of-file indicator, EOF becomes true as soon as that line is read. It does not matter whether the line has a separate end-of-line indicator or not. Consequently, if EOF takes the program out of a processing loop, it will not get a chance to work on any data in that last line.

On the other hand, if a line in a noninteractive textfile is followed by an end-of-file indicator, EOF for that file does not become TRUE until that line has been read and the program has tried to fill the window from the *next* line (which is not there). We shall be able to see this difference more precisely after developing Example 14.1.

Example 14.1

We shall perform exactly the same processing as in Example 11.1. The only change will be in the way the input is delivered: Instead of submitting it from the standard INPUT file, we shall read the data from a file named chemfile. We can consider this to be a *batch process*.

The procedures sortrd, mstdev, and update are not affected since they do not "know" how the data arrive. Consequently, we shall just indicate their positions in the overall program. Our main program needs to declare the file chemfile and establish its existence in the PROGRAM statement. We shall expect testid on a separate line, followed by 21 readings on a second line. The relevant parts of the resulting program are shown in Figure 14.2. Note that the file name appears ahead of the input variable in the READLN call.

14.2.3 Writing Textfiles

WRITE and WRITELN are applicable to all textfiles. The underlying mechanism is based on a textfile's sequential structure in that the window is assumed to be at the end of the file. Consequently, when we send output to a textfile, we are *appending* data to that file. This notion certainly is not new to us: Every time we wrote on the screen or the printer, we added a new line (or a new value) rather than inserting it between existing ones.

14.2.4 The REWRITE Procedure

The initialization of an output file is established via the REWRITE procedure. For instance, the sequence

```
VAR
    chemoutfile  :   TEXT
    • • • • • • • • • • • • • •
    REWRITE (chemoutfile)
```

defines the file chemoutfile and instructs the system to create an empty file with that name, position its window at the end, and set its end-of-file indicator to TRUE. Then, whenever the program performs a WRITE or WRITELN on file chemoutfile, the output values are appended to the new file, and its end-of-file indicator continues to show a value of TRUE.

```
PROGRAM ex1401 (OUTPUT, chemfile) ;
CONST
   numofreads = 21 ;
TYPE
   testgroup = ARRAY [1..numofreads] OF REAL ;
VAR
   chemfile : TEXT ;
   acidity : testgroup ;
   median, avgacidity, maxmed, maxmean,
                       minmed, minmean : REAL ;
   testid, numoftests, maxmedtest, minmedtest,
                       maxmntest, minmntest : INTEGER ;

   sw : BOOLEAN ;
```

descriptions of sortrd, stdev, and update procedures

```
(***              THE MAIN PROGRAM                    ***)
BEGIN
   RESET (chemfile) ;
   maxmed := -200.0 ;  minmed := 200.0 ;  maxmean := -200.0 ;  minmean := 200.0 ;
   numoftests := 0 ;  sw :=TRUE ;
   WHILE sw DO
   BEGIN
      READLN (chemfile,testid) ;
      FOR i := 1 TO numofreads DO
```

```
      READ (chemfile,acidity[i])        ;
    READLN (chemfile)  ;
    sortrd (acidity)  ;
    mstdev (acidity, avgacidity, stdevacid)  ;
    median := acidity[i]  ;
    update (median, avgacidity, testid, maxmed, maxmean, minmed, minmean,
            maxmedtest, maxmntest, minmedtest, minmntest)  ;
    numoftests := numoftests + 1  ;
    WRITELN  ;
    WRITELN ('TEST NO.: ',testid  ;
    WRITELN ('MEDIAN ACIDITY: ',median:7:3,' MEAN ACIDITY: ',
             avgacidity:7:3,' STD DEV.: ',stdevacid:7:3  ;
    WRITELN  :
    IF EOF (chemfile)  THEN sw := FALSE
  END  ;
  WRITELN  ;  WRITELN  ;
  WRITELN ('SUMMARY :')  ;
  WRITELN ('NO. OF TESTS THIS RUN:   ',numoftests)  ;
  WRITELN ('TEST NUMBER ',maxmedtest,' HAD A HIGH MEDIAN OF  ',maxmed:7:3)  ;
  WRITELN ('TEST NUMBER ',maxmntest,' HAD A HIGH MEAN OF  ',maxmean:7:3)  ;
  WRITELN ('TEST NUMBER ',minmedtest,'HAD A LOW MEDIAN OF ',minmed:7:3)  ;
  WRITELN ('TEST NUMBER ',minmntest,' HAD A LOW MEAN OF  ',minmean:7:3)  ;
  WRITELN ('END OF RUN.')
END.
```

Fig. 14.2 ——— Program for Example 14.1

Example 14.2

We can illustrate the file creation process conveniently by modifying Example 14.1. In addition to producing the previous results, the modified version also will deliver output to a new file named chemoutfile. Two lines will be written for each test; the first will contain the test number (a three-digit integer), and the second will show the median, mean, and standard deviation.

The program's basic processing remains as it was. We need only attend to the new file. This requires:

1. Declaration of chemoutfile
2. A call to REWRITE to set up chemoutfile
3. The WRITE and WRITELN statements to transmit output to chemoutfile

The changes are incorporated in the revised program shown in Figure 14.3, shown on pp. 310 and 311.

14.3 DATAFILES

Not all files have to be textfiles. Recall (Figure 14.1) that files may consist of different data values. For example, the declaration

```
VAR
    mydata  :  FILE OF INTEGER
```

is a legitimate one. It sets up an internal *datafile* named mydata consisting of a sequence of integer values. When information is written on such a file, it is represented using the processor's internal data formats and not as human-readable characters. Consequently, its storage is more compact, and its input or output proceeds more rapidly than that of a textfile. Operations other than READ, WRITE, READLN, and WRITELN are used to perform input/output on such files.

The requirement to restrict membership in such a file to a single data type (i.e., with INTEGER, REAL, or BOOLEAN as its sole components) limits its utility. Instead, a much more common practice is to combine data types in any desired combination to form a *record*, and then define that structure as a new data type. This is how we shall use datafiles. The pertinent discussion is presented in the next section.

14.3.1 Records and Record Processing

As Chapter 4 indicated, the RECORD construction gives the Pascal programmer an opportunity to deal with collections of data consisting of any combination of types. In this section we shall use the facility as a convenient and powerful vehicle for constructing data files.

Records are defined as specific data types using Pascal's TYPE declaration. For instance, referring to Example 14.2, suppose we wanted to construct a collection of chemical test data so that each member of this collection were to consist of an integer test number, 21 real test readings, and median, mean, and standard deviation values (all real). This construction can be defined as follows:

```
CONST
   numofreads = 21  ;
TYPE
   testrec = RECORD
                testnum : INTEGER ;
                hydro : ARRAY[1..numofreads] OF REAL ;
                medianacidity : REAL ;
                meanacidity : REAL ;
                stdacidity : REAL
             END
```

testnum, etc. are the *field names* that make up this structure. As is true with any other TYPE declaration, this is only bookkeeping. There are no records yet, nor is there a mechanism for recognizing them. This situation changes when we declare a variable of type testrec, e.g.,

```
VAR
   chemrslt : testrec
```

Now we have a variable named chemrslt associated with sufficient storage to accommodate values denoted by the field names listed in the TYPE declaration.

14.3.2 Internal Manipulation of Records

Each item in a record variable can be manipulated like any other single-valued variable. (We cannot place values in all of a record's items with a single assignment.) When we process a record's items, we must make sure that we identify each item unambiguously. For instance, assuming the testrec data type defined before, we are well within our rights to declare

```
VAR
   chemrslt, foodrslt, paintrslt : testrec
```

As a result of this declaration, it would appear that there are three different items named testnum, three named meanacidity, etc. This is true, but

```
PROGRAM ex1402 (chemfile, chemoutfile, INPUT, OUTPUT) ;
CONST
   numofreads = 21 ;
TYPE
   testgroup = ARRAY [1..numofreads] OF REAL  ;
VAR
   chemfile, chemoutfile   :   TEXT ;
   acidity   :   testgroup ;
   median, avgacidity, stdevacid, maxmed, maxmean,
                            minmed, minmean : REAL  ;
   testid, numoftests, maxmedtest, minmedtest,
                  i, maxmntest, minmntest : INTEGER ;

   sw : BOOLEAN ;
```

descriptions of sortrd, mstdev, and update procedures

```
(***              THE MAIN PROGRAM                ***)
BEGIN
   REWRITE(chemoutfile) ;
   RESET(chemfile) ;
   maxmed := -200.0 ; minmed := 200.0 ; maxmean := -200.0 ; minmean := 200.0 ;
   numoftests := 0 ;   sw := TRUE ;
   WHILE sw DO
      BEGIN
         READLIN (chemfile,testid) ;
```

```
FOR i := 1 TO numofreads DO
   READ (chemfile,acidity[i])    ;
   READLN (chemfile)    ;
   sortrd (acidity)    ;
   mstdev (acidity, avgacidity, stdevacid)    ;
   median := acidity[i]    ;
      update (median, avgacidity, testid, maxmed, maxmean, minmed,
         minmean, maxmedtest, maxmntest, minmedtest, minmntest)    ;
   numoftests := numoftests + 1    ;
   WRITELN    ;
   WRITELN ('TEST NO.:  ',testid)    ;
   WRITELN ('MEDIAN ACIDITY:  ',median:7:3,  '  MEAN ACIDITY:  ',
      avgacidity:7:3,  '  STD DEV.:  ',stdevacid:7:3)    ;
   WRITELN    ;
   WRITE (chemoutfile, testid:3)    ;
   FOR i := 1 TO numofreads DO
      WRITE (chemoutfile, acidity[i]:3:1)    ;
   WRITE (chemoutfile, median:7:3,avgacidity:7:3,stdevacid:7:3)    ;
   WRITELN (chemoutfile)    ;
   IF EOF(chemfile) THEN sw := FALSE
END
WRITELN :  WRITELN ;
WRITELN ('SUMMARY:')    ;
WRITELN ('NO. OF TESTS THIS RUN:  ',numoftests)    ;
WRITELN ('TEST NUMBER  ',maxmedtest,' HAD A HIGH MEDIAN OF  ',maxmed:7:3)    ;
WRITELN ('TEST NUMBER  ',maxmntest,' HAD A HIGH MEAN OF  ',maxmean:7:3)    ;
WRITELN ('TEST NUMBER  ',minmedtest,' HAD A LOW MEDIAN OF  ',minmed:7:3)    ;
WRITELN ('TEST NUMBER  ',minmntest,' HAD A LOW MEAN OF  ',minmean:7:3)    ;
END.
```

Fig. 14.3 ————— Program for Example 14.2

311

the replicate names can be distinguished from each other by attaching the proper record name. Thus, the statement

```
foodrslt.testnum := 409
```

leaves no doubt as to which testnum we mean.

When numerous computations are to be done on items from the same record variable, we can avoid having to specify the record name repeatedly. This is done using the WITH...DO statement whose syntax is shown in Figure 14.4, shown on pp. 314 and 315. For example, the statement

```
WITH   chemrslt   DO
   BEGIN
     TESTNUM := 409 ;
     FOR i := 1 TO numofreads   DO
        hydro[i] := 1.0 ;
     medianacidity := 1.0 ;
     meanacidity := 1.0 ;
     stdacidity := 0.0
   END
```

refers specifically to chemslt.testnum, chemrslt.hydro, chemrslt.meanacidity, and chemrslt.stdacidity.

Entire records may be compared with each other as long as their respective constructions are identical and the type of comparions is either "=" or " <>." Thus,

```
IF   chemrslt = foodrslt   THEN......
```

is acceptable, but

```
IF chemrslt <= foodrslt   THEN.....
```

is not.

14.3.3 Files of Records

A collection of records can be defined as a datafile by an ordinary file declaration. Thus,

```
VAR
   foodfile : FILE OF testrec
```

defines an internal file in which each record is to consist of the items described in testrec's TYPE definition. Since this is not a textfile, its values cannot be transmitted via READ, READLN, WRITE, or WRITELN. Records for such files are transmitted by the special procedures GET and PUT, as explained in the next section. When it is not necessary for the user to view the data directly (i.e., the data are to be read by a program rather than a human being), it is advantageous to use datafiles (rather than textfiles) because the former are more compact and their transmission is more rapid.

14.3.4 Input/Output of Datafiles

RESET and REWRITE operate on datafiles as they do on textfiles. Accordingly, the previous discussion of these procedures applies here as well. Since all the records in a given datafile have the same basic organization (more complex alternatives are possible, but they are beyond the scope of this book), their transmission is simplified by dealing with entire records rather than individual values. A datafile record is read by calling the GET procedure:

GET (internalfilename)

Whenever a datafile's record is read, its values become available in the file's window variable, whose name is ↑ internalfilename. For example, if foodfile is a previously prepared datafile consisting of records of type testrec, the statement

GET(foodfile)

places foodfile's next record in the window variable ↑foodfile.* As a result, ↑foodfile contains the integer value ↑foodfile.testnum, 21 real values ↑foodfile.hydro[1] through ↑foodfile.hydro[21], and real values ↑foodfile.medianacidity, ↑foodfile.meanacidity, and ↑foodfile.stdacidity. These values may be assigned to other variables, written as part of another datafile (using PUT), or written as part of a textfile (using WRITE or WRITELN). Similarly, we can read data from a textfile, prepare a datafile record by assigning values to a window variable, and then send the record off to the datafile with a PUT. This latter process is illustrated in the next section.

---

*The "up arrow" symbol may not be available on your system, in which case another character is assigned to represent it. For example, the carat (^) is used on the IBM Personal Computer and the "at sign" (@) is used in IBM VS Pascal.

```
PROGRAM ex1403 (OUTPUT, chemfile, testfile) ;
CONST
    numofreads = 21 ;
TYPE
    testgroup = ARRAY [1..numofreads] OF REAL ;
    testrec = RECORD
                  testnum : INTEGER ;
                  midval : REAL ;
                  acidity : testgroup ;
                  meanacidity, stdacidity : REAL
              END ;
VAR
    chemfile  :  TEXT ;
    testfile  :  FILE OF testrec ;
    acidity  :  testgroup ;
    median, avgacidity, stdevacid, maxmed, maxmean, minmed, minmean : REAL ;
    testid, numoftests, maxmedtest, minmedtest,
                       maxmntest, minmntest : INTEGER ;

    sw : BOOLEAN ;
```

descriptions of sortrd, mstdev, and update procedures

```
(****               THE MAIN PROGRAM                  ****)
BEGIN
    RESET(chemfile) ;
    REWRITE(testfile) ;
    maxmed := 200.0 ; minmed := 200.0 ; maxmean := -200.0 ; minmean := 200.0 ;
    numoftests := 0 ; sw := TRUE ;
    WHILE sw DO
    BEGIN
        READLN (chemfile,testid) ;
        FOR i := 1 TO numofreads DO
```

```
      READ (chemfile,acidity[i])       ;
      READLN(chemfile)       ;
      sortrd (acidity)       ;
      mstdev (acidity, avgacidity, stdevacid)       ;
      median := acidity[i]       ;
      update (median, avgacidity, testid, maxmed, maxmean, minmed,
              minmean, maxmedtest, maxmntest, minmedtest, minmntest)       ;
      numoftests := numoftests + 1       ;
      WRITELN ;
      WRITELN ('TEST NO.: ',testid)       ;
      WRITELN ('MEDIAN ACIDITY:    ',median:7:3, ' MEAN ACIDITY:    ',
               avgacidity:7:3, ' STD DEV.: ',stdevacid:7:3)       ;
      WRITELN ;
      [BUILD THE OUTPUT FILE RECORD]
      WITH —.243testfile  DO
      BEGIN
         testnum := testid
         FOR i := 1 TO numofreads  DO
            hydro[i] := acidity[i]       ;
         midval := median ;
         meanacidity := avgacidity ;
         stdacidity := stdevacid
      END
      PUT(testfile)       ;
      IF  EOF(chemfile)  THEN  sw := FALSE
   END ;
   WRITELN ; WRITELN ;
   WRITELN ('SUMMARY:')       ;
   WRITELN ('NO OF TESTS THIS RUN: ',numoftests)       ;
   WRITELN ('TEST NUMBER  ',maxmedtest,' HAD A HIGH MEDIAN OF  ',maxmed:7:3)       ;
   WRITELN ('TEST NUMBER  ',maxmntest,' HAD A HIGH MEAN OF  ',maxmean:7:3)       ;
   WRITELN ('TEST NUMBER  ',minmedtest,' HAD A LOW MEDIAN OF  ',minmed:7:3)       ;
   WRITELN ('TEST NUMBER  ',minmntest,' HAD A LOW MEAN OF  ',minmean:7:3)       ;
   WRITELN ('END OF RUN.')
END.
```

Fig. 14.4   Program for Example 14.3

Figure 14.5

Syntax for the WITH Statement

14.3.5 Example 14.3

We are going the use the textfile c h e m f i l e from Example 14.1 to prepare a datafile named t e s t f i l e. Each of t e s t f i l e's records will contain the test number, the 21 acidity readings, the median, mean, and the standard deviation.

   As was the case in the previous two examples, we do not need to change any of the computations. The main program now will include a TYPE declaration for t e s t r e c (and the corresponding file declarations for c h e m f i l e and t e s t f i l e), and the internal processing to prepare the record for the window variable ↑ t e s t f i l e. The resulting program is shown in Figure 14.5. (One of the problems at the end of the chapter asks you to simplify the program.)

Problems

1. Modify Example 14.2 so that, before it shows the computed results for each test, it displays the test number and the 21 readings.
2. Produce a version of Example 10.3 in which the input values are read from a textfile named l a k e f i l e. Run your program using the data given below.

117.0 86.5	123.5 81.1	127.2 92.0LAKE LACKALOOK
31.4 22.8	36.6 23.4	38.8 18.9LAKE LOOKALIKE
45.5 56.7	49.6 61.1	52.2 53.3LAKE LACKALOCK
71.5 19.8	73.4 15.7	72.8 24.6LAKE LACKALICK
204.4 6.7	209.9 18.5	211.3 8.7LAKE LOCALLOX

3. The Nineveh Ice Cream Company ("A Whale of a Treat") makes ice cream in eight incredible flavors: Chocomarsh, Vanillatron, Zoonegeberry, Colonial Mist, Cumulus, Barcarolle, Broccoli, and HehHeh. These delights are sold in Nineveh's three retail stores. At the end of each month, the home office receives a sales report from each store showing, for each flavor, the number of liters sold and the number of ice cream cones sold. (Nineveh has a special interest in ice cream cones.) From this information, the office prepares a textfile in which the first line shows the month and year (e.g., 8 1982), and each subsequent line shows the store number (1, 2, or 3), the number of

liters sold (to the nearest liter), the number of ice cream cones sold (to the nearest cone), and the name of the flavor. (The ice cream sold as cones is part of the total liters.) Thus, the line

2   3140   12473CUMULUS

shows that store number 2 sold 3140 liters of Cumulus ice cream, including 12473 cones. Now, all the company needs is a program to operate on such a file. Write a program that shows the total sales (in liters) and the total number of cones sold for each flavor (one line for each flavor). In addition, the program is to show the total sales and total number of cones for each store regardless of flavor (one line per store). A final line of output shows the grand totals.

We have managed (at great expense and personal risk) to acquire Nineveh's textfile for June 1982. The lines are in no particular order as can be seen below:

8	1982		
1	2178	9888	CHOCOMARSH
1	2234	5676	VANILLATRON
1	5443	13887	COLONIAL MIST
1	3223	4452	BARCAROLLE
1	4568	10095	ZOONEGEBERRY
1	1088	2220	CUMULUS
1	2121	2500	BROCCOLI
1	6644	23888	HEHHEH
2	3140	12473	CUMULUS
2	3385	12500	CHOCOMARSH
2	4665	2875	VANILLATRON
2	3854	1006	ZOONEGEBERRY
2	1172	766	COLONIAL MIST
2	5766	12448	BARCAROLLE
2	6979	34554	HEHHEH
2	6176	344	BROCCOLI
3	8860	96554	HEHHEH
3	3424	6578	COLONIAL MIST
3	4176	9767	BARCAROLLE
3	998	1085	ZOONEGEBERRY
3	2898	4658	VANILLATRON
3	5433	5789	CHOCOMARSH
3	6497	13884	CUMULUS
3	7250	2548	BROCCOLI

4. Modify the program in Problem 3 so that its output appears in the following order: The eight lines showing total sales by flavor are to be

arranged in descending order (highest sales first). The three lines showing sales by store are to appear in descending order (highest sales first).

5. Modify the program in Problem 3 or 4 so that each line also includes a dollar amount for sales. The sales price is the same for all flavors in all stores (a typical value is $2.88 per liter), and it is entered interactively in response to a request from the program. (it is a good idea to display the price on the first line of output, along with the month.)

6. Modify the program in Problem 5 so that, in addition to displaying the results described before, it produces a datafile named `icefile` in which each of the eight records contains the month, year and flavor, liters sold, cones sold, and dollar amount of sales for each store, and total liters sold, cones sold, and dollar amount for that flavor. (Thus, each record would have 15 items.

7. Simplify the main program in Example 14.3 (For instance, are `tes-tid` and `↑textfile.testnum` both necessary?) Input and output requirements are unchanged.

8. Modify the program in Example 10.1 so that the unsorted arrays are read from the textfile `infile`. Each line of `infile` consists of an (integer) array number followed by the six integer values. In addition to displaying the sorted arrays, the program is to produce a datafile named `outdfile` in which each record consists of the array number, the six values in descending order, and the mean value. Here are some test data:

```
304  6   7    4   18   5   9
226  8   4   -2    3   9   5
343  21  20   18   17  16  12
497 -41 -28  -17   -8  -6  -2
568  76  44  32  -76 -44 -32
```

9. Modify the program in Problem 8 so that the first record in `out-dfile` is the one with the lowest mean value, the second is the one with the second lowest mean, etc. Design the program so that the number of arrays to be processed is not fixed, but it does not exceed 10.

10. (*Special Challenge*): Expand the program in Problem 8 as follows: After all the data for `infile` have been processed, the program asks for additional array data to be submitted interactively. Each additional array (along with its array number) is processed as before, and the results (in addition to being displayed are appended to `outdfile`.

Chapter Fifteen

Sets

Our dealings with arrays, records, and files have pointed up the convenience that can be gained from treating data values as organized groups and collections. Another useful type of data organization is the set. Unlike the array, whose elements are ordered and usually fixed in number (for a given situation), the set accommodates more flexible construction in which the number of members may vary arbitrarily, and their order may or may not be important.

Pascal's SET organization is designed to convey this flexibility. We can define sets by declaring them and specifying the criteria that make a data value eligible for membership. (The basic rules for doing this were introduced in Chapter 4, and you may want to check back there for a quick review.) Once declared, a set variable can be processed in a variety of ways, all of which treat the set as a unit of information. This chapter discusses these facilities and illustrates their use.

15.1 DECLARATION OF SETS

Declaration of a set variable (first defined in Figure 5.7) is described diagrammatically in Figure 15.1. Various Pascal implementations set different limits on the maximum number of elements in a set (UCSD Pascal, for example, accepts up to 4080 of them), their values all must differ from each other, and they all must be of the same data type. (Recall from Chapter 4 that this underlying data type is called the *base type*.) Since the base type may be any simple type except REAL, this means that Pascal extends an open invitation to create a set for any coherent collection of items whose processing is facilitated by this kind of organization.

For example, suppose we define a data type named weeks as follows:

```
TYPE
   weeks = 1..52
```

weeks now can serve as the base type for another data type. The declaration

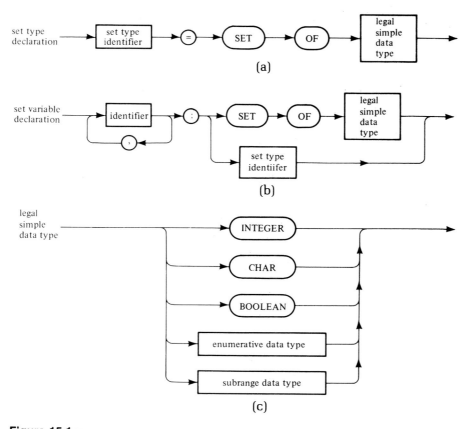

Figure 15.1

Declaration of Sets

```
TYPE
    season = SET OF weeks
```

defines a set type named season such that each declared variable of this type can be a collection of anywhere from 0 to 52 values. We can have any kind of season we want. For example,

```
VAR
    theaterseason, hockeyseason, matingseason,
    papayaseason, symphonyseason, slackseason : season
```

gives us six different kinds of seasons. (There is no doubt that you can think of many more.) The values that these variables may take on are drawn from those defined for the data type weeks. 49 is such a value, and to denote its use as a member of a set, we enclose it in square brackets. Based on our

TYPE declarations, any value from [1] to [52] is a legitimate constant. For example, the assignment

```
papayaseason := [31]
```

tells Pascal that the set papayaseason is to consist of the single value 31. (This is a mighty short papaya season.) A more optimistic assignment might be

```
papayaseason := [31, 32, 33, 34, 35, 36]
```

which gives us a nice 6-week season. Since these values are consecutive, we can say the same thing using Pascal's subrange notation:

```
papayaseason := [31..36]
```

If the crop fails and there is no papaya season (*ay, que cosa,* can this happen?), we can describe the sad event by saying

```
papayaseason := []
```

15.2 MANIPULATION OF SETS

Pascal accepts several types of set operations. Although they are specified by some of the same operator symbols (e.g., +, *) used to describe arithmetic processing, Pascal has no difficulty in determining how to interpret the appearance of a particular operator. Ambiguity is avoided by Pascal's rule that allows sets and set constants to be the only legal operands in set expressions.

To facilitate the discussion of Pascal's set operations, we shall assume the following declarations:

```
TYPE
   weeks = 1..52 ;
   season = SET OF weeks ;
VAR
   theaterseason, hockeyseason, huntingseason,
   symphonyseason, danceseason, operaseason,
   footballseason, baseballseason, rockseason,
   dramaseason, homeseason, awayseason
   busyseason  :  season
```

15.2.1 Set Assignment

We have already seen the operation of set assignment for constant values (with our papayaseason). The same process can be applied to a variable as well. For example, the sequence

```
operaseason := [21..26] ;
danceseason := opera season
```

produces a situation in which the 6-week opera and dance season coincide. (Who are these schedulers anyway?)

15.2.2 Set Addition (Union)

Larger set memberships can be constructed by combining sets via the + operator. For instance, if we define the symphony season by saying

```
symphonyseason := [33..52, 1..16]
```

the statement

```
rockseason := symphonyseason + [17..20, 22]
```

specifies rockseason as consisting of all the weeks in symphony- season as well as weeks 17 through 20, and week 22. The sequence

```
dramaseason := [37, 40..43, 48..50, 2, 6, 7] ;
danceseason := [41..46] ;
theaterseason := dramaseason + danceseason
```

assigns the set [37, 40..46, 48..50, 2, 6, 7] to theaterseason. This is the set of elements found in either dramaseason or danceseason or both. Each constant value appears only once, and the order is immaterial.

15.2.3 Set Differences

The − operator forms sets whose elements constitute the difference between two sets. For instance, the sequence

```
footballseason := [33..48] ;
homeseason := [34, 35, 38, 41, 43, 44, 46, 47] ;
awayseason := footballseason - homeseason
```

assigns the set [33, 36, 37, 39, 40, 42, 45, 48] to awayseason. These are all the elments in footballseason that are not in homeseason.

15.2.4 Set Multiplication (Intersection)

The * operator uses the elements common two specified sets to form a third set. Thus, if we specify the sets

```
footballseason := [33,48] ;
baseballseason := [13,,39] ;
rockseason := [21,,26, 30, 32,,34, 36, 37, 40,,44]
```

the statement

```
busyseason := footballseason * baseballseason * rockseason
```

assigns the set [32..34, 36, 37] to busyseason. (These are the five elements found in all the sets specified in the expression.)

15.3 DECISION OPERATIONS WITH SETS

The IF statement can be used to set up decision rules based on comparisons involving entire sets. Several types of comparisons can be specified, with all of them sharing the same basic property: the outcome is either TRUE or FALSE.

15.3.1 Searching Sets

Pascal's IN operation searches a specified set to determine whether a particular element is present in that set. The element (which itself is *not* a set) must be of the same type as the set's base type. For instance, let us assume the following fragment:

```
CONST
   endgoodnum = 1 ;
TYPE
   tickets = 1,,4000 ;
   winners = SET OF ticket :
VAR
   entrant : INTEGER ;
   number, goodnum : ticket ;
   luckylist : winners ;
   sw : BOOLEAN
   ..............
   sw := TRUE ;
   luckylist := [] ;
   WHILE sw DO
     BEGIN
         READ (goodnum) ;
         IF goodnum < > endgoodnum
           THEN luckylist := luckylist + [goodnum]
           ELSE sw := FALSE
       END
     ..............
```

ticket is defined as a subrange integer data type whose values may range from 1 to 4000. This becomes the base type for a set type named winners. So far we have no variables, just bookkeeping. The variables number and goodnum, both of type ticket, may assume single values in the range 1..4000. Since luckylist is a set variable with ticket as its base type, it may assume combinations of values in this range. So much for the declarations.

luckylist is intended to contain the list of winning numbers in some lottery or sweepstakes. That list is filled by reading each of those numbers (goodnum) in and adding it to the set. Accordingly, luckylist is initialized to empty, and the winning values are read by means of a loop controlled by a terminating value of 1 (which we have given the name endgoodnum. Now the stage is set for the rest of the processing.

If we want to set up a loop in which each entry ticket is brought in to see whether its number is a winner, we are in an excellent position to take advantage of the IN operation:

```
. . . . . . . . . . . . . .
READLN (entrant, number) ;
IF   number IN luckylist
     THEN WRITELN ('NUMBER ',number,' IS A WINNER. HOO HA!')
     ELSE WRITELN ('NUMBER ',number,' DOES NOT WIN. ALAS.')
. . . . . . . . . . . . .
```

Notice that sets or set elements cannot be read or written. When we read a winning number, we read goodnum, not [goodnum].

15.3.2 Comparing Sets with Each Other

Sets having the same base type can be compared with each other using one of four relational operators:

1. The = comparison produces an outcome of TRUE if the two sets being compared contain the same elements (or are both empty). As pointed out earlier, the order is not important. Thus, the comparison

$$[17, 21, 22, 23, 24, 8] = [21..24, 8, 17]$$

would result in a value of TRUE.

2. The < > comparison produces an outcome of TRUE if the two sets being compared differ in their contents. (For example, this is a convenient way to determine whether a set has anything in it.)

3. The >= comparison produces an outcome of TRUE if the first set contains all the second set's elements. Thus, if result is declared as BOOLEAN, the statement

```
result := [18, 23, 6] >= [23, 6, 41, 18, 55]
```

```
PROGRAM   ex1501 (INPUT, OUTPUT) ;   (*IN THIS SYSTEM, <CNTRL>-C *)
TYPE                                 (*INDICATES END-OF-FILE    *)
   weeknum = 1..52 ;
   schedule = SET OF weeknum ;
VAR
   available, booked : schedule ;
   when : weeknum ;
   idnum, i, j : INTEGER ;
   sw : BOOLEAN ;
BEGIN
   available := [1..7, 10..29, 31..52] ;
   booked := [] ;
   sw := TRUE ;
   WRITELN ('HI THERE, WELCOME TO HOTSHOT KNOLLS. THE EXCITEMENT BEGINS!') ;
   WRITELN ;
   WHILE  sw   DO
     BEGIN
       WRITELN ('TYPE IN I.D., DESIRED WEEK NO. (1-52), AND <ENTER>.') ;
       READLN (idnum, when) ;
       IF when IN available
         THEN
           BEGIN
             WRITELN ('WEEK ',when,' IS YOURS, CONGRATULATIONS!') ;
             booked := booked + [when] ;
             available := available - [when]
           END
       ELSE
           WRITELN ('WEEK ',when,' IS ALREADY BOOKED. SORRY.') ;
     WRITELN ('TYPE <ENTER> TO CONTINUE OR <CNTRL>-C TO QUIT.');
     READLN
     IF EOF THEN sw := FALSE
   END ;
WRITELN ; WRITELN ; WRITELN ('BOOKED WEEKS AT THE KNOLLS:') ;
WRITELN ; i := 1 ; j := 1 ;
WHILE i <= 52 DO
  BEGIN
    IF i IN booked
      THEN
        BEGIN
          WRITE (i:4) ;
          IF  j = 10
            THEN
              BEGIN
                WRITELN ;
                j := 1
              END
```

Fig. 15.2

Program for Example 15.1

```
            ELSE
                j := j + 1
            END ;
        i := i + 1
    END;
  WRITELN ;  WRITELN ('END OF RUN.')
END.
```

Figure 15.2

Program for Example 15.1 (continued)

will place a value of FALSE in result, but the statement

result := [23, 6, 41, 18, 55] >= [18, 23, 61]

will assign the value TRUE to result.

4.   The <= comparison produces a value of TRUE if all the elements in the first set are contained in the second set. Thus, the expression

['A'..'F','a..f','*'] <= ['a..h','*','D','F','A..C','E']

is TRUE.

Example 15.1

Hotshot Enterprises, eager to enjoy the benefits of modern business practices and methodologies, arranged for their staff to go to Lake Lackalooka-like for an Intensive Interdisciplinary Dynamic Management Seminar Workshop Conference. They have not reported on the outcome of that historic IIDMSWC (as we in the Management Dynamics set refer to it), but there is strong evidence that the group liked Lake Lackalookalike. Shortly after their return to the home base in Cranepool's Cavity, Hotshot announced a new addition to their business ventures: They have purchased a Luxury Sport Condominium on the lake and are ready to lease its use, 1 week at a time, to qualified clients. Imagine.

In response to a request from Hotshot, we shall write a program to help keep track of the bookings for Hotshot Knolls (as they like to call it). Each client requesting to lease the condominium is given an i.d. number, and each request consists of this i.d. number and a week number (1 through 52; weeks 8 and 9 are reserved for maintenance and refurbishing, and week 30 is reserved for Hotshot). The program is to respond by indicating whether the reservation is accepted (i.e., the Knolls are available) or whether that week had been taken earlier. After the final request (for that run), the program is to display a list of the weeks that have been booked.

Organization of this program pivots around a set data type called a schedule whose values are drawn from the base type weeknum. Two schedules, available and booked, will keep track of the open and reserved week numbers, respectively. Consequently, when processing begins, available is initialized to its maximum number of elements, representing the situation in which all the weeks are available. Conversely, booked is initialized to the empty set to signify that nothing is booked. Then, as each request is brought in, a simple check (with the IN operation) determines whether to process it (i.e., move that week from available to booked) or to turn it down.

To display the results at the end of the run, we have to work our way around Pascal's refusal to read or write set data. Instead, we relate the set values to the base type and display the latter values. The interactive program is shown in Figure 15.2, and a modest sample run is shown in Figure 15.3

Sets can be processed by subprograms, so that the organizational advantages of program modularity can be exploited fully. To illustrate,

HI THERE, WELCOME TO HOTSHOT KNOLLS. THE EXCITEMENT BEGINS!

TYPE IN I.D., DESIRED WEEK NO. (1–52), AND <ENTER>.
222 6
WEEK 6 IS YOURS. CONGRATULATIONS!
TYPE <ENTER> TO CONTINUE OR <CNTRL>-C TO QUIT

3131 7
WEEK 7 IS YOURS. CONGRATULATIONS!
TYPE <ENTER> TO CONTINUE OR <CNTRL>-C TO QUIT.

TYPE IN I.D., DESIRED WEEK NO.(1–52), AND <ENTER>.
4217 8
WEEK 8 IS IS ALREADY BOOKED. SORRY.
TYPE <ENTER> TO CONTINUE OR <CNTRL>-C TO QUIT.
614 51
WEEK 51 IS YOURS. CONGRATULATIONS!
TYPE <ENTER> TO CONTINUE OR <CNTRL>-C TO QUIT.

TYPE IN I.D., DESIRED WEEK NO. (1–52), AND <ENTER>.
7841 6
WEEK 6 IS ALREADY BOOKED. SORRY.
TYPE <ENTER> TO CONTINUE OR <CNTRL>-C TO QUIT.

BOOKED WEEKS AT THE KNOLLS:

  6   7   51
END OF RUN.

Figure 15.3 Sample Run for Example 15.1

```
PROGRAM   ex1501 (INPUT, OUTPUT)            {revised}

    {the TYPE and VAR declarations are exactly as before}

  PROCEDURE addnum ;
  BEGIN
    IF  when IN available
      THEN
        BEGIN
          WRITELN ('WEEK ',when,' IS YOURS, CONGRATULATIONS!') ;
          booked := booked + [when] ;
          available := available - [when]
        END
      ELSE
        WRITELN ('WEEK ',when,' IS BOOKED, SORRY,')
  END;

BEGIN

    {initialization of available, booked, and sw as before}
    {hearty message still appears as in the initial version}

  WHILE  sw  DO
    BEGIN
      WRITELN ('TYPE IN I.D., DESIRED WEEK NO.(1-52), and <ENTER>,');
      READLN (idnum, when) ;
      addnum ;
      WRITELN ('TYPE <ENTER> TO CONTINUE OR <CNTRL>-C TO QUIT,')
      READLN ;

        {the rest is the same}
```

Figure 15.4

Revision of Example 15.1 Showing Set-Processing Subprogram

Figure 15.4 shows Example 15.1's program reorganized so that the processing of each request is handled by a separate procedure named addnum. The use of the program and its results are unaffected.

Problems

1. Assume the following declarations and assignments:

```
TYPE
    letter = 'A','Z' ;
    ltrgroup = SET OF letter ;
```

```
VAR
    alphabet, alpha1, alpha2, alpha3 : ltrgroup
    ................
    alphabet := ['A'..'Z']
```

Write the statement(s) to produce the results specified below. You may use any of the declared variables for intermediate purposes.

(a) Assign the consonants to `alpha1`.

(b) Assign the letters I through N to `alpha1` and `alpha2` and the rest to `alpha3`.

(c) Show the value of `alpha3` after the following sequence:

```
alpha1 := alphabet - ['B'..'G','T'..'Z'] ;
alpha2 := alphabet - alpha1 + ['J'] ;
alpha3 := alphabet * alpha1 + ['R'] - ['K'..'M']
```

2. This question is for those of you with some formal musical background. Assume the following declarations and assignments:

```
TYPE
    tone = (c, csharp, d, dsharp, e, f, fsharp, g,
            gsharp, a, asharp, b ;
    notes = SET OF tone ;
VAR
    row, cluster, scale, tune, chord3, chord4 : notes
    ...................
    row := [c..b]
```

(a) Assign to `scale` the notes of the D major scale.

(b) Assign to `tune` the notes not in the A major scale.

(c) Assign to `scale` the notes in the harmonic e minor scale.

(d) Assign to `chord3` the notes in the F-sharp major triad.

(e) Assign to `chord4` the notes in the D7 chord.

(f) Assign to `cluster` the notes in the E7 and A7 chords.

(g) Assign to `cluster` the notes that are neither in Dm7 nor G7.

The following problems pertain to Example 15.1. Each of them specifies a modification or extension to that program. Consequently, these may be treated singly or in combination.

3. Reorganize the program in Example 15.1 so that, if a particular client submits a request for a week that is already taken, he or she can submit another request without having to resubmit the i.d. number.

4. Revise the program in Example 15.1 to take care of the following deficiency: In its original version, the program will continue to take requests (and turn them down) when all the weeks are booked. In the

revised version, the program is to display a special message and terminate when the last available week is booked.

5. Revise the program (we still are talking about Example 15.1 or any of its modifications) so that when a client submits his or her i.d. number, the program displays a list of the available weeks.

6. A small extension to the version of Problem 5 is to include a feature that allows a client to decide not to book a week after looking at the list of available weeks. In response, the program is to issue a polite message thanking him or her for their interest and inviting them to come back next year.

7. Revise the program so that it can take care of special clients who want to book several consecutive weeks. In this version, the client is asked to submit his or her i.d. number and the number of consecutive weeks desired. If the number is 1, the program proceeds as before. If it is greater than 1, the program checks the available weeks to determine whether the request can be filled. If it can, the program displays the available groups of weeks and asks the client to select. (Remember to break up the ranges as necessary. For example, if the client wants to book for 2 weeks, and weeks 14 through 19 are available, the program must display this information as five separate choices, i.e., 14–15, 15–16, 16–17, etc.)

8. Revise the program so that the summary information includes a line showing the number of weeks booked in each quarter (1..13, 14..26, etc.) and a second line showing the total number of weeks booked.

9. The condominium has worked out so well that Hotshot bought three more units and is ready to lease all of them. Unit 1 (the first one they bought) is still their favorite. Consequently, they will continue to use that one during week 30. Weeks 8 and 9 are still reserved for unit 1's maintenance; weeks 10 and 11 are reserved for unit 2 for the same purpose; similarly, weeks 12 and 13, and weeks 14 and 15 are set aside for units 3 and 4, respectively. To manage the reservations, Hotshot wants a batch version of Example 15.1 that will work as follows: Requests are taken as they come in, but they are not processed immediately. At the end of each day, that day's requests are recorded (on a first come first serve basis) on a file named `newrequests`. Each record in `newsrequests` contains an i.d. number and the requested week number. Even though any client may book more than 1 week, each week's request must be prepared as a separate record. This file is to be processed in conjunction with another file named `currentbookings`. Each record in `currentbookings` shows an i.d. number, the week number booked by that client, and the unit number (1, 2, 3, or 4) reserved for that client. The program is to produce a new file named `totalbookings` consisting of the original records from `currentbookings` and the records created by

processing the information from newrequests. (In a subsequent run, of course, the file created here as totalbookings will be used as the latest currentbookings.) In addition, the program is to print (display) the following summary:

1. The total number of weeks booked in each unit before this run
2. The total number of requests submitted during this run
3. The total number of requests accepted during this run
4. The total number of requests rejected during this run
5. The total number of weeks booked in each unit after this run
6. The list of available weeks for each unit after this run

The records in newrequests, currentbookings, and/or totalbookings may be in arbitrary order or in any order you specify. If a particular order is required, it is up to you to provide the processing necessary to produce that order.

10. *(Special Challenge)* During the stage of initial enthusiasm, it did not occur to Hotshot that somebody might actually want to cancel a reservation. Sad to say, such requests were encountered. Accordingly, modify the program in the previous problem so that the records in newrequests include requests for cancellations as well as reservations. The output file totalbookings remains as before, i.e., a record for each week booked in each unit. However, the printed (displayed) output is to include an additional line showing the number of cancellations received during that run.

11. Since there was no explicit specification in the previous versions of the Hotshot program, it is possible for such a program to take a request for a multiweek booking and process it so that the client is not assigned to the same unit for the entire reserved stay. Prepare a version of the program that prevents this from happening. If the client requests more than 1 consecutive week and Hotshot cannot fill the request without moving the client from one unit to another, the request is to be rejected with an explanatory message.

Chapter Sixteen

Dynamic Data Structures

Data structures such as arrays are said to be *static* because their size is defined when they are declared, and Pascal reserves storage for them as part of the compilation process. That storage is a permanent part of the program regardless of the number of elements actually used. If we use an array in a situation where the entire array may not always be occupied, we are compelled to carry the entire array. Moreover, if arbitrarily different parts of the array are occupied at different times, we are burdened with the additional task of keeping track of the array's pertinent sections.

When there is considerable disparity between the full size of an array and the fraction currently in use, the situation often becomes intolerably cumbersome. Such circumstances are by no means exotic; the Pascal compiler is an example of a program whose operation on small computer systems would be much less assured if it had to rely on static data structures.

An effective way to handle situations with unpredictably extensive data requirements is to use *dynamic data structures*. Dynamic structures may assume a wide variety of forms; however, they share one common property: Storage for dynamic data structures is not allocated until the program is executing and it explicitly asks for such storage. Moreover, storage usually is requested (and allocated) in small increments, so that there is a close relationship between the storage actually needed and that made available.

From what warehouse is this storage allocated? After all, the processor has a certain amount of storage, and that is what it has. Why should it make a difference whether the storage is allocated when the program is compiled or the allocation is deferred until the running program asks for it? We can only introduce some of the reasons here, but the discussion will suffice to point up some of the major benefits of dynamic data structures. Further insight can be developed through usage and experimentation.

After taking care of its essential storage requirements, the software system makes the remaining storage available to Pascal. Supporting this generosity are software facilities that keep track of how much is available, where it is located, and how the situation changes with each allocation. The available storage is not "promised" to any particular data items. Instead, it is totally uncommitted and, therefore, it can be assigned to fulfill whatever request the program may make. Working in conjunction with the allocating mechanism is another facility that enables the program to "return" storage when it is through with it. (In harmony with the exciting world of jet-set travel, where people "deplane," such returned storage is "deallocated.") Deallocation means that the storage is added to the pool of available storage for possible reallocation later in the same program execution. As a result, the program can be designed with any number of dynamic data structures, each with its own unpredictable storage requirements.

From the foregoing description, the allocation of storage would appear to be a haphazard way of doing business. When we declare an array, the storage reserved for that purpose is a cohesive unit of consecutive locations. If wordlist is a one-dimensional array and we refer to wordlist[4, the program "knows" exactly where it is because of its relation to wordlist[4. That relationship will exist for the entire life of the program. With dynamic structures, however, there cannot be such a relationship because no one (not the programmer, nor the program, nor the system) "knows" what will be needed when. The program, of course, contains the requests for storage, together with descriptions of the conditions under which such requests can be made. The frequency with which those conditions are met depends on the situation that develops during a particular run. Consequently, we must reconcile this apparent chaos with the fundamental need to know where everything is (and *what* everything is).

This knowledge is established and maintained by using a type of data item called a *pointer*. As the name implies, a pointer (the data item, not the doggie) tells us where something is. The something, which may be a velocity, a price, a weight, or any other value (or collection of values) we might want to represent, is made available to a program by tying it to a pointer. We always know where the pointer is because it is declared like any other static variable. (We shall start with that fundamental notion; a little later we shall see that the pointers themselves can be dynamically allocated if we make the proper arrangements.) Consequently, the pointer exists throughout the program's execution, and we can use it as a figurative hook (or Velcro, if you prefer) to grasp a dynamically allocated item.

If we say that nose is the name of a pointer, and density is the name of a variable for which storage is to be allocated dynamically, we can describe the basic dynamic allocation mechanism simply and clearly. When we want a newly allocated piece of storage for density, we make the following request:

"Please find an appropriate amount of available storage and let me use it for
density. When you decide which one it is, store its *location* in nose.
Thank you. (Have a good day.)"

Once the storage is allocated, we still do not know where it is. (Neither
does the program or the system.) As a result, we cannot say, "Store a 12.24
in density" via a normal assignment. However, we do know how to find
density's whereabouts because *we* made the arrangements. Consequently, we can gain access to density by referring to it as "the place that nose
points to" (or "the place to which nose points" for those people wounded
by any protruding prepositions).

This is the essence of Pascal's dynamic allocation mechanism. In
subsequent sections we shall see exactly how these facilities are presented
to the programmer and how to make them work for us.

16.1 POINTERS AND POINTEES

16.1.1 Declaration of Pointers

A pointer in Pascal is declared by giving it a name and defining the *data
type* of the pointee (i.e., the item to which it will point). This does not mean
that the pointer is inexorably tied to one variable. However, it is true that
the pointer is *bound to* (can only be associated with) variables having the
data type specified in its declaration.

The syntax for a pointer declaration is given in Figure 16.1. For instance, if we say

```
VAR
      nose :  ↑REAL
```

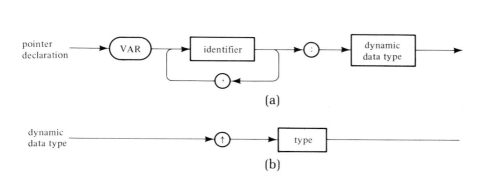

(a)

(b)

Figure 16.1

Construction of a Pointer Declaration

we reserve storage for a variable named n o s e whose value will represent the address of a real variable. (Although it is up to the programmer to make sure that n o s e's contents are consistent with its declaration, Pascal helps by making it difficult to violate this restriction.) The "up arrow" symbol may not be available on your keyboard and some other symbol may be assigned to represent the up arrow [for instance, the carat (^) is used to indicate the up arrow in the p-System Pascal implementation on the IBM Personal Computer].

16.1.2 Allocation of Dynamic Variables

A dynamic variable is allocated by Pascal's NEW procedure. In its basic form, NEW is invoked with a single argument that names the pointer to be associated with the new variable. Thus, using the previous declaration for n o s e

```
NEW (nose)
```

allocates storage for a real variable and stores the address of that variable in n o s e. *The variable thus allocated has no name.* Access to the variable is gained only via its pointer. (If we want to associate a pointer with a particular variable name, that association exists in our heads but not in the program. We can show that association by noting it in a comment; as far as Pascal is concerned, the name is irrelevant.)

A pointer points only to one thing at a time. Consequently, the programmer must allocate storage carefully. For instance, the sequence

```
NEW (nose) ;
NEW (nose)
```

is legal. Pascal will allocate storage for a real value (assuming the earlier declaration for n o s e) and set the address of the newly allocated storage in n o s e. Fine. Then, it will go ahead and do the same thing. The result is that the first allocation is lost because there is no pointer to it. Furthermore, the storage is unavailable for other use because it has not been returned to the available pool. That activity takes a separate procedure, as we shall see. If we want to make such multiple allocations, the only way to do it is to arrange for separate pointers. Techniques for doing this, along with the fundamental benefits offered by those techniques, are discussed in Section 16.2.

16.1.3 Assignment of Values to Dynamic Variables

We can store a value in a dynamically allocated variable by assigning it or reading it in. These, of course, are the same mechanisms used for any variable. With dynamic variables, the only difference is that we must refer to the pointer. Pascal uses the form

$$pointername \uparrow$$

to specify a reference to a variable associated with *pointername*. For instance,

```
nose↑ := 12.24
```

stores the value of 12.24 in `nose`'s pointee. Similarly,

```
READLN (nose↑)
```

stores the next input value (if it is a real number) in the variable associated with `nose`. `READ`, `WRITE`, and `WRITELN` also can be applied to dynamic variables.

Once a dynamic variable has been allocated, it can be processed like any other variable. For instance, the sequence

```
VAR
    nose, finger :  ↑REAL ;          (nose → density)
    NEW (nose) ;
    NEW (finger)
    ............                     (finger → hidense)
    READLN (nose ↑ ) ;
    finger↑ := nose↑
```

is legal. The result is that the value read into the variable pointed to by `nose` (i.e., the variable *we* choose to regard as `density`) is copied into the variable pointed to by `finger`.

16.1.4 Assignment of Pointer Values

As explained earlier, part of the activity performed by the `NEW` procedure is to assign an address to a pointer. This is an automatic process, inseparable from the other work done by that procedure. In addition, it is possible for the program to assign an explicit value to a pointer. Of course, that value must be consistent with a pointer's usage, so that the only assignable value is that taken from another pointer. Since we have no direct knowledge of the actual values stored in pointers, we cannot read in such values (nor can they be written out). This leaves us with the assignment operation. Thus, in the sequence

```
VAR
    nose, finger :  ↑REAL ;
    NEW (nose) ;
    NEW (finger)
      · · · · · · · · · ·
    READLN (nose↑) ;
    finger   := nose
      · · · · · · · · · · ·
```

We end up with a situation where the variable associated with nose has a value in it, and both nose and finger point to that same unnamed variable.

16.1.5 A Name for Nowhere

Thus far, we have discussed the use of pointers to help us find dynamic variables. It also is necessary to have a way to denote the fact that a pointer points nowhere. This is handled by Pascal's built-in constant NIL. Thus, if we say

```
finger := NIL
```

we set the contents of the pointer finger to a particular value that is used consistently whenever NIL is mentioned. That means that we can test for it and use it as a basis for subsequent decisions.

16.1.6 Returning Dynamically Allocated Storage

When the programmer is through with some dynamically allocated storage and wishes to return it to the pool of available storage, he or she does so by invoking Pascal's DISPOSE procedure.

```
                    DISPOSE(pointername)
```

returns the variable *pointername* ↑ to unallocated storage and sets *pointername* to NIL. Consequently, the programmer must make sure that *pointername* ↑ *is allocated before he or she refers to it.* (*pointername* itself, of course, still is there, waiting for a pointee.)

16.2 LINKED LISTS

Now that we have become acquainted with Pascal's facilities for defining, allocating, and assigning dynamic data, we shall apply these features to the construction and processing of a powerful dynamic data structure, the linked list.

16.2.1 Properties of a Linked List

We can use dynamic data allocation to build data structures that expand and contract as needs dictate. Since we cannot count on consecutive elements being next to each other in storage, we have to construct explicit connections to join them. Such *links* are provided by pointers, and a collection of data joined by pointers is called a *linked list*. There are endless varieties of linked lists. Our concentration on the most basic type will enable us to become acquainted with its properties and develop insights into some of the more intricate possibilities.

The essential ingredients of a linked list are shown in Figure 16.2. Each element, usually called a *cell* or a *node*, consists of the data and a *forward pointer* that ties the cell to the next one in the list. As is true with any other data structure, it is up to the programmer to define the criteria for determining the cells' order. A list's first cell is called the *head*, and a separate *head pointer* points to it. This pointer generally is static since it is likely to be the only way to get hold of the list. The last cell, called the *tail*, is marked as such by having its forward pointer point nowhere. Since it is the only pointer in the list with this ephemeral destination, we have a convenient way of identifying the tail. (Some lists may be equipped with a separate tail pointer.)

The nature and extent of a cell's contents are not subject to any particular restrictions. Nor is there any conceptual limit on the number of cells in a list. (Certain limitations may be imposed by a particular programming language, but those are not intrinsic to the data structure itself.) We shall keep things simple for our discussion by considering lists in which each cell may contain several values of arbitrarily different data types, but all cells in a list must be constructed identically.

16.2.2 Fundamental Operations on Linked Lists

Manipulation of a list requires three basic operations: insertion, deletion, and searching, the latter being required to support the other two. Since the location of a cell bears no relation to that of its immediate (conceptual) neighbors, there is no movement of data when the list's structure changes.

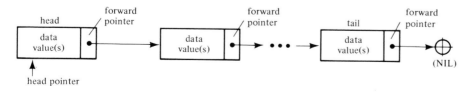

Figure 16.2

Components of a Simple Linked List

To facilitate the definition of these operations, we shall use a simple list in which each cell consists of a forward pointer, a part number, and a price. The assumption is that the list is to be in ascending order by price (i.e., the head contains the lowest priced item). This is shown in Figure 16.3(a).

As Figure 16.3(b) indicates, addition of a new cell to a list involves the following steps:

1. Allocating storage for the new cell and filling it with data
2. Finding where the new cell belongs
3. "Opening" the list to accommodate the new addition by adjusting the appropriate pointers

The addition (insertion) operation must include provisions for handling the special cases where the new cell is to be installed at the head or tail of

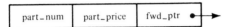

(a) Components of the list cell for section 16.2.2

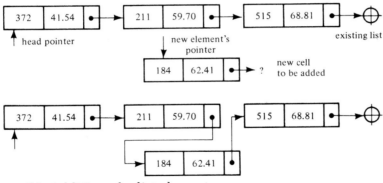

(b) Addition of a list element

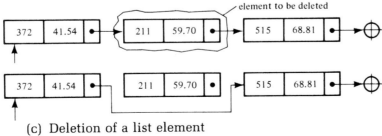

(c) Deletion of a list element

Figure 16.3

the list. Another special case occurs when the list is empty and the element in question is the first one.

Deletion from a list can be viewed as the "mirror image" of insertion. It involves

1. Finding the element to be deleted
2. "Unhooking" the pointers from the unwanted cell and reconnecting the cells around it
3. Returning the newly deleted cell to available storage

This type of transaction is shown in Figure 16.3(c).

There are numerous ways to search a list for a cell containing a given value. The applicability of a particular technique depends on how the list is organized and on the kinds of supporting mechanisms with which the list is equipped. In our case, the search starts at the head of the list and systematically examines the specified data item in each cell until it finds what it is looking for or determines that the desired value is not there. With this type of list we have no choice: Its facilities make it impossible to start anywhere except the head; moreover, given a particular element, the only one we can reach is the next one.

16.2.3 Implementation of List-Processing Operations

Now that we are acquainted with the basic properties of linked lists, we are ready to use Pascal's dynamic data facilities to define, build, and process such lists.

Construction of a List Element   Since there are virtually endless possibilities for the constituents of a list element, we need a flexible vehicle for its construction. Pascal's RECORD data type is well suited for this use, and we can apply it conveniently. To illustrate, let us say that we want each cell to consist of an integer named part num, a real variable named part price, and a forward pointer named fwdptr. Remember that fwdptr will point either to another list element (consisting, in turn, of a partnum and partprice, and a fwdptr) or it will point to NIL. With these requirements in mind, consider the following declarations:

```
TYPE
   partcell = RECORD
   partnum : INTEGER ;
   partprice : REAL ;
   fwdptr : listpointer
END ;
listpointer = ^partcell
```

The newly defined `partcell` data type describes the required list element. (Pascal is able to deal with the fact that `listpointer` appears inside a declaration prior to its own definition.)

We shall not declare a variable of type `partcell` because the resulting record would be static, and we want each cell to be allocated on demand. Consequently, we shall declare a pointer named `newpart` as follows:

```
VAR
    newpart : listpointer
```

Now, whenever we want storage to be allocated for a list element, the invocation

```
NEW (newpart)
```

will get it for us, and `newpart` will point to it.

Assignment of Values to a List Element   The newly allocated cell is of little use as it is. Invocation of the `NEW` procedure obtained the storage, but it is an island accessible through its pointer. It has no values in it of interest to us, nor is the cell part of a list. This section takes care of providing values for a new cell, and the ensuing sections show how to bring that cell into the warmth and comfort of the linked list.

Once the cell is allocated, each constituent can be treated like an ordinary variable, as long as we remember that we must refer to it via its pointer. Thus, the statement

```
READLN (newpart^.partnum, newpart^.partprice)
```

reads two values and stores them in the indicated components of the newly allocated cell. Alternatively, we could have stored values by means of ordinary assignment statements. For instance,

```
newpart↑.partprice  := 386.79
```

is a legitimate assignment. That is all there is to it.

Initializing a List   As indicated earlier, a head pointer is a crucial component of a list structure. Let us define one for our example:

```
VAR
    hdptr : listpointer
```

Initially, the head pointer has no pointee (the list has no members yet). Consequently, `NIL` is a reasonable value with which to initialize it. (Later, we shall use the value as a test to determine whether a list is empty.)

Now we can add the first element to the list. All that is required is to set the head pointer so that it points to the newly allocated cell:

```
hdptr  := newpart
```

Remember that we do not use the up arrow (↑) here because we want to refer to the pointers and not the cell. Assuming all the TYPE and VAR declarations given before, let us review the processing needed to initialize the head pointer, allocate a cell, fill in its data values, and establish the cell as the sole member of the list:

```
hdptr  := NIL ;
NEW (newpart)
READLN (newpart↑.partnum, newpart↑.partprice) ;
hdptr := newpart ;
newpart↑.fwdptr  := NIL    (the head also is the tail)
```

Searching a List   The most direct way to construct a search for a simple linked list is to set up a loop that starts at the head and works its way through the list. To help manage this process, we shall define another

```
VAR
  . . . . . . . . . . . . . . . . . .
  next : listpointer
  testvalue : REAL ;
  testpart : INTEGER ;
  sw : BOOLEAN
    . . . . . . . . . . . . . . . . . .
    READLN (testvalue) ;
    next  := hdptr ;                {next —> head of the list}
    testpart  := 0 ;
    sw := TRUE ;
    WHILE sw DO
       IF next↑.partprice = testvalue
          THEN
             BEGIN
                testpart := next↑.partnum ;
                 sw  := FALSE
             END
        ELSE
           IF next↑.fwdptr = NIL          {end of list?}
             THEN
                 sw := FALSE
             ELSE
             next  := next↑.fwdptr
```

Figure 16.4

Outline for a List Search to Find a Matching Value

pointer named next. Initially, next will point to the head of the list. Then, as we go through each cycle and finish with a given cell, the value in that cell's forward pointer is assigned to next, thereby enabling the program to examine the next cell.

We shall illustrate the technique by setting up a loop that looks through a list of partcells to find a partprice equal to a static real variable named testvalue. The value of partnum for the matching cell will be stored in testpart. If there is no match, testpart will be zero. Figure 16.4 shows Pascal statements. For the sake of brevity, only next, testvalue, testpart, and sw (a switch for loop control) are explicitly declared in the figure; the earlier declarations are assumed. Furthermore, we assume an existing list with hdptr pointing to its first cell.

Adding an Element to a List   There are two basic steps involved in adding an element to a list: finding where it belongs and installing it there. The first step can be handled by a slight variation of the search described in Figure 16.4. This time, instead of looking for a matching price, we shall be interested in finding two adjacent (i.e., linked) cells such that the price value in the new cell falls between their respective price values. In addition, we shall be alert for the special situations in which the new cell's price value compels us to install that cell as the new head or tail of the list. Further help will be sought from another pointer named prior. If a new cell is to be installed between two members of the current list, we shall

```
{ASSUME DECLARATIONS FOR PARTCELL, LISTPOINTER, NEWPART ;      }
{ASSUME THAT A CELL HAS BEEN ALLOCATED AND NEW VALUES WERE     }
{ASSIGNED, THUS, NEWPART POINTS TO THE NEW CELL TO BE ADDED,   }
VAR
    hdptr, prior, next : listpointer ;
    testvalue  : REAL ;
    testpart : INTEGER ;
    sw1, sw2 : BOOLEAN
        . . . . . . . . . . . .
        sw1   := TRUE ;
        prior := hdptr ;
        next  := hdptr↑.fwdptr ;
        WHILE sw1 DO
            IF hdptr = NIL          {IS LIST EMPTY?}
                THEN
                    BEGIN
                        hdptr := newpart ;         {INSTALL FIRST}
                        newpart↑.fwdptr : NIL ; {ELEMENT}
                        sw1 := FALSE
                    END
```

Figure 16.5

Process for Addition to a Linked List

arrange for P r i o r and n e x t to point to these two members. This process is outlined in Figure 16.5.

Deleting an Element from a List   The two basic steps in this operation consist of finding the element and removing it from the list. To find the cell, we can go back to the search technique outlined in Figure 16.4 and expand it to take care of the special situation where there is an attempt to remove a cell from an empty list. Actual deletion simply requires the adjustment of the preceding cell's forward pointer so that it points to the cell following the one to be deleted. A special case is one where the cell to be deleted turns out to be the head of the list.

We shall organize the deletion process as a procedure that handles the same list structure we have been using all along. The cell to be deleted is the one whose P a r t P r i c e matches t e s t v a l u e. We shall use n e x t to point to the unfortunate cell (if it is in the list). P r i o r will point to the cell preceding the one to be deleted. It will be P r i o r's cell, of course, whose forward pointer has to be changed. An additional variable, the integer [r e s u l t, will be used to report the subprogram's activity to an invoking program: A r e s u l t of 1 means that the requested deletion was performed; zero means that there was no such cell in the list; when r e s u l t is -1, it means that the list was empty. The resulting subprogram is shown in Figure

```
ELSE
    IF newpart↑.partprice < hdptr↑.partprice
    THEN
        {INSTALL NEW CELL AS HEAD OF LIST}
        BEGIN
            newpart↑.fwdptr  := hdptr ;
            hdptr := newpart ;
            sw1 := FALSE
        END
    ELSE
        BEGIN
            sw2 := TRUE ;
            WHILE sw2 DO
                IF next = NIL
                    THEN
                        {INSTALL NEW CELL AS THE TAIL}
                        BEGIN
                            newpart↑.fwd.ptr  := NIL ;
                            next↑.fwdptr := newpart ;
                            sw2 := FALSE ;
                            sw1 := FALSE
                        END
```

Figure 16.6

Procedure for Deletion from a List

```
                            ELSE
                                IF (newPart↑.partprice >
                                    prior↑.partprice)      AND
                                    (newPart↑.partprice <
                                    next↑.partprice)
                                    THEN
                                        {INSTALL NEW CELL BETWEEN}
                                        {PRIOR AND NEXT          }
                                        BEGIN
                                            newPart↑.fwdptr  :=
                                            prior↑.fwdptr ;
                                            prior↑.fwdptr := newpart ;
                                            sw1 := FALSE ;
                                            sw2 := FALSE
                                        END
                                    ELSE
                                        BEGIN     {SHIFT POINTER}
                                            prior := next ;
                                            next := next↑.fwdptr
                                        END
END
END
{ASSUME THE FOLLOWING DECLARATIONS IN THE INVOKING PROGRAM:}
{TYPE                                                       }
{    Partcell = RECORD                                      }
{        Partnum : INTEGER ;                                }
{        Partprice : REAL ;                                 }
[        fwdptr : listpointer                               }
{    END ;                                                  }
{    listpointer = ↑Partcell ;                              }
{VAR                                                        }
{    testvalue : REAL ;                                     }
{    result : INTEGER ;                                     }
{    hdptr, prior, next : listpointer                       }
        • • • • • • • • • • • • • • • • • • • • • • • • • • • •
        • • • • • • • • • • • • • • • • • • • • • • • • • • • •




PROCEDURE  delete ;
VAR
    sw : BOOLEAN ;
BEGIN
    result := 0 ;
    IF  hdptr = NIL
```

Figure 16.6

Procedure for Deletion from a List (continued)

```
THEN
    result := -1              (LIST IS EMPTY)
ELSE
    BEGIN
        sw := TRUE ;
        next := hdptr ;
        prior := NIL ;
        WHILE  sw  DO
            IF  next↑.partprice = testvalue
                THEN
                    BEGIN
                        sw := FALSE ;
                        result := 1              (SUCCESSFUL MATCH)
                    END
                ELSE
                    IF  next↑.fwdptr = NIL
                        THEN
                            sw := FALSE          (NOT IN LIST)
                        ELSE
                            BEGIN
                                prior := next;
                                next := next↑.fwdptr
                            END ;
        (END OF SEARCH)
        IF  result = 1
            THEN
                IF  prior := NIL              (DELETE HEAD OF LIST)
                    THEN
                        hdptr := hdptr↑.fwdptr
                    ELSE
                        prior↑.fwd.ptr := next↑.fwdptr
    END
END
```

Figure 16.6

Procedure for Deletion from a List (continued)

16.6. Declarations from a hypothetical invoking program are included to provide context.

Problems

1. Using the partcell structure, assume that we want to construct a list in which the cells are in order by increasing partnum. Write a procedure named addcell that adds a new cell to the list. Assume

that the new cell is allocated and that newPart points to it. Furthermore, when n is invoked, the new cell's values already are assigned. The existing list may be empty, or a cell with that partnum may already be in it.

2. Write a program named listbuild that uses addcell to construct a list of partcells in order by increasing part number. Design your program so that it asks for a part number and price. When the user submits the values; the program adds the new cells to the list and displays the number of cells currently in the list. Run your program with the following data:

Part Number	Price
121	38.71
86	40.40
218	36.05
271	41.70
250	65.37
321	59.50
308	72.14
265	68.00

3. Write a version of the program in Problem 2 that reads the data from a text file.

4. Revise the program in either of the preceding two problems so that each cell includes a part name up to 12 letters long.

5. Using the data structure from Problem 1, write a procedure named pricechange that finds a cell with a specified partnum and replaces its partprice value with a new one. There is no guarantee that the list contains a cell with the indicated part number.

6. Here is the grand finale for partcell: Combine the appropriate components from previous problems and illustrations to write the following interactive program: Using partnum, partprice, and fwdptr, and starting with an empty list, the program asks the user whether he or she wishes to add to the list, delete from the list, change a price in the list, or quit. After the user indicates the desired activity, the program requests the appropriate data, reads the value(s), and reports what it did.

7. Now we shall call on our newly acquired prowess with simple linked lists to build and process more intricate structures. One such structure is the *double linked* list in which each cell is equipped with two pointers: a *forward pointer* to the next cell (or to NIL) and a *backward pointer* (or *back pointer*) to the previous cell (or to NIL). The basic structure is depicted in Figure 16.7.

As a starting point in our examination of double linked-list structures, define a data type named aquacell whose constituents con-

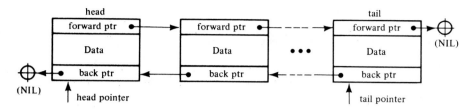

Figure 16.7

Basic Components of a Double-Linked List

sist of a string of 12 letters or less named fishname, an integer named fishref, and two pointers named fwdfish and bkwdfish.

8. Using the data structure developed for the previous problem, write a program that builds a doubly linked list in which the cells are arranged in alphabetical order by fishname. Design your program to operate interactively and run it with the following data:

Fish Name	Ref
guppy	181
mollie	109
betta	265
oscar	347
swordtail	216
angelfish	452
tetra	146

(*Loaded Question*) Is there any advantage in setting up and maintaining a pointer that points to the center of the list?

9. Write a version of the program for the previous problem that reads the input from a textfile.

10. Expand the program of Problem 8 or 9 so that it will handle a series of intermixed additions and deletions.

Railroad Diagrams for Pascal

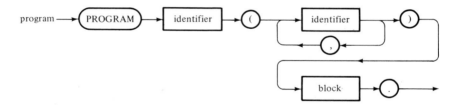

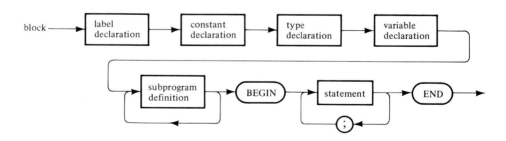

label
declaration

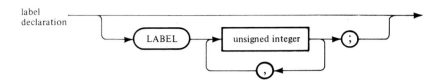

constant
declaration

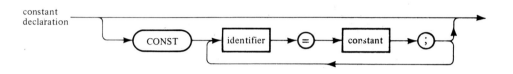

type
declaration

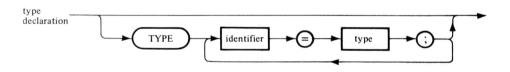

variable
declaration

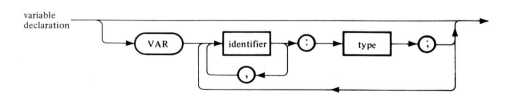

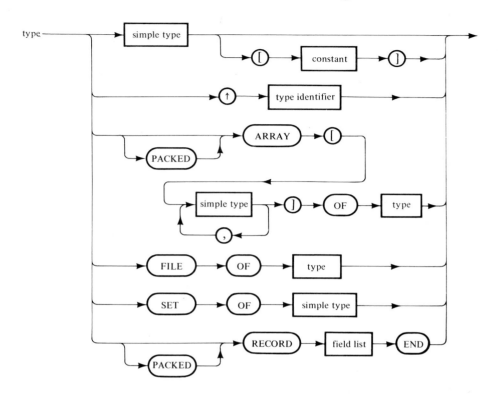

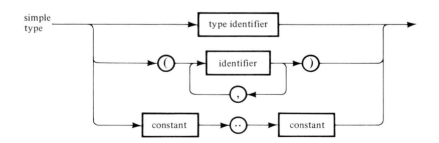

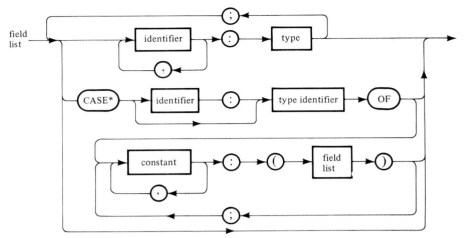

*Not covered in the text.

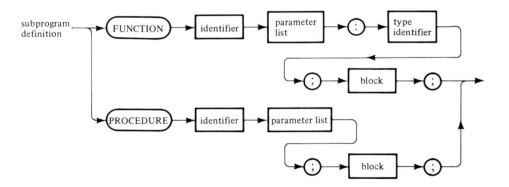

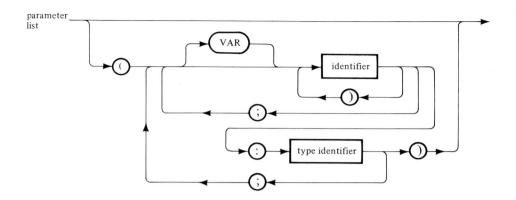

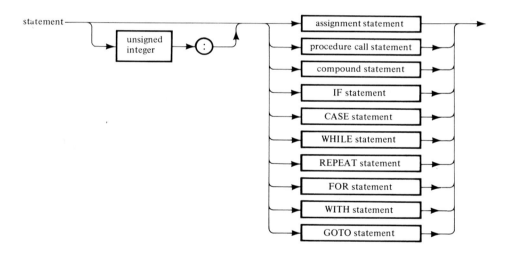

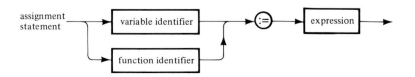

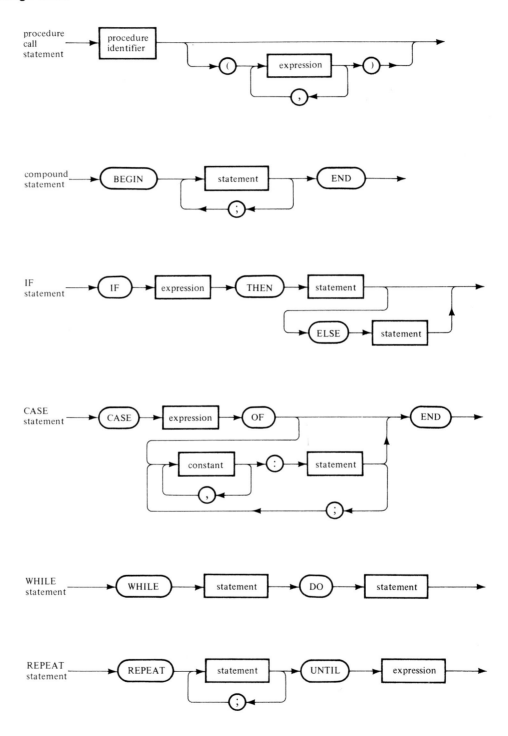

FOR
statement

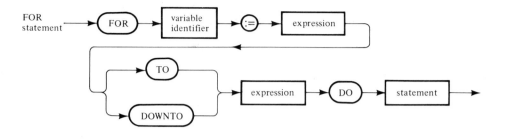

WITH
statement

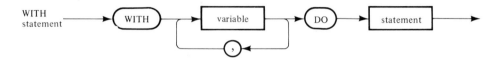

GOTO
statement

expression

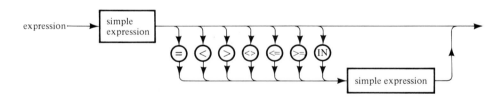

simple
expression

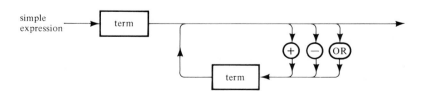

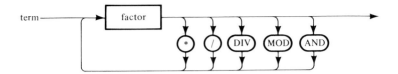

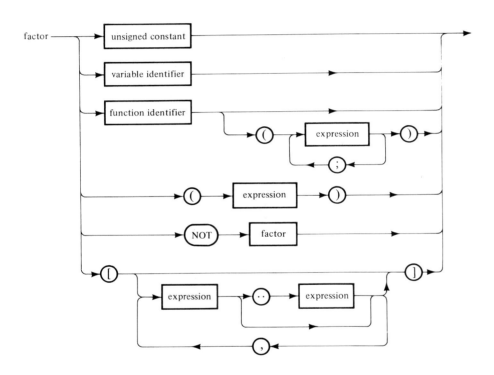

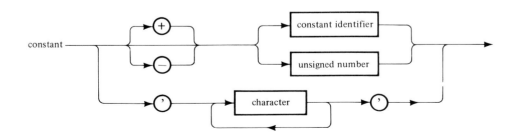

unsigned number

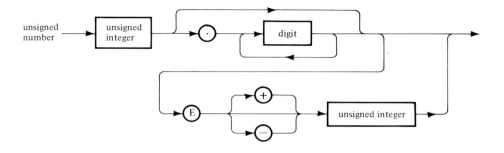

unsigned integer

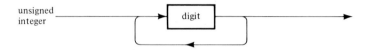

unsigned constant

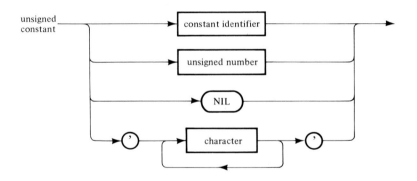

identifier

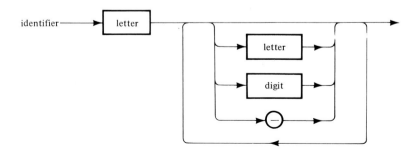

ASCII and EBCDIC Coding Systems

Table B.1 ASCII Codes

Internal Value	ASCII Character	Internal Value	ASCII Character	Internal Value	ASCII Character
32	blank	65	A	97	a
33	!	66	B	98	b
34	"	67	C	99	c
35	#	68	D	100	d
36	$	69	E	101	e
37	%	70	F	102	f
38	&	71	G	103	g
39	'	72	H	104	h
40	(	73	I	105	i
41	)	74	J	106	j
42	*	75	K	107	k
43	+	76	L	108	l
44	,	77	M	109	m
45	-	78	N	110	n
46	.	79	O	111	o
47	/	80	P	112	p
48	0	81	Q	113	q
49	1	82	R	114	r
50	2	83	S	115	s
51	3	84	T	116	t
52	4	85	U	117	u
53	5	86	V	118	v
54	6	87	W	119	w
55	7	88	X	120	x
56	8	89	Y	121	y
57	9	90	Z	122	z
58	:	91	[	123	{
59	;	92	\	124	|
60	<	93	]	125	}
61	=	94	^	126	~
62	>	95	—		
63	?	96	`		
64	@				

Notes: (1) 0–31 are used for internal control signals, as are 127–255. (2) In some ASCII systems the internal values for these characters are 128 greater than those shown. In such cases, 0–159 are used for internal control.

Table B.2 EBCDIC Codes

Internal Value	EBCDIC Character	Internal Value	EBCDIC Character	Internal Value	EBCDIC Character	Internal Value	EBCDIC Value
64	blank	98	↑	129	a	193	A
65	↑	99		130	b	194	B
66		100		131	c	195	C
67		101		132	d	196	D
68	internal	102	internal	133	e	197	E
69	control	103	control	134	f	198	F
70		104	↑	135	g	199	G
71		105		136	h	200	H
72		106		137	i	201	I
73	↓	107	,	138	↑	202–208	control
74	¢	108	%	139		209	J
75	.	109	_	140	internal	210	K
76	<	110	>	141	control	211	L
77	(	111	?	142		212	M
78	+	112	↑	143		213	N
79	|	113		144	↓	214	O
80	&	114		145	j	215	P
81	↑	115	internal	146	k	216	Q
82		116	control	147	l	217	R
83		117		148	m	218–225	control
84		118		149	n	226	S
85	internal	119		150	o	227	T
86	control	120		151	p	228	U
87		121		152	q	229	V
88		122	↓ :	153	r	230	W
89	↓	123	#	154–161	control	231	X
90	:	124	@	162	s	232	Y
91	$	125	'	163	t	233	Z
92	*	126	=	164	u	234–239	control
93	)	127	"	165	v	240	0
94	;	128	control	166	w	241	1
95	¬			167	x	242	2
96	-			168	y	243	3
97	/			169	z	244	4
				170–192	control	245	5
						246	6
						247	7
						248	8
						249	9
						250–255	control

Caution: In EBCDIC systems, SUCC (i) ≠ j, pred (s) ≠ r, etc.

Permanent Words and Identifiers in Standard Pascal

C.1 Language Constants

MAXINT   NIL   TRUE   FALSE

C.2 Data Types

REAL   INTEGER   CHAR   BOOLEAN   TEXT

C.3 Standard Files

INPUT   OUTPUT

C.4 Standard Operations

+   -   *   /   DIV   MOD   AND   OR   NOT   IN

C.5 Reserved Words

ARRAY	END	OF	THEN
BEGIN	FILE	PACKED	TO
CASE	FOR	PROCEDURE	TYPE
CONST	FUNCTION	PROGRAM	UNTIL
DO	GOTO	RECORD	VAR
DOWNTO	IF	REPEAT	WHILE
ELSE	LABEL	SET	WITH

C.6 Built-in Functions

Function Name and Argument	Action	Data Type of Result
ABS(*integer*) ABS(*real*)	Absolute value of argument	INTEGER REAL
ARCTAN(*integer*) ARCTAN(*real*)	Arctangent of argument	REAL REAL
CHR(*integer*)	Determines character whose ordinal value is *integer*	CHAR
COS(*integer*) COS(*real*)	Cosine of argument	REAL REAL
EOF(*filename*)	Returns TRUE if *filename*'s end of file is reached	BOOLEAN
EOLN(*filename*)	Returns TRUE if end of line is reached in filename	BOOLEAN
EXP(*integer*) EXP(*real*)	$e^{argument}$	REAL REAL
LN(*integer*) LN(*real*)	Natural log of *argument*	REAL REAL
ODD(*integer*) ORD(*character*) ORD(*boolean*) ORD(*user-defined*)	Returns TRUE if argument is odd Ordinal value of argument	BOOLEAN INTEGER INTEGER INTEGER
PRED(*integer*) PRED(*character*) PRED(*boolean*) PRED(*user-defined*)	Predecessor of argument	INTEGER CHAR BOOLEAN *user-defined*
ROUND(*real*)	Round to nearest integer	INTEGER
SIN(*integer*) SIN(*real*)	Sine of argument	REAL REAL
SQR(*integer*) SQR(*real*)	Square of the argument	INTEGER REAL

C.6 Built-in Functions

Function Name and Argument	Action	Data Type of Result
SQRT(*integer*)	$\sqrt{argument}$	REAL
SQRT(*real*)		REAL
SUCC(*integer*)	Successor of the argument	INTEGER
SUCC(*character*)		CHAR
SUCC(*boolean*)		BOOLEAN
SUCC(*user-defined*)		*user-defined*
TRUNC(*real*)	Truncated value of argument	INTEGER

C.7 Built-in Procedures

Procedure Name and Argument(s)	Action
DISPOSE(*pointername*)	Takes the variable pointed to by *pointername* out of use by returning it to the pool of available storage.
GET(*filename*)	Moves the next component (record) of file *filename* to the window and places the new value(s) in variable *filename*^.
NEW(*pointername*)	Allocates storage from the available pool for a dynamic variable pointed to by *pointername*.
PACK(*arraynm, startpoint, packedarray*)	Packs *arraynm [startpoint]* into *packedarray* [1], etc.
PAGE(*filename*)	Starts a new page before printing the next line of textfile *filename*.
PUT(*filename*)	Appends the value of variable *filename*^ to the file *filename*.
READ(*filename, list*)	Reads data items from the textfile *filename* into the variables in *list*.
READLN(*filename, list*)	Reads data items from the textfile *filename* into the variables in *list* and moves to the next end-of-line indicator.
RESET(*filename*)	Positions file *filename* to its beginning.
REWRITE(*filename*)	Empties file *filename* and prepares it to accept output.
UNPACK(*arraynm, packedarray, startpoint*)	Unpacks, element *packedarray[1]* into *arraynm[startpoint]*, etc.
WRITE(*filename, list*)	Writes data from *list* to the textfile *filename*.
WRITELN(*filename, list*)	Writes data items from *list* to the textfile *filename* and concludes with an end-of-line indicator.

Index

ABS built-in function, 118
Algorithms
    and programs, 3
    description of, 15
    implementation of, 8
    properties of, 4–6
ALU, 11
Arithmetic operations, 99–107, 322, 336
Arguments for subprograms, 215
Arrays
    characteristics of, 84
    declaration of, 85, 255–256, 272, 353
    dimensionality of, 256–258
    identification of elements in, 85
    indexes for, 87, 261
    input/output of, 148, 282, 288
    loops for processing, 86, 142
    packed, 286–288
    sorting of, 201–203
ASCII character set, 361
Assignment operation, 33, 78, 287, 321, 342
Assignment statement, 33, 97, 103, 355

Bensonhurst, I Scungili di, 95
Blanks in output formats, 153
Blue paint, 5, 22
Blocks, structure of, 30, 355
Boolean data
    declaration of variables for, 72, 291
    expressions with, 292
    formatting for output of, 155
    input/output of, 293

Built-in functions
    ABS, 118
    ARCTAN, 122
    CHR, 290
    COS, 122
    EXP, 120
    EXPO, 124
    FLOAT, 124
    LN, 120
    LOG, 120
    MAX, 124
    MIN, 124
    ODD, 119
    ORD, 290
    PRED, 291
    RANDOM, 125
    ROUND, 118
    SIN, 122
    SQR, 120
    SQRT, 120
    SUCC, 291
    TRUNC, 119

Call by value, *see* Transfer by value
CASE construction, 177–179
CASE statement, 180, 356
Character data
    arrays of, 259–260, 272, 286
    comparisons with, 171, 278
    conversion from, 290
    conversion to, 290
    declaration of variables for, 71, 271

367